C0-AVR-684

PROGRESS IN BEHAVIOR MODIFICATION

Volume 3

DISCARD

CONTRIBUTORS TO THIS VOLUME

Henry E. Adams

L. Michael Ascher

Theodore X. Barber

Thomas D. Borkovec

Ruth E. Clifford

Rodney Copeland

Brian G. Danaher

R. Vance Hall

Howard H. Hughes

Benjamin B. Lahey

Edward Lichtenstein

David Marholin II

Gerald T. O'Brien

David Phillips

Lawrence J. Siegel

Nicholas P. Spanos

BF 637
.B4 P66
V. 3

PROGRESS IN BEHAVIOR
// **MODIFICATION**

EDITED BY

Michel Hersen

Department of Psychiatry
Western Psychiatric Institute and Clinic
University of Pittsburgh School of Medicine
Pittsburgh, Pennsylvania

Richard M. Eisler

Department of Psychiatry and Human Behavior
University of Mississippi Medical Center
Jackson, Mississippi

Peter M. Miller

Weight Control Center
Hilton Head Hospital
Hilton Head Island, South Carolina

Volume 3

ACADEMIC PRESS   NEW YORK   SAN FRANCISCO   LONDON   1976

A Subsidiary of Harcourt Brace Jovanovich, Publishers

INDIANA
UNIVERSITY
LIBRARY
MAY 1 6 1978
NORTHWEST

COPYRIGHT © 1976, BY ACADEMIC PRESS, INC.
ALL RIGHTS RESERVED.
NO PART OF THIS PUBLICATION MAY BE REPRODUCED OR
TRANSMITTED IN ANY FORM OR BY ANY MEANS, ELECTRONIC
OR MECHANICAL, INCLUDING PHOTOCOPY, RECORDING, OR ANY
INFORMATION STORAGE AND RETRIEVAL SYSTEM, WITHOUT
PERMISSION IN WRITING FROM THE PUBLISHER.

ACADEMIC PRESS, INC.
111 Fifth Avenue, New York, New York 10003

United Kingdom Edition published by
ACADEMIC PRESS, INC. (LONDON) LTD.
24/28 Oval Road. London NW1

LIBRARY OF CONGRESS CATALOG CARD NUMBER: 74-5697

ISBN 0-12-535603-X

PRINTED IN THE UNITED STATES OF AMERICA

CONTENTS

Modification of Smoking Behavior:
A Critical Analysis of Theory, Research, and Practice
Edward Lichtenstein and Brian G. Danaher

Methodological and Target Behavior Issues in
Analogue Therapy Outcome Research
Thomas D. Borkovec and Gerald T. O'Brien

Behavior Modification with Learning Disabilities
and Related Problems
Benjamin B. Lahey

Animal Analogues of Behavioral Treatment Procedures: A Critical Evaluation
Henry E. Adams and Howard H. Hughes

Behavioral Considerations in the Treatment of Sexual Dysfunction
L. Michael Ascher and Ruth E. Clifford

Treatment and Transfer: A Search for Empirical Procedures
David Marholin II, Lawrence J. Siegel, and David Phillips

LIST OF CONTRIBUTORS

Numbers in parentheses indicate the pages on which the authors' contributions begin.

HENRY E. ADAMS (207), Department of Psychology, University of Georgia, Athens, Georgia

L. MICHAEL ASCHER (241), Behavior Therapy Unit, Department of Psychiatry, Temple University, Philadelphia, Pennsylvania

THEODORE X. BARBER (1), Medfield Foundation, Medfield, Massachusetts

THOMAS D. BORKOVEC (133), Department of Psychology, University of Iowa, Iowa City, Iowa

RUTH E. CLIFFORD (241), Department of Psychology, Temple University, Philadelphia, Pennsylvania

RODNEY COPELAND (45),* Department of Human Development and Family Life, University of Kansas, Lawrence, Kansas

BRIAN G. DANAHER (79), Stanford University Medical Center, Stanford, California

R. VANCE HALL (45), Department of Human Development and Family Life, University of Kansas, Lawrence, Kansas

HOWARD H. HUGHES (207), Department of Psychology, North Texas State University, Denton, Texas

BENJAMIN B. LAHEY (173), Department of Psychology, University of Georgia, Athens, Georgia

EDWARD LICHTENSTEIN (79), Department of Psychology, University of Oregon, Eugene, Oregon

DAVID MARHOLIN II (293), Department of Special Education, Boston University, Boston, Massachusetts

GERALD T. O'BRIEN (133), Department of Psychology, University of Iowa, Iowa City, Iowa

DAVID PHILLIPS (293), Department of Psychology, University of Illinois at Urbana-Champaign, Champaign, Illinois

Present address: Department of Psychology, Southwest Missouri State University, Springfield, Missouri.

LAWRENCE J. SIEGEL (293),[†] Department of Psychology, Case Western Reserve University, Cleveland, Ohio

NICHOLAS P. SPANOS (1), Department of Psychology, Carleton University, Ottawa, Ontario, Canada

[†]*Present address:* Mid-Missouri Mental Health Center and University of Missouri Medical School, Columbia, Missouri.

PREFACE

Progress in Behavior Modification is a multidisciplinary serial publication encompassing the contributions of psychology, psychiatry, social work, speech therapy, education, and rehabilitation. In an era of intense specialization, it is designed to bring to the attention of all workers in behavior modification, in a yearly review format, the most timely issues and developments in the field. Inasmuch as several journals are presently devoted entirely to publishing articles on behavior modification, and in consideration of the fact that numerous other journals are now allowing an increased allotment of pages to articles dealing with behavioral techniques, even the most diligent reader will find it difficult to keep abreast of all new developments in the field. In light of the publication explosion in behavior modification, there is a real need for a review publication that undertakes to present yearly in-depth evaluations that include a scholarly examination of theoretical underpinnings, a careful survey of research findings, and a comparative analysis of existing techniques and methodologies. In this serial publication we propose to meet this need.

Theoretical discussion, research methodology, assessment techniques, treatment modalities, control of psychophysiological processes, and ethical issues in behavioral control will be considered. Discussions will center on a wide spectrum of child and adult disorders. The range of topics will include, but will not be limited to, studies of fear behavior, measurement and modification of addictive behaviors, modification of classroom behaviors, remedial methods for the retarded and physically handicapped, descriptions of animal analogs, the effects of social influences on behavior, the use of drugs in behavioral approaches, and the contribution of behavior therapy to the treatment of physical illness.

Progress in Behavior Modification will present a diversity of views within the field. We will, on occasion, solicit discussions from theoreticians, researchers, or practitioners not directly associated with behavior modification. Cross-fertilization of ideas, *when maintained at the empirical level,* can be most rewarding and often leads to refinements in theory, research, and practice. In short, we propose not only to review critically developments in behavior modification at a particular point in time, but also to identify new directions and point toward future trends at all levels of inquiry.

Michel Hersen
Richard M. Eisler
Peter M. Miller

CONTENTS OF PREVIOUS VOLUMES

BEHAVIOR MODIFICATION
AND HYPNOSIS[1]

NICHOLAS P. SPANOS

Department of Psychology
Carleton University
Ottawa, Ontario, Canada

AND

THEODORE X. BARBER

Medfield Foundation
Medfield, Massachusetts

I. INTRODUCTION

A number of investigators (Fuchs, Hoch, Paldi, Abramovici, Brandes, Timor-Tritsch, & Kleinhaus, 1973; Moss & Bremer, 1973; Spanos, DeMoor, & Barber, 1973a; Weitzenhoffer, 1972; Woody, 1973) have pointed out that the hypnotic situation and various

[1] Work on this paper was supported in part by research grant MH 21294 from the National Institute of Mental Health. We are indebted to Wilfried DeMoor for invaluable assistance in conceptualizing the relationships between behavior modification and hypnosis and to William C. Coe, John F. Chaves, and Richard F. Q. Johnson for critically reading the manuscript.

behavior modification procedures (particularly systematic desensitization) include several overlapping variables. Furthermore, a number
of clinicians (Astor, 1973; Dengrove, 1973; Fuchs *et al.*, 1973; Lang,
Lazovik, & Reynolds, 1965; Larsen, 1966; Lazarus, 1973; Wolpe,
1958; Wolpe & Lazarus, 1966), who employ hypnotic procedures as
adjuncts to behavior therapy, believe that such procedures facilitate
relaxation or heighten the vividness of imagery. For example, Wolpe
and Lazarus (1966) argue that hypnosis may "enable certain patients
to achieve more vivid and realistic images, and/or deeper and more
satisfactory levels of relaxation" [p. 135]. Similarly, Fuchs *et al.*
(1973) combine hypnosis with systematic desensitization "because
[hypnosis] is an easy and smooth method of achieving a deep state
of relaxation, and because imagery and visualization of suggested
content under hypnosis is much more vivid and plastic" [p. 146].

On the basis of considerations such as those above, several
investigators (Litvak, 1970; Murray, 1963; Woody, 1973) concluded
that some of the successful results of desensitization and other
behavior modification procedures may be due to hypnosis. Woody
(1973), for instance, stated that "Hypnosis has been very much a
part of systematic desensitization, yet seldom has it been acknowledged as contributing to the behavioral changes attributed to the
reciprocal inhibition principle" [p. 252]. In like fashion, Litvak
(1970) also hypothesized that an hypnotic state may be important in
mediating the therapeutic gains seen with systematic desensitization.
In fact, he argued that hypnosis may be at work in systematic
desensitization even when a formal hypnotic induction procedure has
not been employed. In such cases, contended Litvak, the patient
undergoing desensitization may inadvertently enter an hypnotic state
which facilitates therapeutic gain.

The purpose of the present paper is threefold. *First,* we shall cast
a critical eye on the notion that the construct "hypnotic state" or
"trance" is useful for understanding the results of any behavior
modification procedure. In fact, we shall go further and argue that
the "hypnotic state" construct is not even useful for achieving a
parsimonious understanding of the phenomena traditionally subsumed under the rubric of hypnotism. *Second,* we shall contend that
the hypnotic *situation* (as opposed to the hypothetical construct
"hypnotic state" or "trance") and many behavior modification situations share a number of variables in common, and that these common variables play an important role in effecting the behavioral
changes seen in both types of situation. *Finally,* we shall argue that
research in both hypnosis and behavior modification is converging

toward a view of human social behavior that is at variance with and more fruitful than traditional notions concerning personality.

Behavior modification is a general term that subsumes a wide variety of processes and procedures. In this paper we shall consider parallels between hypnosis and those behavior modification techniques which employ subjects' imaginings as the pivot for behavioral change. Thus, we shall be comparing hypnosis with systematic desensitization (Wolpe, 1958), implosion therapy (Stampfl & Levis, 1967, 1968), and Cautela's (1967, 1969, 1970, 1971) covert procedures, which include covert reinforcement, covert extinction, and covert sensitization. Systematic desensitization has been more extensively studied than other behavior modification techniques, and for this reason much of our discussion will focus on this procedure. Behavior modification procedures which do not focus on subjects' imaginings (e.g., operant conditioning, chemical or electrical aversion therapy) will not be discussed, despite the fact that many of the psychosocial antecedents important in the hypnotic situation may well be equally important in these procedures. We shall first provide a logical and empirical critique of the "hypnotic state" construct, and then we shall delineate the commonalities in hypnotic and behavior modification situations.

II. CRITIQUE OF THE "HYPNOTIC STATE" CONSTRUCT

The behavioral phenomena which are currently grouped together under the rubric of hypnotism have been associated with the notion of an "altered state" since Puységur popularized the concept of somnambulism in 1784. In the early nineteenth century the most popular account of these phenomena (which among other behaviors included amnesia, analgesia, catalepsy, hallucination, and hyperesthesia) held that unusual behaviors occurred when subjects were placed in a "magnetic state" (Deleuze, 1879). In the mid-nineteenth century James Braid emphasized the role played by suggestion in eliciting these phenomena (Bramwell, 1903). Misled by the lethargic, sleeplike appearance of his subjects, Braid substituted the notion of "hypnosis" for that of "magnetic state" (Sarbin, 1962).

Many contemporary formulations of hypnotic phenomena continue to revolve around the nineteenth century notion of an "hypnotic trance state." According to these formulations, various ritualistic procedures labeled hypnotic inductions produce such a "trance state" in susceptible individuals (Evans, 1968; Hilgard, 1965; Orne, 1959, 1966; Reyher, 1967). Although hypnotic induction procedures can vary widely in content, they usually include interrelated suggestions that the subject will become increasingly relaxed and sleepy, will enter an unusual (an hypnotic) state, and will be able to respond maximally to further suggestions. The "altered state" believed to be produced by the induction procedures is thought to possess special properties that enable the subject to engage in "hypnotic behaviors." Typically, hypnotic behaviors are thought to include: (a) heightened responsiveness to suggestions for analgesia, amnesia, age-regression, limb catalepsy, and the like (Hilgard, 1965; Hilgard & Tart, 1966); (b) reports of unusual experiences [e.g., illogical thinking, distortions of perception (Orne, 1959, 1966)]; (c) hypnotic appearance [e.g., lethargy, passivity, fixity of gaze (Gill & Brenman, 1959)]; and (d) reports of having been hypnotized (Hilgard & Tart, 1966; Tart, 1972).

Criticism of the notion that a "magnetic" or "hypnotic" state must be postulated to explain the behaviors associated with these concepts also has a long history. Beginning with the French Commission of 1784 and continuing through the work of Faria (1906), Bertrand (1826), and Hall (1845), this tradition criticized the notion that magnetic or hypnotic procedures produced extraordinary behavioral "feats" and instead attempted to explain the phenomena that did occur with more naturalistic concepts such as attention, concentration, and imagination. This tradition has culminated in the logical and empirical criticisms of the "hypnotic state" notion proffered by contemporary investigators (Barber, 1964b, 1969, 1970a, 1970b; Barber, Spanos, & Chaves, 1974; Chaves, 1968; Coe, 1973; McPeake, 1968; Sarbin & Coe, 1972; Spanos, 1970a, 1970b; Spanos & Chaves, 1969, 1970).

A. Logical Criticisms

One important criticism of the hypnotic state notion stems from the fact that it is often denoted by the very behaviors that it seeks to explain (Barber, 1964b, 1969; Chaves, 1968; Spanos, 1970a; Spanos & Chaves, 1970, 1971). Thus, the so-called hypnotic state is deemed to be present when subjects respond to suggestions for analgesia, amnesia, hallucination, and the like, and in a circular fashion the occurrence of these very behaviors is "explained" by stating that the subject is in an hypnotic state. Circular "explanations" of this type explain nothing and, in fact, retard the development of scientific theory construction.

In the last decade advocates of the hypnotic state notion have, themselves, become aware of the construct's circularity. They have attempted to develop multiple behavioral indices with which to "converge" on the "trance state" and, thereby, eliminate the problem of circularity (Hilgard, 1965, 1969). The behavioral indices most commonly employed for this purpose are subjects' reports of having been hypnotized and heightened responsivity to suggestion. However, the use of these two indices leads to more problems than it solves. Subjects' reports of having been hypnotized and heightened responsiveness to suggestion can vary independently of one another; that is, subjects may report that they were hypnotized but fail to respond to suggestions, or conversely, that may respond well to suggestions but state that they were not hypnotized (Barber, 1969, 1970b; Barber & DeMoor, 1972; Conn & Conn, 1967). Furthermore, reports of having been hypnotized can be easily influenced by the wording of the questions used to elicit such reports (Barber, Dalal, & Calverley, 1968). Other behavioral indices such as "hypnotic appearance" have also been shown to vary independently of response to suggest (Barber, 1969).

Another approach toward finding an index of the so-called hypnotic state has been the search for physiological correlates of hypnotic behavior. Many investigators have attempted to relate hypnotic suggestibility to physiological activities occurring: (a) outside of the hypnotic situation [e.g., spontaneous EEG alpha activity (Engstrom, 1970; Galbraith, London, Leibovitz, Cooper, & Hart, 1970; Hartnett, Nowlis, & Svorad, 1969; London, Hart & Leibovitz, 1968)]; or (b) as an accompaniment to hypnotic responding [e.g., slow eye movements during hypnotic induction (Weitzenhoffer, 1969)]. Studies of this type address two separate issues, one empirical and one theoretical. The empirical issue, of course, is simply whether relationships between hypnotic suggestibility and physiological indices can be reliably demonstrated. The theoretical issue revolves around the meaning of any such correlation. In this regard it is important to note that the existence of a correlation between a physiological index and hypnotic suggestibility would not, in and of itself, constitute evidence in favor of hypnotic state conceptualizations. Such a correlation might be equally compatable, or even more compatable, with nonstate formulations of hypnosis.

Let us give a hypothetical example to indicate how correlations between physiological variables and hypnotic suggestibility might be congruent with a conceptualization of hypnosis that does not revolve around the notion of an altered state. As we shall see in some detail later, a good deal of evidence indicates that hypnotic suggestibility is, in part, a function of certain imaginative skills or abilities (Sarbin & Coe, 1972; Spanos & Barber, 1974). It is certainly possible that a generalized proclivity toward engaging in certain types of imaginative behavior may well have a physiological correlate. If this were the case we might find a correlation between the physiological variable and hypnotic suggestibility because they are both correlated with a third variable (generalized proclivity toward imaginative behavior). In brief, the demonstration of a physiological correlate of hypnotic suggestibility does not necessarily support an hypnotic state conceptualization and may even be more congruent with an alternative conceptualization.

Critical reviews of the available research literature (Barber, 1969; Evans, 1972; Sarbin & Slagle, 1972) have failed to uncover consistent evidence for physiological correlates to hypnotic suggestibility. Although several attempts to provide such evidence have been made since these reviews were written, reliable findings have yet to be clearly demonstrated. For example, Morgan (1973) found that hypnotic suggestibility was more highly correlated among identical than among fraternal twins. However, Thorkelson (1973) was unable to replicate these findings. Spiegel (1972, 1973, 1974) claimed to demonstrate a correlation between hypnotic suggestibility and subjects' ability to roll their eyes up into their heads while closing their lids. However, Spiegel's experimental methodology contained a number of serious flaws, and three independent teams of investigators have failed to confirm his findings (Eliseo, 1974; Switras, 1974; Wheeler, Reis, Wolff, Grupsmith, & Mordkoff, 1974). Some very recent findings (Gur & Gur, 1974) relating laterality of eye-movements to hypnotic suggestibility look promising. However, firm conclusions must await their replication. In brief, there is as yet little consistent evidence suggesting physiological correlates of hypnotic suggestibility. Furthermore, while such correlations would prove interesting, they would not by themselves constitute evidence in favor of the traditional hypnotic state conceptualization.

Sarbin and Coe (1972) have advanced still another criticism of the hypnotic state notion. They have pointed out that the hypnotic state construct functions primarily as a pseudoexplanation to fill gaps in empirical knowledge. They contend that such constructs: (a) develop when complex behavior cannot be readily explained in terms of easily observable antecedents; and (b) tend to drop out of scientific discourse as empirical information about the phenomena in question becomes increasingly available. Unfortunately, explanations in terms of such reified unobservables may lead investigators to believe they have explained what they do not, in fact, understand. Recently even Hilgard (1971, 1973), a major advocate of the hypnotic state notion, has conceded that the term is merely a convenient label for denoting an interrelated set of empirical phenomena and should not be used as an explanation of those phenomena.

B. Empirical Criticisms

The notion that a special "state" is required to explain hypnotic behavior has been fostered by two persistent but largely mythical propositions: (a) hypnotic subjects exhibit markedly higher levels of suggestibility than control subjects; (b) hypnotic subjects have unique and unusual experiences that are unavailable to control subjects.

During the nineteenth century the notion of heightened suggestibility among "mesmerized" or "hypnotized" subjects was associated with the belief that these individuals could perform amazing feats such as suspended animation, seeing with the back of the head, and communication with the dead (Deleuze, 1879; Dods, 1847; Haddock, 1849; Newman, 1847). Although these fanciful notions have largely disappeared from the hypnosis literature (Chaves, 1972), occasional remnants of these myths can still be found in the writings of a few contemporary investigators (e.g., Estabrooks, 1971). The more mundane notion that hypnotic procedures are associated with heightened responsiveness to more "conventional" suggestions, like those for amnesia, analgesia, catalepsy, and hallucination, persisted until quite recently. However, an extensive series of studies (Barber, 1965, 1969, 1970a, 1970b; Barber & Calverley, 1968; Barber & Ham, 1974; Barber et al., 1974; Spanos, 1970a) indicate that short instructions designed to motivate subjects' performance (task-motivational instructions) produce increments in suggestibility that equal those produced by an hypnotic induction procedure. For example, in one large-scale study (Barber, 1965) subjects administered either an hypnotic induction procedure or task motivational instructions exhibited equally high levels of responsiveness on a standardized suggestibility scale which assessed such behaviors as arm levitation, body immobility, and selective amnesia. Similar results were obtained when hypnotic and task-motivated subjects were tested for response to other suggestions. For instance, a series of studies (Barber & Hahn,

1962; Evans & Paul, 1970; Spanos, Barber, & Lang, 1974) indicated that suggestions for pain reduction are as effective in reducing physiological and verbal indices of pain in task-motivated subjects as in hypnotic subjects. Similar findings were also reported when hypnotic and task-motivated subjects were given suggestions for amnesia and for visual and auditory hallucinations (Barber & Calverley, 1964a, 1966a; Ham & Spanos, 1974; Norris, 1973; Spanos & Barber, 1968; Spanos & Ham, 1973; Spanos, Ham, & Barber, 1973b).

Another series of studies comparing unsuggestible subjects asked to fake hypnosis with highly suggestible hypnotic subjects demonstrates that faking subjects are as likely as hypnotic subjects to enact convincing performances of suggested age-regression (O'Connell, Shor, & Orne, 1970) or to perform dangerous or "immoral" suggested behaviors (Coe, Kobayashi, & Howard, 1972, 1973; Levitt, Aronoff, Morgan, Toner, Overley, & Parrish, 1975; Orne & Evans, 1965). Although some of the theoretical interpretations imposed on the results of such studies are debatable (Barber, 1969; Coe, 1973; Sheehan, 1971; Spanos & Barber, 1973; Spanos & Chaves, 1970), it is clear that the overt behavior of hypnotic subjects is well within normal limits.

Earlier in this chapter it was pointed out that some clinicians combine hypnotic and behavior modification procedures because they believe that hypnotic techniques produce more profound levels of relaxation than do other procedures. There is no experimental evidence to support this contention. On the contrary, Dunwoody and Edmonston (1974), Edmonston (1972), and McAmmond, Davidson, and Kovitz (1971) reported that hypnotic subjects and control subjects administered conventional relaxation procedures did not differ on electrodermal or electroocular indices of relaxation. In a related study, Paul (1969) found that a progressive relaxation technique produced greater levels of tension reduction on some physiological indices óf relaxation than did hypnotic procedures.

The history of hypnosis is replete with reports of highly unusual subjective experiences thought to be characteristic of the "trance state." For instance, many early mesmerists believed that religious visions were characteristic of somnambulism and that these visions provided firm evidence for the existence of God and the immortality of the human soul (Deleuze, 1879; Grimes, 1845). Some mesmerists believed that their subjects could "mentally travel" to planets and report back accurate information concerning terrestrial inhabitants. The following report concerning the moon and its inhabitants was given by a "mesmerized" subject who, while mentally traveling there, was asked if she saw any water:

Yes: but it does not look like our water, but more like milk and water, and yet it is clear ... It lies in the bottom of hollows and down the steep precipices. The "little folks" can walk upon this water and not sink; they are very light. They wear clothes; but they are very simple and all alike. They seem good sort of people. They have a curious way of jumping on the back of each other. (Haddock, 1849, pp. 91–92)

While contemporary proponents of the hypnotic state notion have modified such outlandish contentions, they often continue to argue that hypnosis produces various distortions of perception and memory and gives rise to an illogical pattern of thinking labeled "trance logic" (Evans, 1968; Hilgard, 1965; Orne, 1959, 1966). The evidence in support of these contentions is, however, largely anecdotal. Studies employing the appropriate methodological controls (Blum & Graef, 1971; Johnson, Maher, & Barber, 1972; McDonald & Smith, 1975; Spanos & Ham, 1973; Spanos et al., 1973b) indicate that hypnotic and task-motivated control subjects proffer highly similar reports concerning their experiences of perceptual and memory distortions. These studies further indicate that reports of so-called trance logic do not occur any more frequently among hypnotic than among control subjects.

At the beginning of this paper we saw that numerous clinicians contend that hypnotic procedures are particularly useful in facilitating the vividness and subjective "reality" of subjects' images. Although only three experimental studies (Ham & Spanos, 1974; Spanos et al., 1973b; Starker, 1974) relating to this contention have been carried out, all of them contradict the hypothesis. Spanos et al. (1973b) gave hypnotic and task-motivated subjects a visual hallucination suggestion and assessed the following dimensions of their visual imagery: subjective location (whether subjects' experienced their images as being "out there" or inside of their heads); vividness; transparency; differential clarity (whether or not the suggested image was uniformly clear and detailed); and belief in the "reality" of their images. Hypnotic and task-motivated subjects did not differ on any of these dimensions of visual imagery. In a related study concerning auditory hallucinations, Ham and Spanos (1974) again found that hypnotic and task-motivated subjects failed to differ on the vividness ratings assigned to their images. However, the task-motivated subjects assigned higher "belief in reality" ratings to their images than did the hypnotic subjects. Starker (1974) also found that hypnotic and task-motivated subjects did not differ in the vividness with which they rated various suggested scenes.

Taken as a whole, we believe that these logical and empirical considerations indicate that the hypnotic state construct is an inadequate conceptual tool for integrating the available data in the area of hypnosis research. For this reason, any ad hoc extension of this construct to "explain" the data of behavior therapy would be gratuitous at best.

The above considerations do not imply that hypnotic induction procedures fail to produce changes in behavior. Instead, these considerations simply indicate that the behavioral changes observed are neither a unique function of hypnotic induction procedures nor readily explicable by postulating an hypnotic state as a causal variable. Nor should the above considerations be taken to mean that there is little agreement in the area of hypnosis research concerning the antecedent variables important in eliciting hypnotic phenomena. In a recent paper (Spanos & Barber, 1974) we pointed out that theoretical controversies in this area have sometimes overshadowed substantial agreement among investigators concerning the factors that mediate hypnotic suggestibility. In fact, most contemporary investigators agree that at least two factors must be postulated to explain hypnotic phenomena.

The first [factor] can be conceptualized as a willingness on the part of the subject to cooperate with the experimenter in fulfilling the aims of the suggestions. The second can be described as a shift in cognitive orientation from an objective or pragmatic perspective to one of involvement in suggestion-related imagining. (Spanos & Barber, 1974, p. 500)

Stated more concretely, a growing body of empirical findings is converging on the view that hypnotic behavior is largely a function of cognitive variables—involvement or absorption in suggestion-related imaginings—that are engendered by the wording of specific suggestions, supported by subjects' attitudes, expectancies, and motivations toward the task, and fostered by preexisting imaginative skills or abilities. In the next section we shall suggest that these factors are also important in achieving positive behavior change with those behavior therapy techniques that utilize subjects' imaginings as an integral part of the therapeutic procedure.

III. COMPARISON OF HYPNOTIC AND BEHAVIOR MODIFICATION SITUATIONS

When the typical hypnotic situation is compared to many behavior modification situations, a number of interesting commonalities are brought to light. By specifying these commonalities we hope to elucidate the processes responsible for behavior change in both types of situations. In an earlier publication (Spanos *et al.*, 1973a) we argued that the behavioral and experiential changes occurring in hypnotic situations and in those behavior modification situations that employ subjects' imaginings can, in part, be accounted for in terms of four sets of variables: "(*a*) subjects' motivations toward both the general situation and the specific suggestions to which they are exposed, (*b*) subjects' attitudes and expectancies with regard to the suggestions they receive, (*c*) the wording of the specific suggestions they are administered, and (*d*) subjects' involvement in circumscribed patterns of imagining that are congruent with the specific suggestions or instructions that are received" [p. 50].[2]

The two years following publication of that paper have witnessed a mushrooming of empirical data in both the hypnosis and behavior modification literature. The new data in both areas have tended to corroborate the importance of the four sets of variables. In the remainder of this chapter we shall review the literature concerning each of the four sets of variables and then point out some theoretical implications.

Before proceeding further it is important to state that we are *not* contending that these four sets of variables are the only ones important in producing therapeutic change. Each of the many behavior modification techniques now in use constitutes a complex composite of interacting variables. The delineation of these variables and their effects is still in its infancy, and all of them cannot be specified with precision at this time. Many variables related to therapeutic change may turn out to be unrelated to behavioral change in the hypnotic situation. Our aim is simply to point out that there are significant commonalities in hypnotic situations and in some behavior modification situations, and these commonalities may account for at least some of the behavioral and experiential changes that occur in each situation.

At this point, it is worthwhile to discuss a variable common to hypnotic and behavior modification situations that does *not* appear as critical as was once believed in effecting behavioral changes in these situations, namely, suggestions or instructions for relaxation.

---

[2] Some of the major *differences* between hypnosis and behavior modification have been delineated by Cautela (1966b). Also, Cautela (1966a), Johnston and Donaghue (1971), and Weitzenhoffer (1972) have presented arguments to support the contention that the therapeutic benefits that occur in the hypnotic treatment of phobias are due to the use of *un*systematic desensitization (rather than to a hypothesized "trance state").

A. Relaxation Instructions

A number of investigators (Astor, 1973; Dengrove, 1973; Fuchs
et al. 1973; Litvak, 1970; Woody, 1973) have suggested theoretical
relationships between hypnosis and behavior modification on the
basis of the fact that both hypnotic induction procedures and systematic desensitization usually include explicit instructions or suggestions for relaxation. For this reason it is important to note that
response to hypnotic suggestion is not seriously affected when relaxation instructions are deleted from hypnotic induction procedures
(Barber, 1969). Similarly, an impressive series of studies indicates
that successful desensitization can be accomplished without first
relaxing subjects (Agras, Leitenberg, Barlow, Curtis, Edwards, &
Wright, 1971; Lazarus, 1971; LoPiccolo, 1971; McGlynn & Davis,
1971; Myerhoff, 1967; Rachman, 1968; Sue, 1972; Vodde & Gilner,
1971; Wilkins, 1971; Wolpin, 1966; Wolpin & Raines, 1966).

Although instruction in relaxation is not *necessary* for successful
hypnotic responding or for successful desensitization, it may sometimes play an important role in both procedures. Wickramasekera
(1973), for example, found that hypnotic suggestibility was enhanced when subjects had been first taught to relax via an electromyographic feedback procedure. Similarly, a number of investigators
have provided data indicating that relaxation may enhance the vividness of phobic imagery and the degree of affective arousal elicited by
such imagery (Chapman & Feather, 1971; Mathews, 1971; Singer,
1974; Van Egeren, 1970; Van Egeren, Feather, & Hein, 1971; Wolpe
& Flood, 1970). Furthermore, there is some evidence that relaxation
instructions may be important in reducing the fears of certain types
of patients (Brown, 1970; Davison, 1968; Farmer & Wright, 1971;
Howlett & Nawas, 1971; Lomont & Edwards, 1967; Rachman,
1966). Unfortunately, many investigators in both hypnosis and behavior therapy have *assumed a priori* that relaxation procedures do,
in fact, significantly decrease subjects' level of physiological arousal.
For example, numerous studies have compared desensitization accompanied by relaxation instructions to desensitization without
prior relaxation. In studies of this type it has been assumed that the
subjects receiving instruction in relaxation actually relax to a greater
degree than do those who fail to receive such instruction. However,
the validity of this assumption is questionable. For instance, Barber
and Hahn (1963) found that an hypnotic induction procedure failed
to produce significant decrements in arousal level. Grossberg (1965)
and Van Egeren *et al.* (1971) obtained similar negative results when

assessing the effects of progressive relaxation procedures. On the other hand, Paul (1969) found that both hypnotic and progressive relaxation techniques produced significant reductions on various indices of arousal. Reasons for the contradictory findings obtained by these studies are far from clear. Nonetheless, the unreliability with which hypnotic and progressive relaxation techniques actually produce significant degrees of relaxation may account for some of the inconsistent findings concerning the therapeutic efficacy of relaxation techniques. In short, although there are a number of complex issues to be considered (Agras *et al.*, 1971; Budzynski & Stoyva, 1973; Edmonston, 1972; Farmer & Wright, 1971; Lang, 1969; Mathews, 1971; Persely & Leventhal, 1972; Schubot, 1966; Singer, 1974; Stoudenmire, 1972; Wickramasekera, 1973), the available data seem to suggest that relaxation instructions or suggestions may not be as crucial as was once believed for eliciting the behavior changes seen in either hypnotic or behavior therapy situations. We shall now turn to some of the commonalities in hypnosis and behavior therapy that appear to be more closely tied to behavior change.

B. Motivation

All major theorists in the area of hypnosis research have stressed the importance of subjects' motivations in determining response to suggestion (Spanos & Barber, 1974). Both clinical experience and recent experimental data also point to the importance of this variable in behavior therapy situations (Lazarus, 1971; McPeake, 1975).

As was mentioned earlier, an extensive series of studies indicates that brief, task-motivational instructions substantially augment subjects' response to a wide variety of test suggestions (Barber, 1969; Barber *et al.*, 1974; Spanos & Chaves, 1970, 1971). Task-motivational instructions of this type involve the use of statements like the following: "[Try] to imagine and to visualize the things I will ask you to imagine. . . . What I ask is your cooperation. . . . [Try] to imagine vividly what I describe to you . . ." (Barber, 1969, p. 46). Very similar instructions aimed at motivating subjects to become involved in their imaginings are employed by behavior therapists. Cautela (1970, 1971, 1975), for example, does not simply ask subjects passively to imagine a particular scene when conducting covert sensitization or covert reinforcement. Instead, he exhorts subjects to become maximally involved in their imaginings with the following types of statements: "Try to imagine everything as vividly as possible, as if you were really there" (Cautela, 1970), and "Try to imagine the scene I am going to describe. Try to imagine that you are really there. Try not to imagine that you are simply seeing what I describe; try to use your other senses as well. . . . [The] main point is you are actually there experiencing everything" (Cautela, 1971, p. 192). Similar exhortations are also employed with subjects undergoing implosion therapy (DeMoor, 1969) and systematic desensitization (Wolpe, 1958). The use of similar motivational exhortations in hypnotic and various behavior therapy situations indicates that (a) subjects' motivations are probably important determinants of their response in these situations, and (b) subjects' motivations may be manipulated effectively to enhance their performance.

A recent study by McPeake (1975) has provided data which support the contention that subjects' motivations may play an important role in determining the results of behavior therapy procedures. This investigator employed several behavioral criteria to differentiate test-anxious students who were motivated to improve their school performance from test-anxious students who were unmotivated in this regard. Both groups were administered systematic desensitization for test anxiety, but only the motivated group showed posttest increments in grade point average. Numerous clinical reports also indicate that unmotivated subjects fail to change their maladaptive behavior when exposed to procedures like desensitization (Davison, 1969; Lazarus, 1971). Lazarus (1971), for example, noted that systematic desensitization can be expected to be effective only with subjects "who do not derive too many primary or secondary gains from their avoidance behavior" and "who are not strongly averse to the method" [p. 95]. Of course, motivation is not the only variable effecting changes in hypnosis and behavior modification situations. Attitudes and expectancies also appear to play an important role in this respect. These variables will be examined next.

C. Attitudes and Expectancies

A growing body of evidence from both hypnosis and behavior modification research indicates that subjects' attitudes and expectancies concerning the procedures they will undergo play an important role in determining their response in these situations. In hypnosis research two methodological procedures have been employed to assess the effects of subjects' attitudes and expectancies on their performance. When the first procedure is used, subjects' attitudes and expectancies are assessed on various self-report scales and then correlated with their hypnotic suggestibility. In the second procedure, subjects' attitudes and expectancies are experimentally manipulated and then the effects of such manipulations on hypnotic performance are noted.

Studies employing the correlational procedure have consistently indicated that subjects holding positive attitudes toward hypnosis achieve higher hypnotic suggestibility scores than those holding negative attitudes (Andersen, 1963; Barber, Ascher, & Mavroides, 1971; Barber & Calverley, 1966b; Derman & London, 1965; Diamond, Gregory, Lenney, Steadman, & Talone, 1974; London, 1961; London, Cooper, & Johnson, 1962; Melei & Hilgard, 1964; Rosenhan & Tomkins, 1964; Shor, Orne, & O'Connell, 1966; Spanos & McPeake, 1975a). Similar results have been obtained when subjects' expectations of their hypnotic performance has been correlated with their actual hypnotic performance. Subjects who expected to respond positively to hypnosis achieved higher levels of hypnotic suggestibility than those who did not expect to respond positively (Barber & Calverley, 1969; Derman & London, 1965; Diamond, 1970; Gregory & Diamond, 1973; Melei & Hilgard, 1964; Shor, 1971).

Studies that manipulated subjects' attitudes and expectancies have also consistently demonstrated the importance of these variables for hypnotic suggestibility. In one such study (Cronin, Spanos, & Barber, 1971) a group of subjects was given information aimed at producing positive attitudes and expectancies by correcting common misconceptions about hypnosis, while a second group was given no information. Subjects in the information group exhibited higher levels of hypnotic suggestibility than those in the no-information group. Several other investigators (Diamond, 1972; Shor & Cobb, 1968) obtained similar results in comparable studies.

Along the same lines, a number of clinical reports (Heron, 1953; Kroger, 1963; Pattie, 1956; Sarbin, 1950; Secter, 1957; Wolberg, 1948) indicate that subjects who are initially refractory to hypnotic procedures become more suggestible as the hypnotist inculcates positive attitudes and expectancies about hypnosis.

Just as hypnotic suggestibility can be augmented by inculcating subjects with favorable attitudes, it can be reduced by inculcating them with unfavorable attitudes. Spanos and McPeake (1975b) informed a group of subjects that hypnotic suggestibility was associated with "weak-mindedness." The subsequent hypnotic performance of these subjects was below that of subjects who did not receive such information. In two related experiments Barber and

Calverley (1964b, 1964c) found that nonhypnotic subjects were much less likely to respond to suggestions when the experimental context was defined for them as a test of *gullibility* rather than a test of *imagination*. In still another study these investigators (Barber & Calverley, 1964d) varied the tone of voice in which the experimenter presented suggestions. In one condition he spoke in a firm, positive manner designed to engender cooperation and favorable attitudes. In the other condition he spoke lackadaisically, implying that subjects need not take the experiment seriously. Subjects exposed to the firm tone of voice achieved higher suggestibility scores than those administered the suggestions lackadaisically. These studies, and others reviewed in detail elsewhere (Barber, 1970b; Barber *et al.*, 1974; Diamond, 1974) clearly indicate that subjects' attitudes and expectations toward the test situation play an important role in effecting their response to suggestion. Next, we turn to an examination of attitudes and expectancies in behavior modification.

The study of patients' attitudes and expectancies in the context of conventional psychotherapy is well established as an area of inquiry. Despite this, the role played by these variables in behavior therapy has come under experimental scrutiny only relatively recently. Nonetheless, many behavior therapists acknowledge the importance of these variables in their day-to-day clinical work. To cite but a single example, Wolpe (1958) makes a point of describing the procedures he will employ with each subject in detail. While describing these procedures, Wolpe (1969): (*a*) goes to great lengths to correct any misconceptions that could engender unfavorable attitudes toward the therapeutic procedures; (*b*) constructs favorable attitudes and expectancies by providing the patient with a learning theory rationale for the procedures he will undergoe; and (*c*) draws attention to the effectiveness of behavior therapy as compared to psychoanalytically oriented procedures.

Clinical observers of behavior therapy procedures (Brown, 1967; Klein, Dittman, Parloff, & Gill, 1969) have also stressed the fact that behavior therapists regularly manipulate their patients' attitudes and expectancies. For instance, Klein *et al.* (1969) made the following observations concerning the procedures employed by Wolpe and his associates:

Perhaps the most striking impression we came away with was how much use behavior therapists make of suggestion and how much the patient's expectations and attitudes are manipulated. . . . [The] therapist tells the patient at length about the power of the treatment method, pointing out that it has been successful with comparable patients and all but promising similar results for him too. . . . [Treatment] plans and goals were laid out in such detail that the patient was taught precisely how things would proceed and what responses and changes were expected of him along the way. (Klein *et al.*, 1969, p. 262)

Lazarus (1973) has provided an interesting clinical study which bears on the importance of subjects' expectancies in behavior therapy. Patients requesting hypnosis as a therapy were randomly assigned to two behavior therapy treatment conditions, one defined as hynosis and the other as relaxation. Two other groups who showed no preference for either type of treatment were also assigned to the two conditions. The patients requesting and receiving hypnosis showed more improvement than those who requested hypnosis but received relaxation. However, the hypnosis and relaxation conditions did not produce differential improvement for subjects who showed no initial preference for either treatment. Lazarus (1973) tentatively concluded from these findings that "the fulfilling of clients' expectations will tend to enhance their response to therapy" [p. 29]. Lazarus (1971) has also cited numerous other instances in which subjects' unfavorable attitudes and expectations toward behavior therapy techniques appear to have interfered with success of procedures such as desensitization.

Several clinical studies with implosion therapy also point to the role of patients' expectations in determining the effects of treatment. Rachman (1966), for example, found that exposure to implosion led to no improvement for spider phobics. Wolpin and Raines (1966), on the other hand, found that implosion reduced snake phobias. The discrepancy between these results could be due to expectancy differences engendered by preliminary instructions. Wolpin and Raines (1966) informed their patients that implosion was a treatment designed to help them overcome their fears and then provided the patients with a rationale for the procedures they were to undergo. None of Rachman's (1966) patients was so informed. As Wilson (1967) put it, Rachman's patients were simply imagining frightening situations and rehearsing fear responses.

Recently, a number of experimental studies have tested the hypothesis that attitudes and expectancies play an important role in the success of behavior modification procedures. In one set of experiments (Leitenberg, Agras, Barlow, & Oliveau, 1969; Oliveau, Agras, Leitenberg, Moore, & Wright, 1969) subjects were exposed to a systematic desensitization procedure that was defined to them in one of two ways: desensitization was defined as "therapy" to one group, and as an experimental technique for studying imagination to the other. In short, the former group was led to expect that desensitization would result in a reduction of their fears, whereas the other group was not. The results indicated that desensitization leads to reduction in fear only when subjects expect that it will do so. The subjects exposed to desensitization defined as an experiment in imagination did not show a reduction in their phobias.

Several other recent studies (Borkovec, 1972; Miller, 1972; Persely & Leventhal, 1972; Rosen, 1974) have also found that desensitization defined as therapy led to greater fear reduction than the same procedure defined in a nontherapeutic manner. Similar results have been obtained with implosion techniques presented in either a therapeutic or nontherapeutic context (Borkovec, 1972; Jaffe, 1968). Jaffe (1968) also found that subjects' pretreatment expectations of therapeutic success correlated highly (.70) with posttreatment approach to the feared object. Furthermore, he found that pretreatment expectations of success were highly correlated with therapeutic change in subjects exposed to a "pseudotherapy" treatment. Tori and Worell (1973) also exposed subjects to a counterconditioning procedure defined as nontherapy or to a highly convincing pseudotherapy condition. Subjects given the pseudotherapy exhibited greater posttest fear reduction than those administered the nontherapy procedure.[3]

Pseudotherapy as a control against which to compare the effects of behavior therapy has been used fairly frequently in this research area. Most studies employing this control have found that desensitization defined as therapy produced greater fear reduction than

---

[3] Another series of studies (Cataldo, 1970; Howlett & Nawas, 1971; Lomont & Brock, 1971; McGlynn, 1971, 1972; McGlynn & Mapp, 1970; McGlynn, Mealiea, & Nawas, 1969; McGlynn, Reynolds, & Linder, 1971; McGlynn & Williams, 1970; Woy & Efran, 1972) examined the effects of subjects' expectancies in a different way. In these studies the desensitization procedures were *always* defined to the subjects as therapy. However, instructions were administered to inculcate different groups with varying expectancies concerning the effectiveness of the therapy. Conflicting results were obtained in these studies: some studies found that expectancy instructions had no effect; others found that expectancy instructions had an effect; and in three studies (Cataldo, 1970; Howlett & Nawas, 1971; Lomont & Brock, 1971) the results appear to be equivocal.

The majority of these studies failed to assess the success of their attitude-change manipulations in actually changing subjects' attitudes about the therapy they were to undergo. This is an important deficiency because several reports (Cataldo, 1970; Gelder, Bancroft, Gath, Johnston, Mathews, & Shaw, 1973; Marcia, Rubin, & Efran, 1969) indicated that subjects often forget or "cognitively neutralize" information designed to change their attitudes about behavior therapy. Thus, the contradictions in the above studies may be due to an unequal effectiveness of the various attitude-change manipulations in changing subjects' attitudes.

pseudotherapy (Davison, 1968; Jaffe, 1968; Lang *et al.*, 1965; Paul, 1966). The conventional explanation of these results holds that expectations cannot account for the results of behavior therapy. However, McReynolds and Tori (1972) provide data indicating that desensitization therapy procedures contain greater expectancy-inducing properties than do the typical pseudotherapy treatments employed in previous studies. Thus, the greater fear reductions typically found when behavior therapy is compared to pseudotherapy may be due to the greater expectancy enhancing properties of the behavior therapy procedures. Foreyt and Hagen (1973) provided data consistent with this hypothesis when comparing covert sensitization with a convincing pseudotherapy procedure in a study dealing with weight loss. These investigators found that subjects in both treatments reported equal decrements in the palatability of their favorite foods. However, in an important clinical study relating to the issue of pseudotherapy, a group of British investigators found more complex results (Gelder *et al.*, 1973). Implosion and desensitization treatments did not differ either from each other or from a convincing pseudotherapy condition in alleviating delimited phobias. However, the pseudotherapy condition was not as effective as either of the "real" therapies in reducing the generalized fears of agoraphobic patients. In brief, the results of this study taken together with the other studies cited here support the hypothesis that subjects' attitudes and expectancies foster some, but certainly not all, of the therapeutic gains achieved by behavior therapy procedures.[4]

D. The Wording of Suggestions

While motivations, attitudes, and expectancies play an important role in determining subjects' response to suggestion, it is the wording of the suggestions themselves that provides specific information

---

[4] The studies cited above indicate that the definition of the situation as "therapy" is extremely important in generating expectancies that lead to therapeutic benefit. Recent research has also begun to specify other antecedent variables that function in this regard. For example, a series of studies (Bernstein, 1973, 1974; Bernstein & Nietzel, 1973; Blom & Craighead, 1974; Miller & Bernstein, 1972; Nietzel, 1973) indicate that significant reductions in phobic behavior can be achieved *without* therapeutic procedures like desensitization, simply by manipulating various situational variables (e.g., strong demands to approach the feared object as opposed to weak demands). In fact, one of these studies (Nietzel, 1973) found that strong interpersonal demands to approach the feared object were as effective as systematic desensitization in reducing fear.

concerning the overt behavior and cognitive activity expected in both hypnotic and behavior modification situations.

Hypnotic suggestions, and the instructions typically employed by behavior therapists, do *not* direct subjects to engage in overt behavior. On the contrary, these suggestions usually provide subjects with a cognitive strategy; they instruct subjects to imagine certain hypothetical events, and imply that these imaginings will produce changes in behavior. The following suggestion for arm heaviness, taken from the Stanford Hypnotic Susceptibility Scale, is typical of those used in hypnotic situations:

Imagine you are holding something heavy in your hand. . . . Now the hand and arm feel heavy as if the [imagined] weight were pressing down . . . as it feels heavier and heavier and heavier the imagined weight begins to move down. . . . (Weitzenhoffer & Hilgard, 1962, p. 17)

The wording of this suggestion clearly imparts two expectations to the subject: (*a*) that his arm is to lower; (*b*) that the arm lowering is to be experienced as an involuntary movement rather than as a self-guided volitional act. This suggestion also provides a cognitive strategy for meeting these expectations; it asks subjects to become involved in imagining a specific situation—a weight pressing on their arm—which, if it were a real situation rather than imaginary, would be expected to produce an involuntary lowering of the arm.

Behavior therapists often use instructions that are similar to hypnotic suggestions in at least two ways. *First,* these instructions explicitly specify the overt behavior changes expected from the subject. *Second,* they instruct subjects to imagine events which, if they in fact existed, would lead to the behavioral change. Cautela (1967), when engaged in covert sensitization with alcoholics, defines avoidance of alcohol as the specific behavioral change that is expected, and then instructs patients to imagine a series of behaviors culminating in the involuntary avoidance of alcohol (e.g., vomiting while raising a drink to the lips). Other behavior modification procedures, such as covert reinforcement and desensitization, also instruct patients to imagine situations designed to mediate specific overt behaviors. In sum, both hypnotic and behavior therapy suggestions provide a cognitive strategy for mediating overt behavior.

Naturally, there are differences as well as similarities in the suggestions used in hypnotic and behavior modification situations. For instance, subjects in most hypnosis research are seen for only a single session, during which they are administered numerous suggestions instructing them to imagine relatively unrelated events (e.g., imagine your arm is being pulled upward by a balloon; imagine your hands are two pieces of steel welded together). On the other hand, patients in behavior therapy situations are usually seen over several sessions, and during that time they are typically instructed to imagine a series of events relating to the same situational theme (e.g., imagining progressive approach responses to a feared object). Differences of this type are, of course, important for mediating the different kinds of behavior elicited by hypnotic and behavior therapy situations. Nonetheless, such differences should not obscure a basic commonality. In both situations, suggestions instruct subjects to engage in specific patterns of imagining in order to achieve specific behavioral results.

Other commonalities can also be noted in the suggestions used in hypnotic and behavior therapy situations. For instance, in both situations the suggestions employed often vary along a dimension of concreteness. Some hypnotic suggestions specify concrete and detailed situations (e.g., instructing subjects to imagine a cast on their arm that makes the arm rigid), whereas others specify only the behaviors and experiences expected and leave the details of the imaginings up to the subject (e.g., instructing subjects simply to imagine that the arm is rigid). Behavior therapy suggestions can also vary along an abstract-concrete dimension. For example, desensitization hierarchies are sometimes highly individualized and specific, whereas at other times more general, standardized hierarchies are employed. In these latter cases subjects must employ their imaginings to tailor the relatively abstract instructions to their own specific circumstances.

In the last few years a number of studies have begun to investigate the structure of hypnotic suggestions (Barber & Hahn, 1962; Chaves & Barber, 1974; Coe, Allan, Krug, & Wurzmann, 1974; Evans & Paul, 1970; Spanos & Barber, 1972; Spanos et al., 1974; Spanos, Horton, & Chaves, 1975; Spanos, Spillane, & McPeake, 1976). These studies have either assessed or manipulated (a) the extent to which a strategy for imagining is provided by various types of suggestions (e.g., suggestions for analgesia and for arm levitation), or (b) the congruence between the suggested imaginings and the behavioral effects that are sought. Recently, the results of these studies have been summarized in the following manner: "Suggestions that provide the subject with an explicit strategy for imagining—that ask him to direct his imaginings along specific channels that are congruent with the aims of the suggestions—are more likely to be experienced than suggestions that do not provide such a strategy" (Spanos & Barber, 1974, p. 507).

The role played by the structure of the suggestions employed in behavior therapy has yet to be systematically investigated. However, the results of four studies indicate that the structure of suggestions may play an important role in behavior therapy procedures (Gibbons, Kilbourne, Saunders, & Castles, 1970; Marks, Gelder, & Edwards, 1968; Moore, 1965; Woody & Schauble, 1969). In two of these studies (Gibbons et al., 1970; Woody & Schauble, 1969) a typical desensitization procedure was compared to a hypnotic-desensitization procedure in which (a) extra fear-reducing suggestions were given in addition to typical desensitization hierarchy items, and/or (b) the hierarchy items were much more elaborately worded for the hypnosis groups. In both of these studies the hypnosis-desensitization treatment reduced fear to a greater extent than did the more traditional desensitization procedure. In a third study by Marks et al. (1968) a hypnotic induction procedure followed by direct (nonimaginal) suggestions for fear reduction was compared to a desensitization procedure containing more elaborate, imagery-inducing hierarchy items. The desensitization group exhibited greater fear reduction than the hypnosis group. A fourth study, carried out by Moore (1965), did not involve hypnosis. Instead, asthmatic patients were assigned to one of three treatments: standard desensitization; relaxation plus direct (nonimaginal) suggestion; or relaxation alone. Only the desensitization group showed significant improvement on physiological measures of respiratory capacity.

Unfortunately, all but one of these studies (Moore, 1965) confounded the type of suggestions employed with the presence or absence of an hypnotic induction procedure. Taken as a group, however, they suggest the following hypotheses that need to be tested in further research: (a) Other things being equal, the presence of an hypnotic induction procedure will not facilitate the effects of systematic desensitization. (b) The length and elaborateness of hierarchy suggestions will significantly effect the level of fear reduction achieved with desensitization.

Subjects in both hypnotic and behavior therapy situations differ widely in the extent to which they respond to the suggestions they are administered. Next, we shall examine some of the cognitive processes that appear to be related to such differential responding.

E. Involved Imagining

Before examining data relating to the concept of involved imagining in hypnosis and behavior therapy, it behooves us to look more closely at the notion of imagining. Some behavior therapists define imaginings as covert *stimuli* eliciting discrete responses such as relaxation and anxiety. However, in order to understand the data of hypnosis and behavior therapy, we believe it is more profitable to focus on the response rather than on the stimulus aspects of subjects' imaginings. Suggested imagining consists of covert but active responding; it involves an ongoing synthesis of diverse sensory information with information retrieved from memory, for the purpose of constructing and representing the hypothetical events refered to or implied by the suggestions (Neisser, 1972; Pavio, 1971; Sarbin, 1972; Spanos, 1973). Thus, imagining includes not only sensory imagery but a more general change in cognitive focus.

In recent years, the general change in cognitive focus associated with the term imagining has been of major theoretical interest to many investigators. Evidence from a wide variety of sources appears to be converging on the notion that information is processed in the nervous system along two separate but complementary and interacting channels (Bower, 1970; Neisser, 1967; Pavio, 1971). One channel, specialized for the processing of sequential and linear aspects of information, is of primary importance for what is usually classified as propositional, critical, or analytical thinking (Bogen, 1969; Horowitz, 1970; Levy, 1969; Ornstein, 1972). The other channel, specialized for processing spatial and "representational" aspects of information, is of importance for what is classified as holistic, synthetic, intuitive, or appositional thinking or imagining (Benton, 1972; Bogen, 1969; Horowitz, 1970; Klinger, 1971; Ornstein, 1972). Obviously, any complex cognitive activity involves the continual interaction of processes associated with both channels. Nonetheless, imagining, which has traditionally been associated with holistic and spatial modes of cognitive representation, consists predominantly of those processes classified in terms of the "appositional" channel.

Recent work has also supported the hypothesis that propositional or analytic modes of cognition are subserved primarily by the dominant (usually the left) cerebral hemisphere, while imaginative or appositional modes are subserved primarily by the nondominant hemisphere (Bogen, 1969; Galin, 1974; Kocel, Galin, Ornstein, & Merrin, 1972; Ornstein, 1972; Seamon, 1972). Furthermore, there is evidence to indicate that laterality of eye movement (i.e., the tendency of subjects to move their eyes to the left while engaging in reflective thought) constitutes a reliable measure of the extent of right-hemisphere activity (Bakan, 1969; Kocel *et al.*, 1972; Singer, 1974).

Subjects differ in the extent to which they can call up and attend consistently to their imaginings; that is, they differ in their ability to become involved or absorbed in their imaginings (Singer, 1974;

Singer & Antrobus, 1972). The more a subject becomes involved in suggested imaginings, the more he simultaneously fails to maintain a critical stance toward his experience—and therefore the more he fails to indicate to himself that his imaginings are not actual, external occurrences (Sarbin & Coe, 1972; Shor, 1959, 1970; Spanos, 1973; Spanos & Barber, 1974; Spanos & McPeake, 1974). In this respect, involvement in imagining is more closely related to active role rehearsal or involved play acting than to the passive reception of external events traditionally connoted by the term stimulus (Horowitz, 1970; Klinger, 1971; Pavio, 1971; Ryle, 1949; Sarbin, 1970; Singer, 1974; Skinner, 1953).

It will be recalled that the suggestions employed in both hypnosis and behavior therapy implicitly or explicitly instruct subjects to carry out patterns of imagining consistent with those overt behaviors preestablished as the goals of either the experiment or the therapy. In both areas of investigation, evidence is accumulating that subjects tend to engage in the desired behavior when they become absorbed or involved in imaginings that are consistent with the suggestions given. For example, a series of studies (Spanos, 1971, 1973; Spanos & Ham, 1975; Spanos et al., 1973b; Spanos & McPeake, 1974) indicate that for the duration of their responding, hypnotic subjects who pass suggestions: (a) tend to engage in suggestion-related imaginings; and simultaneously (b) fail to critically analyze or contradict the reality of their imaginings. Conversely, subjects who fail suggestions tend to report that they: (a) were not motivated to or did not expect to pass; or (b) continuously contradicted the reality of their imaginings; that is, they indicated to themselves that their imaginings were not actual occurrences.

A second line of evidence pointing to the importance of involved imagining in hypnotic performance comes from studies that attempted to enhance suggestibility in unresponsive subjects. A number of these reports (Comins, Fullam, & Barber, 1975; Diamond, 1972; Kinney & Sachs, 1974; Sachs, 1969, 1971; Sachs & Anderson, 1967) indicate that suggestibility can be enhanced when subjects are trained, through direct instruction and with the use of modeling procedures, to engage in suggestion-related imagining and to exclude competing thoughts and sensory imputs from their focus of awareness.

Finally, a third line of evidence relating imagining and hypnotic suggestibility comes from studies which have assessed nonhypnotic imaginative involvements. Various procedures including self-report scales, semistructured interviews, and several behavioral indices have been devised to assess the extent to which individuals become absorbed or involved in such every-day imaginative activities as watching a movie, listening to poetry, dramatic role playing, or observing a sunset. Put somewhat differently, these procedures appear to be tapping an aspect of subjects' generalized proclivity to engage in appositional types of cognitive activity. An extensive series of studies have consistently indicated that these measures of involved imagining, or appositional cognition, correlate with hypnotic suggestibility (As, 1962; As, O'Hara, & Munger, 1962; Barber & Glass, 1962; Coe, 1964; Coe & Sarbin, 1966; J. R. Hilgard, 1970, 1974; Lee-Teng, 1965; Sarbin & Lim, 1963; Shor, Orne, & O'Connell, 1962; Spanos & McPeake, 1975a,b; Tellegen & Atkinson, 1974). These positive results are particularly impressive when it is noted that imaginative involvement is the only "trait" or cognitive skill measure that has correlated consistently with hypnotic suggestibility (Spanos & Barber, 1974). Dovetailing neatly with these findings, a number of recent studies (Bakan, 1971; Meskin & Singer, 1974) indicate that measures of imaginative predisposition similar to those that relate to hypnotic suggestibility also correlate with laterality of eye movement. As mentioned above, laterality of eye movement provides an index of right-hemisphere functioning and appears to correlate with hypnotic suggestibility (Bakan, 1969; Gur & Gur, 1974). Also consistent with these findings are recent electroencephalographic (EEG) data indicating that hypnotic responsivity, like other spatial and imaginative tasks, is associated with the relative predominance of right-hemispheric functioning (Morgan, Macdonald, & Hilgard, 1974).

In summary, evidence accumulated in widely different experimental contexts with a variety of methodological procedures, converges with a high degree of consistency on the following proposition: responsiveness to suggestion is closely related to a particular type of cognitive activity; subjects who respond to suggestions tend to become involved in imaginings that are consistent with the themes that are suggested, whereas those who are unresponsive fail to become involved in suggestion-related imaginings.

Systematic research concerning the role played by such cognitive factors as imagining and thinking in mediating the beneficial changes observed in behavior therapy is still of relatively recent origin (Breger & McGaugh, 1965; D'Zurilla & Goldfried, 1971; Goldfried, 1971; Jacobs & Wolpin, 1971; Locke, 1971; Meichenbaum, 1976; Valins & Ray, 1967; Wilkins, 1971). Nonetheless, the importance of involved imagining is intimated by the insistence of many behavior therapists that vivid and realistic imagery is a prerequisite to therapeutic success with treatments like desensitization (Cautela, 1971; Nawas, Mealiea, & Fishman, 1971; Wolpe, 1958, 1969). Oftentimes, behavior therapists appear to employ the term imagery to refer to the broader concept of *involved imagining*. For instance, when carrying out implosion therapy, Stampfl and Levis (1967, 1968) do not simply ask the patient to imagine a particular scene. Instead, they try to involve him in the activity by instructing him to play-act and to "live" the scene with genuine emotion. After repeating a particular scene in imagination, the patient is encouraged to act out the scene, and is given every opportunity to verbalize his role-playing behavior. Sometimes, sound effects are added to make the patient's imaginings as realistic as possible (Kirchner & Hogan, 1966). Similarly, noxious-smelling substances are sometimes used in covert sensitization to "assist" subjects' imaginings (Maletzky, 1974).

Recent data (McLemore, 1972) suggest that *vividness of imagery per se* is not as important in behavior therapy as is sometimes indicated. Several studies (J. Hilgard, 1970; Morgan & Lam, 1969; Perry, 1973; Spanos, Valois, Ham, & Ham, 1973c; Sutcliffe, Perry, & Sheehan, 1970) also indicate that vividness of imagery is, at best, only inconsistently related, and at times completely unrelated, to hypnotic suggestibility. From our perspective, subjects who report imagery but remain uninvolved in their imaginings will tend to show little behavior change either in treatments such as desensitization or in hypnotic situations. Danaher and Thoresen (1972) have reached a similar conclusion concerning desensitization: "Simply visualizing an imaginal scene is not sufficient in most therapeutic regimens; rather, actual involvement in the scene itself with patient-as-actor is more often required" [p. 137]. Janda and Rimm (1972) provide data which point to the importance of "involvement in the imagined scene" in behavior therapy. These investigators found that the extent of discomfort experienced when imagining noxious scenes during covert sensitization was correlated ($r = .53$) with improvement on the criterion measure (weight loss).

At this point it is worth noting that both hypnotic and behavior therapy subjects often respond successfully when they imagine situations that are quite different from those suggested. For instance, hypnotic subjects given the suggestion that their arm was being pulled upward by an attached, helium-filled balloon tended to show arm levitation and to describe this response as an involuntary act, when they imagined situations such as the following: the wrist attached to a pulley that was raising the arm; air being pumped into the hollowed-out arm; or the hand pushed upward by a gust of wind

(Spanos, 1971; Spanos & Barber, 1972). Although these imagined situations differ from one another and from the situation contained in the suggestion, they are all consistent with the overt behavior and subjective experience required by the suggestion; that is, they are all consistent with arm rising experienced as involuntary occurrence. In short, these and other data indicate that subjects tend to pass hypnotic suggestions when they become involved in imaginings that are consistent with the aims of the suggestions, regardless of whether or not their imaginings correspond closely to the specific suggested contents (Spanos, 1971, 1973; Spanos & Barber, 1972; Spanos & Ham, 1973; Spanos & McPeake, 1974). These findings do not, of course, indicate that imaginings of any kind lead subjects to pass suggestions. Subjects whose imaginings are unrelated to the aims of the suggestions tend to fail (Spanos, 1973).

The imaginings of behavior therapy patients, like those of hypnotic subjects, can mediate change even when they are markedly different from the situations described in the instructions or suggestions. Weitzman (1967), for example, interviewed six patients undergoing systematic desensitization about their imaginings. He reported that when closely questioned, all six patients reported a flow of visual imagery. In addition, he noted: "The initiating scene, once visualized, shifted and changed its form. Moreover, these transformations took place continuously and, when the imagining was terminated by the therapist, had produced images which were quite removed in their content from the intended stimulus" (Weitzman, 1967, p. 305). Similar results have also been reported by Brown (1967), Barrett (1969), Singer (1974), and Weinberg and Zaslove (1963). In a pilot study Spanos, Kosloff, and Chaves (1971) also found that desensitization subjects sometimes reported experiences that differed considerably from the scenes that were suggested. For instance, one of these subjects, asked to imagine herself progressively approaching a snake at the end of a corridor, instead visualized the following: "When you asked me to imagine the snake, I started thinking about millions of these little snakes coming up through the sand. When I thought about millions of snakes, I was scared to death. I started to imagine the snake, but I was still on the beach and they all started crawling. Oh, it was terrible. It was crawling all over me." Reports such as these indicate that subjects undergoing behavior therapy, like hypnotic subjects, at times imagine situations that are quite different from those suggested.

Unfortunately, data concerning the range of content in patients' imaginings that is congruent with therapeutic change have yet to be systematically gathered. Nonetheless, it is interesting that some behavior therapists (e.g., Wolpe, 1969) regularly ask subjects about their imaginings in order to make sure that they have not strayed too far from the intent of the suggestions. When viewed in the light of findings from hypnosis research, this indicates that imaginings may fail to effect therapeutic change when their contents are inconsistent with or unrelated to the aims of the suggestions.

The interrelationships between imaginings and overt behavior are only beginning to be studied in both hypnosis and behavior modification. It is our belief, however, that focused research attention on such interrelationships will reap important theoretical benefits for both areas.

IV. THEORETICAL TRENDS IN HYPNOSIS AND BEHAVIOR THERAPY

Thus, far, we have delineated a number of variables that appear to be related to behavioral change in both hypnotic and behavior modification situations. Here we will address ourselves briefly to the theoretical implications of these commonalities for both areas of investigation.

Techniques for the direct and systematic modification of problem behaviors were employed regularly during the latter half of the last century. Both Braid and Bramwell employed hypnotic procedures and direct suggestions for the treatment of such problems as alcoholism and impotence (Bramwell, 1903). Similarly, at the turn of the century, American psychologists were using Pavlovian conditioning theory to develop behavioral treatments for obsessive-compulsive disorders and for phobias (Freedberg, 1973). However, with the rise of psychoanalytic theorizing, these early approaches were largely superseded and forgotten. For most of the present century psychological thinking has been dominated by theories of personality and psychotherapy that conceptualize human behavior as resulting from relatively permanent "traits" or "underlying dynamic dispositions" (Bandura, 1969; Mischel, 1968, 1973; Ullmann & Krasner, 1969). The trait approach to personality has promulgated a number of highly influential (though not necessarily useful) premises that have guided both psychological research and the practice of psychotherapy. These premises include the notions that: (a) behavior is of primary theoretical importance as an index of broad, internal dispositions; (b) behavior will be successfully predicted when valid indices of an individual's most important traits can be discerned; (c) situational influences on adult behavior are relatively unimportant, perhaps producing superficial alterations in behavior, but leaving the "underlying dynamics" uneffected; and (d) important psychotherapeutic change can only occur in a relatively long-term relationship aimed at reorganizing the "internalized dynamic equilibrium" of the patient (Mischel, 1968).

Research in behavior therapy, with its demonstrations of therapeutic success and its emphasis on both the careful delineation of the behavior to be changed and the specification of situational contingencies used to produce change, has constituted one of the major challenges to traditional trait conceptualizations. The success of behavior therapy implies more than the continued development of useful behavior-changing procedures. It also portends a view of human functioning that differs fundamentally from traditional trait conceptualizations, a view that emphasizes the modifiability of complex human behavior in terms of situational contingencies.

The theoretical underpinnings of contemporary behavior therapy developed largely from conceptual models used to explain animal behavior (Bandura, 1969; Franks, 1969). It is from the animal laboratory that behavior therapists learned the value of stressing the objective delineation of specific behaviors and the manipulation of discrete stimulus contingencies. Nonetheless, traditional theories of learning, which view the development of human behavioral repertoires as the gradual and automatic buildup of specific stimuli with specific responses, have proven inadequate for handling such complex cognitive behavior as language acquisition and imagining (Miller, Galanter, & Pribram, 1960; Sarbin, 1970; Spielberger & DeNike, 1966).

The inadequacies of traditional learning theories have led contemporary social-learning theorists (Bandura, 1974; Mischel, 1973; Rotter, 1954) to reinterpret the results of behavior therapy in terms of conceptual models that stress the primary importance of human cognitive functioning. These contemporary social-learning approaches emphasize the role played by subjects' expectations and meanings in mediating the behavioral effects produced by situational contingencies. Within these conceptual frameworks subjects' imaginings are seen as playing a crucial role in determining both the meanings that they attach to situations and the behavior that they display. To cite but one example, Mischel (1973) has reviewed his own studies which indicate that the behavior of children attempting to delay gratification can be markedly altered by instructing them to imaginatively reconstruct the objective delay situation in various ways. Social learning theorists do not, of course, deny the importance of subject characteristics in influencing behavior, nor do they state that behavior is a function *only* of situational variables (Ekehammar, 1974). Instead, they have attempted to develop theoretical models sufficiently comprehensive to deal with the interactive effects of subjects' characteristics and situational contingencies (Endler & Hunt, 1966, 1968, 1969; Magnusson, 1974; Mischel, 1973; Mischel, Zeiss, & Zeiss, 1974; Moos, 1969).

The development of hypnosis in the twentieth century parallels that of personality theory in a number of respects. As was the case with personality theory, the rise of psychoanalytic movement led to conceptualizations of hypnotic responsivity in terms of "underlying dynamic dispositions" (Ferenczi, 1950; Freud, 1953; Gill & Brenman, 1959; Kubie & Margolin, 1944; Schilder, 1956). However, personality trait indices derived from such theories have consistently failed to correlate with hypnotic suggestibility (Barber, 1964a; Hilgard, 1965). On the other hand, much of the work reviewed earlier clearly indicates the importance of situational variables on hypnotic suggestibility. In this regard, however, it is important to note that contemporary hypnotic theorists, like social learning theorists, do not contend that situational variables are the *only* factors influencing subjects' response. Instead, they argue that situation-specific attitudes, expectancies, and motivations effect hypnotic suggestibility through interaction with particular subject characteristics [e.g., imaginative skills (Spanos & Barber, 1974)]. One corollary of this perspective indicates that situational variables like attitudes and expectancies may moderate the relationship between subject characteristics and hypnotic suggestibility (Barber, 1969; Hilgard, 1965). Recent support for this contention was obtained by Spanos and McPeake (1975b), who found a significant correlation between imaginative involvement and hypnotic suggestibility when subjects had been given favorable information about hypnosis, but no correlation when they received unfavorable information. A number of other studies (Bowers, 1971; Gur & Reyher, 1973; Rosenhan, 1969; Silver, 1974) have also demonstrated the occurrence of complex interactions among situational variables, subject characteristics, and hypnotic suggestibility.

In short, social learning conceptualizations of behavior therapy and contemporary theories of hypnotic behavior appear to be converging on a view of human functioning that stresses the role of complex cognitive factors in mediating situational influences on behavior. Therefore, a free flow of information between these two areas, unencumbered by the unnecessary notion of an "hypnotic state," could prove mutually enhancing. In both areas of inquiry continued research based on this common perspective can be expected to lead to more fruitful and comprehensive generalizations concerning human social behavior.

REFERENCES

Agras, W. S., Leitenberg, H., Barlow, D. H., Curtis, N. A., Edwards, J., & Wright, D. Relaxation in systematic desensitization. *Archives of General Psychiatry*, 1971, **25**, 511–514.

Andersen, M. L. Correlates of hypnotic performance: An historical and role-theoretical analysis. Unpublished doctoral dissertation, University of California, Berkeley, 1963.

As, A. Non-hypnotic experiences related to hypnotizability in male and female college students. *Scandinavian Journal of Psychology*, 1962, 3, 112–121.

As, A., O'Hara, J. W., & Munger, M. P. The measurement of subjective experiences presumably related to hypnotic susceptibility. *Scandinavian Journal of Psychology* 1962, 3, 47–64.

Astor, M. H. Hypnosis and behavior modification combined with psychoanalytic psychotherapy. *International Journal of Clinical and Experimental Hypnosis*, 1973, **21**, 18–24.

Bakan, P. Hypnotizability, laterality of eye movement and functional brain asymmetry. *Perceptual and Motor Skills*, 1969, **28**, 927–932.

Bakan, P. The eyes have it. *Psychology Today*, 1971, 4, 64–68.

Bandura, A. *Principles of behavior modification*. New York: Holt, 1969.

Bandura, A. Behavior theory and the models of man. *American Psychologist*, 1974, **29**, 859–869.

Barber, T. X. Hypnotizability, suggestibility, and personality. V. A critical review of research findings. *Psychological Reports*, 1964, 14, 299–320. (a)

Barber, T. X. "Hypnosis" as a causal variable in present-day psychology: A critical analysis. *Psychological Reports*, 1964, 14, 839–842. (b)

Barber, T. X. Measuring "hypnotic-like" suggestibility with and without "hypnotic induction"; psychometric properties, norms, and variables influencing response to the Barber Suggestibility Scale (BSS). *Psychological Reports*, 1965, 16, 809–844.

Barber, T. X. *Hypnosis: A scientific approach*. Princeton, N.J.: Van Nostrand-Reinhold, 1969.

Barber, T. X. *LSD, marihuana, yoga, and hypnosis*. Chicago: Aldine, 1970. (a)

Barber, T. X. Suggested ("hypnotic") behavior: The trance paradigm versus an alternative paradigm. Medfield, Mass.: Medfield Foundation, 1970. (b)

Barber, T. X., Ascher, L. M., & Mavroides, M. Effect of practice on hypnotic suggestibility: A re-evaluation of Hull's postulates. *American Journal of Clinical Hypnosis*, 1971, **14**, 48–53.

Barber, T. X., & Calverley, D. S. An experimental study of "hypnotic" (auditory and visual) hallucinations. *Journal of Abnormal and Social Psychology*, 1964, 63, 13–20. (a)

Barber, T. X., & Calverley, D. S. Empirical evidence for a theory of "hypnotic" behavior:

Effects of pretest instructions on response to primary suggestions. *Psychological Record*, 1964, **14**, 457–467. (b)

Barber, T. X., & Calverley, D. S. The definition of the situation as a variable affecting "hypnotic-like" suggestibility. *Journal of Clinical Psychology*, 1964, **20**, 438–440. (c)

Barber, T. X., & Calverley, D. S. Effect of E's tone of voice on "hypnotic-like" suggestibility. *Psychological Reports*, 1964, **15**, 139–144. (d)

Barber, T. X., & Calverley, D. S. Toward a theory of "hypnotic" behavior: Experimental analysis of suggested amnesia. *Journal of Abnormal Psychology*, 1966, **71**, 95–107. (a)

Barber, T. X., & Calverley, D. S. Toward a theory of hypnotic behavior: Experimental evaluation of Hull's postulate that hypnotic susceptibility is a habit phenomenon. *Journal of Personality*, 1966, **34**, 416–433. (b)

Barber, T. X., & Calverley, D. S. Toward a theory of "hypnotic" behavior: Replication and extension of experiments by Barber and co-workers (1962-65) and Hilgard and Tart (1966). *International Journal of Clinical and Experimental Hypnosis*, 1968, **16**, 179–195.

Barber, T. X., & Calverley, D. S. Multidimensional analysis of "hypnotic" behavior. *Journal of Abnormal Psychology*, 1969, **74**, 209–220.

Barber, T. X., Dalal, A. S., & Calverley, D. S. The subjective reports of hypnotic subjects. *American Journal of Clinical Hypnosis*, 1968, **11**, 74–88.

Barber, T. X., & DeMoor, W. A theory of hypnotic induction procedures. *American Journal of Clinical Hypnosis*, 1972, **15**, 112–135.

Barber, T. X., & Glass, L. B. Significant factors in hypnotic behavior. *Journal of Abnormal and Social Psychology*, 1962, **64**, 222–228.

Barber, T. X., & Hahn, K. W., Jr. Physiological and subjective responses to pain-producing stimulation under hypnotically suggested and waking-imagined "analgesia." *Journal of Abnormal and Social Psychology*, 1962, **65**, 411–418.

Barber, T. X., & Hahn, K. W. Hypnotic induction and "relaxation." *Archives of General Psychiatry*, 1963, **8**, 295–300.

Barber, T. X., & Ham, M. W. *Hypnotic phenomena*. Morristown, N.J.: General Learning Press, 1974.

Barber, T. X., Spanos, N. P., & Chaves, J. F. *Hypnosis, imagination, and human potentialities*. Oxford: Pergamon, 1974.

Barrett, C. L. Systematic desensitization versus implosive therapy. *Journal of Abnormal Psychology*, 1969, **74**, 587–592.

Benton, A. L. The "mirror" hemisphere. *Journal of the History of Medicine and Allied Sciences*, 1972, **27**, 5–14.

Bernstein, D. A. Situational factors in behavioral fear assessment. *Behavior Therapy*, 1973, **4**, 41–48.

Bernstein, D. A. Manipulation of avoidance behavior as a function of increased or decreased demand on repeated behavioral tests. *Journal of Consulting and Clinical Psychology*, 1974, **42**, 896–900.

Bernstein, D. A., & Nietzel, M. T. Procedural variation in behavioral avoidance tests. *Journal of Consulting and Clinical Psychology*, 1973, **41**, 165–174.

Bertrand, A. J. F. *Du magnétisme animal en France*. Paris: Baillière et Fils, 1826.

Blom, B. E., & Craighead, E. W. The effects of situational and instructional demands on indices of speech anxiety. *Journal of Abnormal Psychology*. 1974, **83**, 667–675.

Blum, G. S., & Graef, J. R. The detection over time of subjects simulating hypnosis. *International Journal of Clinical and Experimental Hypnosis*, 1971, **14**, 211–224.

Bogen, J. E. The other side of the brain. II. An appositional mind. *Bulletin of the Los Angeles Neurological Societies*, 1969, **34**, 135–162.

Borkovec, T. D. Effects of expectancy on the outcome of systematic desensitization and implosive treatments for analogue anxiety. *Behavior Therapy*, 1972, 3, 29–40.

Bower, G. H. Analysis of a mnemonic device. *American Scientist*, 1970, 58, 496–510.

Bowers, K. S. Sex and susceptibility as moderator variables in the relationship of creativity and hypnotic susceptibility. *Journal of Abnormal Psychology*, 1971, 78, 93–100.

Bramwell, J. M. *Hypnotism: Its history, practice, theory.* London: Grant Richards, 1903.

Breger, L., & McGaugh, J. L. Critique and reformulation of "learning-theory" approaches to psychotherapy and neurosis. *Psychological Bulletin*, 1965, 63, 338–358.

Brown, B. M. Cognitive aspects of Wolpe's Behavior Therapy. *American Journal of Psychiatry*, 1967, 124, 854–859.

Brown, H. A. Systematic desensitization: Counterconditioning or expectancy manipulation? Unpublished doctoral dissertation, State University of New York at Stony Brook, 1970.

Budzynski, T. H., & Stoyva, J. M. Biofeedback techniques in behavior therapy. In D. Shapiro *et al.* (Eds.), *Biofeedback and self control: 1972* Chicago: Aldine, 1973. Pp. 437–459.

Cataldo, J. F. Systematic desensitization: A cognitive-expectancy approach. Unpublished doctoral dissertation, State University of New York at Buffalo, 1970.

Cautela, J. R. Desensitization factors in the hypnotic treatment of phobias. *Journal of Psychology*, 1966, 64, 277–289. (a)

Cautela, J. R. Hypnosis and behavior therapy. *Behaviour Research and Therapy*, 1966, 4, 219–224. (b)

Cautela, J. R. Covert sensitization. *Psychological Record*, 1967, 20, 459–468.

Cautela, J. R. Behavior therapy and self-control: Techniques and implications. In C. M. Franks (Ed.), *Behavior therapy: Appraisal and status.* New York: McGraw-Hill, 1969. Pp. 323–340.

Cautela, J. R. Covert reinforcement. *Behavior Therapy*, 1970, 1, 33–50.

Cautela, J. R. Covert extinction. *Behavior Therapy*, 1971, 2, 192–200.

Cautela, J. The use of covert conditioning in hypnotherapy. *International Journal of Clinical and Experimental Hypnosis*, 1975, 23, 1–14.

Chapman, C. R., & Feather, B. W. Sensitivity to phobic imagery: A sensory decision theory analysis. *Behaviour Research and Therapy*, 1971, 9, 161–168.

Chaves, J. F. Hypnosis reconceptualized: An overview of Barber's theoretical and empirical work. *Psychological Reports*, 1968, 22, 587–608.

Chaves, J. F. Tasachen und spekulationen im bereich der hypnose. *Archiv fuer Psychologie*, 1972. 124, 62–69.

Chaves, J. F., & Barber, T. X. Cognitive strategies, experimenter modeling and expectation in the attenuation of pain. *Journal of Abnormal Psychology*, 1974, 83, 356–363.

Coe, W. C. The heuristic value of role theory and hypnosis. Unpublished doctoral dissertation, University of California, Berkeley, 1964.

Coe, W. C. Experimental designs and the state-nonstate issue in hypnosis. *American Journal of Clinical Hypnosis*, 1973, 16, 118–128.

Coe, W. C., Allen, J. L., Krug, W. M., & Wurzmann, A. G. Goal-directed fantasy in hypnotic responsiveness: Skill, item wording, or both? *International Journal of Clinical and Experimental Hypnosis*, 1974, 22, 157–166.

Coe, W. C., Kobayashi, K., & Howard, M. L. An approach toward isolating factors that influence anti-social conduct: Personal relationship, knowledge of an experiment, hypnosis. *International Journal of Clinical and Experimental Hypnosis*, 1972, 20, 118–131.

Coe, W. C., Kobayashi, K., & Howard, M. L. Experimental and ethical problems of evaluating the influence of hypnosis in antisocial conduct. *Journal of Abnormal Psychology,* 1973, **82,** 476–482.

Coe, W. C., & Sarbin, T. R. An experimental demonstration of hypnosis as role enactment. *Journal of Abnormal Psychology,* 1966, **71,** 400–405.

Comins, J. R., Fullam, F., & Barber, T. X. Effects of experimenter modeling, demands for honesty, and initial level of suggestibility on response to "hypnotic" suggestions. *Journal of Consulting and Clinical Psychology,* 1975, **43,** 668–675.

Conn, J. H., & Conn, R. N. Discussion of T. X. Barber's "Hypnosis as a causal variable in present-day psychology: A critical analysis." *International Journal of Clinical and Experimental Hypnosis,* 1967, **15,** 106–110.

Cronin, D. M., Spanos, N. P., & Barber, T. X. Augmenting hypnotic suggestibility by providing favorable information about hypnosis. *American Journal of Clinical Hypnosis,* 1971, **13,** 259–264.

Danaher, B. G., & Thoresen, C. E. Imagery assessment by self-report and behavioral measures. *Behaviour Research and Therapy,* 1972, **10,** 131–138.

Davison, G. C. Systematic desensitization as a counterconditioning process. *Journal of Abnormal Psychology,* 1968, **73,** 91–99.

Davison, G. C. Appraisal of behavior modification techniques with adults in institutional settings. In C. M. Franks (Ed.), *Behavior therapy: Appraisal and status.* New York: McGraw-Hill, 1969. Pp. 220–278.

Deleuze, J. P. F. *Practical instruction in animal magnetism.* New York: Wells, 1879.

DeMoor, W. Reciprocal inhibition versus unreinforced response evocation in behavior therapy. Unpublished doctoral dissertation, Katholieke Universiteit te Leuven, 1969.

Dengrove, E. The uses of hypnosis in behavior therapy. *International Journal of Clinical and Experimental Hypnosis,* 1973, **21,** 13–17.

Derman, D., & London, P. Correlates of hypnotic susceptibility. *Journal of Consulting Psychology,* 1965, **29,** 537–545.

Diamond, M. J. The use of observationally presented information to modify hpnotic susceptibility. Unpublished doctoral dissertation, Stanford University, 1970.

Diamond, M. J. The use of observationally presented information to modify hypnotic susceptibility. *Journal of Abnormal Psychology,* 1972, **79,** 174–180.

Diamond, M. J. Modification of hypnotizability: A review. *Psychological Bulletin,* 1974, **81,** 180–198.

Diamond, M. J., Gregory, J., Lenney, E., Steadman, C., & Talone, J. M. An alternative approach to personality correlates of hypnotizability: Hypnosis-specific mediational attitudes. *International Journal of Clinical and Experimental Hypnosis,* 1974, **22,** 346–353.

Dods, J. B. *Philosophy of mesmerism.* Originally published: 1847. (Reprinted in *Library of mesmerism.* Vol. 2. New York: Fowler & Wells, 1865.)

Dunwoody, R. C., & Edmonston, W. E., Jr. Hypnosis and slow eye movements. *American Journal of Clinical Hypnosis,* 1974, **16,** 270–274.

D'Zurilla, T. J., & Goldfried, M. R. Problem solving and behavior modification. *Journal of Abnormal Psychology,* 1971, **78,** 107–126.

Edmonston, W. E., Jr. Relaxation as an appropriate experimental control in hypnosis studies. *American Journal of Clinical Hypnosis,* 1972, **14,** 218–228.

Ekehammar, B. Interactionism in personality from a historical perspective. *Psychological Bulletin,* 1974, **81,** 1026–1047.

Eliseo, T. S. The hypnotic induction profile and hypnotic susceptibility. *International Journal of Clinical and Experimental Hypnosis,* 1974, **22,** 320–326.

Endler, N. S., & Hunt, J. McV. Sources of behavioral variance as measured by the S-R inventory of anxiousness. *Psychological Bulletin,* 1966, **65,** 338–346.

Endler, N. S., & Hunt, J. McV. S-R inventories of hostility and comparisons of the proportions of variance from persons, responses, and situations for hostility and anxiousness. *Journal of Personality and Social Psychology*, 1968, **9**, 309–315.

Endler, N. S., & Hunt, J. McV. Generalizability of contributions from sources of variance in the S-R inventory of anxiousness. *Journal of Personality*, 1969, **37**, 1–24.

Engstrom, D. R. The enhancement of EEG alpha production and its effects on hypnotic susceptibility. Unpublished doctoral dissertation, University of Southern California, 1970.

Estabrooks, G. H. Hypnosis comes of age. *Science Digest*, 1971, **69**, 44–50.

Evans, F. J. Recent trends in experimental hypnosis. *Behavioral Science*, 1968, **13**, 477–487.

Evans, F. J. Hypnosis and sleep: Techniques for exploring cognitive activity during sleep. In E. Fromm & R. E. Shor (Eds.), *Hypnosis: Research developments and perspectives.* Chicago: Aldine (Atherton), 1972. Pp. 43–83.

Evans, M. B., & Paul, G. L. Effects of hypnotically suggested analgesia on physiological and subjective responses to cold stress. *Journal of Consulting and Clinical Psychology*, 1970, **35**, 362–371.

Faria, J. C. A. de. In D. G. Dalgado (Ed.), *De le cause du sommeil lucide ou étude de la nature de l'homme.* (2nd ed.) Paris: Henri Jouve, 1906.

Farmer, R. G., & Wright, J. M. C. Muscular reactivity and systematic desensitization. *Behavior Therapy*, 1971, **2**, 1–10.

Ferenczi, S. Introjection and transference. *Sex and psychoanalysis.* New York: Brunner, 1950.

Foreyt, J. P., & Hagen, R. L. Covert sensitization: Conditioning or suggestion? *Journal of Abnormal Psychology*, 1973, **82**, 17–23.

Franks, C. M. Behavior therapy and its Pavlovian origins: Review and perspectives. In C. M. Franks (Ed.), *Behavior therapy: Appraisal and status.* New York: McGraw-Hill, 1969. Pp. 1–28.

Freedberg, E. J. Behavior therapy: A comparison between early (1890–1920) and contemporary techniques. *Canadian Psychologist*, 1973, **14**, 225–240.

Freud, S. *Three essays on the theory of sexuality.* (Stand. ed.) Vol. 7. London: Hogarth, 1953.

Fuchs, K., Hoch, A., Paldi, E., Abramovici, H., Brandes, J. M., Timor-Tritsch, I., & Kleinhaus, M. Hypno-desensitization therapy of vaginismus. Part I. "In vitro" method. Part II. "In vivo" method. *International Journal of Clinical and Experimental Hypnosis*, 1973, **21**, 144–156.

Galbraith, G. C., London, P., Leibovitz, M. P., Cooper, L. M., & Hart, J. T. EEG and hypnotic susceptibility. *Journal of Comparative and Physiological Psychology*, 1970, **72**, 125–131.

Galin, D. Implications for psychiatry of left and right cerebral specialization. *Archives of General Psychiatry*, 1974, **31**, 572–583.

Gelder, M. G., Bancroft, J. H. J., Gath, D. H., Johnston, D. W., Mathews, A. M., & Shaw, P. M. Specific and non-specific factors in behavior therapy. *British Journal of Psychiatry*, 1973, **123**, 445–462.

Gibbons, D., Kilbourne, L., Saunders, A., & Castles, C. The cognitive control of behavior: A comparison of systematic desensitization and hypnotically-induced "directed experience" techniques. *American Journal of Clinical Hypnosis*, 1970, **12**, 141–145.

Gill, M. M., & Brenman, M. *Hypnosis and related states.* New York: International Universities Press, 1959.

Goldfried, M. R. Systematic desensitization as training in self-control. *Journal of Consulting and Clinical Psychology*, 1971, **37**, 228–234.

Gregory, J., & Diamond, M. J. Increasing hypnotic susceptibility by means of positive expectancies and written instructions. *Journal of Abnormal Psychology*, 1973, 82, 363–367.

Grimes, J. S. *Eterology: or the philosophy of mesmerism and phrenology: including a new philosophy of sleep and of consciousness, with a review of the pretensions of neurology and phreno-magnatism.* New York: Saxton & Miles, 1845.

Grossberg, J. M. The physiological effectiveness of brief training in differential muscle relaxation. (Tech. Rep. No. 9) La Jolla, Calif.: Western Behavioral Sciences Institute, 1965.

Gur, R. C., & Gur, R. E. Handedness, sex, and eyedness as moderating variables in the relation between hypnotic susceptibility and functional brain asymmetry. *Journal of Abnormal Psychology*, 1974, 83, 635–643.

Gur, R. E. & Reyher, J. Relationship between style of hypnotic induction and direction of lateral eye movements. *Journal of Abnormal Psychology*, 1973, 82, 499–505.

Haddock, J. *Psychology: Or the science of the soul, considered physiologically and philosophically.* Originally published: 1849. (Reprinted in *Library of mesmerism.* Vol. 2, New York: Fowler & Wells, 1865.)

Hall, C. R. *Mesmerism: Its rise, progress and mysteries.* London Burgess, Stringer & Co., 1845.

Ham, M. W., & Spanos, N. P. Suggested auditory and visual hallucinations in task-motivated and hypnotic subjects. *American Journal of Clinical Hypnosis*, 1974, 17, 94–101.

Hartnett, J., Nowlis, D., & Svorad, D. Hypnotic susceptibility and EEG alpha: Three correlations. (Hawthorne House Res. Memo. No. 97) Stanford University: Stanford, California, 1969.

Heron, W. T. *Clinical applications of suggestion and hypnosis.* Springfield, Ill.: Thomas, 1953.

Hilgard, E. R. *Hypnotic susceptibility.* New York: Harcourt, 1965.

Hilgard, E. R. Altered states of awareness. *Journal of Nervous and Mental Disease*, 1969, 149, 68–79.

Hilgard, E. R. Hypnotic phenomena: The struggle for scientific acceptance. *American Scientist*, 1971, 59, 567–577.

Hilgard, E. R. The domain of hypnosis: With some comments on alternative paradigms. *American Psychologist*, 1973, 28, 972–982.

Hilgard, E. R., & Tart, C. T. Responsiveness to suggestions following waking and imagination instructions and following induction of hypnosis. *Journal of Abnormal Psychology*, 1966, 71, 196–208.

Hilgard, J. R. *Personality and hypnosis.* Chicago: University of Chicago Press, 1970.

Hilgard, J. R. Imaginative involvement: Some characteristics of the highly hypnotizable and the non-hypnotizable. *International Journal of Clinical and Experimental Hypnosis*, 1974, 22, 138–156.

Horowitz, M. J. *Image formation and cognition.* New York: Appleton, 1970.

Howlett, S. C., & Nawas, M. M. Exposure to aversive imagery and suggestion in systematic desensitization. In R. D. Rubin, H. Fensterheim, A. A. Lazarus, & C. M. Franks (Eds.), *Advances in behavior therapy 1969.* New York: Academic Press, 1971. Pp. 123–135.

Jacobs, A., & Wolpin, M. A second look at systematic desensitization. In A. Jacobs & L. B. Sachs (Eds.), *The psychology of private events.* New York: Academic Press, 1971. Pp. 78–108.

Jaffe, L. W. Non-specific factors and deconditioning in fear reduction. Unpublished doctoral dissertation, University of Southern California, 1968.

Janda, L. H., & Rimm, D. C. Covert sensitization in the treatment of obesity. *Journal of Abnormal Psychology*, 1972, 80, 37–42.

Johnson, R. F. Q., Maher, B. A., & Barber, T. X. Artifact in the "essence of hypnosis"; An evaluation of trance logic. *Journal of Abnormal Psychology*, 1972, **79**, 212–220.

Johnston, E., & Donoghue, J. R. Hypnosis and smoking: A review of the literature. *American Journal of Clinical Hypnosis*, 1971, **13**, 265–274.

Kinney, J. M., & Sachs, L. B. Increasing hypnotic susceptibility. *Journal of Abnormal Psychology*, 1974, **83**, 145–150.

Kirchner, J. H., & Hogan, R. A. The therapist variable in the implosion of phobias. *Psychotherapy: Theory, Research and Practice*, 1966, **3**, 102–104.

Klein, M. H., Dittman, A. T., Parloff, M. B., & Gill, M. M. Behavior therapy: Observations and reflections. *Journal of Consulting and Clinical Psychology*, 1969, **33**, 259–266.

Klinger, E. *Structure and functions of fantasy*. New York: Wiley, 1971.

Kocel, K., Galin, D., Ornstein, R., & Merrin, E. L. Lateral eye movement and cognitive mode. *Psychonomic Science*, 1972, **27**, 223–228.

Kroger, W. S. *Clinical and experimental hypnosis: In medicine, dentistry, and psychology*. Philadelphia: Lippincott, 1963.

Kubie, L. S., & Margolin, S. The process of hypnotism and the nature of the hypnotic state. *American Journal of Psychiatry*, 1944, **100**, 611–622.

Lang, P. J. The mechanics of desensitization and the laboratory study of human fear. In C. M. Franks (Ed.), *Behavior therapy: Appraisal and status*. New York: McGraw-Hill, 1969. Pp. 160–191.

Lang, P. J., Lazovik, A. D., & Reynolds, D. J. Desensitization, suggestibility and pseudo-therapy. *Journal of Abnormal Psychology*, 1965, **70**, 395–402.

Larsen, S. Strategies for reducing phobic behavior. *Dissertation Abstracts*, 1966, **26**, 6850.

Lazarus, A. A. *Behavior therapy and beyond*. New York: McGraw-Hill, 1971.

Lazarus, A. A. "Hypnosis" as a facilitator in behavior therapy. *International Journal of Clinical and Experimental Hypnosis*, 1973, **21**, 25–31.

Lee-Teng, E. Trance-susceptibility, induction susceptibility, and acquiescence as factors in hypnotic performance. *Journal of Abnormal Psychology*, 1965, **70**, 383–389.

Leitenberg, H., Agras, W. S., Barlow, D. H., & Oliveau, D. C. Contribution of selective positive reinforcement and therapeutic instructions to systematic desensitization therapy. *Journal of Abnormal Psychology*, 1969, **74**, 113–118.

Levitt, E. E., Aronoff, G., Morgan, C. D., Toner, M., Overley, M., & Parrish, M. Testing the coercive power of hypnosis: Committing objectionable acts. *International Journal of Clinical and Experimental Hypnosis*, 1975, **23**, 59–67.

Levy, J. Possible basis for the evolution of lateral specialization of the human brain. *Nature (London)*, 1969, **224**, 614–615.

Litvak, S. B. Hypnosis and the desensitization behavior therapies. *Psychological Reports*, 1970, **27**, 787–794.

Locke, E. A. Is "behavior therapy" behavioristic? (An analysis of Wolpe's psychotherapeutic methods.) *Psychological Bulletin*, 1971, **76**, 318–327.

Lomont, J. F., & Brock, L. Cognitive factors in systematic desensitization. *Behaviour Research and Therapy*, 1971, **9**, 187–195.

Lomont, J. F., & Edwards, J. E. The role of relaxation in systematic desensitization. *Behaviour Research and Therapy*, 1967, **5**, 11–25.

London, P. Subject characteristics in hypnosis research. I. A survey of experience, interest, and opinion. *International Journal of Clinical and Experimental Hypnosis*, 1961, **9**, 151–161.

London, P., Cooper, L. M., & Johnson, H. J. Subject characteristics in hypnosis research. II. Attitudes toward hypnosis, volunteer status, and personality measures. III. Some correlates of hypnotic susceptibility. *International Journal of Clinical and Experimental Hypnosis*, 1962, **10**, 13–21.

London, P., Hart, J. T., & Leibovitz, M. P. EEG alpha rhythms and susceptibility to hypnosis. *Nature (London)*, 1968, 219, 71–72.

LoPiccolo, J. Effective components of systematic desensitization. Department of Psychology, University of Oregon, 1971. (Mimeo)

Magnusson, D. The individual in the situation: Some studies on individuals' perception of situations. *Studia Psychologia*, 1974, 16, 124–132.

Maletzky, B. M. "Assisted" covert sensitization in the treatment of exhibitionism. *Journal of Consulting and Clinical Psychology*, 1974, 42, 34–40.

Marcia, J. E., Rubin, B. M., & Efran, J. S. Systematic desensitization: Expectancy change or counterconditioning? *Journal of Abnormal Psychology*, 1969, 74, 382–387.

Marks, I. M., Gelder, M. G., & Edwards, G. Hypnosis and desensitization for phobias: A controlled prospective trial. *British Journal of Psychology*. 1968, 114, 1263–1274.

Mathews, A. Psychophysiological approaches to the investigation of desensitization and related procedures. *Psychological Bulletin*, 1971, 76, 73–91.

McAmmond, D. M., Davidson, P. O., & Kovitz, D. M. A comparison of the effects of hypnosis and relaxation training on stress reactions in a dental situation. *American Journal of Clinical Hypnosis*, 1971, 13, 233–242.

McDonald, R. D., & Smith, J. R. Trance logic in tranceable and simulating subjects. *International Journal of Clinical and Experimental Hypnosis*, 1975, 23, 80–89.

McGlynn, F. D. Experimental desensitization following three types of instructions. *Behaviour Research and Therapy*, 1971, 9, 367–369.

McGlynn, F. D. Systematic desensitization under two conditions of induced expectancy. *Behaviour Research and Therapy*, 1972, 10, 229–234.

McGlynn, F. D., & Davis, D. J. A factorial study of cognitive exposure and relaxation in experimental desensitization. Department of Psychology, State College, Mississippi, 1971. (Mimeo)

McGlynn, F. D., & Mapp, R. H. Systematic desensitization of snake-avoidance following three types of suggestion. *Behaviour Research and Therapy*, 1970, 8, 197–201.

McGlynn, F. D., Mealiea, W. L., & Nawas, M. M. Systematic desensitization of snake-avoidance under two conditions of suggestion. *Psychological Reports*, 1969, 25, 220–222.

McGlynn, F. D., Reynolds, J. E., & Linder, L. H. Systematic desensitization with pretreatment and intra-treatment therapeutic instructions. *Behaviour Research and Therapy*, 1971, 9, 57–63.

McGlynn, F. D., & Williams, C. W. Systematic desensitization of snake-avoidance under three conditions of suggestion. *Journal of Behavior Therapy and Experimental Psychiatry*, 1970, 1, 97–101.

McLemore, C. W. Imagery in desensitization. *Behaviour Research and Therapy*, 1972, 10, 51–57.

McPeake, J. D. Hypnosis, suggestion, and psychosomatics. *Diseases of the Nervous System*, 1968, 29, 536–544.

McPeake, J. D. Factors effecting test anxiety in two year college students. Unpublished doctoral dissertation, Boston College, 1975.

McReynolds, W. T., & Tori, C. A. A further assessment of attention-placebo effects and demand characteristics in studies of systematic desensitization. *Journal of Consulting and Clinical Psychology*, 1972, 38, 261–264.

Meichenbaum, D. Toward a cognitive theory of self-control. In G. Schwartz & D. Shapiro (Eds.), *Consciousness and self-regulation: Advances in research*. New York: Plenum, 1976, in press.

Melei, J. P., & Hilgard, E. R. Attitudes toward hypnosis, self-predictions, and hypnotic susceptibility. *International Journal of Clinical and Experimental Hypnosis*, 1964, **12**, 99–108.

Meskin, B., & Singer, J. L. Daydreaming, reflective thought and laterality of eye movements. *Journal of Personality and Social Psychology*, 1974, **30**, 64–71.

Miller, B. V., & Bernstein, D. A. Instructional demand in a behavioral avoidance test for claustrophobic fears. *Journal of Abnormal Psychology*, 1972, **80**, 206–210.

Miller, G. A., Galanter, E., & Pribram, K. H. *Plans and the structure of behavior*. New York: Holt, 1960.

Miller, S. B. The contribution of therapeutic instructions to systematic desensitization. *Behaviour Research and Therapy*, 1972, **10**, 159–169.

Mischel, W. *Personality and assessment*. New York: Wiley, 1968.

Mischel, W. Toward a cognitive social learning reconceptualization of personality. *Psychological Review*, 1973, **80**, 252–283.

Mischel, W., Zeiss, R., & Zeiss, A. Internal-external control and persistence validation and implications of the Stanford preschool internal-external scale. *Journal of Personality and Social Psychology*, 1974, **29**, 265–278.

Moore, N. Behavior therapy in bronchial asthma: A controlled study. *Journal of Psychosomatic Research*, 1965, **9**, 257–276.

Moos, R. H. Sources of variance in responses to questionnaires and in behavior. *Journal of Abnormal Psychology*, 1969, **74**, 405–412.

Morgan, A. H. The heritability of hypnotic susceptibility in twins. *Journal of Abnormal Psychology*, 1973, **82**, 55–61.

Morgan, A. H., & Lam, D. The relationship of the Betts vividness of imagery questionnaire and hypnotic susceptibility: Failure to replicate. (Hawthorne House Res. Memo. No. 103) Unpublished manuscript. 1969.

Morgan, A. H., Macdonald, H., & Hilgard, E. R. EEG alpha: Lateral asymmetry related to task and hypnotizability. *Psychophysiology*, 1974, **11**, 275–282.

Moss, C. S., & Bremer, B. Exposure of a "medical modler" to behavior modification. *International Journal of Clinical and Experimental Hypnosis*, 1973, **21**, 1–12.

Murray, E. J. Learning theory and psychotherapy: Biotropic versus sociotropic approaches. *Journal of Counseling Psychology*, 1963, **10**, 250–255.

Myerhoff, L. Tension and anxiety in deconditioning. Unpublished doctoral dissertation, University of Southern California, 1967.

Nawas, M. M. Mealiea, W. L., Jr., & Fishman, S. T. Systematic desensitization as counterconditioning: A retest with adequate controls. *Behavior Therapy*, 1971, **2**, 345–356.

Neisser, U. *Cognitive psychology*. New York: Appleton, 1967.

Neisser, U. Changing conceptions of imagery. In P. W. Sheehan (Ed.), *The function and nature of imagery*. New York: Academic Press, 1972. Pp. 234–249.

Newman, J. B. *Fascination, or the philosophy of charming illustrating the principles of life in connection with spirit and matter*. Originally published: 1847. (Reprinted in *Library of mesmerism*. Vol. 1. New York: Fowler & Wells, 1865.)

Nietzel, M. T. The effects of assessment and treatment mediated demand characteristics in a psychotherapy analogue study. Doctoral dissertation, University of Illinois, 1973.

Norris, D. L. Barber's task-motivational theroy and post-hypnotic amnesia. *American Journal of Clinical Hypnosis*, 1973, **15**, 181–190.

O'Connell, D. N., Shor, R. E., & Orne, M. T. Hypnotic age regression: An empirical and methodological analysis. *Journal of Abnormal Psychology*, 1970, 76(Monogr. 3, Pt. 2).

Oliveau, D. C., Agras, W. S., Leitenberg, H., Moore, R. C., & Wright, D. E. Systematic desensitization, therapeutically oriented instructions and selective positive reinforcement. *Behaviour Research and Therapy*, 1969, **7**, 27–33.

Orne, M. T. The nature of hypnosis: Artifact and essense. *Journal of Abnormal and Social Psychology*, 1959, 58, 277–299.

Orne, M. T. Hypnosis, motivation and compliance. *American Journal of Psychiatry*, 1966, 122, 721–726.

Orne, M. T., & Evans, F. J. Social control in the psychological experiment: Antisocial behavior and hypnosis. *Journal of Personality and Social Psychology*, 1965, 1, 189–200.

Ornstein, R. E. *The psychology of consciousness*. New York: Viking Press, 1972.

Pattie, F. A. Methods of induction, susceptibility of subjects and criteria of hypnosis. In R. M. Dorcus (Ed.), *Hypnosis and its therapeutic applications*. New York: McGraw-Hill, 1956. Chapter 2.

Paul, G. L. *Insight vs. desensitization in psychotherapy: An experiment in anxiety reduction*. Stanford, Calif.: Stanford University Press, 1966.

Paul, G. L. Physiological effects of relaxation training and hypnotic suggestion. *Journal of Abnormal Psychology*, 1969, 74, 425–437.

Pavio, A. *Imagery and verbal processes*. New York: Holt, 1971.

Perseley, G., & Leventhal, D. B. The effects of therapeutically oriented instructions and of the pairing of anxiety imagery and relaxation in systematic desensitization. *Behavior Therapy*, 1972, 3, 417–424.

Perry, C. Imagery, fantasy and hypnotic susceptibility: A multidimensional approach. *Journal of Personality and Social Psychology*, 1973, 26, 217–221.

Rachman, S. Studies in desensitization. II. Flooding. *Behaviour Research and Therapy*, 1966, 4, 1–6.

Rachman, S. The role of muscular relaxation in desensitization therapy. *Behaviour Research and Therapy*, 1968, 6, 159–166.

Reyher, J. Hypnosis in research on psychopathology, In J. E. Gordon (Ed.), *Handbook of clinical and experimental hypnosis*. New York: Macmillan, 1967. Pp. 110–147.

Rosen, G. M. Therapy set: Its effects on subjects' involvement in systematic desensitization and treatment outcome. *Journal of Abnormal Psychology*, 1974, 83, 291–300.

Rosenhan, D. Hypnosis and personality: A moderator variable analysis. In L. Chertok (Ed.), *Psychophysiological mechanisms of hypnosis*. Berlin & New York: Springer-Verlag, 1969. Pp. 193–198.

Rosenhan, D. L., & Tomkins, S. S. On preference for hypnosis and hypnotizability. *International Journal of Clinical and Experimental Hypnosis*, 1964, 12, 109–114.

Rotter, J. B. *Social learning and clinical psychology*. Englewood Cliffs, N.J.: Prentice-Hall, 1954.

Ryle, G. *The concept of mind*. London: Hutchinson, 1949.

Sachs, L. B. Modification of hypnotic behavior without hypnotic inductions. Unpublished study, West Virginia University, 1969.

Sachs, L. B. Construing hypnosis as modifiable behavior. In A. Jacobs & L. B. Sachs (Eds.), *The psychology of private events*. New York: Academic Press, 1971. Pp. 61–75.

Sachs, L. B., & Anderson, W. L. Modification of hypnotic susceptibility. *International Journal of Clinical and Experimental Hypnosis*, 1967, 15, 172–180.

Sarbin, T. R. Contributions to role-taking theory. I. Hypnotic behavior. *Psychological Review*, 1950, 57, 255–270.

Sarbin, T. R. Attempts to understand hypnotic phenomena. In L. Postman (Ed.), *Psychology in the making*. New York: Alfred A. Knopf, 1962. Pp. 745–785.

Sarbin, T. R. Toward a theory of imagination. *Journal of Personality*, 1970, 38, 52–76.

Sarbin, T. R. Imagining as muted role-taking: A historical-linguistic analysis. In P. W.

Sheehan (Ed.), *The function and nature of imagery*. New York: Academic Press, 1972. Pp. 333–353.

Sarbin, T. R., & Coe, W. C. *Hypnotic behavior: The psychology of influence communication*. New York: Holt, 1972.

Sarbin, T. R., & Lim, D. T. Some evidence in support of the role-taking hypothesis in hypnosis. *International Journal of Clinical and Experimental Hypnosis*, 1963, 11, 98–103.

Sarbin, T. R., & Slagle, R. W. Hypnosis and psychophysiological outcomes. In E. Fromm & R. E. Shor (Eds.), *Hypnosis: Research developments and perspectives*. Chicago: Aldine (Atherton), 1972; Pp. 185–214.

Schilder, P. *The nature of hypnosis*. New York: International Universities Press, 1956.

Schubot, E. D. The influence of hypnotic and muscular relaxation in systematic desensitization of phobias. Unpublished doctoral dissertation, Stanford University, 1966.

Seamon, J. Imagery codes and human information retrieval. *Journal of Experimental Psychology*, 1972, 96, 468–470.

Secter, I. I. Considerations in resistances to initial inductions of hypnosis. *Journal of Clinical and Experimental Hypnosis*, 1957, 5, 77–81.

Sheehan, P. W. A methodological analysis of the simulating technique. *International Journal of Clinical and Experimental Hypnosis*, 1971, 19, 83–99.

Shor, R. E. Hypnosis and the concept of the generalized reality orientation. *American Journal of Psychotherapy*, 1959, 13, 582–602.

Shor, R. E. The three factor theroy of hypnosis as applied to the book reading fantasy and to the concept of suggestion. *International Journal of Clinical and Experimental Hypnosis*, 1970, 18, 89–98.

Shor, R. E. Expectancies of being influenced and hypnotic performance. *International Journal of Clinical and Experimental Hypnosis*, 1971, 19, 154–166.

Shor, R. E., & Cobb, J. C. An exploratory study of hypnotic training using the concept of plateau responsiveness as a referent. *American Journal of Clinical Hypnosis*, 1968, 10, 178–197.

Shor, R. E., Orne, M. T., & O'Connell, D. N. Validation and cross-validation of a scale of self-reported personal experiences which predict hypnotizability. *Journal of Psychology*, 1962, 53, 55–75.

Shor, R. E., Orne, M. T., & O'Connell, D. N. Psychological correlates of plateau hypnotizability in a special volunteer sample. *Journal of Personality and Social Psychology*, 1966, 3, 80–95.

Silver, M. J. Hypnotizability as a function of repression, adaptive regression, and mood. *Journal of Consulting and Clinical Psychology*, 1974, 42, 41–46.

Singer, J. L. *Imagery and daydream methods in psychotherapy and behavior modification*. New York: Academic Press, 1974.

Singer, J. W., & Antrobus, J. S. Daydreaming, imaginal processes, and personality: A normative study. In P. W. Sheehan (Ed.), *The function and nature of imagery*. Academic Press, 1972. Pp. 175–201.

Skinner, B. F. *Science and human behavior*. New York: Macmillan, 1953.

Spanos, N. P. Barber's reconceptualization of hypnosis: An evaluation of criticisms. *Journal of Experimental Research in Personality*, 1970, 4, 241–258. (a)

Spanos, N. P. A reply to Tellegen's "Comments of Barber's reconceptualization of hypnosis." *Journal of Experimental Research in Personality*, 1970, 4, 268–269. (b)

Spanos, N. P. Goal-directed fantasy and the performance of hypnotic test suggestions. *Psychiatry*, 1971, 34, 86–96.

Spanos, N. P. Hypnosis: A sociological and phenomenological perspective. Unpublished doctoral dissertation, Boston University, 1973.

Spanos, N. P., & Barber, T. X. "Hypnotic" experiences as inferred from subjective reports: Auditory and visual hallucinations. *Journal of Experimental Research in Personality,* 1968, 3, 136–150.

Spanos, N. P., & Barber, T. X. Cognitive activity during "hypnotic" suggestibility: Goal-directed fantasy and the experience of non-volition. *Journal of Personality,* 1972, 40, 510–524.

Spanos, N. P., & Barber, T. X. A review of Orne's "Hypnosis, motivation and the ecological validity of the psychological experiment." *American Journal of Clinical Hypnosis,* 1973, 16, 138–141.

Spanos, N. P., & Barber, T. X. Toward a convergence in hypnosis research. *American Psychologist,* 1974, 29, 500–511.

Spanos, N. P., Barber, T. X., & Lang, G. Cognition and self-control: Cognitive control of painful sensory input. In H. London and R. E. Nisbett (Eds.), *Thought and feeling: Cognitive alteration of feeling states.* Chicago: Aldine, 1974. Pp. 141–158.

Spanos, N. P., & Chaves, J. F. Converging operations and the "hypnotic state" construct. *Proceedings of the American Psychological Association,* 11th Annual convention, 1969, 905–906.

Spanos, N. P., & Chaves, J. F. Hypnosis research: A methodological critique of experiments generated by two alternative paradigms. *American Journal of Clinical Hypnosis,* 1970, 13, 108–127.

Spanos, N. P., & Chaves, J. F. Hypnotismus: Barbers empirische und theoretische Neuformulierung. In A. Katzenstein (Ed.), *Hypnose: Aktuelle probleme in theorie, experiment und klinik.* Jena: Fischer, 1971. Pp. 43–56.

Spanos, N. P., DeMoor, W., & Barber, T. X. Hypnosis and behavior therapy: Common denominators. *American Journal of Clinical Hypnosis,* 1973, 16, 45–64. (a)

Spanos, N. P., & Ham, M. L. Cognitive activity in response to hypnotic suggestion: Goal-directed fantasy and selective amnesia. *American Journal of Clinical Hypnosis,* 1973, 15, 191–198.

Spanos, N. P., & Ham, M. W. Involvement in imagining and the "hypnotic dream." *American Journal of Clinical Hypnosis,* 1975, 18, 43–51.

Spanos, N. P., Ham, M. W., & Barber, T. X. Suggested ("hypnotic") visual hallucinations: Experimental and phenomenological data. *Journal of Abnormal Psychology,* 1973, 81, 96–106. (b)

Spanos, N. P., Horton, C., & Chaves, J. F. The effects of two cognitive strategies on pain threshold. *Journal of Abnormal Psychology,* 1975, 84, 677–681.

Spanos, N. P., Kosloff, M., & Chaves, J. F. *Cognitive activity during systematic desensitization.* Medfield, Mass.: Medfield Foundation, 1971.

Spanos, N. P., & McPeake, J. D. Involvement in suggestion-related imaginings, experienced involuntariness, and credibility assigned to imaginings. *Journal of Abnormal Psychology,* 1974, 83, 687–690.

Spanos, N. P., & McPeake, J. D. Involvement in everyday imaginative activities, attitudes toward hypnosis, and hypnotic suggestibility. *Journal of Personality and Social Psychology,* 1975, 31, 594–598. (a)

Spanos, N. P., & McPeake, J. D. The interaction of attitudes toward hypnosis and involvement in everyday imaginative activities on hypnotic suggestibility. *American Journal of Clinical Hypnosis,* 1975, 17, 247–252. (b)

Spanos, N. P., Spillane, J., & McPeake, J. D. Cognitive strategies and response to suggestion in hypnotic and task-motivated subjects. *American Journal of Clinical Hypnosis*, 1976, **18**, 254–262.

Spanos, N. P., Valois, R., Ham, M. W., & Ham, M. L. Suggestibility, and vividness and control of imagery. *International Journal of Clinical and Experimental Hypnosis*, 1973, **21**, 305–311. (c)

Spiegel, H. An eye-roll test for hypnotizability. *American Journal of Clinical Hypnosis*, 1972, **15**, 25–27.

Spiegel, H. *Manual for hypnotic induction profile: Eye-roll levitation method.* (Rev. ed.) New York: Soni Medica, 1973.

Spiegel, H. The grade 5 syndrome and the highly hypnotizable person. *International Journal of Clinical and Experimental Hypnosis*, 1974, **22**, 303–319.

Spielberger, D. C., & DeNike, L. D. Descriptive behaviorism versus cognitive theory in verbal operant conditioning. *Psychological Review*, 1966, **73**, 306–326.

Stampfl, T. G., & Levis, D. J. Essentials of implosive therapy: A learning-theory-based psychodynamic behavioral therapy. *Journal of Abnormal Psychology*, 1967, **72**, 496–503.

Stampfl, T. G., & Levis, D. J. Implosive therapy: A behavioral therapy? *Behaviour Research and Therapy*, 1968, **6**, 31–36.

Starker, S. Effects of hypnotic induction upon visual imagery. *Journal of Nervous and Mental Disease*, 1974, **159**, 433–437.

Stoudenmire, J. Effects of muscle relaxation training on state and trait anxiety in introverts and extraverts. *Journal of Personality and Social Psychology*, 1972, **24**, 273–275.

Sue, D. The role of relaxation in systematic desensitization. *Behaviour Research and Therapy*, 1972, **10**, 153–158.

Sutcliffe, J. P., Perry, C. W., & Sheehan, P. W. Relation of some aspects of imagery and fantasy to hypnotic susceptibility. *Journal of Abnormal Psychology*, 1970, **76**, 279–287.

Switras, J. E. A comparison of the eye-roll test for hypnotizability and the Stanford Hypnotic Susceptibility Scale: Form A. *American Journal of Clinical Hypnosis*, 1974, **17**, 54–55.

Tart, C. T. Measuring the depth of an altered state of consciousness, with particular reference to self-report scales of hypnotic depth. In E. Fromm & R. E. Shor (Eds.), *Hypnosis: Research developments and perspectives.* Chicago: Aldine (Atherton), 1972. Pp. 445–477.

Tellegen, A., & Atkinson, G. A. Openness to absorbing and self-altering experiences ("absorption"), a trait related to hypnotic susceptibility. *Journal of Abnormal Psychology*, 1974, **83**, 268–277.

Thorkelson, K. E. The relationship between hypnotic susceptibility and certain personality, physiological and electroencephalographic variables in monozygotic and disygotic twin pairs. Unpublished doctoral dissertation, University of Minnesota, 1973.

Tori, C., & Worell, L. Reduction of human avoidant behavior: A comparison of counterconditioning, expectancy, and cognitive information approaches. *Journal of Consulting and Clinical Psychology*, 1973, **41**, 269–278.

Ullmann, L. P., & Krasner, L. *A psychological approach to abnormal behavior.* Englewood Cliffs, N.J.: Prentice-Hall, 1969.

Valins, S., & Ray, A. A. Effects of cognitive desensitization on avoidance behavior. *Journal of Personality and Social Psychology*, 1967, **7**, 345–350.

Van Egeren, L. F. Psychophysiology of systematic desensitization: Individual differences and the habituation model. *Journal of Behavior Therapy and Experimental Psychiatry,* 1970, 1, 249–255.

Van Egeren, L. F., Feather, B. W., & Hein, P. L. Desensitization of phobias: Some psychophysiology propositions. *Psychophysiology,* 1971, 8, 213–228.

Vodde, T. W., & Gilner, F. H. The effects of exposure to fear stimuli on fear reduction. *Behaviour Research and Therapy,* 1971, 9, 169–175.

Weinberg, N. H., & Zaslove, M. "Resistance" to systematic desensitization of phobias. *Journal of Clinical Psychology,* 1963, 14, 179–181.

Weitzenhoffer, A. M. Hypnosis and eye movements. I. Preliminary report on a possible slow eye movement correlate of hypnosis. *American Journal of Clinical Hypnosis,* 1969, 11, 221–227.

Weitzenhoffer, A. M. Behavior therapeutic techniques and hypnotherapeutic methods. *American Journal of Clinical Hypnosis,* 1972, 15, 71–82.

Weitzenhoffer, A. M., & Hilgard, E. R. *Stanford hypnotic susceptibility scale, form C.* Palo Alto, Calif.: Consulting Psychologists Press, 1962.

Weitzman, B. Behavior therapy and psychotherapy. *Psychological Review,* 1967, 74, 300–317.

Wheeler, L., Reis, H. T., Wolff, E., Grupsmith, E., & Mordkoff, A. M. Eye-roll and hypnotic susceptibility. *International Journal of Clinical and Experimental Hypnosis,* 1974, 22, 327–334.

Wickramasekera, I. Effects of electromyographic feedback on hypnotic susceptibility. *Journal of Abnormal Psychology,* 1973, 82, 74–77.

Wilkins, W. Desensitization: Social and cognitive factors underlying the effectiveness of Wolpe's procedure. *Psychological Bulletin,* 1971, 76, 311–317.

Wilson, G. D. Efficacy of "flooding" procedures in desensitization of fear: A theoretical note. *Behaviour Research and Therapy,* 1967, 5, 138.

Wolberg, L. R. *Medical hypnosis.* Vol. 1. New York: Grune & Stratton, 1948.

Wolpe, J. *Psychotherapy by reciprocal inhibition.* Stanford, Calif.: Stanford University Press, 1958.

Wolpe, J. *The practice of behavior therapy.* Oxford: Pergamon, 1969.

Wolpe, J., & Flood, J. The effect of relaxation on the galvanic skin response to repeated phobic stimuli in ascending order. *Journal of Behavior Therapy and Experimental Psychiatry,* 1970, 1, 195–200.

Wolpe, J., & Lazarus, A. A. *Behavior therapy techniques.* Oxford: Pergamon, 1966.

Wolpin, M. The application of modified conditioning procedures to clinical problems: Three case histories. Unpublished manuscript, Camarillo State Hospital, Camarillo, California, 1966.

Wolpin, M., & Raines, J. Visual imagery, expected roles and extinction as possible factors in reducing fear and avoidance behavior. *Behaviour Research and Therapy,* 1966, 4, 25–37.

Woody, R. H. Clinical suggestion and systematic desensitization. *American Journal of Clinical Hypnosis,* 1973, 15, 250–257.

Woody, R. H., & Shauble, P. G. Desensitization of fear by video tapes. *Journal of Clinical Psychology,* 1969, 25, 102–103.

Woy, R. J., & Efran, J. S. Systematic desensitization and expectancy in the treatment of speaking anxiety. *Behaviour Research and Therapy,* 1972, 10, 43–49.

BEHAVIOR MODIFICATION
IN THE CLASSROOM[1]

RODNEY COPELAND[2] AND R. VANCE HALL

Department of Human Development and Family Life
University of Kansas
Lawrence, Kansas

I. INTRODUCTION

Widespread applications of behavior modification procedures in classroom settings have occurred in a relatively short time, and the

[1] The preparation of this manuscript was supported in part by the following grants: Research Grant HD 03144 from the National Institute of Child Health and Human Development and Research Grant MH 13296 from the National Institute of Mental Health.

[2] *Present address:* Department of Psychology, Southwest Missouri State University, Springfield, Missouri.

acceptance and implementation of systematic behavioral procedures seem to be accelerating. Not only has behavior modification had an impact on education in the United States, but it is becoming widespread in Canada, Australia, New Zealand, Mexico, Panama, Brazil, and other Latin American countries. The authors have received personal communications from Israel, Great Britain, The Netherlands, West Germany, and other European countries where teachers are beginning to apply operant procedures in classroom settings.

It is unusual for such a rapid implementation of procedures to occur in the field of education. It usually takes 50 years for a new development in education to be widely adopted. In the case of behavior modification this time lag has been reduced. Perhaps the reason is that the effectiveness of behavior modification techniques has been undeniably demonstrated with significant research data. Another probable reason is that the procedures have been applied to many practical areas. Teachers have seen that they provide programmatic solutions to learning and behavior problems. It is also likely that educators relate to the applications of behavior modification procedures which deal specifically and directly with learning and motivation problems. Behavior modification is less encumbered with theoretical orientations far removed from the classroom and ongoing environment than most other approaches. Therefore, teachers have been quick to sense how they could apply the procedures.

For whatever reasons, behavioral approaches are being widely used, and their acceptance has been very rapid. This chapter will trace the progress of behavior modification from the laboratory to the classroom. It will also outline the development of teacher training programs and present one approach (Responsive Teaching) that trains teachers to implement behavior modification procedures. Another section suggests directions for future research and applications in education. The concluding sections deal with moral and ethical issues and the changing roles of educators as they learn to apply behavior modification procedures to learning and behavior problems of students.

II. EARLY APPLICATIONS

A. Research with Institutionalized Populations

Skinner and his colleagues clearly delineated the principles of operant conditioning in laboratory investigations involving animals

(Ferster & Skinner, 1957; Skinner, 1938, 1953). Their work has been followed by an orderly progression of experiments from the laboratory to the classroom. Following Skinner's work in the 1940's and 1950's, reports of experimental programs carried out in institutions and laboratory settings (with extremely deviant children) began appearing. These were followed by studies with normal preschool children in laboratory school settings and, finally, by studies carried out in the public schools. The latter research projects took place first in special classes and, by the late 1960's, in regular classes with normal children. By the 1970's widespread interest among educators had been generated. Hundreds of behavior modification research studies had been published, and behavior modification training programs for teachers were being developed.

There have been accounts in which operant procedures were systematically applied to severely handicapped or deviant children in laboratory or institutional settings (Ayllon & Michael, 1959; Lovaas, Schaeffer, & Simmons, 1965; Wolf, Risley, & Mees, 1964). In these early studies, alleviating deviant or deficient behavior was the primary emphasis. The behaviors were often severely dehabilitating to the child and prevented the occurrence of normal interactions. Thus, while the behaviors dealt with were not necessarily school oriented, they evoked the interest of educators. This is understandable because, regardless of the philosophy of an educational approach, all educators want children to develop behavior patterns with a minimum of deviant or destructive behavior (e.g., tantrums) and a maximum of useful behavior (e.g., reading). These studies revealed an approach that: (1) reduced undesirable behavior; (2) established desirable behavior; and (3) permitted the ready acquisition of procedures for implementing this system by trainers and teachers. Other attractive features were that emphasis was placed on developing positive and rewarding settings rather than punitive ones, the approach was highly individualized, and the emphasis was on bringing about behavioral change by changing the environment.

B. Research with Preschool Children

At about the same time as the studies conducted with deviant children in institutional or laboratory settings, a series of experiments were carried out, primarily at the University of Washington, with normal preschool children (Allen, Hart, Buell, Harris, & Wolf, 1964; Allen, Henke, Harris, Baer, & Reynolds, 1967; Buell, Stoddard, Harris, & Baer, 1968; Bushell & Jacobson, 1968; Bushell,

Wrobel, & Michaelis, 1968; Harris, Johnston, Kelley, & Wolf, 1964a; Harris, Wolf, & Baer, 1964b; Hart, Allen, Buell, Harris, & Wolf, 1964; Hart & Risley, 1968; Wolf, Risley, Johnston, Harris, & Allen, 1967).

Allen *et al.* (1964) systematically studied the effects of adult attention directed toward a nursery school child who excessively isolated herself from peers. Most of the adult attention being given to the child was contingent upon isolate behavior. When the adults were instructed to ignore the girl during isolate behavior and attend to her when she played with peers, her rate of playing with peers increased. Hart *et al.* (1964) demonstrated similar effects when they instructed the teacher of two preschool boys to ignore the boys when they engaged in crying behavior and to attend to them when they handled stressful situations without crying. As a result of differential attention, the rate of crying diminished to near zero. Harris *et al.* (1964a) reduced crawling while simultaneously increasing the walking behavior of a 3-year-old girl by attending to her when she walked and ignoring her when she crawled. As can be seen, much of this research applied extensive use of adult attention to modify the behavior of preschoolers. It also marked the progress being made in bringing operant procedures from laboratory and institutional settings to more applied settings with normal populations.

C. Research in Special Classrooms

1. EARLY STUDIES

The first studies carried out in school settings generally involved children in special classrooms (Hanley, 1967). Just as with early institutional research, the initial behaviors dealt with in special classrooms were frequently deviant social behaviors that prevented children from functioning in normal environments.

Early studies in special classrooms included attempts to decrease tantrums through systematic teacher attention (Zimmerman & Zimmerman, 1962) or by using candy and stars contingent on appropriate behavior (Carlson, Arnold, Becker, & Madsen, 1968).

Other treatment strategies were designed to improve conduct and attention-to-task behavior of hyperactive children (Knowles, Prutsman, & Raduege, 1968; Quay, Sprague, Werry, & McQueen, 1967) and autistic children (Hudson & DeMyer, 1968; Rabb & Hewett, 1967).

Patterson (1965) increased the in-seat behavior of a hyperactive boy by making candy reinforcement for the boy and his peers contingent on having him remain appropriately seated at his desk.

Straughn, Potter, and Hamilton (1965) increased verbalizations in an elective deaf mute by making points the pupil could earn for an all class party contingent on his talking in the classroom. Sulzbacher and Houser (1968) reduced the frequency of a disruptive obscene classroom gestures through contingent loss of recess time. Other researchers reported improved study or attending to task behavior for underachievers (Broden, Hall, Dunlap, & Clark, 1970; McKenzie, Clark, Wolf, Kothera, & Benson, 1968; O'Leary & Becker, 1967; Walker & Buckley, 1968) and retardates (Zimmerman, Zimmerman, & Russel, 1968).

Early academic studies carried out in special classrooms involved the use of token systems in which tokens or points were earned contingently on some specific academic response. These tokens were later exchanged for back up reinforcers such as edibles, toys, extra recess, or classroom privileges.

Token systems were used to improve assignment completion and correct answers on assignments (Birnbrauer & Lawler, 1964; Birnbrauer, Wolf, Kidder, & Tague, 1965; Cohen, Filipczak, & Bis, 1968; Tyler & Brown, 1968), improved grades (Tyler, 1967) and achievement scores (Martin, Burkholder, Rosenthal, Tharp, & Thorne, 1968; Wolf, Giles, & Hall, 1968).

In the study by Birnbrauer *et al.* (1965) a special classroom was devised for 15 institutionalized retardates. Token reinforcement was dispensed contingently on the percentage of errors on assignments and the number of academic items completed. Time-out for inappropriate behavior and contingent social reinforcement were used to increase appropriate behavior.

2. BEHAVIORAL SYSTEMS IN SPECIAL EDUCATION

The number of studies involving special classrooms has steadily increased and several new behavior modification remedial strategies have been devised. Behavioral strategies for exceptional children have been employed, not only with individual children or single classrooms, but also on a district, state, or national scale.

Examples of school or district-wide systems are the Center at Oregon for Research and the Behavioral Education of the Handicapped (CORBEH) (Walker & Hops, in press) system developed in Eugene, Oregon, and the Responsive Teaching approach (Hall, Copeland, & Clark, 1976), which is outlined later in this chapter. The

Consulting Teacher Model of the State of Vermont (McKenzie, Egner, Knight, Perelman, Schneider, & Garvin, 1970), the Applied Behavior Analysis (Bushell & Ramp, 1974), and Engelmann-Becker (Becker, 1972) Follow Through Programs are also statewide and national in scope.

These stytems have several features in common which identify them as behavior modification programs: *First,* they all include procedures that define or pinpoint desirable behaviors as well as deviant behavior. *Second,* they all measure on a daily or repeating basis the occurrence of those behaviors; the behavioral definitions are in clear, observable terms. *Third,* the systems are all dependent on clearcut consequences administered for the occurrence or nonoccurrence of specific behaviors.

Distinct differences do exist, however, between various approaches. The differences occur in many instances because of methodological variations such as differing measurement strategies or differing modes of contingency delivery. For instance, the Consulting Teacher Model in Vermont (Fox, Egner, Paolucci, Perelman, McKenzie, & Garvin, 1972) relies heavily on measurement, develops detailed minimum objectives for each special child, especially in academic areas, and uses operant principles in developing individual and group treatment strategies.

The CORBEH (Walker & Hops, in press) system also depends on precise measurement procedures and the use of operant principles for treatment strategies. However, CORBEH is not significantly involved in academic goals for children. It suggests detailed strategies that teachers can incorporate in their classrooms to manage the entire spectrum of deviant or disruptive behaviors. Project Follow Through (Bushell & Ramp, 1974) has developed a token economy that deals with both disruptive and academic behavior and suggests a very specific classroom curriculum. Responsive Teaching (Hall & Copeland, 1972) focuses on measurement procedures and operant psychology for educators and encourages individual teachers and staffs to devise their own systems and approaches to deal with educational problems. The Responsive Teaching Model stresses the use of scientific verification procedures by teachers.

D. Research in the Regular School Classroom

1. RESEARCH DESIGNS

In a relatively short time, basic research moved from the laboratory to the normal classrooms. A number of factors facilitated this transition. The research designs and methodologies used by operant researchers allow single subjects or single groups to be investigated on a continuous basis and also to serve as their own controls (Baer, Wolf, & Risley, 1968). The reversal, multiple baseline (Baer *et al.*, 1968), and changing criterion (Hall, 1971; Hall & Fox, in press) designs were developed by behavior analysts for classroom research. All three designs involve collecting preexperimental or baseline levels of observable behaviors and then systematically programming changes in the environment to observe the effects of those changes on the subjects' behavior. The primary goal in operant research is to collect evidence that the programmed environmental changes are in fact responsible for changes in behavior.

In a reversal design, the programmed change, once applied and effective over a period of time, is withdrawn briefly to note the resultant trend in the target behavior. If the target behavior reverts back to its preexperimental or baseline level, a functional relationship has been demonstrated between the environmental change and the target behavior.

A multiple baseline design is one in which two or more behaviors are measured simultaneously prior to instituting experimental procedures. An experimental procedure is then introduced on one of the behaviors, and at subsequent intervals the same procedure is instituted for the second behavior, and then for the third. If there are successive changes in each behavior when experimental procedures are instituted, a functional relationship has been demonstrated between the procedure and each of the behaviors.

In a changing criterion design (Hall, 1971; Hall & Fox, in press), control of behavior is demonstrated if the behavior being modified changes as a function of changing criteria of reinforcement.

Another factor facilitating the transition to the classroom can be seen in analyzing the aims of education and operant research. Both attempt to discover ways in which children's functioning can be improved on a day-to-day basis. Educators are charged with the responsibility of developing and supervising the learning process. Therefore, a measurement technology that provides an avenue for the precise recording of children's ongoing behavior is important.

In addition to the metholological attributes of behavioral analysis research strategies, data-based principles of operant psychology provide a justification for teaching itself. Skinner has stated, ". . . the variables that affect human behavior lie outside the organism in its environmental history. We undertake to predict and control behavior by discovering the external conditions of which behavior is a function" (Skinner, 1953, p. 35).

What has school research revealed concerning the external conditions of which behavior is a function? The consequences of behavior thus far investigated in school research can be placed into three categories: (1) social attention systems; (2) direct contingency systems; and (3) token systems. All three approaches involve some social contact, and all involve delivering consequences for specific behaviors.

In social attention systems, contingencies are arranged so that a teacher's or peer's social attention is delivered or withheld following a specific observable behavior.

In direct contingency systems, children are given opportunities to engage in certain behaviors or to receive tangible items contingent on emitting specific behaviors. The Premack Principle is often involved in direct contingency systems. Briefly, the Premack Principle states: "of any two responses, the independently more probable one will reinforce the less probable one" (Premack, 1963, p. 31). In direct contingency systems, a high probability behavior (e.g., participation in extra gym class) is made contingent on a low probability behavior (e.g., working arithmetic problems).

In token systems, subjects receive tokens (any exchangeable item such as points, marks, chips, etc.) for emitting specific behaviors and then exchange their tokens for tangible items or the opportunity to engage in certain behaviors.

2. DEVIANT BEHAVIOR IN THE REGULAR CLASSROOM

As in other populations, many of the first studies carried out in regular school classrooms focused on disruptive, uncooperative, or inattentive behaviors. Among the earliest studies reported and the most thoroughly researched were those in which teachers were instructed to use attention, praise, and approval as social reinforcers to increase study or appropriate behavior (Becker, Madsen, Arnold, & Thomas, 1967; Hall, Lund, & Jackson, 1968a; Hall, Panyan, Rabon, & Broden, 1968b; Madsen, Becker, & Thomas, 1968; Schmidt & Ulrich, 1969; Thomas, Becker, & Armstrong, 1968; Ward & Baker, 1968). The study by Hall et al. (1968a) took place in two elementary schools in an inner city school system. Experiments were conducted with students who were identified as disruptive or nonproductive by their teachers. Trained observers recorded three behaviors on a daily basis, using an interval-recording method. The three behaviors measured were (1) study behavior of the subjects; (2) teacher verbalizations directed toward the pupils; and (3) teacher proximity to the pupils. The definition of study behavior differed for each student but generally involved the student being oriented toward the appropriate object, person, or assigned course materials, and the student participating in class activities when requested by the teacher.

Experiment 1 involved a student (Robbie) who emitted study behavior in 25% of the intervals in which he was observed during the class spelling period. It was noted that 55% of the teacher attention Robbie received followed nonstudy behavior. Following the baseline phase, whenever Robbie was engaged in 1 min of continuous study the observer signaled the teacher. On this cue the teacher approached Robbie and praised him for his study behavior. Robbie's rate of study behavior increased to a rate of 71% during this experimental phase. A brief reversal was instituted in which the teacher discontinued praising the child for study behavior. Robbie's rate of study behavior decreased to a mean of 50%. However, when reinforcement for study was reinstated, his study rate again increased, stabilizing at a rate ranging between 70% and 80% of the observational sessions. Follow-up checks made after 14 weeks indicated that study behavior was being maintained at a mean rate of 79%.

Similar results were obtained with four other children. An analysis of the attention directed to the subjects by one teacher in the study of Hall et al. (1968a) demonstrated that it was not the amount of attention the teacher directed toward the subject but its delivery contingent on study behavior that produced the changes in behavior.

Numerous other studies have been conducted using direct contingencies or token reinforcement systems to decrease disruptive or nonattending behaviors in regular classrooms. Hall, Fox, Willard, Goldsmith, Emerson, Owen, Davis, and Porcia (1971c) used games, privileges, and feedback to decrease talkouts. Other investigators used procedures such as contingent free time (Long & Williams, 1973), time-out from social reinforcement (Brown, Nesbitt, Purvis, & Cossairt, 1973; Hall & Fox, 1973; Ramp, Ulrich, & Dulaney, 1971; Waisk, Senn, Welch, & Cooper, 1969), self-recording (Broden, Hall & Mitts, 1971), a good behavior game (Barrish, Saunders, & Wolf, 1969), and vicarious reinforcement (Kazdin, 1973). However, published accounts of research with token systems in regular classrooms are limited (O'Leary, Becker, Evans, & Saudargas, 1969). There are probably varied reasons for this, with the most obvious being the response cost of token systems. If a regular classroom teacher, with 25 children or more, implements a token system it must be manageable so that the teacher can carry on regular teaching duties.

McLaughlin and Malaby (1972) gathered promising data suggesting that token systems can be implemented in regular classrooms. In their research, procedures were developed and tested with allowed teachers to implement token systems in rooms of 25 children or more. The token system these authors devised was used throughout the day and had several significant features. *First,* their token system was cost free. The backup reinforcers used were natural to the regular classroom environment. *Second,* this system was applicable to large groups. *Third,* a single teacher without outside observers or recorders could manage all of the features of the token economy.

In the first step in the McLaughlin and Malaby (1972) system, a list of privileges was developed for which contingent tokens (points) could be exchanged. The types of privileges for which the children could spend points were selected by the students and teacher and included sharpening pencils, playing games, being on a committee, etc. The privileges selected by the students were then ranked in terms of desirability, and point values were assigned to the privileges. Next, behaviors which earned points were determined as well as behaviors which lost points, and records were developed so that the students themselves kept track of points earned and lost. At the first of each week a 15-min period was spent in which points earned the previous week were exchanged for privileges for the present week. The analysis of data gathered in a regular classroom revealed higher rates of completed assignments when the token system was in effect.

3. INCREASING ACADEMIC PERFORMANCE

Few early behavior modification studies focused on academic behaviors. The number of such studies has increased steadily, however, until today the emphasis is less on controlling disruptive and deviant behavior and more on increasing academic performance. Among the first to attempt to directly increase academic accuracy and output were Evans and Oswalt (1968). They used reinforcement procedures to increase spelling accuracy in fourth-grade students. Lovitt and Curtiss (1969b) found that pupil-arranged reinforcement resulted in greater academic output than teacher-arranged reinforcement. Felixbrod and O'Leary (1973) found self-determined reinforcement and teacher-determined reinforcement of equal effect in increasing the learning of history and geography material. The amount and accuracy on written assignments in kindergarten, first-grade, and second-grade students was increased through contingent access to a playroom (Hopkins, Schutte, & Garton, 1971; Salzberg,

Wheeler, Devar, & Hopkins, 1971). Harris and Sherman (1973) found that peer tutoring and access to recess were effective in increasing math scores of fourth- and fifth-grade students. Tribble and Hall (1972) discovered that the percent of assigned math problems completed by a third-grade boy increased when he was allowed to lead the class in a favorite game contingent on completion of assignments. Lahey, McNees, and Brown (1973) increased the number of correct answers to reading-comprehension questions by two sixth-grade students by paying them money contingent on correct answers. Ayllon and Roberts (1974) found that by increasing academic performance in reading through token reinforcement, discipline problems were eliminated.

A few recent studies have reported increased creative responses of students through reinforcement procedures (Goetz & Baer, 1973; Goetz & Salmonson, 1972; Maloney & Hopkins, 1973). This seems to be a continuation of the research trend away from the laboratory and deviant behaviors toward more normal and/or gifted populations with more complex and sophisticated behaviors.

While most of the studies that have researched the academic responding of school children have dealt with the consequence side of the response chain, a limited number of studies have systematically investigated the antecedent events preceding an academic response. Lovitt and Curtiss (1969a) experimented with the procedure of verbalizing a problem before a child was expected to make a written response. Rieth, Axelrod, Hathaway, Wood, and Fitzgerald (1974) manipulated the way in which spelling words were presented to students for study and observed the effects on weekly spelling tests. Broden, Copeland, Beasley, and Hall (in press) assessed the effects of instructions and questions requiring multiple word responses on the kind and length of discussion answers given by students in a junior high school class.

III. TEACHER TRAINING

The studies outlined in the preceding section of this chapter were important because they demonstrated that the basic behavior modification principles initially developed in the laboratory could be used in applied settings to solve significant behavioral and learning problems. They were also important because they conclusively demonstrated to educators that teacher attention, classroom privileges, games, and token reinforcement systems could be used in regular as well as special public school classrooms.

A. The Outside Researcher as Teacher Trainer

As was pointed out by Patterson (1969), these early studies were merely demonstrations because they were carried out under the direct supervision of skilled researchers. Although some of the teachers who participated in these experiments continued to use the practices that had resulted in improved pupil performance after the experiments were terminated, there was also evidence that some teachers reverted to less effective practices once the experimenters withdrew (Kuypers, Becker, & O'Leary, 1968).

It is not difficult to understand why teachers involved in experiments contrived by someone outside the classroom have failed to continue carrying out experimental procedures after the experimenters have departed. One reason is that the experiments often depended on systems requiring equipment, observers, research assistants, and others not available in normal classroom situations. Such systems collapse when the equipment and outside assistance are withdrawn. Another probable reason is that some of the procedures, including complex token systems, require so much effort and energy on the part of the teacher that gains in pupil performance which result are not enough to maintain the teacher's participation once the reinforcers that are provided by the experimenters are no longer available.

This does not mean that experimenter-conducted investigations are unimportant. Such investigations by skilled researchers have and will continue to make an important contribution to the development of behavior modification procedures. The publication of this research in the literature has helped create the great interest in the use of these techniques, but even if all teachers were to continue to carry on the behavior modification procedures after formal investigations were concluded, the research study directed by an outside experimenter is not a good model for training individual teachers.

Training teachers in this way is prohibitively expensive. Furthermore, even if all the trained researchers available were to devote full time to working with teachers in their classrooms, only a small fraction could be reached. Individual research studies were an excellent place to begin training teachers, but the approach was not likely to result in training large numbers of teachers to use ongoing behavior modification procedures in their classrooms. To accomplish this goal, other teaching strategies are necessary.

B. The Lecturer as Trainer

In recent years many teachers have been "taught" basic learning theory principles which are the foundation of behavior modification in the schools. However, there is little evidence that exposure to concepts of social learning theory through lectures in college classes or in-service workshops has done more than result in an increased interest in behavior modification. It has been the authors' experience that very few teachers, counselors, principals, and school psychologists translate what has been presented in lectures and workshops into actual practice. Thus, learning about learning theory principles and behavior modification studies in the usual college lecture class, or through school in-service workshops, does not seem to be a good model for rapidly training teachers, principals, and other educators to become expert in using behavior modification.

C. The Bag of Tricks Model

Another approach is the "bag of tricks model." This model takes a number of forms. They all lack one or more elements of a program which will allow teachers to independently solve problems beyond the narrow training they receive.

Some bag of tricks programs that identify themselves as behavior modification approaches present lockstep token reinforcement systems. They provide training in implementing a token system without providing a background in behavioral principles and applied behavioral analysis procedures that will allow the flexibility necessary for those carrying out the system to revise or supplant the program if it becomes outmoded or unnecessary. It is similar in aspect to the cookbook approaches which advocate, "If faced with this problem, do this."

Other bag of tricks programs stress precise measurement and recording procedures of a certain type but fail to give a well-rounded background in social learning theory and applied behavior analysis that would allow their practitioners to understand and assess what they are doing. Some such programs may help teachers within a limited range, and may in fact prove effective over the short term, but they are unlikely to result in new programs that will meet requirements beyond those for which they were originally designed.

In order for a program to be truly viable over the long term it must allow its practitioners to apply procedures in new and different situations as they arise. It must not only go beyond the "lecture model" in which people are told what they should do but receive no opportunity to practice doing it. It must provide training which will allow them to generalize what they learn to new and different situations.

D. The Consultant Teacher Model and Training of Support Personnel

One approach already noted that has proved effective in increasing the use of behavior modification procedures by teachers has been the Consulting Teacher Model developed by McKenzie and his colleagues (McKenzie *et al.*, 1970) at the University of Vermont. Special education consultants are trained to assist teachers, principals, and parents to observe and measure behavior, set behavioral goals, and use systematic reinforcement procedures to assist children with behavior or learning problems in the regular classroom.

Other models that have focused on training teachers (as well as support personnel) to use behavioral procedures are the Follow Through programs by Bushell and Englemann-Becker. Bushell's Behavior Analysis Follow Through program has trained and employed over 2,000 parent teachers for the primary grades (Bushell & Ramp, 1974). The Englemann-Becker program (Becker, 1972) has trained over 750 teacher aides for grades K-3 in behavior analysis skills. Moore and Sanner (1969) have also developed a behavioral consultation program for elementary school teachers.

The Consulting Teacher Model and programs for training of support personnel which have focused on an applied behavior analysis approach have generated data indicating that they have been successful in bringing about positive changes in pupil behavior. One strength of the model developed by McKenzie and associates is the emphasis upon on-the-job training of teachers and parents to use behavior modification procedures which are based on applied behavior analysis.

E. The Responsive Teaching Approach

Another approach for training teachers to use behavior modification techniques has been described previously by Hall and Copeland (1972) and Hall, Copeland, and Clark (1976). Called *Responsive Teaching,* it is a program for teaching educators to use a behavior modification approach that emphasizes the precise observation and measurement of behavior, the application of social learning theory principles, and applied behavior analysis research designs.

The Responsive Teaching approach is designed for training teachers, principals, school psychologists, and other staff during the school year while they are on the job. Whether presented as an after-school university credit course, or a district credit in-service training program or workshop, this approach combines lectures and discussion sessions designed to teach principles and procedures with practical applications of the procedures in the classroom.

Its primary purpose is to provide participants with a foundation for understanding and using behavior modification principles and skills so they will continue to practice and build on what they have learned after completing the course. Since the first Responsive Teaching class, more than 2,000 educators have been trained. It has been adapted for training parents (Responsive Parenting), social workers, institutional staff members, nurses, businessmen, psychologists, speech clinicians, and other professionals interested in learning behavior modification skills.

1. FORMAT FOR RESPONSIVE TEACHING TRAINING SESSIONS

The Responsive Teacher program was originally designed as a three-credit course taught over one semester. Depending on circumstances, the number of weekly sessions has varied from 10 to 14. (On occasion the course has been given as a 1-week workshop with follow-up practicum experience in carrying out a study subsequent to the workshop.) Ideally, however, weekly sessions lasting about 3 hr are held right after public school classes have ended for the day, preferably where participants are working. Such arrangements are not always possible, and participants must sometimes travel a considerable distance to the weekly sessions.

The 3-hr weekly sessions are divided into two parts. The first half is used to present basic information through lectures and films. The lectures cover the material outlined in the next subsection of this chapter. The instructor's verbal presentation is supplemented by overhead transparencies that have been developed for that purpose (Hall & Fox, 1973). The transparencies provide cues to the instructor to remind him of the points to be covered in the lecture. They also provide a visual outline of the most important elements of the lecture for the participant. The first half of the weekly sessions is also used for films, demonstrations, role playing, and other activities designed for presenting basic concepts and principles to the entire group being trained.

During the second part of each weekly session the participants are divided into groups of no more than ten persons. Each group is led by someone who has previously taken the course. The small groups allow participants to ask questions about the material covered in the lectures and to receive feedback and reinforcement regarding individual progress in meeting the requirements.

In each weekly small-group session, the participants engage in several activities that help to accomplish this goal. First a discussion is held in which questions and comments regarding lecture material or assigned reading are answered and clarified. Then a quiz is given by the group leader based on the lecture. This quiz is graded in class, and kept by the participant. Thus, almost immediate feedback is provided regarding whether or not the participant has grasped the course content for the week.

The remainder of the small-group session focuses on assignments the participant is to carry out. These include reports on assigned readings and activities such as assignments to measure and record behavior or to design and carry out a shaping procedure. The major portion of time, however, is used for the participant to report on the study he or she is carrying out in conjunction with the course. Each week the participants discuss the progress of their studies and receive feedback and advice from their group leader and, if necessary, from the course instructor.

Each group member follows the progress of all studies carried out within their group.

2. THE COURSE CONTENT

The Responsive Teaching approach is designed to provide participants with a background of information and with basic skills that will prepare them to use behavior modification procedures:

1. Background readings of previous research.
2. Practical observation and recording procedures.

3. Applied behavior analysis research designs.
4. Basic reinforcement principles.
5. An applied behavior modification study.

3. BACKGROUND READINGS

Participants are asked to read a number of journal articles in order to acquaint themselves with some of the previous research, including some historically significant studies (e.g., Patterson, 1965; Wolf *et al.*, 1964), and to familiarize them with acceptable models for reporting their own research. Since it is sometimes difficult for participants to have access to the journals themselves, a book of selected readings (Rieth & Hall, 1974) and Part III of the *Behavior Management Series* (Hall, 1971) contain resource articles.

4. PRACTICAL OBSERVATION AND RECORDING PROCEDURES

The foundation of behavior modification research and application is based on precise observation and measurement of behavior. Therefore, beginning in the first session, participants are taught to define and measure behavior and are asked to practice observing and recording behavior. Emphasis is placed on methods teachers can use while they reach. These include direct measurement of permanent products, frequency counting, duration, and time sampling. Once recording of behavior begins, participants are taught to present their data on simple graphs.

5. APPLIED BEHAVIOR ANALYSIS RESEARCH DESIGNS

Applied behavior analysis research designs (Baer *et al.*, 1968) are a distinguishing feature of Responsive Teaching. Participants learn to assess the credibility of other research as well as that of their own efforts by using reversal, multiple baseline, and changing criterion designs. The test used in conjunction with the lectures on observation and measurement and applied behavior analysis research designs is in the *Behavior Management Series:* Part I, *The measurement of behavior* (Hall, 1971).

6. BASIC REINFORCEMENT PRINCPLES

Once measurement and applied behavior analysis research designs have been introduced and participants have begun measuring behaviors of concern, they are taught the basic social learning theory principles that underly behavior modification procedures. These behavior modification principles and concepts are presented during weekly lectures and are also made available to participants in the *Behavior Management Series:* Part II, *Basic principles* (Hall, 1971). Among the principles and procedures covered are operant and respondent behavior, reinforcement, extinction, satiation, shaping, reinforcement schedules, token reinforcement, contingency contracting, generalization, discrimination, chaining, prompting, fading, instructional control, punishment, time-out, response cost, and overcorrection. Emphasis is placed on recognizing and applying natural contingencies rather than those extrinsic to school settings.

The course is organized so that participants can easily comprehend these principles and procedures. Group leaders assign readings related to the material to be covered a week prior to its presentation in class. During the lecture the instructor presents the material in lecture and demonstrations. At the same time the material is presented in outline form through overhead transparencies. Immediately after the lecture the material is discussed in the small-group sessions. Weekly quizzes are administered and participants receive feedback concerning their written responses. Two exams are also administered. These exams are essentially composites of the weekly quizzes. The first is used as a means of assessing whether the participants have learned the material and allows for review and reteaching if errors are made. The final exam is another form of the same test. Most participants score 90% or better on the final examination.

7. CARRYING OUT A BEHAVIOR MODIFICATION STUDY

The main vehicle for encouraging participants to use and to begin practicing systematic behavior modification procedures in their classrooms is the study each is asked to carry out. Through these experiments the participants learn to use what they have been taught in practical situations. They learn to incorporate Responsive Teaching procedures into their repertoires by using them in their classrooms. By following the progress of others in the small group and seeing them succeed, each person participates vicariously in studies carried out by peers.

Through their experiments, participants define and record behaviors, arrange for and carry out reliability checks, graph, employ reversal, multiple baseline, or changing criterion research designs, and write up and present their research studies.

Guide sheets distributed to participants help them through each stage of carrying out and writing up their studies. The group leaders and the instructor monitor the studies weekly. This is one of the most important functions of the small-group sessions. A preliminary draft of the study is checked by the group leader and instructor and returned the following week with feedback about its strengths and deficiencies.

To date, approximately 60 Responsive Teaching studies carried out in schools and homes have been published in books and professional journals. Several appear in Part III of the *Behavior Management Series* (Hall, 1971). Those presented in Hall, Cristler, Cranston, and Tucker (1970) illustrate the three basic multiple baseline designs. Those appearing in Hall and Fox (in press) illustrate changing criterion designs. Others illustrate the effects of using systematic reinforcement, extinction, and punishment procedures (e.g., Fox, Copeland, Harris, Rieth, & Hall, 1974; Hall, 1971, Part II & Part III; Hall, Axelrod, Foundopolous, Shellman, Campbell, & Cranston, 1971a; Hall, Ayala, Copeland, Cossairt, Freeman, & Harris, 1971b; Hall, Cossairt, & Crowder, 1973b; Hall *et al.,* 1971c).

Other studies illustrating that the Responsive Teaching model can be adapted for training parents include Hall, Axelrod, Tyler, Grief, Jones, and Robertson (1972) and the Responsive Parenting studies generated by Clark (see Hall, Copeland, & Clark, 1976).

8. SUMMARY

The Responsive Teaching approach outlined here is not presented as the only valid approach for training teachers in behavior modification. It is presented, however, as one that has been used successfully by an increasing number of individuals in the United States as well as in other countries.

In addition to the considerable number of individuals trained in the Responsive Teaching approach in the Kansas City area, many others have reported success in other areas, including Canada, Panama (Hall, Copeland, Chavez, & Alvarado, 1973a), and Brazil. The *Managing Behavior Series* booklets have been translated into Spanish and Portuguese for use in Latin American countries.

We would not contend, however, that the Responsive Teaching approach is unique. There are a number of other programs being conducted that incorporate its essential elements, including the aforementioned ones developed by McKenzie and Bushell. The elements that Responsive Teaching and these programs have in common which differentiate them from the "experimenter as trainer," the "lecture," and the "bag of tricks" models is that the former programs include training in: (1) observing and measuring behavior; (2) using applied behavior analysis research designs; and (3) principles and procedures of basic social learning theory. They all also require the participants to practice the concepts.

Programs that lack these elements hold much less promise as vehicles for training school personnel to learn to apply behavior modification procedures successfully.

IV. FUTURE DIRECTIONS FOR RESEARCH

Research has demonstrated beyond question that behavior modification procedures are effective in increasing social and academic behaviors. It seems certain that research will continue on the effects of systematic consequences on behaviors in the classroom. However, a number of other research areas should lend themselves to applied behavior analysis investigations.

A. Creativity, Self-Control, and Other Complex Behaviors

Forthcoming studies should deal with creativity, self-control, and other complex behaviors. As previously mentioned, Maloney and Hopkins (1973) and Brigham, Graubard, and Stans (1972) have begun to investigate ways of increasing creative student behaviors. The application of behavior modification in the area of self-management or -control is gaining attention (Bolstad & Johnson, 1972; Drabman, Spitalnik, & O'Leary, 1973; Thoresen & Mahoney, 1974). The fact that researchers moved from an emphasis on reducing disruptive and deviant behaviors to increasing academic behaviors such as those involved in mathematics and spelling is encouraging. It is perhaps even more exciting that there seems to be a trend toward investigating increasingly complex behaviors such as those involving original written compositions and spoken language during class discussions (Broden et al., in press).

One problem associated with such research is that because it is more complex, it is usually more difficult to define the behaviors and to obtain reliable measurements. When such measurement problems are overcome, there will be an increasing number of studies that will explore ways to teach such complex behaviors more effectively.

Another area of educational research concerns antecedent stimuli (e.g., Lovitt & Curtiss, 1969a). However, there are a few other examples of research describing how materials are presented to the learner. Robie, Copeland, and Hall (1974) investigated the effects of using a mechanical device to teach two-digit borrowing (regrouping) in subtraction, and Rieth *et al.* (1974) have investigated the effects of distributed versus massed practice in spelling.

B. Some Unanswered Questions

Unfortunately, many educational practices to date have been based upon intuitive guesses and/or traditions. There are few data available to help the educator determine which teaching techniques are most effective, which stimulus materials are best to use, and in what ways they should be presented. Among the questions that need to be answered empirically are the following:

1. How long should learning sessions be?
2. How much practice is optimal for various learning tasks?
3. How often should review sessions occur in order to maintain skills?
4. What sequence of skills is necessary for optimal learning?
5. What are the schedules of feedback and reinforcement that will optimize learning and retention?

Another future direction for educational research is related to the training of parents to assist teachers and the school in educating their children through cooperative behavior modification projects. McKenzie *et al.* (1968) demonstrated that parent-delivered reinforcement was effective in increasing attending behavior and achievement in pupils who had been labeled "learning disabled." Subsequently, Clark (1975) and her colleagues have explored the results of teaching groups of parents applied behavior analysis (Responsive Parenting) skills in order for them to better communicate with the school staff and to allow for cooperative school-home intervention using behavior modification procedures to increase learning and to decrease problem behaviors.

V. MORAL AND ETHICAL ISSUES IN EDUCATION

It can be argued that in the past it probably did not make too much difference what teachers chose as their educational goals because they were frequently unable to achieve them. The situation has changed. It has been conclusively demonstrated that operant procedures are effective and powerful and, if used systematically, will bring about rapid changes in most behaviors.

Because of this, many persons have raised questions not only about what behaviors and skills are being taught but also about the procedures themselves. Among the questions one hears are the following:

1. If you reinforce children for appropriate behavior is it not just a system of bribery?
2. If you use these procedures are you not controlling and manipulating others in a way that makes them automatons, since they are powerless to resist?
3. Even though you are changing the behavior, are you not merely treating symptoms rather than the underlying causes of the behavior?
4. What right do you have to determine what behaviors will be modified?

A. A System of Bribery?

The dictionary definition of a bribe is ". . . anything given or promised to induce a person to do something illegally wrong or normally reprehensible." Are we bribing public officials, teachers, ministers, and physicians when we pay them salaries or monies for services rendered? Is it not also appropriate and logical that we reward children for performing the learning tasks we designate for them and expect them to master? Why should children be on a different system than adults? Not many adults would continue to go to work day after day if they were not paid *both* monetarily and with some kind of social recognition or reinforcement.

Some critics say that children should learn for learning's sake, that learning should be internalized, and that the child should take pride in a job well done and that in itself should be reward enough. Although this is the ideal situation, what about the child who does not respond in this way? Behaviorists accept the fact that for many children, praise, attention, privileges, or other reinforcers must be used in the beginning as new skills are taught.

Others have said that behaviorism is wrong because we are manipulating innocent children by offering them rewards they cannot resist, thus forcing them to do things they would not do ordinarily. In answer to this criticm it should be pointed out that those who object to using positive reinforcement to get children to strive for appropriate social and academic behavior have not hesitated to try to coerce children to do the same things by scolding them, spanking them, or by removing privileges. Anyone who looks at the question objectively must admit that teachers and parents are charged with the responsibility of changing the behavior of their children. In bringing about these changes, if we must choose between reinforcing appropriate responses or coercing through punishing inappropriate behavior, we ask, "Which is more humane?"

B. Automatons, Control, and Manipulation

Behavior modification techniques are extremely powerful and do permit educators to reach objectives effectively. It is sometimes argued, however, that procedures used in applied behavior analysis are amoral. They are not good, nor are they bad. They can be used for uplifting social purposes or for evil. This puts a great responsibility upon us as to how they should be used and applied. Educators should *not* ignore these powerful procedures and abdicate responsibility for molding the lives of our children. They should rather accept the responsibility for changing children's lives and make certain educational goals are in the best interests of children and society.

To do this it is necessary that all segments of society be involved in determining educational goals. This process is already in practice in the Consulting Teacher program in Vermont (Fox *et al.*, 1972), wherein teachers, parents, and community people develop minimum learning objectives for each child in the elementary school, and together monitor children's progress toward attaining those objectives.

As can be seen recent research and applications of behavior modification techniques reveal a trend away from reducing talk-outs and out-of-seat behavior to increasing academic performance, creative responses, participation in discussions, and self-control. Behavior modification can be used to reach humanistic goals as well as ones which feature elements of imposed control. If it is possible for us to define what is meant by independent thinking and creativity, it seems certain that by using systematic behavior modification techniques we can teach people to become more independent and creative.

C. Symptoms

Behaviorists are sometimes accused of treating symptoms and not underlying causes of behavior. It is true that we have focused on behaviors that can be observed and measured. If we change these overt behaviors, will the basic problem remain or result in symptom substitution while the underlying cause remains untreated? Our data have not borne this out. This is especially true since in most cases our objective has been to substitute an adaptive behavior for a maladaptive one. In case after case when children have had their behavior modified in more appropriate directions, the subjective judgments have been almost unanimous in indicating that they have become happier persons in the process.

Obviously the debate concerning the ethical use of behavior modification techniques with children will continue. This is a healthy development, especially if open debate results in facilitating improved educational practices. Educators who have had the opportunity to use behavior modification techniques have resolved the conflict regarding its ethical use. Its rapid acceptance is continuing at an accelerated pace. Systematic behavior modification procedures *can* and *do* work. Properly applied, they bring about improved behavior and learning on the part of children. Since educators are charged with the responsibility for improving the behavioral and academic repertoires of students, it would be immoral and unethical for them not to use procedures which allow them to do so more effectively.

VI. CHANGING ROLES FOR THE APPLIERS OF BEHAVIOR MANAGEMENT

A. The Teacher

We have outlined ways that teachers are being trained and have suggested some areas for future research. As we develop better procedures for training teachers, they will become more effective in determining educational goals, providing appropriate stimulus materials, arranging opportunities for pupils to make correct responses, and providing systematic feedback and differential reinforcement for those responses. The teacher's role will shift from that of one who frequently fails to provide pupils with a good learning environment to one who is successful. More specifically, teachers will become more aware of the importance of providing reinforcement for appropriate responses. As they become skilled in doing so, their roles will shift to being primarily agents for providing reinforcement rather than, as is now too often true, agents who use aversive controls in the classroom.

As teachers learn to observe and measure behavior and to use applied behavior analysis, they become practicing researchers whose decisions regarding materials and teaching techniques are based on data rather than on intuition, traditional practice, or convenience. This, of course, occurs only if strategies can be arranged that make it possible for the teacher to do so without being overwhelmed (punished) by a great deal of extra work, and if the school administrators, parents, and others in the community reinforce teachers for their efforts in this direction. When this shift in role does occur we can expect that pupils will be increasingly motivated and enthusiastic toward academic tasks. The quality of education will increase as programs designed to help individual students are implemented.

B. The Principal

As the role of the teacher changes as a function of behavior modification studies and procedures, a similar change can be predicted for the principal, director, or headmaster of the school. Research by Brown and Copeland and their colleagues indicates that the principal can use behavior modification to bring about changes in pupil behaviors, including school attendance, tardiness, disruptions, school phobic behavior, and academic behaviors (Brown, Copeland, & Hall, 1972, 1974; Copeland, Brown, & Hall, 1974).

Other studies have indicated that principals can positively affect teacher behavior. Cossairt, Brown, Copeland, and Hall (1973) demonstrated that modeling, feedback, and praise were effective in increasing teacher praise for attending behavior in pupils. Copeland, Brown, Axelrod, and Hall (1972) used verbal praise to parents via the telephone to increase attendance in chronically absent pupils. This research has indicated that it is possible for the principal to be an effective reinforcing agent for students, teachers, and parents. In fact, data showed that the principal became more effective by shifting his role from that of a disciplinarian who is primarily a dispenser of punishment to an agent of reinforcement.

In addition to changing his role from one who contacts others primarily when problems occur to one who has frequent reinforcing contacts for appropriate behavior, an applied behavior analysis approach holds promise for the principal to better fulfill his role as instructional leader. He will be able to make better decisions regarding curriculum materials and procedures based on behavioral records and research.

Another application is in the area of evaluation of teaching competence. Principals have long been required to evaluate and rate teachers. This rating has usually been done subjectively. As improved observation and measurement techniques are developed, it will be possible for principals to evaluate teachers objectively and to provide them with specific feedback and reinforcement regarding their teaching performances.

One reason principals spend as much time as they do in routine administrative tasks rather than in supervising instruction is that they have received little training or reinforcement for interacting with pupils, teachers, and parents. Therefore, tasks related to the instructional programs have been relatively punishing. As principals develop skills which allow them to receive more reinforcement for instructional leadership, their role is sure to change.

C. The School Psychologist

The school psychologist has traditionally been someone who is consulted when pupils have learning or behavior problems which the teacher, principal, and other school staff cannot handle. Usually he reviews the records of the pupil, interviews the teacher, pupil, and parents, and administers various educational and psychological tests. From the information obtained he usually attempts to identify or label the student's problem and to recommend special placement or some other therapy. All too frequently further contact is quite limited, and the psychologist has little time to help implement or follow up on recommendations.

In recent years, however, a number of school psychologists have demonstrated that their role can be shifted from one who tests, labels, and recommends to that of one who assists teachers, principals, and parents in applying behavioral techniques designed to remediate the problem behaviors. An even greater shift in the role of the school psychologist is possible. Armed with a knowledge of behavior modification principles and procedures, the school psychologist can become an agent for implementing preventative rather than remedial programs. Through training in using behavior modification procedures, teachers will be able to apply those procedures with other pupils, and the number of referrals will decrease. Perhaps even more important is the movement that now exists in some school districts which allows the school psychologist to teach teachers and other school staff members to use behavior modification procedures during in-service training sessions. Such teachers and principals will be better able to deal with the problems they face and will be able to use the school psychologist as a behavioral consultant rather than someone who removes the child from the classroom or recommends other remedial solutions difficult or impossible to implement.

D. Teacher Aides

Behavior modification research has demonstrated quite conclusively that one does not need a professional degree in education or psychology in order to teach a child new skills (Hall *et al.,* 1972; Wolf *et al.,* 1964). This demonstration is significant in that it provides a rationale and justification for the extensive use of paraprofessionals. Teacher aides provide the schools with a tremendous potential for delivering more individual attention to children. With proper training, aides can play a vital role in providing quality learning experiences for students.

Two programs that have been developed as outgrowths of the Responsive Teaching Model train paraprofessionals how to deal effectively with problem children and the parents of the children (Copeland, Terry, Hardin, & Alvarado, 1975; Crowder, Marquesen, & Peterson, 1974). Other behavior modification programs make extensive use of persons without degrees (Bushell & Ramp, 1974; Clark, 1975).

The future will see further development of this trend. It will be important that the increased use of paraprofessionals in direct educational roles with children does not result in a lessening of the quality of services. A safeguard for this will be the development of paraprofessional training sequences and the formats that provide professionals with evaluative instruments to assess the functioning of paraprofessionals

VII. SUMMARY

We have briefly outlined the historical progression which traced behavior modification from the laboratory to the classroom. The progression was marked by an initial emphasis on deviant social behaviors. Recently, emphasis has shifted to increasing academic behaviors and more complex responses. At the same time it was marked by movement from special classroom settings to normal preschool and regular public school classrooms.

We have also outlined how the guidance of educators has developed from training which was incidental to applied research to the "lecture," "bag of tricks," and other defective models, and then to the Consulting Teacher and Responsive Teaching approaches which hold promise as ways of insuring that behavior modification procedures will be learned and correctly implemented.

We have also suggested some areas of future research emphasis and have outlined how the roles of various persons involved in education may be expected to change as a result of the behavior modification movement.

Finally, we have briefly raised some moral and ethical issues and have suggested how they might be solved. Whatever one's view of behavior modification and its place in the field of education, it is important to be informed regarding what has happened in the field. Rarely has a movement made itself felt in education so rapidly. Whether one is convinced that behavior modification approaches are destined to become a dominant force in the field, or whether one is of the opinion that this is merely another short-lived innovation, it will be important to look at it closely so that decisions made regarding its implementation or rejection can be made on the basis of understanding and knowledge of what is involved. Otherwise it is possible that behavior modification will be misapplied and will fail to realize its promise for education, or that it will be rejected out of hand due to a lack of information regarding all that it encompasses.

REFERENCES

Allen, E., Hart, B., Buell, J., Harris, F., & Wolf, M. M. Effects of social reinforcement on isolate behavior of a nursery school child. *Child Development*, 1964, **35**, 511–518.

Allen, E., Henke, L., Harris, F., Baer, D., & Reynolds, N. Control of hyperactivity by social reinforcement of attending behavior. *Journal of Educational Psychology*, 1967, **58**, 231–237.

Ayllon, T., & Michael, J. The psychiatric nurse as a behavioral engineer. *Journal of the Experimental Analysis of Behavior*, 1959, **2**, 323–334.

Ayllon, T., & Roberts, M. P. Eliminating discipline problems by strengthening academic performance. *Journal of Applied Behavior Analysis*, 1974, 7, 71–76.

Baer, D., Wolf, M. M., & Risley, T. R. Some current dimensions of applied behavior analysis. *Journal of Applied Behavior Analysis*, 1968, 1, 91–97.

Barrish, H., Saunders, M., & Wolf, M. M. Good behavior game: Effects of individual contingencies for group consequences on disruptive behavior in a regular classroom. *Journal of Applied Behavior Analysis*, 1969, 2, 119–124.

Becker, W. C. Some effects of direct instruction methods in teaching disadvantaged children in Project Follow Through. *Proceedings of the International Symposium on Behavior Therapy, 1972.*

Becker, W. C., Madsen, C., Arnold, C., & Thomas, D. The contingent use of teacher attention and praise in reducing classroom behavior problems. *Journal of Special Education*, 1967, 1, 287–307.

Birnbrauer, J. S., & Lawler, J. Token reinforcement for learning. *Mental Retardation*, 1964, 2, 275–579.

Birnbrauer, J. S., Wolf, M. M., Kidder, J. D., & Tague, C. E. Classroom behavior of retarded pupils with token reinforcement. *Journal of Experimental Child Psychology*, 1965, 2, 219–235.

Bolstad, O. D., & Johnson, S. M. Self-regulation in the modification of disruptive classroom behavior. *Journal of Applied Behavior Analysis*, 1972, 5, 443–454.

Brigham, T. A., Graubard, P. S., & Stans, A. Analysis of the effects of sequential reinforcement contingencies on aspects of composition. *Journal of Applied Behavior Analysis*, 1972, 5, 421–429.

Broden, M., Copeland, G., Beasley, A., & Hall, R. V. Altering student responses through changes in teacher verbal behavior. *Journal of Applied Behavior Analysis*, in press.

Broden, M., Hall, R. V., Dunlap, A., & Clark, R. Effects of teacher attention and a token reinforcement system in a junior high school special education class. *Exceptional Children*, 1970, 36, 341–349.

Broden, M., Hall, R. V., & Mitts, B. The effect of self-recording on the classroom behavior of two eighth grade students. *Journal of Applied Behavior Analysis*, 1971, 4, 191–199.

Brown, L., Nesbitt, J., Purvis, G., & Cossairt, A. The control of severe tantrum behavior through the use of a one-minute time-out procedure on three early stage tantrum symptoms. In R. V. Hall & R. G. Fox (Eds.), *Instructor's manual for the Responsive teaching model transparency kit.* Lawrence, Kans.: H & H Enterprises, Inc., 1973. Pp. 32–33.

Brown, R., Copeland, R., & Hall, R. V. The school principal as a behavior modifier. *Journal of Educational Research*, 1972, 66, 175–180.

Brown, R., Copeland, R., & Hall, R. V. School phobia: Effects of behavior modification treatment applied by an elementary school principal. *Child Study Journal*, 1974, 4, 125–133.

Buell, J., Stoddard, P., Harris, F., & Baer, D. Collateral social development accompanying reinforcement of outdoor play in a preschool child. *Journal of Applied Behavior Analysis*, 1968, 1, 167–173.

Bushell, D., & Jacobson, J. The simultaneous rehabilitation of mothers and their children. Paper read at the meeting of the American Psychological Association, San Francisco, September 1968.

Bushell, D., & Ramp, E. A. *The behavior analysis classroom.* Lawrence, Kans.: University of Kansas Behavior Analysis Follow Through Project, 1974.

Bushell, D., Wrobel, P., & Michaelis, M. Applying "group" contingencies to the classroom study behavior of preschool children. *Journal of Applied Behavior Analysis*, 1968, 1, 55–61.

Carlson, C., Arnold, C., Becker, W., & Madsen, C. The elimination of tantrum behavior of a
    child in an elementary classroom. *Behaviour Research and Therapy*, 1968, 6, 117–119.
Clark, M. L. Teaching parents applied behavior analysis: A training program for the
    prevention and remediation of behavior problems. Unpublished doctoral dissertation,
    University of Kansas, 1975.
Cohen, J., Filipczak, J., & Bis, J. Case project: Contingencies applicable to special educa-
    tion. In J. M. Shlien (Ed.), *Research in psychotherapy*. Vol. 3. Washington, D.C.:
    American Psychological Association, 1968. Pp. 134–148.
Copeland, R. E., Brown, R., Axelrod, S., & Hall, R. V. Effect of a school principal praising
    parents for student attendance. *Educational Technology*, 1972, 12, 56–59.
Copeland, R. E., Brown, R., & Hall, R. V. The effects of principal implemented techniques
    on the behavior of pupils. *Journal of Applied Behavior Analysis*, 1974, 1, 77–86.
Copeland, R. E., Terry, B. J., Hardin, T. R., & Alvarado, F. The paraprofessional as a special
    team member. Paper read at the National Association for School Psychologists Conven-
    tion, Atlanta, Georgia, March, 1975.
Cossairt, A., Brown, R. E., Copeland, R. E., & Hall, R. V. Effects of principal supervision
    package on positive teaching methods and the subsequent effects on student attending,
    instruction following and academic performance in the classroom. Paper read at the
    81st Annual American Psychological Association, Montreal, Canada, Sept. 1973.
Crowder, J., Marquesen, V., & Peterson, M. Responsive teaching for the paraprofessional.
    Workshop presentation at the annual meeting of the Association for Advancement of
    Behavior Therapy, Chicago, November 1974.
Drabman, R., Spitalnik, R., & O'Leary, K. D. Teaching self-control to disruptive children.
    Journal of Abnormal Child Psychology, 1973, 1, 68–87.
Evans, G., & Oswalt, G. Acceleration of academic progress through the manipulation of peer
    influence. *Behavior Research and Therapy*, 1968, 6, 189–195.
Felixbrod, J. J., & O'Leary, K. D. Effects of reinforcement on children's academic behavior
    as a function of self-determined and externally imposed contingencies. *Journal of
    Applied Behavior Analysis*, 1973, 6, 241–250.
Ferster, C. B., & Skinner, B. F. *Schedules of reinforcement*. New York: Appleton, 1957.
Fox, R. G., Copeland, R., Harris, J. W., Rieth, H. J., & Hall, R. V. A computerized system
    for selecting responsive teching studies catalogued along twenty-eight important dimen-
    sions. *Behavior analysis in education*. New York: Appleton, 1974. Pp. 124–158.
Fox, W. L., Egner, A. N., Paolucci, P. E., Perelman, P. P., McKenzie, H. S., & Garvin, J. S.
    An introduction to a regular classroom approach to special education. In E. N. Deno
    (Ed.), *Instructional alternatives for exceptional children*. Arlington, Virginia: Council
    for Exceptional Children, 1972. Pp. 22–46.
Goetz, E. M., & Baer, D. M. Social control of form diversity and the emergence of new
    forms in children's blockbuilding. *Journal of Applied Behavior Analysis*, 1973, 6,
    209–217.
Goetz, E. M., & Salmonson, M. M. The effect of general and descriptive reinforcement on
    "creativity" and easel painting. In G. B. Semb (Ed.), *Behavior analysis in education*.
    Lawrence: University of Kansas Press, 1972. Pp. 33–61.
Hall, R. V. *Behavior management series: Part I. The measurement of behavior; Part II. Basic
    principles; Part III. Applications in school and home*. Lawrence, Kans.: H & H
    Enterprises, 1971.
Hall, R. V., Axelrod, S., Foundopoulos, M., Shellman, J., Campbell, R. A., & Cranston, S. S.
    The effective use of punishment to modify behavior in the classroom. *Educational
    Technology*, 1971, 11, 24–26. (a)

Hall, R. V., Axelrod, S., Tyler, L., Grief, E., Jones, F. C., & Robertson, R. Modification of behavior problems in the home with a parent as observer and experimenter. *Journal of Applied Behavior Analysis*, 1972, 5, 53–64.

Hall, R. V., Ayala, H., Copeland, R., Cossairt, A., Freeman, J., & Harris, J. Responsive teaching: An approach for training teachers in applied behavior analysis techniques. In E. A. Ramp & B. L. Hopkins (Eds.), *A new direction for education: Behavior analysis 1971.* Lawrence: University of Kansas Support and Development Center for Follow Through, Department of Human Development, 1971. Pp. 127–157. (b)

Hall, R. V., & Copeland, R. The responsive teaching model: A first step in shaping school personnel as behavior modification specialists. In F. W. Clark, D. R. Evans, & L. A. Hamerlynck (Eds.), *Implementing behavioral programs for schools and clinics.* Champaign, Ill.: Research Press, 1972. Pp. 125–150.

Hall, R. V., Copeland, R., Chavez, A., & Alvarado, F. *Responsive teaching in Panama.* Paper presented at the 2nd International Workshop on Behavior Analysis, Lawrence, Kans., 1973. (a)

Hall, R. V., Copeland, R., & Clark, M. L. Management strategies for teachers and parents: Responsive teaching. In N. G. Haring & R. L. Schiefelbusch (Eds.), *Teaching special children.* New York: McGraw-Hill, 1976. Pp. 157–196.

Hall, R. V., Cossairt, A., & Crowder, J. Responsive teaching: A practical behavior modification approach for schools. *Challenge*, 1973, 2, No. 4/5. (b)

Hall, R. V., Cristler, C., Cranston, S. S., & Tucker, B. Teachers and parents as researchers using multiple baseline designs. *Journal of Applied Behavior Analysis*, 1970, 3, 247–255.

Hall, R. V., & Fox, R. (Eds.) *Instructors Manual for the Responsive teaching model transparency kit.* Lawrence, Kans.: H & H Enterprises, Inc., 1973.

Hall, R. V., & Fox, R. G. Changing criterion designs: An alternative applied behavior analysis procedure. In B. C. Etzel, J. M. Le Blanc, & D. M. Baer (Eds.), *New developments in behavioral research: Theory, method and application* (In honor of Sidney W. Bijou). Hillsdale, N.J.: Lawrence Erlbaum Associates, in press.

Hall, R. V., Fox, R., Willard, D., Goldsmith, L., Emerson, M., Owen, M., Davis, F., & Porcia, E. The teacher as observer and experimenter in the modification of disputing and talking out behaviors. *Journal of Applied Behavior Analysis*, 1971, 4, 141–149. (c)

Hall, R. V., Lund, D., & Jackson, D. Effects of teacher attention on study behavior. *Journal of Applied Behavior Analysis*, 1968, 1, 1–12. (a)

Hall, R. V., Panyan, M. Rabon. D., & Broden, M. Instructing beginning teachers in reinforcement procedures which improve classroom control. *Journal of Applied Behavior Analysis*, 1968, 1, 315–322. (b)

Hanley, E. M. Review of research involving applied behavior analysis in the classroom. *Review of Educational Research*, 1967, 40, 597–625.

Harris, F., Johnston, M., Kelley, C., & Wolf, M. M. Effects of social reinforcement on regressed crawling of a nursery school child. *Journal of Educational Psychology*, 1964, 55, 35–41. (a)

Harris, F., Wolf, M. M., & Baer, D. Effects of adult social reinforcement on child behavior. *Young Children*, 1964, 20, 8–17. (b)

Harris, J. W., & Sherman, J. A. Use and analysis of the "Good Behavior Game" to reduce disruptive classroom behavior. *Journal of Applied Behavior Analysis*, 1973, 6, 405–418.

Hart, B., Allen, E., Buell, J., Harris, F., & Wolf, M. M. Effects of social reinforcement on operant crying. *Journal of Experimental Child Psychology*, 1964, 1, 145–153.

Hart, B., & Risley, T. R. Establishing use of descriptive adjectives in the spontaneous speech of disadvantaged preschool children. *Journal of Applied Behavior Analysis*, 1968, **1**, 109–120.

Hopkins, B. L., Schutte, R. C., & Garton, K. L. The effects of access to a playroom on the rate and quality of printing and writing of first and second-grade students. *Journal of Applied Behavior Analysis*, 1971, **4**, 77–88.

Hudson, E., & DeMyer, M. Food as a reinforcer in educational therapy of autistic children. *Behaviour Research and Therapy*, 1968, **6**, 37–43.

Kazdin, A. E. The effect of vicarious reinforcement on attentive behavior in the classroom. *Journal of Applied Behavior Analysis*, 1973, **6**, 71–78.

Knowles, P., Prutsman, T., & Raduege, V. Behavior modification of simple hyperkinetic behavior and letter discrimination in a hyperactive child. *Journal of School Psychology*, 1968, **6**, 157–160.

Kuypers, D., Becker, W., & O'Leary, K. How to make a token system fail. *Exceptional Children*, 1968, **35**, 101–111.

Lahey, B. B., McNees, M. P., & Brown, C. C. Modification of deficits in reading for comprehension. *Journal of Applied Behavior Analysis*, 1973, **6**, 475–480.

Long, J. D., & Williams, R. L. The comparative effectiveness of group and individually contingent free time with inner city junior high school students. *Journal of Applied Behavior Analysis*, 1973, **16**, 465–474.

Lovaas, O. I., Schaeffer, B., & Simmons, J. Q. Building social behavior in autistic children by use of electric shocks. *Journal of Experimental Research and Personality*, 1965, **1**, 99–109.

Lovitt, T. C., & Curtiss, K. A. Effects of manipulating an antecedent event on mathematics response rate. *Journal of Applied Behavior Analysis*, 1969, **1**, 329–333. (a)

Lovitt, T. C., & Curtiss, K. A. Academic response rate as a function of teacher and self-imposed contingencies. *Journal of Applied Behavior Analysis*, 1969, **3**, 49–53. (b)

Madsen, C., Becker, W., & Thomas, D. Rules, praise and ignoring: Elements of elementary classroom control. *Journal of Applied Behavior Analysis*, 1968, **1**, 139–150.

Maloney, K. B., & Hopkins, B. L. The modification of sentence structure and its relationship to subjective judgments of creativity in writing. *Journal of Applied Behavior Analysis*, 1973, **6**, 425–433.

Martin, G., England, G., Kaprowy, E., Kilgour, K., & Pilek, V. Operant conditioning of kindergarten-class behavior in autistic children. *Behaviour Research and Therapy*, 1968, **6**, 281–294.

Martin, M., Burkholder, R., Rosenthal, T., Tharp, R., & Thorne, G. Programming behavior change and reintegration into school milieux of extreme adolescent deviates. *Behaviour Research and Therapy*, 1968, **6**, 371–383.

McKenzie, H. S., Clark, M., Wolf, M. M., Kothera, R., & Benson, C. Behavior modification of children with learning disabilities using grades as tokens and allowances as back-up reinforcers. *Exceptional Children*, 1968, **34**, 745–753.

McKenzie, H. S., Egner, A. N., Knight, M. F., Perelman, P. P., Schneider, B. M., & Garvin, J. S. Training consulting teachers to assist elementary teachers in the management and education of handicapped children. *Exceptional Children*, 1970, **37**, 137–143.

McLaughlin, T. F., & Malaby, J. Intrinsic reinforcers in a classroom token economy. *Journal of Applied Behavior Analysis*, 1972, **5**, 263–270.

Moore, R. K., & Sanner, K. Helping teachers analyze and remedy problems. In J. D. Krumboltz & C. E. Thoresen (Eds.), *Behavioral counseling: Cases and techniques*. New York: Holt, 1969. Pp. 152–166.

O'Leary, K. D., & Becker, W. C. Behavior modification of an adjustment class: A token reinforcement program. *Exceptional Children,* 1967, 37, 637–642.

O'Leary, K. D., Becker, W. C., Evans, M. B., & Saudargas, R. A. A token reinforcement program in a public school: A replication and systematic analysis. *Journal of Applied Behavior Analysis,* 1969, 2, 3–13.

Patterson, G. R. An application of conditioning techniques to the control of a hyperactive child. In L. P. Ullmann & L. H. Kranser (Eds.), *Case studies in behavior modification.* New York: Holt, 1965. Pp. 370–375.

Patterson, G. R. A community mental health program for children. In L. A. Hamerlynck, P. O. Davidson, & L. E. Acker (Eds.), *Behavior modification and ideal mental health services.* Calgary, Alberta: University of Calgary, 1969. Pp. 130–172.

Premack, D. Rate differential reinforcement in monkey manipulation. *Journal of the Experimental Analysis of Behavior,* 1963, 6, 81–89.

Quay, H., Sprague, R., Werry, J., & McQueen, M. Conditioning visual orientation of conduct problem children in the classroom. *Journal of Experimental Child Psychology,* 1967, 5, 512–517.

Rabb, E., & Hewett, F. Developing appropriate classroom behaviors in a severely disturbed group of institutionalized kindergarten-primary children utilizing a behavior modification model. *American Journal of Orthopsychiatry,* 1967, 1, 275–285.

Ramp, E., Ulrich, R., & Dulaney, S. Delayed timeout as a procedure for reducing disruptive classroom behavior: A case study. *Journal of Applied Behavior Analysis,* 1971, 4, 235–240.

Rieth, H. J., Axelrod, S., Hathaway, F., Wood, K., & Fitzgerald, C. Influence of distributed practice and daily testing on weekly spelling tests. *Journal of Educational Research,* 1974, 68, 13–22.

Rieth, H. J., & Hall, R. V. *Responsive teaching model readings in applied behavior analysis.* Lawrence, Kans.: H & H Enterprises, 1974.

Robie, E. R., Copeland, R. E., & Hall, R. V. Calcumate. Part I. The effects of using a mechanical device to teach two digit subtraction with borrowing, to children across various socio-economic populations. Paper read at the International Council for Exceptional Children Convention, New York, April 1974.

Salzberg, B. H., Wheeler, A. A., Devar, L. T., & Hopkins, B. L. The effect of intermittent feedback and intermittent contingent access to play on printing of kindergarten children. *Journal of Applied Behavior Analysis,* 1971, 4, 163–172.

Schmidt, G. W., & Ulrich, R. E. Effects of group contingent events upon classroom noise. *Journal of Applied Behavior Analysis,* 1969, 2, 171–179.

Skinner, B. *The behavior of organisms.* New York: Appleton, 1938.

Skinner, B. *Science and human behavior.* New York: Wiley, 1953.

Straughn, J., Potter, W., & Hamilton, S. Behavior treatment of an elective mute. *Journal of Child Psychology and Psychiatry,* 1965, 6, 125–130.

Sulzbacher, S., & Houser, J. A tactic to eliminate disruptive behaviors in the classroom: Group contingent consequences. *American Journal of Mental Deficiency,* 1968, 73, 88–90.

Thomas, D., Becker, W., & Armstrong, M. Production and elimination of disruptive classroom behavior by systematically varying teacher's behavior. *Journal of Applied Behavior Analysis,* 1968, 1, 35–45.

Thoresen, C. E., & Mahoney, M. J. *Behavioral self-control.* New York: Holt, 1974.

Tribble, A., & Hall, R. V. Effects of peer approval on completion of arithmetic assignments. Appendix I of Hall, R. V., & Copeland, R. The responsive teaching model: A first step in shaping school personnel as behavior modification specialists. In F. W. Clark, D. R. Evans, & L. A. Hamerlynck (Eds.), *Implementing behavioral programs for schools and clinics.* Champaign, Ill.: Research Press, 1972. Pp. 125–150.

Tyler, V. Application of operant token reinforcement to academic performance of an institutionalized delinquent. *Psychological Reports,* 1967, **21**, 249–260.

Tyler, V., & Brown, G. Token reinforcement of academic performance with institutionalized delinquent boys. *Journal of Educational Psychology,* 1968, **59**, 164–168.

Waisk, B. H., Senn, K., Welch, R. H., & Cooper, B. R. Behavior modification with culturally deprived school children: Two case studies. *Journal of Applied Behavior Analysis,* 1969, **2**, 181–194.

Walker, H. M., & Hops, H. Increasing academic achievement by reinforcing direct academic performance and/or facilitative non-academic responses. *Journal of Educational Psychology,* in press.

Walker, J., & Buckley, N. The use of positive reinforcement in conditioning attending behavior. *Journal of Applied Behavior Analysis,* 1968, **1**, 245–252.

Ward, M. H., & Baker, B. L. Reinforcement therapy in the classroom. *Journal of Applied Behavior Analysis,* 1968, **1**, 323–328.

Wolf, M. M., Giles, D., & Hall, R. Experiments with token reinforcement in a remedial classroom. *Behaviour Research and Therapy,* 1968, **6**, 51–64.

Wolf, M. M., Risley, T. R., Johnston, M., Harris, F., & Allen, E. Applications of operant conditioning procedures to the behavior of an autistic child: A follow-up and extension. *Journal of the Experimental Analysis of Behavior,* 1967, **5**, 59–60.

Wolf, M. M., Risley, T. R., & Mees, H. L. Application of operant conditioning procedures to the behaviour problems of an autistic child. *Behaviour Research and Therapy,* 1964, **1**, 305–312.

Zimmerman, E., & Zimmerman, J. The alteration of behavior in a special classroom situation. *Journal of the Experimental Analysis of Behavior,* 1962, **5**, 59–60.

Zimmerman, E., Zimmerman, J., & Russel, C. Differential effects of token reinforcement on "attention" in retarded students instructed as a group. Paper read at the meeting of the American Psychological Association, San Francisco, Sept. 1968.

MODIFICATION OF SMOKING BEHAVIOR: A CRITICAL ANALYSIS OF THEORY, RESEARCH, AND PRACTICE

EDWARD LICHTENSTEIN   AND   BRIAN G. DANAHER

Department of Psychology
University of Oregon
Eugene, Oregon

Stanford University
Medical Center
Stanford, California

I. INTRODUCTION

The evidence that cigarette smoking is causally linked to a number of serious physical disorders has given rise to a large literature describing and evaluating methods of modifying smoking behavior. Many methods have been applied to the problem of smoking control: legislation, education, medication, individual and group therapy, hypnosis, and others (Bernstein, 1969; Schwartz, 1969). In particular, workers in behavior modification—who derive their principles and techniques from experimental psychology—have found the study of cigarette smoking of considerable interest.

Outcome research in behavior change is greatly expedited when an objectively measurable target behavior is used as the criterion of success. Smoking behavior is potentially observable, occurs in discrete units, and has a fairly high rate of occurrence. Another useful attribute of cigarette smoking is its absolute zero point. Complete abstinence—no cigarettes smoked—is an undeniable outcome effect however produced, and can suggest directions for further research. There are millions of readily identifiable cigarette smokers, many of whom are willing to participate in research projects. Smoking thus lends itself nicely to the target behavior research strategy that has proved effective in several areas of behavior modification (e.g., Paul, 1969).

Smoking behavior affords several other advantages to behavioral researchers as well. Much behavior modification research with adults is focused on specific fears or anxieties of college students. The small-animal or insect phobias usually studied are not maladaptive for the individuals being treated and may not be representative of more severe clinical problems (Cooper, Furst, & Bridger, 1969). The physical effects of cigarette smoking, however, make this behavior truly maladaptive for the individual and frequently produces considerable subjective discomfort and motivation to change. Public opinion data indicate that about half of current smokers want to quit and have tried to do so without success (AIPO, 1974). In smoking experiments it is usually possible to recruit persons from the community who more closely approximate the general population than is true in most psychological research on college student samples. For the investigator of behavior change, smoking affords an optimal balance between internal and external validity (Campbell & Stanley, 1963). It is an opportunity to study behavior change processes in a meaningful, naturalistic context that still permits adequate measurement and controls.

Cigarette smoking lends itself to a varied range of behavioral strategies. There are several theories and a number of behavioral principles which can be used to derive treatment tactics. Smoking, which occurs under many stimulus conditions and which may be consequated by numerous reinforcers, can be analyzed and treated with a number of different techniques. Thus, one may use smoking behavior to compare the validity and effectiveness of different behavioral principles and strategies rather than to contrast a behavioral technique against a more traditional treatment, as has been done in much of the behavior modification literature.

Recent smoking control research has emphasized self-control strategies. This reflects a more general range of interest in self-control approaches to behavior change (Thoresen & Mahoney, 1974; Watson & Tharp, 1972). Since the smoking performance represents a trade-off of delayed aversive consequences (physical/disease effects) for immediate reinforcement, it provides repeated opportunities for self-control mechanisms to operate. Smoking shares this characteristic with several other appetitive or "behavioral excess" phenomena, most notably obesity and alcohol abuse. Knowledge of the variables involved in maintenance and modification of smoking may enhance our understanding of these other "habit-forming" or "addictive" patterns.

Smoking control research may be focused on practical considerations arising from the health consequences of smoking and/or on conceptual issues such as self-monitoring, attribution, self-control, or parameters of punishment. Given the social importance and experimental convenience of smoking, one is not surprised by the outpouring of the research. This paper will focus on recent work, essentially from 1969 to the present. Several reviews have adequately summarized and evaluated the earlier literature (Bernstein, 1969; Keutzer, Lichtenstein, & Mees, 1968; Lichtenstein & Keutzer, 1971; McFall & Hammen, 1971; Schwartz, 1969). We will first review theoretical issues concerning the maintenance and modification of smoking and then consider methodological requirements of smoking control research. A critical review of recent research will be organized around two broad and not mutually exclusive strategies: aversion and self-control. We will conclude with some speculations and suggestions for future research.

II. MODELS OF SMOKING BEHAVIOR

Modification procedures should be derivable from a valid and useful model of smoking behavior. Several models emphasizing pharmacological, sociological, or psychological variables—or some combination of these—have been put forth. A recent volume edited by Dunn (1973) provides an excellent summary of several of these approaches, especially those emphasizing pharmacological mechanisms. The proceedings of two conferences edited by Hunt (1970, 1973) include descriptions of several psychological models with an emphasis on mechanisms of learning. The papers presented are long on theory but short on data. They represent efforts to conceptualize smoking within the framework of general psychological theory in the hope that this will have theoretical and/or heuristic utility. Much of the theorizing was contributed by workers not personally involved in smoking research. While it is too soon to judge the eventual fruitfulness of these approaches, we are currently pessimistic about their clinical utility. Nevertheless, some of the efforts are worthy of consideration.

A model proposed by Tomkins (1966) relating smoking to affect management is probably the most widely known formulation. Tomkins proposes that smoking achieves regularity only if it is consistently associated (reinforced) by positive affect enhancement or the reduction of negative affect. In many individuals smoking eventually becomes preaddictive or addictive. These two states are characterized by varying intensities of "deprivation negative affect" which the smoker experiences as a state that must be altered by something. A widely used questionnaire has been developed to measure the various types of smoking (Ikard, Green, & Horn, 1969), and factor analysis data have generally been consistent with the formulation. Ikard and Tomkins (1973) presented tentative validity data for the typology, but like all typologies there appears to be considerable overlap. Tomkins (1968) theorized that different cessation methods are necessary for different smoking types but has offered only anecdotal supportive evidence.

Within a learning framework, Hunt and Matarazzo (1970) argue for the utility of construing smoking as a habit. Defining habit as "a fixed behavior pattern overlearned to the point of becoming automatic and marked by decreasing awareness and increasing dependency on secondary, rather than primary, reinforcement" [p. 67], they stress the importance of the phenomenon of overlearning in applying learning principles to smoking. They acknowledge, however, that the experimental study of learning has not concerned itself with the degree of overlearning, in the sense of sheer number of trials, represented by habitual cigarette smoking. In contrast to the Tomkins model, the Hunt and Matarazzo habit formulation minimizes the role of affect in smoking.

Logan (1970, 1973) and Ferraro (1973) conceptualize smoking and the modification of smoking within the framework of incentive theory. Crucial to their analysis is the positing of a learned self-control drive which manifests both individual and situational variability. Logan believes that the practice of successful self-control (i.e., nonsmoking) responses can be learned through standard shaping procedures and must be practiced and reinforced. Gradual reduction and/or successful periods of short-term or situational abstinence are implied as a means of strengthening the self-control drive. As will be seen in a later section of this chapter, however, the evidence on gradual reduction is clearly negative. While gradual reduction or periods of short-term abstinence may strengthen the self-control drive, the incentive value or reinforcement value of cigarettes that are smoked typically increases.

Premack (1970) also focuses on self-control, but within an operant framework, and offers some provocative analyses concerning the apparent failure of behavior modification treatment programs for smokers in contrast to the large numbers of persons who apparently quit smoking on their own. Premack argues that not smoking is reinforced by the reduction of such covert negative reinforcers as humiliation or shame. One avoids the feeling of humiliation that would be felt (and has been felt in the past) if one were to smoke. Only anecdotal evidence is presented in support of these interesting conjectures.

None of these three formulations provides specific guidelines for the modification of smoking in either research or treatment settings. It seems clear that a variety of learning mechanisms can be applied in plausible fashion to cigarette smoking. Bernstein (1969, 1970) offers a general behavioral formulation: "In this view, cigarette smoking is maintained by the observable environmental stimuli (including those originating within the body wall) which elicit it and by those which it produces, that is, by a combination of respondent and operant conditioning." He argues for the flexibility of this formulation in that any environmental variable can be considered as long as it is observable and potentially manipulable. It would be difficult for a behavioral (or any other) psychologist to quarrel with this formulation. It may be excessively general, and Bernstein himself notes the formidable difficulties involved in implementing his conceptualization. Cigarette smoking occurs under such a myriad of different stimulus conditions and in association with so many secondary reinforcers that it is very difficult to specify and control functionally relevant operants and respondents.

The situation is even further complicated by the growing and convincing evidence of the primary reinforcement effects of nicotine. For if the psychological models are long on theory and short on data, then the pharmacological approaches can be said to be data rich and perhaps theory poor. Dunn (1973) summarizes numerous experimental demonstrations of the reinforcing effects of nicotine on animals and man. One approach is represented by a set of studies which demonstrate that humans alter their rate of smoking and rate of puffing in accordance with the nicotine content of their cigarettes (Armitage, 1973; Jarvik, 1973). A second approach reported by

Hutchinson and Emley (1973) is particularly persuasive from a behavioral perspective. Using operant paradigms with both monkeys and men, they show convincingly that nicotine decreases the effects of stressful and unpleasant stimulation (e.g., inhibits pain-elicited aggression) while simultaneously enhancing reactions which permit the organism to reduce or terminate unpleasant or stressful stimuli. Russell (1974a) has summarized the evidence in support of nicotine as a reinforcer and has commented that "there is little doubt that if it were not for the nicotine in tobacco smoke, people would be little more inclined to smoke than they are to blow bubbles or light sparklers" (Russell, 1974b, p. 793).

The implications of this converging pharmacological evidence on the reinforcing effects of nicotine for behavioral treatment of cigarette smoking are not yet clear. The pharmacological data do not preclude an important role for psychological reinforcers but have implications for treatment strategies that will be considered later.

Several writers have attempted to integrate physiological and behavioral data into a composite model of smoking behavior. The models described by Dunn (1973) and Russell (1974a) are essentially descriptive and developmental. They are in basic agreement in describing smoking as being initiated primarily by psychosocial reinforcers but as being later maintained by a learned dependence on nicotine. Psychosocial reinforcers are then seen again as crucial for the termination of smoking, if such is to occur. Russell's is the more detailed and comprehensive effort in that he draws together material on the pharmacology of nicotine, mechanisms of learning, and mechanisms of psychosocial reinforcement similar in substance to those advanced by Tomkins and his associate (see Ikard & Tomkins, 1973; Tomkins, 1966, 1968). While comprehensive and persuasive, Russell's model is not yet sufficiently precise to permit the derivation of specific treatment strategies.

A more complex theoretical integration is attempted by Eysenck (1973), who attempts to encompass behavioral and physiological data on smoking within the framework of his more general theory of personality. Eysenck argues for the necessity of including individual difference dimensions (especially his favorite one—introversion-extroversion) in any comprehensive account of smoking behavior. He hypothesizes that nicotine effects depend on the ongoing degree of cortical arousal and may therefore either be depressing or excitatory depending on that level of arousal. Cortical arousal is, in Eysenck's schema, partly a function of the position of the individual on the extroversion-introversion continuum, as well as of the situational conditions obtaining at a particular time. The theory proposed is too complex to be readily summarized, but one implication, shared by the Tomkins model, is the necessity for tailoring methods of treatment according to relevant characteristics of the particular smoker.

This brief excursion among proposed models of smoking behavior is far from inclusive and has slighted approaches based on decision theory (Mausner & Platt, 1971) and homeostatic models (Solomon & Corbit, 1973). It should serve, however, to acquaint the reader with the major issues that may be pursued further and especially to demonstrate the complexity of the subject.

III. METHODOLOGICAL ISSUES

Methodological requirements for proper evaluation of smoking control methods are no different in principle than those for any other behavioral intervention. The general issues are discussed elsewhere (e.g., Kiesler, 1971; Paul, 1967) and Bernstein (1969, 1970) has provided thoughtful applications to smoking behavior. While it is unfortunately true that much of the published research violates one or more methodological criteria, we see no point in here repeating these criteria in general terms, preferring instead to apply them to particular studies as appropriate. We will, however, consider two issues that are especially relevant to smoking behavior: (1) measurement of smoking, especially reliance on self-monitoring; (2) choice of control group.

A. Self-Reports and Smoking Behavior

With but few exceptions, all smoking control research has relied on self-reports for information about smoking rates. The manner in which these data are collected varies in concreteness and format, ranging from global estimates of cigarettes per day through having subjects tally whenever a cigarette is smoked; but all methods rest on the accuracy or honesty of the subjects' record keeping.

There are two fundamental indices of smoking behavior: *rate,* using days as the unit of time and typically expressed as percentage of baseline smoking; and *abstinence,* the number or percentage of subjects who are abstinent, i.e., not engaging in any smoking whatsoever. These two should always be reported, although abstinence data sometimes are not. The two indices have different metric properties and yield different implications for measurement procedures and practical application.

1. ABSTINENCE

Abstinence is a nominal scale datum that requires less powerful, nonparametric statistical analyses and is less likely to yield statistical significance than are rate data, which can be analyzed with more powerful parametric procedures (e.g., Lichtenstein, Harris, Birchler, Wahl, & Schmahl, 1973). Abstinence, therefore, is a less sensitive indicator of differential treatment effects and for testing conceptually derived hypotheses, but it is an inherently meaningful outcome in that it is the goal of most smokers who seek help. Follow-up reports indicate that persons who substantially decrease but do not stop their smoking subsequently return to baseline levels. In evaluating the absolute effects or practical value of any smoking treatment, the proportion of subjects achieving and maintaining abstinence is a critical index.

Abstinence is also less susceptible to reactivity effects of self-monitoring (Kazdin, 1974) and to variations in the method of obtaining self-report data. Self-monitoring has been shown to affect the rate of smoking at least on a short-term basis (Frederiksen, Epstein, & Kosevsky, 1975; McFall, 1970) but has rarely been shown to produce abstinence and intuitively would not be expected to do so (see Rozensky, 1974, for an exception to this point). Since subjects can readily discriminate whether or not they are smoking at all, it matters little how self-report abstinence data are obtained. Global retrospective reports, daily estimates, or cigarette-by-cigarette record keeping would all be expected to produce equivalent results. Nor would it appear to matter whether the mode of data collection changed during the course of the experiment, as when, for example, subjects keep self-monitoring booklets before and during treatment but provide follow-up smoking rates in gross verbal self-report fashion via telephone interviews. The only real concern about abstinence is the possibility that Ss might not be telling the truth. Abstinence can, however, be corroborated in a manner not possible for rate data. The use of informants or observers who interact with the subjects provides fairly strong verification of whether a subject is smoking or not (Lichtenstein et al., 1973; Schmahl, Lichtenstein, & Harris, 1972). That a subject might be smoking secretly or be in collusion with the informant is possible but unlikely. Unannounced measurement of the subject's carboxyhemoglobin level can provide independent confirmation of the informant's information but is sensitive only to smoking that has occurred very recently (Lando, 1975). Carboxyhemoglobin levels can be estimated from breath samples, which can be collected and analyzed relatively economically (cf. Cohen, Perkins, Ury, & Goldsmith, 1971).

2. RATE

For most investigators, rate remains the datum of choice because it is so integral to the operant research paradigm, permits powerful parametric statistical procedures to be used, and is likely to be a more sensitive index of group differences. Self-monitoring of smoking rates is a reactive procedure (McFall, 1970) consistent with reactive self-monitoring effects reported for obesity and other discrete behavioral phenomena (Kazdin, 1974). Indirect evidence of the reactivity of self-monitoring is found in a number of reports that self-monitored smoking rates are lower than subjects' prior estimates of their smoking behavior. As Kazdin (1974) has noted, self-monitoring effects are usually confounded with the implied demand characteristics involved in volunteering for a smoking control project—the subject clearly expects to lower rather than increase his/her smoking—but the fact remains that self-monitored rate is likely to be less than the "real" baseline.

Smoking rates are also likely to be more susceptible to variations in the self-monitoring procedures. Frederiksen et al. (1975) found continuous reporting to be significantly more reliable than weekly or daily recording, although the mean differences were not large and the subjects may have been aware of the fact that the experimenters had independent information about their smoking. For rate data, it is especially important that data collection procedures remain constant over time within a given experiment. Otherwise, changes in rate may be partly a function of changes in measurement procedures.

In lieu of estimating accuracy of self-reports by making inferences about subjects' veracity on the basis of traitlike personality measures (cf. Gerson & Lanyon, 1972), most behavioral researchers have sought a more objective observational methodology by which smoking could be corroborated. It must be recognized that constant observation is all but impossible except in those few instances involving highly restricted settings and limited daily routines. Some studies have reported the percentage of agreement between the smoker and some observer for occasions when the two are together (Azrin &

Powell, 1968; Powell & Azrin, 1968). In others, rate data are reported as correlations between reports of the subject and those of the observer. These correlational data are difficult to interpret, since it seems likely that the informant must be making inferences about the subject's smoking rate from a limited data base.

A number of studies (Best, 1975; Best & Steffy, 1975; Conway, 1974; Marston & McFall, 1971; Ober, 1968; Steffy, Meichenbaum, & Best, 1970) have employed a refined *tally system* in which the subject makes a friend-observer responsible for: (*a*) counting the available cigarettes before and after every day; (*b*) checking on any discrepancies on self-reported cigarettes; and (*c*) signing his name on the bottom of the page as a voucher of its accuracy.

The enlistment of friends as observers in smoking research probably results in enhanced reactivity. In some cases cooperation is difficult (Ober, 1968), performance is sloppy (Conway, 1974), and bias is obvious (Marrone, Merksamer, & Salzberg, 1970). Although Winett (1973) has suggested that these problems might be handled by placing observers on salary for accurate reporting, this means of establishing observer accuracy poses even more complications.

It is possible that carbon monoxide measurements may be refined to provide estimates of rate of smoking, and this seems well worth pursuing. Since blood carbon monoxide level is affected by atmospheric factors, it provides only a very crude indicator of smoking rate. In spite of limitations noted above, we advise routine use of informants and more frequent use of carboxyhemoglobin measurements.

B. Choice of Control Groups

Bernstein (1969, 1970) has provided the most thorough discussion of possible sources of changes in smoking behavior and the corresponding kinds of control groups that might be employed. He makes an interesting argument for several varieties of no-treatment control in order to evaluate the contribution of expectation and self-effort and has presented data showing the effects of these factors (Bernstein, 1970). However, we are more in agreement with Marston and McFall (1971) that "the critical test of an experimental treatment's efficacy is its ability to reduce smoking significantly more than most minimal-treatment procedures; the minimal-treatment would be compared" [p. 154]. Bernstein's approach is useful for a fine-grain analysis of the nonspecifics of the helping situation. Investigators interested in hypothesis testing and/or the evaluation of a smoking treatment strategy derived from some basic principle or theory would be better advised to follow the Marston and McFall approach.

There are numerous demonstrations that any kind of smoking treatment produces significantly more smoking reduction than does no treatment. The attention-placebo or minimal-treatment control group embodies both subject's self-effort and nonspecific factors in treatment settings and is a stringent comparison for any proposed smoking treatment strategy. Judging by the small Ns often employed in reported research (i.e., smoking subjects often seem in short supply), we recommend increasing the N in the treatment and/or attention-placebo group rather than assigning some of the available subjects to a no-treatment control. Distributing small numbers of subjects over several groups is likely to produce nonsignificant results because of another characteristic of smoking data: large variability in posttreatment smoking rates. Given any treatment, a few smokers are likely to quit completely or nearly completely while some are likely to be relatively unaffected by treatment. Whether the data are expressed in raw number of cigarettes smoked per day or percentage of baseline, there will be large within-group variance that will lead to insignificant between-group differences unless the N is very large or the experimental effect unusually powerful.

IV. REVIEW OF THE LITERATURE

The wide variety of behavioral smoking control strategies employed precludes neat categorization of the research literature. We have chosen to use two broad but not mutually exclusive categories. Aversion strategies aim at suppressing smoking behavior and usually, but not necessarily, emphasize laboratory sessions and minimize homework assignments. Self-control strategies emphasize homework assignments and usually, but not necessarily, minimize aversive control.

Treatment effectiveness will be evaluated from both a relative and an absolute perspective. By a *relative perspective* we mean comparisons between specific behavioral treatments and attention-placebo, nonbehavioral, or no-treatment comparison groups. By an *absolute perspective* we mean the amount of smoking cessation or reduction achieved. A treatment strategy may show statistical superiority (especially to a nontreated control) while producing relatively little abstinence or only modest reduction in smoking rates.

The absolute perspective requires a frame of reference in order to interpret such statements as "relatively little abstinence" or "unimpressive reduction in smoking rates." Hunt and Bespalec (1974) summarized data from 89 smoking control studies representing all manner of approaches. Figure 1 is adapted from their report and displays both the percent of abstainers and percent of baseline for the subjects in these 89 studies at varying follow-up intervals. It can be seen in Fig. 1 that most relapse occurs during the first month after treatment and that the relapse curve is a negatively accelerated one that breaks sharply at the 3- to 6-month point. The percentage of abstinent subjects asymptotes in the 20–30% range, and smoking rate asymptotes around 60% of baseline. Hunt and Bespalec's cautions about wide variability in sample size, treatment procedures, and reporting techniques should be kept in mind. Also, it appears that the curves are based only on subjects who achieved abstinence at termination, thus yielding an overly optimistic picture of total program effectiveness. McFall and Hammen (1971) reviewed a much smaller subset of behavioral studies. At the 4- or 6-month follow-up, percentage of baseline smoking averaged about 75% of baseline, and the percentage of abstinent subjects ranged from 9 to 17% with a mean of 13%.

A. Aversion Strategies

As with other intrinsically rewarding problem behaviors such as alcoholism, aversive strategies are frequently applied to smoking control. Three major kinds of aversive stimuli have been used: electric shock, cigarette smoke itself, and imaginal stimuli. Electric shock has long been the favorite of laboratory researchers, since it is most easily quantified and the temporal arrangements thought to be so crucial for the conditioning process can best be controlled and manipulated. Cigarette smoke is clumsier to work with but produces aversion in those modalities which are directly involved in the smoking act itself (Danaher & Lichtenstein, 1974a). Imaginal stimuli are in one sense easy to work with (no apparatus is needed), but very difficult to control and quantify. The three kinds of aversion tend to be administered in the laboratory but can be adapted to self-administration in the community. Aversive stimuli can also be paired with overt smoking behavior and/or covert behavior—urges or images.

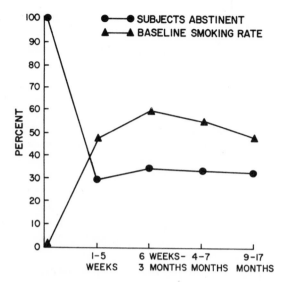

Fig. 1. Relapse rate—percent baseline smoking and percent abstinent—following treatment.
[Adapted and reprinted with permission from Hunt and Bespalec (1974).]

1. ELECTRIC SHOCK

In a previous review of the smoking literature (Lichtenstein & Keutzer, 1971), it was concluded that laboratory-administered shock was ineffective because "human [subjects] appear to be all too capable of discriminating between shock and no-shock situations and the hoped for generalization never materialized" [p. 63]. The studies using shock since that review suggest little need to revise that statement.

Andrews (1970) compared the effects of shocking different responses (e.g., touch cigarette, puff cigarette) and two levels of escape. No significant main effects were found. A noncontingent shock group was not significantly different from the contingent groups, but a minimum shock (attention-placebo) control was significantly different from all shock groups. Absolute smoking reduction and abstinence were minimal.

A comprehensive study by Russell, Armstrong, and Patel (in press) is even more conclusive. Russell (1970) previously reported some encouraging results with electric shock, at least for well-motivated smokers. (Six of nine subjects—out of 23 original referrals—who completed a conditioning program were abstinent at 1-year follow-up.) In a well-controlled extension of this work, 70 heavy smokers (mean = 32 cigarettes per day) were randomly assigned to one of five conditions: electric shock contingent with smoking; noncontingent electric shock; no-shock smoking sessions to control for possible satiation or negative practice effects; simple support and attention from therapists; and no treatment. Treated subjects were seen for ten sessions with 20 shock trials per session. All four treatments were significantly more effective than the no-treatment condition. Contingent and noncontingent shock groups did not differ and were no more successful than the no-shock or simple attention groups. A conditioned motor response was demonstrable in 19 or 28 shock subjects but was irrelevant to treatment outcome.

Two studies that found between-group differences yielded negligible absolute changes in smoking behavior. Using an ambitious 2 × 5 design, Conway (1974) assigned subjects to groups receiving no aversive conditioning, placebo (subthreshold) shock, therapist-delivered shock, subject-delivered shock, and covert sensitization. Within each level of aversion, one-half of the subjects also received a self-control program. The three aversion groups including covert sensitization were significantly more effective than the two control groups. Levine (1974) instructed subjects to smoke at an accelerated pace (every 7.5 sec): one-half received electric shock after every inhalation, and the remaining subjects received a balanced number of shocks between puffs. Significant differences were found between the contingent versus noncontingent shock conditions.

While it seems clear that contingent shock for smoking behavior in the laboratory does not by itself reduce smoking behavior, it is yet possible that shock augmented by other procedures might prove useful. Chapman, Smith, and Layden (1971) combined daily shock sessions with intensive "self-management" training. Six of eleven subjects in one of their studies were abstinent at the 12-month follow-up. The effects of the self-management training were not evaluated and may have been responsible for treatment effects.

Transfer to the natural environment remains a problem for many office-bound treatment methods, especially aversion. Some of the work on alcoholism attempts to overcome this difficulty by surrounding the subject with many cues and stimuli related to his drinking; for example, a simulated barroom situation (Vogler, Lunde, Johnson, & Martin, 1970). This has not been attempted with smoking probably because smoking, in contrast to drinking, can occur in such a wide variety of contexts that it is practically impossible to simulate all or most of them. If one could condition the thoughts, images, or covert verbalizations that smokers are assumed to emit prior to or during the smoking chain, then one might hope for better generalization of conditioning effects. Steffy *et al.* (1970) formed four groups: (1) overt verbalization with smoking; (2) covert verbalization with smoking; (3) overt verbalization with nonsmoking; (4) an insight control group. Contrary to their expectation, the covert verbalization with smoking group was significantly more successful in reduction of smoking than the other groups. However, the absolute level of reduction was not impressive, and the use of relatively light smokers and a fairly high attrition rate further qualify interpretation of this study.

Berecz (1972) had subjects self-administer shock in the laboratory while they were either actually smoking or just imagined themselves smoking. The imagined smoking condition was significantly better for heavy smokers, equal to or greater than 20 cigarettes a day, and comparable to the actual smoking condition for what Berecz termed "moderate smokers," who averaged about 13 cigarettes per day. Berecz (1974a, 1974b) has argued forcefully for the superiority of shocking cognitions about the target behavior itself. We agree that cognitions deserve greater attention, and some of the self-control strategies reviewed below attempt to do so. Berecz presents several pilot cases in support of his contention, but more controlled research is clearly needed.

Another approach to the problem of transfer is to employ apparatus to administer shock contingently in the smoker's natural environment: a special cigarette pack is used which automatically causes a painful shock to be delivered when opened. Powell and Azrin (1968) varied the intensity of shock with three subjects and found, consistent with laboratory data, that smoking reduction was directly related to the intensity of the punishing stimulus. It was also found that the greater the intensity of the shock, the less time subjects wore the apparatus. In addition, subjects refused to participate in the study. However, prior to being approached, these subjects had not indicated any desire to stop smoking. It is possible that with motivated subjects, the negative side effects observed would be greatly diminished.

This appears to have been the case in a report by Whaley, Rosencrantz, and Knowles (personal communication), who used a similar apparatus and reported that nine of ten volunteer subjects were abstinent 1 month after the unit had been removed, and five of ten were still abstinent 18 months after termination. The apparatus requirement limits the practical utility of this approach.

Ober (1968) worked with volunteer subjects and used a simple pocket shocker that subjects activated themselves. All subjects in the self-punishment group were abstinent at termination, suggesting that shock punishment can temporarily suppress smoking behavior. Using a similar device, Whitman (1969) instructed subjects to self-administer three electric shocks after every third cigarette urge. Subjects would also place quinine powder on the tongue if urges persisted. The combined aversive procedure produced significant posttreatment reduction but was not more effective than a self-monitoring control group. The partial reinforcement schedule may have undermined the effects of electrical aversion.

Laboratory pairing of shock with smoking behavior is not effective, but self-administered shock in the natural environment seems to produce temporary suppression. The pairing of laboratory shock with smoking urges and cognition appears promising but requires more controlled research. In contrast to this conclusion, Schick Laboratories operate a commercial smoking control program which features electric shock paired with smoking behavior and which claims considerable success. We suggest that the effectiveness of the Schick program is due to strong motivation engendered by high fees, adroit use of social pressure, and other nonspecific treatment processes.

2. CIGARETTE SMOKE

The choice of cigarette smoke as the aversive stimulus in smoking treatment may be a particularly appropriate one. Excessive smoke affects many of the endogenous cues that characterize smoking, thereby increasing the impact of aversion therapy. Wilson and Davison (1969) summarized the animal literature indicating potent effects for aversion where target responses and associated aversive stimuli exhibit significant topographical similarities, and they contend that this phenomenon has important implications for the choice of aversive stimuli in clinical research. Lublin (1969) reached a similar conclusion based on his clinical experiences in smoking treatment programs. Cigarette smoke as an aversive stimulus has been used in two major ways: rapid smoking and satiation.

a. Rapid Smoking. Requiring subjects to smoke rapidly and continually and/or blowing warm, stale smoke in subject's face is an increasingly popular aversion procedure. A Dutch researcher, Wilde (1964), reported successful results with seven subjects treated by blowing warm, stale smoke at them while they smoked at their normal rate. Franks, Fried, Ashem (1966) improved the apparatus, but their results were equivocal: there was no control group and attrition was high. Meanwhile, Wilde (1965) published a retraction, reporting almost complete relapse in the subjects he had treated. Our laboratory (Grimaldi & Lichtenstein, 1969) replicated the Franks *et al.* procedure with added controls and a 20-dollar deposit which virtually eliminated attrition. There were no significant differences among a contingent smoke group, a noncontingent smoke group, and an attention-placebo control group. In terms of absolute smoking rates, there was considerable posttreatment relapse, and no subject was abstinent 6 months after treatment. Up to this point the procedure emphasized externally delivered smoke blown at the subject while he puffed at his normal rate.

Lublin and Joslyn (1968) apparently increased the effectiveness of the procedure by massing sessions, requiring subjects to smoke rapidly, and offering high levels of encouragement. Lublin and Joslyn reported that 40 of 78 persons who participated in at least three sessions (there were 21 dropouts) stopped smoking entirely, and at 1-year follow-up 15 subjects were abstinent and 16 were smoking less than 50% of baseline. The fact that the subjects in Lublin and Joslyn's work tended to be heavy smokers made their results seem promising and motivated us to standardize the procedure and evaluate the method more carefully.

In our first study (Schmahl *et al.*, 1972), 28 habituated smokers received either warm smoky air or warm mentholated air (a presumed control group) in a paradigm which required them to smoke until they could tolerate no more cigarettes. Both groups puffed at a rapid rate (every 6 sec), received considerable social reinforcement, and were given high expectations of success. Rather than a fixed number of sessions, subjects were seen until they were abstinent and felt they could control their smoking. All subjects were abstinent at termination after an average of eight sessions. Sixteen of the 25 subjects followed up for 6 months remained abstinent, but there were no differences between the smoky-air and menthol-air groups. Paradoxically, subjects contacted for follow-up information every 4 weeks smoked less than did subjects contacted every 2 weeks.

Although both the experimental and control groups did not differ, the absolute amount of smoking reduction and cessation achieved relative to the data summarized in Fig. 1 was encouraging, particularly since these were reasonably habituated smokers (mean years smoking = 9.4; mean baseline smoking = 24.9 cigarettes per day). However, the complexity of the treatment procedure precluded drawing conclusions about what variables were responsible for successful outcome.

In a second study (Lichtenstein *et al.*, 1973), social and relationship variables were kept constant, but at a relatively enriched level, and the nature and degree of the aversive stimulation were varied. Subjects were randomly assigned to one of four treatment groups: warm smoky air plus rapid smoking (the same treatment given experimental subjects in the first study); warm smoky air only; or an attention-placebo group. Three experimenters, also randomly assigned, saw each subject individually for an average of 7.2 sessions, and follow-up data were obtained for 6 months posttreatment. There were no differences among experimenters. All but one subject was abstinent at termination, and 21 subjects remained abstinent 6 months later. A significant treatment group by follow-up interval interaction was observed. The interaction was found to be attributable to the attention-placebo group having a steeper relapse curve. The three aversion groups were very similar in performance: six of ten subjects in each were abstinent at 6-month follow-up.

This study indicated that the aversive stimulation per se contributed to the treatment effect, but there was no additive effect accruing from subjects both smoking rapidly and having smoke blown in their faces. Rapid smoking clearly was just as effective as the smoke-blowing apparatus. Therefore, in our subsequent work we have dropped the smoke-blowing apparatus and used rapid smoking, which is more convenient and can be used with small groups of smokers.

We were impressed and surprised that all subjects in the attention-placebo group stopped smoking during treatment. Apparently, the "nonspecifics" of the treatment situation were quite potent. In a third study (Harris & Lichtenstein, 1971), the level of aversive stimulation was kept constant—using the rapid smoking procedure—while varying three social or relationship variables that we hypothesized were important in the treatment situation. A 2 × 2 design was employed, wherein subjects were seen individually or in groups of three. Half of the subjects received the same level of verbal reinforcement, warmth/friendliness and positive expectations, as had been the case in the first two studies. The other subjects were given instructions intended to convey less favorable expectations, were subjected to a research rather than a clinical atmosphere, and were given little contingent social reinforcement by the experimenter. Both subject ratings and independent ratings of taped treatment sessions verified that these manipulations were successful.

Subjects receiving the same high levels of social interaction and relationship were about as successful as had been smokers in our previous work, independent of whether they were seen individually or in small groups. Subjects given the same aversive procedure but in a barren social context were significantly less successful, both at termination and follow-up. Eight of 18 subjects in this "deprived" group were not smoking at termination, and their posttreatment relapse rate was significantly steeper than for the "enriched" groups.

The criteria for termination in the three previous studies were abstinence and subjects' reported belief that they could control their smoking. We reasoned that many of these subjects might still be experiencing strong urges to smoke and that if subjects continued until they reported no urges they might be less likely to relapse. Weinrobe and Lichtenstein (1975) instructed subjects to self-monitor urges as well as smoking throughout the course of their participation. Twenty-nine smokers received rapid smoking aversion treatment until they achieved abstinence and were terminated either after reporting no smoking urges or while still reporting such urges but believing they could control them. As hypothesized, smoking rates for subjects reporting urges ($N = 11$) were significantly higher. Interestingly, the no-smoking plus zero-urge subjects required fewer sessions than did the subjects run to the smoking criterion only. A yoking procedure was used in order to control for an expected confound in the opposite direction; it was expected that no smoking plus zero-urge subjects would require more sessions. In fact, the number of treatment sessions was related to success at the 3-month follow-up, but this relationship was not quite significant. The overall results of this study were quite consistent with the previous three: all subjects were abstinent at termination; at 3 months posttreatment 17 of 29 subjects were abstinent and percent of baseline smoking was 28%.

Figure 2 presents follow-up data on subjects from the four studies who had received rapid smoking and contingent warmth; that is, all subjects from the first study (Schmahl et al., 1972), the three aversion groups from Lichtenstein et al. (1973), the high social condition subjects from the Harris and Lichtenstein (1971) study, and all of the subjects from the Weinrobe and Lichtenstein (1975) study are included. Given the differences in subjects, the different experimenters, and the variations in procedure, these data seem remarkably consistent. The relapse curves tend to flatten out around the third month, and relapse is clearly most pronounced during the first 3 months and usually during the first month. The shape of the

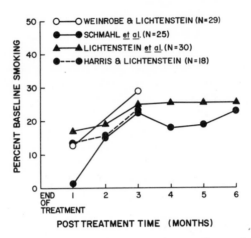

Fig. 2. *Follow-up smoking rates for subjects receiving aversive smoke in a warm, contingently persuasive context.*

relapse curves are quite similar to Hunt and Bespalec's (1974) summary curve depicted in Fig. 1. However, the four rapid-smoking relapse curves are considerably lower in height.

In our last rapid-smoking study, Kopel (1974) adapted the procedure for self-administration in the home in the context of studying the effects of booster session, self-control, and cognitive factors on the maintenance of smoking reduction. This study employed a six-session treatment procedure and an attention-placebo control group similar to that used in Lichtenstein *et al.* (1973), wherein subjects smoked at their normal rate while being instructed to be sensitive to the negative effects of their smoking. Subjects receiving rapid-smoking treatment either in the laboratory or via self-administration were significantly superior to the attention-placebo subjects at the 3-month follow-up. (Attention-placebo subjects were all given six sessions of laboratory treatment.) The overall smoking reduction and cessation achieved was somewhat less than in previous work because of the six-session standardized version employed.

Data from our laboratory appear to justify the conclusion that rapid smoking administered in a warm, contingently persuasive interpersonal context leads to significant smoking reduction and cessation. About half of the subjects so treated remain abstinent from 3 to 6 months after termination. These results are superior to those found generally in the behavior modification literature and compare favorably with the various programs summarized in Fig. 1. These data also permit some tentative conclusions about which factors contribute to the observed effects. Rapid smoking per se seems to be a significant variable. This conclusion is suggested by the significant difference between the aversion groups and the attention-placebo group at follow-up (Lichtenstein *et al.*, 1973) and by the finding that a combined group of laboratory-administered and self-administered rapid smoking was more successful than a stringent laboratory-based attention-placebo condition (Kopel, 1974).

It must be acknowledged that the magnitude of the rapid-smoking effect does not appear to be large. Posttreatment cessation achieved by the attention-placebo group in the two studies just cited, together with the marked differences between receiving high and low levels of "nonspecific social factors" (where all subjects received rapid smoking) in Harris and Lichtenstein (1971), indicate that the interpersonal/persuasive aspects of the treatment setting are a significant source of variance. We have little reason to suppose that a straightforward classical conditioning mechanism is operating in the rapid-smoking procedure. Although subjects will occasionally report that smoking-related cues encountered in their environment are no longer attractive or are even mildly distasteful, we rarely seem to produce repugnance or avoidance. Subjects often look forward to beginning rapid smoking in the laboratory, especially if they have successfully abstained from smoking since the previous session.

At least two processes may underlie the efficacy of the rapid-smoking procedure. Satiation may operate at both a psychological and physiological level to temporarily reduce the intrinsic attractiveness of cigarettes. The physiological aspect may be attributed to the intense dosage of nicotine, the effect being such that the body resists additional intake via further smoking. Smoking in a rapid and continuous manner also produces irritation of the sensitive mucous membrane of the throat, nasal passages, and lungs, thereby contributing to short-term reduction of smoking "pleasure." A second and possibly independent process, one that may operate to prolong abstinence beyond the point presumably accounted for by physiological satiation, involves the cognitive rehearsal of the unpleasant experiences of treatment. According to Bandura (1969, p. 507), aversion therapy may provide the subject with salient unpleasant experiences which he can subsequently reinstate or rehearse cognitively in order to counteract smoking urges after treatment ends. The rapid-smoking procedure facilitates this process by having subjects focus on the unpleasant aspects while smoking and then revivifying these immediately following each trial.

Irrespective of the exact processes operating that make it effective—there is much discussion and some controversy regarding aversion therapy generally (Berecz, 1973, 1974a; Danaher & Lichtenstein, 1974a; Hallam & Rachman, 1972)—the effectiveness, convenience, and simplicity of rapid smoking have made it an increasingly popular treatment option.

Lublin, one of the main developers of the procedure, has maintained a smoking clinic that appears to combine rapid smoking with blown smoky air (Lublin & Joslyn, 1968). Lublin and Barry (1973) reported a 42% abstinence rate at the 6-month follow-up. This work appeared to involve relatively heavy smokers from the community at large. Best (1975) combined rapid smoking and blown smoke and found a 31.5% abstinence rate at the 6-month follow-up. Both Lublin and Best used a "sessions to cessation" procedure similar to that used in the first four studies in our own laboratory. Rapid smoking was also employed in a case report that was partially successful (Gordon & Hall, 1973).

Several recent studies have used a fixed number of rapid-smoking sessions. Morrow, Sachs, Gmeinder, and Burgess (1973) reported a 46% abstinence rate at the 6-month follow-up for a procedure combining five sessions of rapid smoking and a self-control package. A well-designed study by Lando (1975) provides the most notable negative results concerning the effectiveness of rapid smoking. Lando compared rapid smoking with a satiation procedure modeled after Resnick (1968b) and also included a control group that smoked in their usual way. At the 2-month follow-up there were no differences among the groups, and absolute smoking reduction in the rapid-smoking condition was much less than that reported by other investigators. This result may have been partly due to procedural differences in that Lando's subjects were seen in groups of five to ten smokers and were given 3-min trials rather than being required to smoke to tolerance level. Lando also appeared to have intentionally minimized the interpersonal/persuasive components of the treatment in order to illuminate better the effects of rapid smoking. In a more applied context, the incorporation of rapid smoking into a smoking clinic employing group meetings did not add anything to program effectiveness (Curtis, Simpson, & Cole, 1973).

Data on rapid smoking from other laboratories appear to be somewhat positive, though some of the data are from uncontrolled clinical trials and there are negative instances. There is considerable work in progress using rapid-smoking procedures in several laboratories and clinics that should yield more information about the robustness of the procedure and perhaps about some of the underlying mechanisms.

An important consideration in the use of rapid smoking is the need for *medical screening;* also, it is necessary to inform subjects of potential physical risks involved. Cigarette smoking, largely by increasing the body's level of nicotine and carbon monoxide in the blood (COHb), accelerates and stresses the cardiovascular system, and it is reasonable to assume that rapid smoking intensifies these stressful effects. Hauser (1974) has forcefully stated some of the risks involved, and the senior author has replied to these observations (Lichtenstein, 1974). Perusal of the medical and environmental health literatures along with consultations with physicians convinces us that there is considerable diversity of opinion concerning the degree of risk involved and the extent of medical screening required. While much is known about both the acute and chronic effects of regular-paced smoking (cf. Agué, 1973; Cohen et al., 1971; Doyle, 1974; Larson, Haag, & Silvette, 1961; Larson & Silvette, 1968), virtually no evidence is available on the corresponding effects of rapid smoking.

We have recently collected data on this issue, comparing regular and rapid smoking on both heart rate and COHb using a within-subjects design (Danaher, Lichtenstein, & Sullivan, in press). Regular smoking consisted of three 5-min periods of normal smoking interspersed with two 5-min rest periods and concluding with a 15-min final rest period. Rapid smoking was conducted in a manner intended to approximate its current research and clinical application. Subjects were paced every 6 sec and were given either two (or three) trials or 15 min of rapid smoking, whichever came first. Rest periods between trials were 5 min long. Alveolar CO was measured before and after the session (Cohen et al., 1971), while heart rate was obtained continuously throughout the session. Pre- and postsession changes in carbon monoxide levels were essentially comparable in regular and rapid smoking. At the point where the greatest heart-rate changes were observed, rapid smoking produced a mean increase of 28.3 beats per minute (range = 23 to 32), whereas regular smoking produced a mean increase of 13.8 beats per minute (range = 3 to 34). McAlister (1975) reported a modest increase in COHb in a single-subject analysis of rapid smoking.

Proceeding cautiously, it seems prudent and necessary to exclude persons with pulmonary and cardiovascular disease from rapid-smoking treatment. In addition, because their condition may be aggravated by the procedure, individuals with emphysema and asthma should likewise be excluded or seen under medical supervision. It must be recognized that these exclusions encompass a population of individuals most in need of help to stop smoking.

b. Satiation. If a smoker greatly increases his normal consumption of cigarettes for a specified period of time, smoking loses its rewarding properties and may well become aversive. Satiation is especially convenient in that it requires no apparatus and is carried out by the subject in his natural environment. However, it requires medical screening safeguards in that doubling or tripling one's smoking for several days stresses the cardiovascular system similarly to rapid smoking.

Two reports by Resnick (1968a, 1968b) indicated very encouraging results. In a pilot study, Resnick (1968a) described successful treatment of eight smokers with the satiation procedure. In a controlled study (Resnick, 1968b), subjects were instructed either to double or triple their smoking for a week while control subjects were instructed to smoke at their usual rate. All subjects were instructed to stop smoking at the end of the week. Both satiation groups showed significantly more reduction in smoking than did controls, and at the 4-month follow-up 25 of the 40 subjects in the two satiation groups were abstinent compared to only four of 20 in the control group. Resnick supplied no data concerning how faithfully subjects carried out the satiation procedure. His subjects were young, relatively light smokers, and it has been suggested that his control group was not subjected to a plausible attention-placebo procedure (Marston & McFall, 1971). Nevertheless, the impressive absolute results and the efficiency of the procedure stimulated a number of efforts to replicate and extend the satiation procedure.

Unfortunately, the overwhelming weight of the evidence on satiation since Resnick's original studies is clearly negative. In two studies that compared several treatments, one of which included an attention-placebo group, satiation yielded neither significant between-group differences nor impressive reduction or cessation data (Marston & McFall, 1971; McCallum, 1971). In two studies that were intended as essential replications, with methodological improvement, of Resnick's study, the results were again clearly negative: satiation data were not significantly superior to data for control groups, nor again were the absolute rates of smoking cessation or reduction noteworthy (Claiborn, Lewis, & Humble, 1972; Sushinsky, 1972). Lando (1975) instructed subjects to engage in excessive smoking both in the laboratory and between sessions in their natural environment. Satiation subjects were no more successful than a slow-smoking control group which engaged in neither excessive nor rapid smoking. There are five relatively unequivocal failures to replicate Resnick's successful employment of satiation. Therefore, the effectiveness of the procedure seems very much in doubt.

Best and Steffy (1975) reported some interesting data on the interaction effects between a personality dimension—internal versus external locus of control—and satiation. There were no significant main effects such that overall results were similar to previous failures to replicate the Resnick results. However, "internals" (internal-locus subjects) who received satiation were significantly more successful than internals not receiving satiation. Subjects in the Best and Steffy study were drawn from the community, whereas Resnick's original study was run with college students and may have had an unusually high proportion of internals. The possibility that interaction between locus of control and satiation accounts for the failure to replicate Resnick's results does not appear to be very plausible, given that there were five replication failures including a wide range of subjects.

Two studies have employed steady chain smoking under experimenter supervision to produce satiation. Marrone *et al.* (1970) gathered subjects into a motel room and required them to chain-smoke continually. Two different groups were conducted, one receiving 10 hr of satiation and the other, 20 hr. The 20-hr satiation group had significantly more abstinence (six of ten) at the 4-month follow-up than did a no-treatment control group. However, smoking rate data showed no significant differences among the three groups. This study is difficult to compare with other satiation studies because of the unique marathon nature of the procedure and the possibility of group-process effects in such a setting. Young (1973) provided subjects six (twice weekly) sessions of laboratory-based satiation wherein subjects chain-smoked eight cigarettes. Paradoxically, satiation subjects tended to do worse than subjects who were not given satiation. Young's prodecure appears to have been midway between satiation and rapid smoking, and his negative results are puzzling.

The data indicate that satiation is a much less effective treatment procedure than rapid smoking. Given that the two techniques seem functionally similar, one may speculate as to the factors involved in this discrepancy. Rapid smoking typically has been administered in the laboratory during several treatment sessions involving a persuasive interpersonal relationship. In contrast, several satiation studies (e.g., Claiborn *et al.*, 1972; Sushinsky, 1972) repeated Resnick's procedure of having very minimal treatment time and experimenter contact. While Lando's (1975) and Young's (1973) subjects completed six treatment sessions, they intentionally minimized interpersonal persuasiveness. It is possible that the apparent superiority of rapid smoking is in part a function of variables such as treatment time and interpersonal persuasiveness.

Another possible factor involved is the relative emphasis on cognitive focusing and revivification in the two procedures. As noted earlier, rapid smoking typically instructs subjects to focus on negative experiences during the trials and immediately thereafter. Satiation in the natural environment appears to avoid involving such explicit instructional sets to use cognitions and thus may not facilitate generalization and/or maintenance. An exception to this trend is Young's (1973) study in which chain smoking was paired with covert behavior rehearsal in some of the experimental conditions. Increased evidence as to the "follow-through" of satiation also may yield the conclusion that subjects simply are not smoking as much as they have been instructed to do (Lichtenstein, 1971).

3. COVERT SENSITIZATION

Covert sensitization reflects aversion therapy's growing concern with cognitive antecedents and consequences (Cautela, 1967, 1970, 1971). In this procedure, both the target behavior and the aversive stimulus are presented imaginally by having the subject first imagine himself preparing to smoke and then having him imagine himself experience nausea and vomiting. An escape-relief dimension is introduced at this point by instructing the subject to imagine himself feeling better as he turns away and rejects his cigarettes. The subject is usually given training and practice in the procedure in the laboratory and may be encouraged and/or instructed to carry it out in his natural environment, thus permitting it to be used as a self-control precedure. The portability of the procedure and its relative safety (physical risk and discomfort are minimal) are a considerable practical advantage.

Wagner and Bragg (1970) found that a combination of systematic desensitization and covert sensitization was superior to either procedure alone. This was a well-controlled study, but the absolute degree of smoking reduction and cessation was not large. Sachs, Bean, and Morrow (1970) found covert sensitization to be superior to self-control and attention-placebo groups, although again the differences were not substantial. Sachs *et al.* attempted to reduce demand characteristics by instructing subjects not to use their own effort to facilitate treatment, but this may have been somewhat confusing. In several other studies varying in adequacy of controls (Fuhrer, 1971; Lawson & May, 1970; McCallum, 1971; Sipich, Russell, & Tobias, 1974; Weiss, 1974; Wisocki & Rooney, 1974), covert sensitization was not more effective than other treatments or controls and/or the absolute smoking reduction achieved was relatively minimal.

The overall evidence in support of covert sensitization in the modification of smoking behavior appears to be relatively weak. The economy and portability of the procedure suggest, however, that it deserves additional empirical study. Effectiveness might be enhanced by programming (and monitoring) in a more thorough manner the continued imaginal conditioning beyond the point of abstinence, as has been suggested by Cautela (1970). Recent evidence by Goguen (1974) tends to support the necessity of this "overlearning" component. It may also be worth attempting to enhance the effectiveness of imaginal covert sensitization by augmenting it with strong olfactory stimuli in a manner analogous to that already found to have some importance for obesity (Foreyt & Kennedy, 1971; Kennedy & Foreyt, 1968) and sexual dysfunction (Maletzky, 1973, 1974; Maletzky & George, 1973).

The three classes of aversive stimuli here discussed—electrical, cigarette smoke, and covert—do not exhaust the possibilities. Olfactory and gustatory aversive stimuli might be particularly useful (and safe) for smoking (cf. Wilson & Davison, 1969). Thus far, only Whitman (1969, 1972) has explored the use of gustatory aversion, in one study with quinine powder on the tongue and in another with bitter-tasting lozenges taken just before smoking. Taste aversion produced minimal, absolute, or relative effects in Whitman's studies, perhaps because subjects were seen in large groups or worked on their own. Whitman also found that subjects infrequently used the lozenges as directed, a potential problem for any self-administered procedure.

4. LIMITATIONS OF AVERSION

Aversion control has a number of inherent limitations. It concerns many people on esthetic and ethical grounds. The physical riskiness involved with certain aversive stimuli limits its use and may preclude its application to the individuals most in need of treatment.

A more general question concerning aversive strategies relates to what we can fairly expect of them. Although there are instances of having the subject take an aversion procedure home for self-administration in normal surroundings, many of the aforementioned aversion regimens assume (at least tacitly) that the laboratory-based treatment will effect some significant impact on general smoking performance. As the data indicate, this optimistic assumption has not received widespread support. In his excellent overview of the literature of behavior modification, Bandura (1969) specifies that optimal application of "counterconditioning" involves the reduction of the targeted response with the concurrent acceleration of suitable substitute behaviors (incompatible at best). However, acceptable substitutes to smoking are not easily found and, as the later discussion of the self-control packages suggests, those substitutes which have been identified have not evidenced particularly strong effects.

Perhaps a modification of the perspective on aversion therapy seems in order. Certain kinds of aversion do appear to be quite successful in producing short-term cessation. An increasingly evident conclusion, however, is that cognitive variables must be considered in more detail if initial cessation is to be successfully prolonged to the point of long-term abstinence. Viewing the extant aversion strategies as having the limited goal of producing short-term cessation should sharpen our search for other principles and methods that can enable greater maintenance of change. This point echoes Bernstein's (1969, 1974) repeated contention that smoking research should concentrate on the maintenance of nonsmoking rather than on short-term cessation.

B. Self-Control Strategies

The second major class of smoking treatments can be categorized loosely as those involving *self-control*. Compared to standard aversion therapy procedure, the usual self-control program has the client more actively participating in the definitions and implementation of his treatment regimen. The focus of self-control on the individual as change-agent and on the application of the intervention tactics at home (often via "homework assignments") practically ensures that treatment will have some significant impact on the client's "real world." Programmed generalization is a key ingredient in self-control procedures.

Although a number of operational definitions for self-control are available in the literature (e.g., Cautela, 1969; Ferster, 1965, 1970; Kanfer & Karoly, 1972; Kanfer & Phillips, 1970; Skinner, 1953; Thoresen & Mahoney, 1974), we have adopted a more generic definition which stipulates that self-control includes those procedures which the client applies *in situ* to change some aspect of his own behavior. This working definition does not subscribe to any particular theoretical model but allows for any of the possible combinations between covert and overt target behaviors and intervention modalities. Self-control includes completely self-administered treatment programs as well as those more common occasions in which the client works closely with a consultant/therapist during the training phase.

In addition to being susceptible to the same methodological considerations shared by all treatment programs, self-control research must be evaluated in terms of whether the procedures themselves have been applied. Consider the conclusions one draws from an apparently unsuccessful application of self-control. The observed ineffectiveness could be attributed to either of the following causes: (a) the procedures when faithfully employed had little impact on the target behavior; or (b) the procedures were not faithfully applied by the subjects, thereby precluding any conclusion about their clinical utility. Clearly the way one choses to view the same outcome may yield two quite different conclusions and directions for further inquiry. Self-control programs need to be evaluated with respect to "follow-through," i.e., the thoroughness of their application in combination with various outcome criteria (Lichtenstein, 1971; Thoresen & Mahoney, 1974).

With one major modification, we have followed the general outline of self-control provided by Thoresen and Mahoney (1974) in using *environmental planning* and *behavioral programming* as two major categories. We have chosen to use a third category—*cognitive control*—to encompass a set of procedures that seemed to combine elements of both planning and programming.

1. ENVIRONMENTAL PLANNING

One major class of self-control procedures based upon research evidence from the animal laboratory seeks to reduce smoking by rearranging the prevailing circumstances under which it occurs. The client formulates a "game plan" by which he arranges his environment in ways that will contribute to his effort to stop smoking. These arrangements are made prior to possible smoking performances, and they may relieve the client of immediate responsibility for responding to his smoking. Instead, he need only remain vigilant and adhere to his carefully constructed plan while (in theory) preprogrammed environmental forces operate to reduce the frequency of his smoking. Two major types of environmental planning to reduce smoking will be reviewed: stimulus control and contingency management.

a. Stimulus Control. Stimulus control has been the basis for a set of clinical procedures that seek to control maladaptive behavior by systematically changing the prevailing stimulus situations in which the targeted response occurs. From this perspective, smoking is viewed as having become linked with a variety of specific environ-

mental and internal events which have come to serve as discriminative stimuli or cues for the smoking response. The act of
smoking in association with these internal-external cues has been
reinforced on some partial schedule so that presence of cues (e.g., a
glass of beer, a cup of coffee, a feeling of tension) becomes associated with strong subjectively experienced "urges" to smoke. The
prevailing stimulus-response conditions are generally altered via a
two-step stimulus control program: (a) smoking is initially restricted
to novel situations in order to extinguish the power of prior cues; (b)
the novel stimuli are subsequently faded, thereby encouraging a
corresponding reduction/elimination of smoking. Important features
of the stimulus control approach are the emphasis on gradual reduction rather than immediate cessation and the client's responsibility
for carrying out the treatment plan in his natural environment. Three
major strategies for achieving stimulus control of smoking have been
devised.

(1) *Increasing the stimulus interval.* One strategy allows for
continued smoking but limits its performance to particular times,
which are signaled by some cuing device. Once well established, the
new smoking cue is gradually thinned or faded by simply increasing
the time interval between its presentation.

In an elegant example of this approach, Powell and Azrin (1968)
utilized a cigarette case that automatically locked itself for a period
of time following the removal of a cigarette. Distinctive stimuli, both
tactile and auditory, signaled when the device would again open and
came to serve as the cue for smoking, particularly as the interval
between lockings was increased. The smoking rates of five heavy
smokers were gradually reduced from about two and a half packs a
day to a half pack a day by systematically lengthening the time-lock-
ing intervals. The procedure was relatively inoffensive to the participants, but their smoking rates returned to normal after use of the
apparatus was withdrawn. These subjects were recruited and had not
sought help for their smoking. The preprogrammed cigarette case is
an expensive and somewhat cumbersome piece of apparatus, thus
limiting the practical utility of this approach.

Other smoking-on-cue programs have used simple pocket timers.
Upper and Meridith (1971) found that a group using timers was more
successful in gradually reducing smoking than control subjects told
to reduce gradually on their own. However, at the 1-year follow-up
all subjects had resumed baseline smoking levels. This program had
reduction of smoking rather than cessation as the goal of treatment.
Bernard and Efran (1972) assigned subjects to either a timer elimina-

tion, a timer reduction, or a control condition in which subjects were simply told to eliminate their smoking. Contrary to predictions, the two elimination groups returned to baseline smoking by the 2-month follow-up, while the reduction subjects demonstrated minimal recidivism and a 40% abstinence rate. Further analysis revealed that the most successful subjects in the reduction condition had set aside the scheduled reduction and quit smoking "precipitously." Claiborn *et al.* (1972) had subjects smoke only at certain hours and gradually increased the interval between smoking periods. Between-group results were not significant, nor was the amount of smoking reduction impressive.

Shapiro and his colleagues (Levinson, Shapiro, Schwartz, & Tursky, 1971; Shapiro, Tursky, Schwartz, & Schnidman, 1971) utilized a variable interval schedule of cued smoking. A preliminary study (Shapiro *et al.,* 1971) found that subjects who followed the procedure experienced the most reduction (median = 25% baseline). A critical finding was that a substantial percentage of the sample (40%) failed to complete the program and that a number of subjects reported that reduction below 12 cigarettes a day was particularly difficult. In a second and better controlled effort (Levinson *et al.,* 1971), the variable interval procedure was compared to a self-monitoring program with a counter. Both groups received identical reduction requirements. The results showed the timer to be more effective in reducing consumption than the counter. Four of the seven timer subjects were abstinent at the end of treatment, while no counter subjects had quit entirely. Consistent with other research using this procedure, there was substantial attrition and subjects reported 12 cigarettes per day to be a difficult barrier.

(2) *Hierarchical reduction.* In a second major approach to stimulus control, subjects are asked to monitor smoking activity and identify situations in which smoking would have a high and low probability. A hierarchy is developed based on either the presumed difficulty of reducing smoking in a situation or the enjoyment from smoking in the situation. The subject then reduces or eliminates his smoking in cumulative and progressive fashion from the easiest to the hardest situations in the hierarchy. In theory, this program gradually approximates nonsmoking. The absolute number of cigarettes smoked per day need not be regulated as long as no cigarettes are consumed in prohibited situations.

Two early investigations (Gutmann & Marston, 1967; Pumroy & March, 1966) found high attrition and minimal smoking reduction at follow up. Sachs *et al.* (1970) included internal situations (thoughts and feelings) in their application of the hierarchy reduction approach. No significant differences were found at the 1-month follow-up among the hierarchical reduction group, a covert sensitization condition, or an attention-placebo control condition. Marston and McFall (1971) instructed subjects to divide their day into four equivalent parts and progressively to eliminate smoking from the easiest to the most difficult section. Other self-control strategies such as self-reward were also employed. Treatment and control conditions were found to be equivalently effective at both posttreatment and 6-month follow-up. Smoking rates for all subjects at 6-month follow-up was 69% of baseline, indicating minimal absolute effects.

Flaxman (1974) hypothesized that gradual reduction may be appropriate to a point at which abrupt cessation is necessary. This reasoning is consistent with the findings of Upper and Meridith (1971) and Levinson et al. (1971) that 12 cigarettes a day was a difficult barrier for subjects on a gradual reduction program. In a carefully designed study, subjects all received self-control instructions and were assigned to the following experimental conditions: *gradual quitting*, using a hierarchy method similar to Sachs et al. (1970); *partial-gradual quitting*, where the hierarchy program was used to cut back gradually until half of the steps were completed or smoking had been reduced to half of the baseline, at which time immediate cessation was required; *target-date quitting*, in which subjects were instructed to choose a date (approximately 2 weeks after start of treatment) by which time cessation was required; and *immediate quitting*, where abstinence was required following the first treatment session. Six-month follow-up results clearly favored the target-date condition relative to the hierarchical reduction and immediate quitting conditions. However, process analyses indicated that few subjects in the partial-gradual reduction condition progressed to where they instituted the abrupt cessation program.

(3) *Deprived response performance.* The third major application of stimulus control progressively narrows the discriminative stimuli for smoking by delimiting the circumstances in which smoking is allowed. This procedure requires that all smoking occur in a deprived setting or one devoid of all possible distractions and accompanying reinforcers. A common example has the subjects smoking only while seated in a "smoking chair" located in the garage. The deprived response program also includes significant aspects of self-punishment. Removing oneself from an ongoing social interaction in order to withdraw to a "smoking chair" can be viewed as a self-imposed time-out procedure. Two $N = 1$ case reports presented successful

application of the procedure to smoking (Nolan, 1968; Roberts, 1969). In these cases, however, the subject was either the experimenter's wife or the experimenter himself. In both cases smoking cessation occurred abruptly toward the end and appeared to be a function of other than stimulus control processes. Further, these successes were not replicated in a more controlled project by Karen and Bogardus (1973), who found both high attrition and consistent return to baseline of those subjects who did participate. Although direct tests of the "smoking chair" technique have been mixed, the procedure has been employed in numerous self-control packages (e.g., Morrow et al., 1973), probably because of its convenience and face validity.

In contrast to reported successes in controlling other behavioral excesses, stimulus control approaches to smoking reduction and cessation have not been at all impressive. Subjects appear to find many of the procedures burdensome and terminate treatment. Gradual reduction below a certain level, approximately 12 cigarettes per day, appears to be quite difficult, and this may be a point at which the primary reinforcement of nicotine becomes paramount. Gradual quitting may serve to establish an aperiodic reinforcement schedule which interferes with extinction (Flaxman, 1974), or may serve to *increase* the reinforcement value and thereby the attractiveness of the remaining cigarettes (Mausner, 1966). Stimulus control procedures have continued to be popular, however, perhaps as a result of the persuasiveness of the proposed underlying model and/or the relatively "painless" focus on allowing smoking while limiting only the situations in which it can occur.

b. Contingency Contracting. Any treatment program includes elements of contracting—either with oneself or others—to supply the incentive needed to produce therapeutic behavior change. In the present discussion, the term *contingency contracting* is limited to those arrangements (contracts) made by the smoker with other individuals to help modify his smoking behavior. Arrangements developed and enforced by individuals/agencies in order to control the smoking behavior of others are omitted because these are not properly considered instances of *self*-control.

Within the usual practice of contingency contracting, the smoker makes arrangements so that he need not be concerned with the appropriate administration of contingent rewards/punishments. The function of providing consequation is the major responsibility of the individual/agency as specified in the contract. The smoker is completely familiar with the terms of the smoking contract, however, and is aware of the costs attached to transgression. Contracting as a method of smoking control has taken two major forms: deposit systems and social contracts.

(1) *Deposit systems.* Deposits are commonly used to promote attendance and gain compliance with program tasks and assignments. Less frequently, deposit return is tied contingently to smoking cessation or reduction. Deposits are usually monetary, although material possessions that lend themselves to partial repayment (e.g., a record collection) may be employed (Nurnberger & Zimmerman, 1970); tokens can be used to facilitate the assignment of tangible rewards for appropriate reduction/abstinence (Bornstein, Carmody, Relinger, Zohn, Devine, & Bugge, 1975). Deposit-contract systems include a strong element of punishment (response cost), since portions of the deposit may be forfeited by transgression. Although both reinforcement and punishment complement each other, it seems clear that the sustained threat of losing one's deposit provides the dominant influence (Tighe & Elliott, 1968).

Two studies present clear examples of the deposit system as the major controlling tactic by returning a portion of subject's deposits contingent on progressively longer periods of abstinence. Elliott and Tighe (1968) found that 84% of their subjects were abstinent following treatment and 37.5% remained abstinent at relatively long follow-up periods. In a more complete factorial design, Winett (1973) found that contingent repayment produced significantly greater smoking cessation than did noncontingent repayment schedules. At the 6-month follow-up, 50% versus 23.5% of the subjects were abstinent in the contingent and the noncontingent group, respectively.

(2) *Social contracts.* Although efforts to stop smoking often include elements of public announcement mixed with encouragement and support from one's family, friends, and associates, one line of smoking research has attempted to make more explicit use of these social contingencies as a means for motivating reduction/abstinence. The emphasis on social contracts can be traced to studies in which subjects simply make a public announcement that they are trying to quit, which presumably sets in motion appropriate social consequation (e.g., Tighe & Elliott, 1968) to cases in which friends and family are described as having acted as "reinforcers" for successful smoking reduction (e.g., Bornstein *et al.*, 1975; Lawson & May, 1970).

Married couples who want to stop smoking together present potentially powerful opportunities for investigation of social contracting as a smoking control tactic. Two studies, neither with formal control groups, worked with married couples as a means of rewarding nonsmoking. Nehemkis and Lichtenstein (1971) trained a small sample of married couples to reciprocally reinforce one another for successfully meeting graduated reduction goals. Cumulative reduction—and cessation for about half the couples—was achieved during treatment and short-term follow-up, but a 6-month follow-up indicated considerable relapse. Gutmann and Marston (1967) were notably less successful in their effort with married couples and graduated reduction, perhaps because they chose to use smoking as a reward for reduction.

Another lightly investigated aspect of social contracting as a means of smoking control can be found in the use of the "buddy system." By systematically programming contacts between smokers and training them in appropriate verbal praise and contingent rewards, it may be possible to increase treatment effectivensss (Janis & Hoffmann, 1970).

In sum, contingency contracting appears to offer a simple and economical method of producing cessation and may be grafted on to other treatment strategies. One problem encountered by Winett (1973) is that smoking sometimes returns to baseline levels once the contracts have expired. Winett suggests that smoking contracts should be interminable for some individuals. Another solution would emphasize the use of social contingencies based on relationships and positive praise that may produce enduring incentives for abstinence. Contingency contracting between two smokers—particularly married ones—provides a promising area for future inquiry. Two possible problems exist, however: (a) the same reciprocal interaction that initially facilitates reduction/abstinence may later produce relapse if one member resumes smoking; (b) the response-cost aspects of the contract may produce hostile, competitive behaviors between the partners that undermine the quality of the social relationship.

Environmental planning efforts to control smoking have had mixed results. Stimulus control procedures fail to produce cessation in most cases. Contingency contracting has shown more promise, but results have not been uniform. One pervasive problem in this research has been the implicit assumption that the gradual reduction of smoking is synonymous with the gradual approximation of nonsmoking. "Nonsmoking" precludes operational definition, since the term describes an absence of behavior rather than the presence of some alternative response. Research should be directed towards identifying and systematically applying substitute behaviors which will both replace smoking and also make its resumption unlikely.

A related perspective suggests increased attention to what the smoker is doing *cognitively* when he is involved in environmental planning programs. If, as Bandura (1969) has suggested, the individual engages in self-evaluation in order to stay within the terms of a contract, then a more explicit focus on shaping these self-statements may increase effectiveness.

2. BEHAVIORAL PROGRAMMING

Thoresen and Mahoney (1974) have stressed that instances of behavioral programming usually occur following the performance of the target behavior. In the present discussion, however, the temporal aspect of the presentation is less critical than the fact that the individual initiates and self-administers the controlling strategy.

Two categories of behavioral programming can be traced directly to the abundant literature of operant learning in that they emphasize self-reward and its converse, self-punishment. Cognitive control is a third and rapidly expanding example of preprogramming.

a. Self-reward. One strategy has the smoker assigning himself a reward contingent upon successfully avoiding smoking. Self-reward lends itself to programs stressing abstinence, those aimed at gradual reduction via a changing criterion design, and those emphasizing the acquisition of nonsmoking skills. While these straightforward applications of self-reward could stand as treatment programs in their own right, they have been used generally as motivational systems in multifaceted treatment programs emphasizing a number of various strategies. It should be noted that self-reward regimens need not be limited to tangible rewards, since covert verbal (self-evaluatory) statements may play an important but as yet unevaluated role in the modification of smoking behavior.

b. Self-punishment. The converse of assigning rewards for appropriate behavior is the application of punishments for transgressions of a self-imposed standard. Axelrod, Hall, Weis, and Rohrer (1974), for example, instructed a smoker to tear up a dollar bill every time he smoked a cigarette; in another case, the smoker contributed 25 cents to a charity for each smoke. These response-cost procedures produced mixed results: the dollar procedure produced abstinence in 50 days without resumption, whereas the 25 cent contribution subjects continued to smoke. While group studies with factorial designs are needed to identify the possible active ingredients suggested by these case reports, it seems safe to conclude that 25 cent fines for smoking are probably not sufficiently aversive.

In one suggested alternative the donation is sent to the smoker's most hated organization (Watson & Tharp, 1972). Irrespective of the method used, it seems clear that strong aversive consequences are required to counteract smoking.

Stronger aversion has been involved in the self-application of some of the procedures discussed earlier, including rapid smoking (e.g., Kopel, 1974) and shock (e.g., Ober, 1968). Technically, any of the self-administered or homework versions of what are otherwise office-bound procedures (rapid smoking, covert sensitization) are instances of self-punishment. The fact that their *in situ* administration does not always follow the target behavior does not cancel this classification. As noted above, self-administered shock or rapid smoking has produced effective posttreatment suppression of smoking.

3. COGNITIVE CONTROLS

In earlier sections we proposed that existing treatment formats (i.e., aversion therapy and contingency contracting) might be modified so as to emphasize their cognitive components. A third category of self-control involves the client's *explicit* manipulation of his cognitive behavior (thoughts, self-instruction, imagery rehearsal, etc.) as a smoking control strategy. The explicit attack on cognitive aspects of behavior modification has received increasing support generally (cf. Mahoney, 1974; Meichenbaum, 1973; Meichenbaum & Cameron, 1974), which has been reflected in smoking research specifically. Attempts to change the manner in which smokers think before and after smoking has proven to be an area for vigorous research. Cognitions incompatible with smoking may be practiced in the clinic [e.g., Chapman and associates' (1971) emotional response routine], as scheduled homework assignments (e.g., Miller & Gimpl, 1971), or on an ad lib basis to combat smoking urges. To date, the greatest research effort in the area of cognitive control of smoking has been directed at a particular set of procedures known as "coverant control."

Homme (1965, 1966) coined the word "coverant" to refer to covert operant behavior or thoughts. While primarily theoretical and anecdotal, Homme's work had been influential as the first systematic effort to include cognition in an operant behavior change framework. Refinements of the original outline have been presented elsewhere (Danaher, 1974; Mahoney, 1970), but the general procedure has the client think about (say to himself) two compelling reasons (covert statements) focusing on different aspects of his attempt to stop smoking. The first covert statement (an antismoking thought) presents some aversive aspect of continued smoking, and the second covert statement (pro-nonsmoking) emphasizes the benefits that will follow from sustained nonsmoking. The strategy is initiated when an urge to smoke is experienced and is followed by the self-assignment of some rewarding activity.

The purpose of coverant control is to eliminate smoking by strengthening self-statements (and associated cognitions) that are incompatible with its performance. The procedure is safe, requires no apparatus, and can be tailored to the individual thoughts, beliefs, and feelings of the smoker, and these factors may account for its relative popularity. A number of studies have compared coverant control strategies with several other behavioral treatments and/or to appropriate self-monitoring or attention-placebo controls (Keutzer, 1968; Lawson & May, 1970; Rutner, 1967; Tooley & Pratt, 1967), and these have received extensive review elsewhere (Mahoney, 1974).

Less well reviewed studies have also appeared. Johnson (1968) found coverant control to be superior both at the end of treatment and at the 3- and 6-month follow-ups to an attention-placebo control group, while a breath-holding group (subjects hold their breath until it becomes mildly uncomfortable whenever they have an urge to smoke) performed about as well as the coverant control groups. Hark (1970) found coverant control to be significantly better than a no-contact control group but was not superior to a nondirective discussion group. Gordon (1971) examined the effects of timing of the negative coverant: (a) prior to touching a package of cigarettes; (b) after lighting but before inhaling a cigarette; or (c) prior to any high-probability behavior. An attention-placebo control was also included. Only 1-month follow-up data were reported and these indicated no differences among groups. All groups demonstrated significant smoking reduction, and the magnitude of the reduction was relatively large in comparison to many behavioral studies. Danaher and Lichtenstein (1974b) compared the efficacy of various combinations of cues and consequences within the coverant control framework. Process data showed that subjects more faithfully carried out the treatment procedure when they assigned themselves valued rewards. Consistent with other research, however, no significant differences emerged between coverant control and attention-placebo subjects at the 8-month follow-up.

The clinical effectiveness of coverant control alone in producing significant smoking reduction and cessation appears to be minimal.

Changes in self-statements fail to produce corresponding changes in smoking. Subvocal and imaginal procedures may, however, be useful in enhancing client's commitment to change behavior and to carry out program requirements (cf. Marston & Feldman, 1972). Many smokers have experienced past failures and frustrations in trying to stop and emit to themselves such negative covert statements as "I guess I'm just addicted," or "I can't do anything when the urge to smoke hits me" (Davidson, 1964). Imagining oneself as a successful nonsmoker may be a necessary but not sufficient step in producing prolonged abstinence. Mahoney (1974) has argued persuasively for directly intervening upon such cognitions in discussing his work with obese clients, and it would appear to be just as appropriate to do so with smokers. Further clinical and research experimentation appears necessary in order to develop the principles and technology required to deal with these covert control processes.

C. Self-Control Treatment Packages

In turning to self-control procedures which have been grouped to form so-called "package treatments," it should be immediately apparent that the components do not demonstrate individual treatment effectiveness. Research on these packages has proliferated at a substantial rate in spite of this state of affairs, probably in the hope that combining procedures may yield a unique and more powerful product (a catalytic effect). One common vehicle used in these research efforts has been the *manual*. This document usually provides an overview of a behavioral perspective of smoking behavior, the general aspects of change technology (shaping, chaining, reward/ punishment, etc.), and specific instructions in the implementation of self-control strategies to aid in the elimination of smoking. Some manuals are designed to be self-administered and are completely self-contained, while others are intended to serve as the basis for intensive discussion and interaction with a consultant/therapist.

A number of research investigations have included self-control package procedures, and Table I presents a selected list including their component processes.

Several programs are notable in reporting impressive absolute results. Brengelmann (1973) in Germany has developed a self-control package composed of up to 37 procedures (e.g., changing brands daily, limiting smoking to certain times and places, delay lighting up after urges). In one study, this package emphasizing stimulus control

TABLE I

Self-Control Treatment Packages

Study	Environmental planning	Behavioral programming	Cognitive control	Substitute behavior
Brengelmann (1973)	Hierarchical reduction Deprived response Deposit system	—	—	—
Chapman et al. (1971)	Hierarchical reduction Deprived response Deposit system	—	Emotional response routine Self-instruction	Time-structured activity
Conway (1974)	Hierarchical reduction Deprived response	Self-reward for nonsmoking and self-control	Self-instruction	—
Flaxman (1974)	Miscellaneous stimulus control procedures Social contracts	Self-reward for nonsmoking	Emotional response routine	Time-structured activity Relaxation
Harris & Rothberg (1972)	Hierarchical reduction Deprived response Social contracts	Self-reward for nonsmoking Self-punishment for smoking	Miscellaneous cognitive control procedures	Time-structured activity Relaxation

Marston & McFall (1971)	Hierarchical reduction	Self-reward for nonsmoking	Self-instruction	Eating
Miller & Gimpl (1971)	—	Self-reward for nonsmoking and self-control	Self-instruction	Relaxation —
Morrow et al. (1973)	Deprived response	Self-satiation	Self-instruction	Eating Physical and/or quiet activity Time-structured activity Exercise Relaxation
Ober (1968)	Miscellaneous stimulus control procedures	Self-reward for nonsmoking	Self-instruction	
Pomerleau & Ciccone (1974)	Hierarchical reduction Miscellaneous stimulus control procedures	Self-satiation	Self-instruction and imagery	—
St. Pierre & Lawrence (1974)	Increasing stimulus interval Reverse hierarchical reduction	Self-reward for nonsmoking Self-satiation	Self-instruction and imagery	

and gradual reduction was found to be superior to various other smoking treatments, including a placebo control condition. Subsequent investigation revealed that the self-control procedures were significantly improved with the addition of a contingency contracting adjunctive arrangement (58% subjects abstinent at the 2-month follow-up). The program is currently under evaluation as a "mail order" treatment. Although the limited follow-up precludes strong conclusions, Brengelmann's efforts do suggest that self-control procedures may require an intensive treatment regimen in order to produce substantial levels of success.

In a study noted earlier, Flaxman (1974) found that setting a target data for quitting greatly enhanced the impact of a self-control package (50% subjects abstinent at the 6-month follow-up). These encouraging results require replication, however, since they were both unexpected and based on a small N.

Three studies have obtained notable success in applying self-control packages with aversion procedures. Pomerleau and Ciccone (1974) used a broad spectrum of self-control and aversion procedures and found that 46% of their subjects were abstinent at the 11-month follow-up. Chapman et al. (1971) used electric shock in the laboratory in conjunction with packaged self-control procedures, and 54% of their subjects were abstinent at the 12-month follow-up. In the Morrow et al. (1973) study, 46% of the subjects remained abstinent 1 year after having received a program combining rapid-smoking aversion (in the office and at home) and a number of self-control procedures. Moreover, of those subjects who also participated in group meetings following the conclusion of the intensive treatment phase, 90% were abstinent 1 year later.

While the above studies are encouraging, the general conclusions regarding the additive or "packaged" self-control procedures is that they have not resulted in improved treatment effectiveness: the combination procedures are no more effective than the individual components in producing cessation. This pattern of results is sobering, but we believe should not discourage further effort in this direction. Theoretical and empirical work in behavioral self-control is still in its infancy. As principles and procedures become refined, applications to smoking reduction should be more effective.

V. CONCLUDING COMMENTS

In his recent book, Yates (1975) titles his chapter on smoking, "When Behavior Therapy Fails." While there are some promising findings, we cannot strongly dispute Yates's observation, nor is it especially comforting that other smoking control methods have done no better. We are not discouraged by this state of affairs and are confident it can and will be improved. Suggestions for so doing have been interspersed throughout the text. Here we offer some additional recommendations for potentially effective treatment procedures and for a research strategy to evaluate them.

A. Suggested Treatment Directions

Instead of focusing stimulus control and other self-control strategies on cessation where they have consistently demonstrated little promise, we propose that these procedures should emphasize the maintenance of nonsmoking. Cessation has been produced reliably (though often for only short periods) by aversion procedures and by contingency contracting. The most powerful package program might well include intensive exposure to aversion therapy with appropriate contingencies for nonsmoking in combination with extensive instruction in self-control procedures which are aimed at helping the ex-smoker successfully *cope* with urges. This program would combine aversion and self-control in order to exploit their respective strength in producing cessation and maintenance.

This proposal follows from the research evidence reported in this chapter and more directly from the studies (Chapman *et al.*, 1971; Morrow *et al.*, 1973; Pomerleau & Ciccone, 1974) that, while probably best regarded as multiple case reports (Bernstein, 1974), indicate the power of this approach. It should be noted that all cases of aversion plus self-control have not been as dramatically effective (e.g., Flaxman, 1974), and more needs to be accomplished in expanding the composition of the self-control components.

More attention needs to be given to training the smoker to cope with deprivation—the urges and discomfort that arise from going without cigarettes. Once deprivation discomfort has been aroused it may not simply disappear by altering the stimulus situation. Cognitive coping strategies can play a particularly critical role here. One such strategy which shares some common elements with coverant control and self-administrered covert sensitization might explicitly shape the vivid recollection of the aversion therapy experience in order to counteract urges. Obsessive preoccupation with smoking might be interrupted by thought stopping and/or replacing by more adaptive self-instructions. The utility of distracting thoughts (thinking about a pleasant scene instead of smoking) has as yet been virtually unexplored.

Coping skills need not be limited to the cognitive variety. It is suggested that relaxation used as a coping skill in the manner described by Goldfried (1971, 1973; also Goldfried & Trier, 1974) may be one effective approach to dealing with deprivation discomfort. Investigators have attempted to desensitize smokers to deprivation. The study by Morganstern and Ratliff (1969) lacked controls and proper follow-up but reported promising results. Gerson and Lanyon (1972) presented suggestive evidence that desensitization to deprivation plus covert sensitization is superior to covert sensitization alone. Relaxation taught as a self-control coping procedure would not involve systematic desensitization per se. After being taught to relax, individuals would be given training and instruction in using relaxation consistently in their natural environment as both a substitute response for smoking and as a means of coping with deprivation discomfort. Once well learned, relaxation can be "turned on" very quickly and in just about any situation, thus making it potentially quite useful. In the only study to employ a "coping-desensitization" procedure (Stein, Sherman, Greenberg, Pippitt, & Reiter, 1975), promising results were obtained although the small sample size (N = 7) precluded definitive results.

Another potentially useful direction, especially suggested by the work of Best (1975) and Best and Steffy (1975), involves tailoring treatment methods to the characteristics of individual smokers. In two studies they have found significant interactions between internal versus external locus of control and type of treatment. Internal subjects were more successful with satiation or rapid smoking; external subjects, with stimulus control procedures. Eysenck (1973) and Ikard and Tomkins (1973) have also argued for tailoring, albeit using different framework and individual difference dimensions. More research is needed to identify the critical individual differences for tailoring treatments.

B. Evaluating Promising Treatment Strategies

Effective behavioral treatments (e.g., desensitization) have often evolved from extensive clinical experience, which then led to controlled experimentation and subsequent interplay between the clinic and the laboratory. Unfortunately, this has not been the case with smoking behavior. Early research on smoking behavior seemed characterized by the premature application of techniques (believed to be effective with other problem behaviors) to smoking behavior and/or the premature freezing of treatment techniques into group programs without sufficient pilot work (Lichtenstein, 1971). It is all too easy to conduct an armchair analysis of smoking behavior and then to conclude that such techniques as systematic desensitization, stimulus control, and thought stopping would be applicable. The convenience of smoking research noted earlier then makes it tempting immediately to mount a group design to test the effectiveness of the treatment technique in question. Little wonder that the typical experiment found results that were unimpressive both in a relative and absolute sense (Lichtenstein & Keutzer, 1971; McFall & Hammen, 1971).

We therefore suggest an alternative strategy that would focus initially on intensive pilot work with individual smokers or very small groups of smokers. When a treatment package is developed that seems promising, a clinical trials evaluation would be appropriate. The treatment would be temporarily "frozen" and administered, either individually or in small groups, to some consecutive number of referred smokers. No control group need be employed at this stage. Instead, careful baseline data are necessary and a form of "effort control" can be employed where, after baseline subjects are instructed to try their best to stop or reduce their smoking for a period of a week or more. The data would be evaluated with respect to both baseline "effort control" smoking rates and in an absolute sense in terms of the sheer degree of cessation and reduction. Single subject statistical analyses might well be employed (e.g., Gottman, 1973). We believe that data of this sort would be much more informative than many "controlled" experiments thus far reported in the literature.

The research strategy described is the implicit procedure that has been followed in the development of effective behavioral treatment strategies. We are somewhat puzzled as to why it has not been adhered to more frequently in work with smokers. One possibility is that much smoking research has been graduate student thesis or dissertation work, and the temporal requirements of such research have precluded the preferred developmental strategy. It is also likely that smokers rarely appear as clients in psychological (or mental health) clinics but instead are recruited for specific research projects or research clinics. The integration of clinical work and clinical research should have a salutary effect on the development of smoking control technologies.

Because one of its defining characteristics is the accurate and thorough collection of data, behavior therapy is exposed to rigorous evaluation. This exposure results in appropriately qualified conclusions and projects a somewhat negative impression. We have not been dissuaded from continuing our efforts as a result of the difficulties in identifying effective treatment methods and suggest that others also be cautioned against doing so. Smoking is a pervasive and serious health hazard. Research efforts aimed at assisting people's efforts to quit must be encouraged.

Several areas for optimism do exist. First, theory and practice of behavior therapy is maturing to the extent that simple conditioning models are being replaced by more comprehensive conceptions of behavior. The notion of absolute environmental control is being amended to more properly include an equal emphasis on personal control. Bandura (1974) has eloquently argued that "people activate and create environments as well as rebut them" [p. 867]. The trend toward developing self-control programs aimed at facilitating personal control over behavior has witnessed an explosion of research interest and practical innovations (Mahoney & Thoresen, 1974; Thoresen & Mahoney, 1974). We have outlined a potentially fruitful new direction integrating the initial suppressive effects of extant aversion procedures with the potentially critical long-term maintenance effects of self-control procedures.

Aversion procedures, too, are being construed in a more complex light. In addition to the critical considerations of the relevance of the aversive stimulus (electrical shock, unpleasant smoke, etc.) and target of aversive stimulation (actual versus imagined smoking), an increasing emphasis has been afforded the function of the client's translation (symbolically) of the aversive experience into an effective "tool" which can help sustain abstinence.

Finally, theory and data from behavior therapy demonstrating the effects of environmental variables on behavior have important practical implications. Legislative, organizational, or individual actions that place situational constraints on smoking, increase response costs for smoking, or increase payoffs for not smoking would be expected to yield constructive outcomes in the long run. Such actions may arouse resistance, some of it legitimate, from persons concerned about encroachments on the rights of smokers. But we believe the potential of environmental planning and organizational use of rewards and response costs is great and has been unduly neglected.

REFERENCES

Agué, C. Smoking patterns, nicotine intake at different times of day and changes in two cardiovascular variables while smoking cigarettes. *Psychopharmacologia*, 1973, **30**, 135–144.

AIPO, American Institute of Public Opinion. Public puffs on after 10 years of warning. *Gallup Opinion Index,* 1974, No. 108, 20–21.

Andrews, D. A. *Aversive treatment procedures in the modification of smoking.* Unpublished doctoral dissertation, Queens University, Ontario, Canada, 1970.

Armitage, A. K. Some recent observations relating to the absorption of nicotine from tobacco smoke. In W. L. Dunn, Jr. (Ed.), *Smoking behavior: Motives and incentives.* Washington, D.C.: Winston & Sons, 1973. Pp. 83–91.

Axelrod, S., Hall, R. V., Weis, L., & Rohrer, S. Use of self-imposed contingencies to reduce the frequency of smoking behavior. In M. J. Mahoney & C. E. Thoresen (Eds.), *Self-control: Power to the person.* Monterey, Calif.: Brooks/Cole, 1974. Pp. 77–85.

Azrin, H. H., & Powell, J. Behavioral engineering: The reduction of smoking behavior by a conditioning apparatus and procedure. *Journal of Applied Behavior Analysis,* 1968, **1,** 193–200.

Bandura, A. *Principles of behavior modification.* New York: Holt, 1969.

Bandura, A. Behavior theory and the models of man. *American Psychologist,* 1974, **29,** 859–869.

Berecz, J. M. Reduction of cigarette smoking through self-administered aversion conditioning: A new treatment model with implications for public health. *Social Science and Medicine,* 1972, **6,** 57–66.

Berecz, J. M. Aversion by fiat: The problem of "face validity" in behavior therapy. *Behavior Therapy,* 1973, **4,** 110–116.

Berecz, J. M. Punishment, placebos, psychophysiology, and polemics in aversion therapy: A reply to Danaher and Lichtenstein. *Behavior Therapy,* 1974, **4,** 117–122. (a)

Berecz, J. M. Smoking, stuttering, sex, and pizza: Is there commonality? Paper presented at the meeting of the Association for Advancement of Behavior Therapy, Chicago, November 1974. (b)

Bernard, H. S., & Efran, J. S. Eliminating versus reducing smoking using pocket timers. *Behaviour Research and Therapy,* 1972, **10,** 399–401.

Bernstein, D. A. The modification of smoking behavior: An evaluative review. *Psychological Bulletin,* 1969, **71,** 418–440.

Bernstein, D. A. The modification of smoking behavior: A search for effective variables. *Behaviour Research and Therapy,* 1970, **8,** 133–146.

Bernstein, D. A. The modification of smoking behavior: Some suggestions for programmed "symptom substitution." Paper presented at the meeting of the Association for Advancement of Behavior Therapy, Chicago, November 1974.

Best, J. A. Tailoring smoking withdrawal procedures to personality and motivational differences. *Journal of Consulting and Clinical Psychology,* 1975, **43,** 1–8.

Best, J. A., & Steffy, R. A. Smoking modification procedures for internal and external locus of control clients. *Canadian Journal of Behavioral Science,* 1975, **7,** 155–165.

Bornstein, P. H., Carmody, T. P., Relinger, H., Zohn, J. C., Devine, D. A., & Bugge, I. D. Reduction of smoking behavior through token reinforcement procedures. Unpublished manuscript, University of Montana, 1975.

Brengelmann, J. C. *Verbesserte methoden zur behandlung des rauchens.* Unpublished manuscript, 1973. (Available from Max-Planck-Institut fur Psychiatrie, Department of Psychology, Munich, West Germany.)

Campbell, D. T., & Stanley, J. C. *Experimental and quasi-experimental designs for research.* Chicago: Rand McNally, 1963.

Cautela, J. R. Covert sensitization. *Psychological Reports,* 1967, **20,** 459–468.

Cautela, J. R. Behavior therapy and self-control: Techniques and implications. In C. M. Franks (Ed.), *Behavior therapy: Appraisal and status.* New York: McGraw-Hill, 1969. Pp. 323–340.

Cautela, J. R. Treatment of smoking by covert sensitization. *Psychological Reports,* 1970, 26, 415–420.

Cautela, J. R. Covert conditioning. In A. Jacobs & L. B. Sachs (Eds.), *The psychology of private events.* New York: Academic Press, 1971. Pp. 109–130.

Chapman, R. F., Smith J. W., & Layden, T. A. Elimination of cigarette smoking by punishment and self-management training. *Behaviour Research and Therapy,* 1971, 9, 255–264.

Claiborn, W. L., Lewis, P., & Humble, S. Stimulus satiation and smoking: A revisit. *Journal of Consulting Psychology,* 1972, 28, 416–419.

Cohen, S. I., Perkins, N. M., Ury, H. K., & Goldsmith, J. R. Carbon monoxide uptake in cigarette smoking. *Archives of Environmental Health,* 1971, 22, 55–60.

Conway, J. B. Aversive conditioning and self-management in the control of smoking. Doctoral dissertation, University of Western Ontario, Canada, 1973; *Dissertation Abstracts International B,* 1974, 34, 1401B–1402B.

Cooper, A., Furst, J. B., & Bridger, W. H. A brief commentary on the usefulness of studying fears of snakes. *Journal of Abnormal Psychology,* 1969, 74, 413–414.

Curtis, B., Simpson, D. D., & Cole, S. G. Rapid puffing as a treatment component of a community smoking program. (Tech. Rep. No. 73-32) Fort Worth, Tex.: Texas Christian University, Institute of Behavioral Research, 1973.

Danaher, B. G. Theoretical foundations and clinical applications of the Premack Principle: Review and critique, *Behavior Therapy,* 1974, 5, 307–324.

Danaher, B. G., & Lichtenstein, E. Aversion therapy issues: A note of clarification. *Behavior Therapy,* 1974, 5, 112–116. (a)

Danaher, B. G., & Lichtenstein, E. An experimental analysis of coverant control: Cuing and consequation. Paper presented at the meeting of the Western Psychological Association, San Francisco, April 1974. (b)

Danaher, B. G., Lichtenstein, E., & Sullivan, J. M. Comparative effects of rapid and normal smoking on heart rate and carboxyhemoglobin. *Journal of Consulting and Clinical Psychology;* in press.

Davidson, H. A. Rationalizations for continued smoking. *New York State Journal of Medicine,* 1964, 24, 2993–3001.

Doyle, J. T. Tobacco and the cardiovascular system. In J. T. Hurst (Ed.), *The heart: Arteries and veins.* (3rd ed.) New York: McGraw-Hill, 1974. Pp. 1563–1567.

Dunn, W. L., Jr. *Smoking behavior: Motives and incentives.* Washington, D.C.: Winston & Sons, 1973.

Elliott, R., & Tighe, T. Breaking the cigarette habit: Effects of a technique involving threatened loss of money. *Psychological Record,* 1968, 18, 503–513.

Eysenck, H. J. Personality and the maintenance of the smoking habit. In W. L. Dunn, Jr. (Ed.), *Smoking behavior: Motives and incentives.* Washington, D.C.: Winston & Sons, 1973. Pp. 113–146.

Ferraro, D. P. Self-control of smoking: The amotivational syndrome. *Journal of Abnormal Psychology,* 1973, 81, 152–157.

Ferster, C. B. Classification of behavior pathology. In L. Krasner & L. P. Ullmann (Eds.), *Research in behavior modification.* New York: Holt, 1965. Pp. 6–26.

Ferster, C. B. Comments on paper by Hunt and Matarazzo. In W. A. Hunt (Ed.), *Learning mechanisms in smoking.* Chicago: Aldine, 1970. Pp. 91–102.

Flaxman, J. Smoking cessation: Gradual vs. abrupt quitting. Paper presented at the meeting of the Association for Advancement of Behavior Therapy, Chicago, October 1974.

Foreyt, J. P., & Kennedy, W. A. Treatment of overweight by aversion therapy. *Behaviour Research and Therapy,* 1971, 9, 29–34.

Franks, C. M., Fried, R., & Ashem, B. An improved apparatus for the aversive conditioning of cigarette smokers. *Behaviour Research and Therapy*, 1966, 4, 301–308.

Frederiksen, L. W., Epstein, L. H., & Kosevsky, B. P. Reliability and controlling effects of three procedures for self-monitoring smoking. *Psychological Record*, 1975, 25, 255–264.

Fuhrer, R. E. *The effects of covert sensitization with relaxation induction, covert sensitization without relaxation instructions, and attention-placebo on the reduction of cigarette smoking*. (Doctoral dissertation, University of Montana) Ann Arbor, Mich.: University Microfilms, 1971. No. 72-13, 449; *Dissertation Abstracts International B*, 1971, 32, 6644B–6645B.

Gerson, P., & Lanyon, R. I. Modification of smoking behavior with an aversion-desensitization procedure. *Journal of Consulting & Clinical Psychology*, 1972, 38, 399–402.

Goguen, L. J. Overlearning of covert conditioning as a variable in the permanent modification of smoking behavior. Paper presented at the meeting of the Association for Advancement of Behavior Therapy, Chicago, November 1974.

Goldfried, M. R. Systematic desensitization as training in self-control. *Journal of Consulting & Clinical Psychology*, 1971, 37, 228–234.

Goldfried, M. R. Reduction of generalized anxiety through a variant of systematic desensitization. In M. R. Goldfried & M. Merbaum (Eds.), *Behavior change through self-control*. New York: Holt, 1973. Pp. 297–304.

Goldfried, M. R., & Trier, C. S. Effectiveness of relaxation as an active coping skill. *Journal of Abnormal Psychology*, 1974, 83, 348–355.

Gordon, S. B. *Self-control with a covert aversive stimulus: Modification of smoking*. (Doctoral dissertation, West Virginia University) Ann Arbor, Mich.: University Microfilms, 1971. No. 72-5154; *Dissertation Abstracts International B*, 1972, 32, 4858B–4859B.

Gordon, S. B., & Hall, L. A. Therapy determined by assessment in the modification of smoking: A case study. *Journal of Behavior Therapy and Experimental Psychiatry*, 1973, 4, 379–382.

Gottman, J. M. N-of-one and N-of-two research on psychotherapy. *Psychological Bulletin*, 1973, 80, 93–105.

Grimaldi, K. E., & Lichtenstein, E. Hot, smoky air as an aversive stimulus in the treatment of smoking. *Behaviour Research and Therapy*, 1969, 7, 275–282.

Gutmann, M., & Marston, A. R. Problems of S's motivation in a behavioral program for reduction of cigarette smoking. *Psychological Reports*, 1967, 20, 1107–1114.

Hallam, R., & Rachman, S. Theoretical problems of aversion therapy. *Behaviour Research and Therapy*, 1972, 10, 341–353.

Hark, R. D. *An examination of the effectiveness of coverant conditioning in the reduction of cigarette smoking*. (Doctoral dissertation, Michigan State University) Ann Arbor, Mich.: University Microfilms, 1970. No. 70, 20; *Dissertation Abstracts International B*, 1970, 31, 2958B.

Harris, D. E., & Lichtenstein, E. Contribution of nonspecific social variables to a successful, behavioral treatment of smoking. Paper presented at the meeting of the Western Psychological Association, San Francisco, April 1971.

Harris, M. B., & Rothberg, C. A self-control approach to reducing smoking. *Psychological Reports*, 1972, 31, 165–166.

Hauser, R. Rapids smoking as a technique of behavior modification: Caution in selection of subjects. *Journal of Consulting and Clinical Psychology*, 1974, 42, 625.

Homme, L. E. Perspectives in psychology. XXIV. Control of coverants, the operants of the mind. *Psychological Record*, 1965, 15, 501–511.

Homme, L. E. Contiguity theory and contingency management. *Psychological Record,* 1966, 16, 233–241.

Hunt, W. A. (Ed.) *Learning mechanisms in smoking.* Chicago: Aldine, 1970.

Hunt, W. A. (Ed.) New approaches to behavioral research on smoking. *Journal of Abnormal Psychology,* 1973, 81(Whole Vol.).

Hunt, W. A., & Bespalec, D. A. An evaluation of current methods of modifying smoking behavior. *Journal of Clinical Psychology,* 1974, 30, 431–438.

Hunt, W. A., & Matarazzo, J. D. Habit mechanisms in smoking. In W. A. Hunt (Ed.), *Learning mechanisms in smoking.* Chicago: Aldine, 1970. Pp. 65–102.

Hutchinson, R. R., & Emley, G. S. Effects of nicotine on avoidance, conditioned suppression and aggression response measures in animals and man. In W. L. Dunn, Jr. (Ed.), *Smoking behavior: Motives and incentives.* Washington, D.C.: Winston & Sons, 1973. Pp. 171–196.

Ikard, F. F., Green, D., & Horn, D. A scale to differentiate between types of smoking as related to the management of affect. *International Journal of Addictions,* 1969, 4, 649–659.

Ikard, F. F., & Tomkins, S. The experience of affect as a determinant of smoking behavior: A series of validity studies. *Journal of Abnormal Psychology,* 1973, 81, 172–181.

Janis, I. L., & Hoffmann, D. Facilitating effects of daily contact between partners who make a decision to cut down on smoking. *Journal of Personality and Social Psychology,* 1970, 17, 25–35.

Jarvik, M. E. Further observations on nicotine as the reinforcing agent in smoking. In W. L. Dunn, Jr. (Ed.), *Smoking behavior: Motives and incentives.* Washington, D.C.: Winston & Sons, 1973. Pp. 33–49.

Johnson, S. S. *The evaluation of self-control techniques upon differing types of smoking behavior.* (Doctoral dissertation, University of Colorado) Ann Arbor, Mich.: University Microfilms, 1968. No. 69-4370; *Dissertation Abstracts International B,* 1969, 29, 3507B.

Kanfer, F. H., & Karoly, P. Self-control: A behavioristic excursion into the lion's den. *Behavior Therapy,* 1972, 3, 398–416.

Kanfer, F. H., & Phillips, J. S. *Learning foundations of behavior therapy.* New York: Wiley, 1970.

Karen, R. L., & Bogardus, L. C. A study of the short-term and long-term effectiveness of a self-control procedure for smoking control. Unpublished manuscript, California State University, San Diego, 1973.

Kazdin, A. E. Self-monitoring and behavior change. In M. J. Mahoney & C. E. Thoresen (Eds.), *Self-control: Power to the person.* Monterey, Calif.: Brooks/Cole, 1974. Pp. 218–246.

Kennedy, W. A., & Foreyt, J. P. Control of eating behavior in an obese patient by avoidance conditioning. *Psychological Reports,* 1968, 22, 571–576.

Keutzer, C. S. Behavior modification of smoking: The experimental investigation of diverse techniques. *Behaviour Research and Therapy,* 1968, 6, 137–157.

Keutzer, C. S., Lichtenstein, E., & Mees, H. L. Modification of smoking behavior: A review. *Psychological Bulletin,* 1968, 70, 520–533.

Kiesler, D. J. Experimental designs in psychotherapy research. In A. E. Bergin & S. L. Garfield (Eds.), *Handbook of psychotherapy and behavior change.* New York: Wiley, 1971. Pp. 36–74.

Kopel, S. A. *The effects of self-control, booster sessions, and cognitive factors on the maintenance of smoking reduction.* (Doctoral dissertation, University of Oregon) Ann Arbor, Mich.: 1974. University Microfilms 1974. No. 75-3895. *Dissertation Abstracts International B,* 1975, 35, 4182B–4183B.

Lando, H. A. A comparison of excessive and rapid smoking in the modification of chronic smoking behavior. *Journal of Consulting and Clinical Psychology*, 1975, 43, 350–355.

Larson, P. S., Haag, H. B., & Silvette, H. *Tobacco: Experimental and clinical studies.* Baltimore: Williams & Wilkins, 1961.

Larson, P. S., & Silvette, H. *Tobacco: Experimental and clinical studies.* Suppl. I. Baltimore: Williams & Wilkins, 1968.

Lawson, D. M., & May, R. B. Three procedures for the extinction of smoking behavior. *Psychological Record*, 1970, 20, 151–157.

Levine, B. A. Effectiveness of contingent and non-contingent electric shock in reducing cigarette smoking. *Psychological Reports*, 1974, 34, 223–226.

Levinson, B. L., Shapiro, D., Schwartz, G. E., & Tursky, B. Smoking elimination by gradual reduction. *Behavior Therapy*, 1971, 2, 477–487.

Lichtenstein, E. Modification of smoking behavior: Good designs—ineffective treatments. *Journal of Consulting and Clinical Psychology*, 1971, 36, 163–166.

Lichtenstein, E. Lichtenstein replies. *Journal of Consulting and Clinical Psychology*, 1974, 42, 625–626.

Lichtenstein, E., Harris, D. E., Birchler, G. R., Wahl, J. M., & Schmahl, D. P. Comparison of rapid smoking, warm, smoky air, and attention placebo in the modification of smoking behavior. *Journal of Consulting and Clinical Psychology*, 1973, 40, 92–98.

Lichtenstein, E., & Keutzer, C. S. Modification of smoking behavior: A later look. In R. D. Rubin, H. Fensterheim, A. A. Lazarus, & C. M. Franks (Eds.), *Advances in behavior therapy 1969.* New York: Academic Press, 1971. Pp. 61–75.

Logan, F. A. The smoking habit. In W. A. Hunt (Ed.), *Learning mechanisms in smoking.* Chicago: Aldine, 1970. Pp. 131–145.

Logan, F. A. Self-control as habit, drive, and incentive. *Journal of Abnormal Psychology*, 1973, 81, 127–136.

Lublin, I. Principles governing the choice of unconditioned stimuli in aversive conditioning. In R. D. Rubin & C. M. Franks (Eds.), *Advances in behavior therapy 1968.* New York: Academic Press, 1969. Pp. 73–81.

Lublin, I., & Barry, J. Aversive counter-conditioning of cigarette addiction. Paper presented at the meeting of the Western Psychological Association, Anaheim, California, April 1973.

Lublin, I., & Joslyn, L. Aversive conditioning of cigarette addiction. Paper presented at the meeting of the Western Psychological Association, Los Angeles, September 1968.

Mahoney, M. J. Toward an experimental analysis of coverant control. *Behavior Therapy*, 1970, 1, 510–521.

Mahoney, M. J. *Cognition and behavior modification.* Boston: Ballinger Press, 1974.

Mahoney, M. J., & Thoresen, C. E. (Eds.) *Self-control: Power to the person.* Monterey, Calif.: Brooks/Cole, 1974.

Maletzky, B. M. "Assisted" covert sensitization: A preliminary report. *Behavior Therapy*, 1973, 4, 117–119.

Maletzky, B. M. "Assisted" covert sensitization in the treatment of exhibitionism. *Journal of Consulting and Clinical Psychology*, 1974, 42, 34–40.

Maletzky, B. M., & George, F. S. The treatment of homosexuality by "assisted" covert sensitization. *Behaviour Research and Therapy*, 1973, 11, 655–657.

Marrone, R. L., Merksamer, M. A., & Salzberg, P. M. A short duration group treatment of smoking behavior by stimulus satiation. *Behaviour Research and Therapy*, 1970, 8, 347–352.

Marston, A. R., & Feldman, S. E. Toward the use of self-control in behavior modification *Journal of Consulting and Clinical Psychology*, 1972, 39, 429–433.

Marston, R. M., & McFall, R. M. Comparison of behavior modification approaches to smoking reduction. *Journal of Consulting and Clinical Psychology*, 1971, 36, 153–162.

Mausner, B. Report on a smoking clinic. *American Psychologist*, 1966, 21, 251–255.

Mausner, B., & Platt, E. S. *Smoking: A behavioral analysis.* Oxford: Pergamon, 1971.

McAlister, A. Helping people quit smoking: Current progress. In A. J. Enelow & J. B. Henderon (Eds.), *Applying behavioral science to cardiovascular risk.* Bethesda, Maryland, American Heart Association, 1975. Pp. 147–165.

McCallum, R. N. The modification of cigarette smoking behavior: A comparison of treatment techniques. Paper presented at the meeting of the Southwestern Psychological Association, San Antonio, Texas, April 1971.

McFall, R. M. Effects of self-monitoring on normal smoking behavior. *Journal of Consulting and Clinical Psychology*, 1970, 35, 135–142.

McFall, R. M., & Hammen, C. L. Motivation, structure, and self-monitoring: Role of nonspecific factors in smoking reduction. *Journal of Consulting and Clinical Psychology*, 1971, 37, 80–86.

Meichenbaum, D. Cognitive factors in behavior modification: Modifying what clients say to themselves. In C. M. Franks & G. T. Wilson (Eds.), *Annual review of behavior therapy theory and practice.* Vol. 1. New York: Brunner/Mazel, 1973. Pp. 416–431.

Meichenbaum, D., & Cameron, R. The clinical potential of modifying what clients say to themselves. In M. J. Mahoney & C. E. Thoresen (Eds.), *Self-control: Power to the person.* Monterey, Calif.: Brooks/Cole, 1974. Pp. 263–290.

Miller, A., & Gimpl, M. Operant conditioning and self-control of smoking and studying. *Journal of Genetic Psychology*, 1971, 119, 181–186.

Morganstern, K. P., & Ratliff, R. G. Systematic desensitization as a technique for treating smoking behavior: A preliminary report. *Behaviour Research and Therapy*, 1969, 7, 397–398.

Morrow, J. E., Sachs, L. B., Gmeinder, S., & Burgess, H. Elimination of cigarette smoking behavior by stimulus satiation, self-control techniques, and group therapy. Paper presented at the meeting of the Western Psychological Association, Anaheim, California, April 1973.

Nehemkis, A. M., & Lichtenstein, E. Conjoint social reinforcement in the treatment of smoking. Paper presented at the meeting of the Western Psychological Association, San Francisco, April 1971.

Nolan, J. D. Self-control procedures in the modification of smoking behavior. *Journal of Consulting and Clinical Psychology*, 1968, 32, 92–93.

Nurnberger, J. I., & Zimmerman, J. Applied analysis of human behavior: An alternative to conventional motivational inferences and unconscious determination in therapeutic programming. *Behavior Therapy*, 1970, 1, 59–69.

Ober, D. C. Modification of smoking behavior. *Journal of Consulting and Clinical Psychology*, 1968, 32, 543–549.

Paul, G. L. Strategy of outcome research in psychotherapy. *Journal of Consulting Psychology*, 1967, 31, 104–118.

Paul, G. L. Outcome of systematic desensitization. II. Controlled investigations of individual treatment, technique variations, and current status. In C. M. Franks (Ed.), *Behavior therapy: Appraisal and status.* New York: McGraw-Hill, 1969. Pp. 105–199.

Pomerleau, O. F., & Ciccone, P. Preliminary results of a treatment program for smoking cessation using multiple behavior modification techniques. Paper presented at the meeting of the Association for Advancement of Behavior Therapy, Chicago, November 1974.

Powell, J. R., & Azrin, N. The effects of shock as a punisher for cigarette smoking. *Journal of Applied Behavior Analysis*, 1968, 1, 63–71.

Premack, D. Mechanisms of self-control. In W. A. Hunt (Ed.), *Learning mechanisms in smoking.* Chicago: Aldine, 1970. Pp. 107–123.

Pumroy, D. K., & March, B. The evaluation of a cigarette smoking reduction method. Paper presented at the meeting of the Eastern Psychological Association, New York City, April 1966.

Resnick, J. H. The control of smoking by stimulus satiation. *Behaviour Research and Therapy,* 1968, 6, 113–114. (a)

Resnick, J. H. Effects of stimulus satiation on the overlearned maladaptive response of cigarette smoking. *Journal of Consulting and Clinical Psychology,* 1968, 32, 501–505. (b)

Roberts, A. H. Self-control procedures in the modification of smoking behavior: Replication. *Psychological Reports,* 1969, 24, 675–676.

Rozensky, R. H. The effect of timing and self-monitoring on reducing cigarette consuption. *Journal of Behavior Therapy and Experimental Psychiatry,* 1974, 5, 301–303.

Russell, M. A. H. Effect of electrical aversion on cigarette smoking. *British Medical Journal,* 1970, 1, 82–86.

Russell, M. A. H. Realistic goals for smoking and health: A case for safer smoking. *Lancet,* 1974, 1, 254–258. (a)

Russell, M. A. H. The smoking habit and its classification. *Practicioner,* 1974, 212, 791–800. (b)

Russell, M. A. H., Armstrong, E., & Patel, U. A. The role of temporal contiguity in electric aversion therapy for cigarette smoking: Analysis of behaviour changes. *Behaviour Research and Therapy,* in press.

Rutner, I. T. The modification of smoking behavior through techniques of self-control. Unpublished master's thesis, Wichita State University, 1967.

Sachs, L. B., Bean, H., & Morrow, J. E. Comparison of smoking treatments. *Behavior Therapy,* 1970, 1, 465–472.

Schmahl, D. P., Lichtenstein, E., & Harris, D. E. Successful treatment of habitual smokers with warm, smoky air and rapid smoking. *Journal of Consulting and Clinical Psychology,* 1972, 38, 105–111.

Schwartz, J. L. A critical review and evaluation of smoking control methods. *Public Health Reports,* 1969, 84, 489–506.

Shapiro, D., Tursky, B., Schwartz, G. E., & Schnidman, S. K. Smoking on cue: A behavioral approach to smoking reduction. *Journal of Health and Social Behavior,* 1971, 12, 108–113.

Sipich, J. F., Russell, R. K., & Tobias, L. L. A comparison of covert sensitization and "nonspecific" treatment in the modification of smoking behavior. *Journal of Behavior Therapy and Experimental Psychiatry,* 1974, 5, 201–203.

Skinner, B. F. *Science and human behavior.* New York: Macmillan, 1953.

Solomon, R. L., & Corbit, J. D. An opponent-process theory of motivation. II. Cigarette addiction. *Journal of Abnormal Psychology,* 1973, 81, 158–171.

Steffy, R. A., Meichenbaum, D., & Best, J. A. Aversive and cognitive factors in the modification of smoking behavior. *Behaviour Research and Therapy,* 1970, 8, 115–126.

Stein, N., Sherman, M., Greenberg, D., Pippitt, M., & Reiter, S. Self-control training for the modification of smoking. Unpublished manuscript, Syracuse University, 1975.

St. Pierre, R., & Lawrence, P. S. Smoking modification: The effects of combining positive and aversive treatment and maintenance procedures. Paper presented at the meeting of the Association for Advancement of Behavior Therapy, Chicago, November 1974.

Sushinsky, L. W. Expectation of future treatment, stimulus satiation, and smoking. *Journal of Consulting and Clinical Psychology,* 1972, 39, 343.

Thoresen, C. E., & Mahoney, M. J. *Behavioral self-control.* New York: Holt, 1974.

Tighe, T. J., & Elliott, R. A. A technique for controlling behavior in natural life settings. *Journal of Applied Behavior Analysis,* 1968, **1**, 263–266.

Tomkins, S. S. Psychological model for smoking behavior. *American Journal of Public Health,* 1966, **12**, 17–20.

Tomkins, S. S. Psychological model for smoking behavior. In E. Borgatta & R. Evans (Eds.), *Smoking, health and behavior.* Chicago: Aldine, 1968. Pp. 165–186.

Tooley, J. T., & Pratt, S. An experimental procedure for extinction of smoking behavior. *Psychological Record,* 1967, **17**, 209–218.

Upper, D., & Meredith, L. A timed-interval procedure for modifying cigarette-smoking behavior. Unpublished manuscript, Veterans Administration Hospital, Brockton, Massachusetts, 1971.

Vogler, R. E., Lunde, S. E., Johnson, G. R., & Martin, P. L. Electrical aversion conditioning with chronic alcoholics. *Journal of Consulting and Clinical Psychology,* 1970, **34**, 258–263.

Wagner, M. K., & Bragg, R. A. Comparing behavior modification approaches to habit decrement–smoking. *Journal of Consulting and Clinical Psychology,* 1970, **34**, 258–263.

Watson, D. L., & Tharp, R. G. *Self-directed behavior: Self-modification for personal adjustment.* Monterey, Calif.: Brooks/Cole, 1972.

Weinrobe, P. A., & Lichtenstein, E. The use of urges as termination criterion in a rapid smoking program for habitual smokers. Paper presented at the meeting of the Western Psychological Association, Sacramento, April 1975.

Weiss, J. I. *An experimental examination of Cautela's covert sensitization as a smoking reduction technique.* (Doctoral dissertation, University of North Dakota) Ann Arbor, Mich.: University Microfilms, 1974. No. 74-24, 540; *Dissertation Abstracts International B,* 1974, **35**, 2454B.

Whitman, T. L. Modification of chronic smoking behavior: A comparison of three approaches. *Behaviour Research and Therapy,* 1969, **7**, 257–263.

Whitman, T. L. Aversive control of smoking behavior in a group context. *Behaviour Research and Therapy,* 1972, **10**, 97–104.

Wilde, G. J. S. Behavior therapy for addicted smokers. *Behaviour Research and Therapy,* 1964, **2**, 107–110.

Wilde, G. J. S. Erratum. *Behaviour Research and Therapy,* 1965, **3**, 313.

Wilson, G. T., & Davison, G. C. Aversion techniques in behavior therapy: Some theoretical and metatheoretical considerations. *Journal of Consulting and Clinical Psychology,* 1969, **33**, 327–329.

Winett, R. A. Parameters of deposit contracts in the modification of smoking. *Psychological Record,* 1973, **23**, 49–60.

Wisocki, P. A., & Rooney, E. J. A comparison of thought stopping and covert sensitization techniques in the treatment of smoking: A brief report. *Psychological Record,* 1974, **24**, 191–192.

Yates, A. J. *Theory and practice in behavior therapy.* New York: Wiley, 1975.

Young, F. D. The modification of cigarette smoking by oversatiation and covert behavior rehearsal. Unpublished doctoral dissertation, University of Windsor, Ontario, Canada, 1973.

METHODOLOGICAL AND TARGET BEHAVIOR ISSUES IN ANALOGUE THERAPY OUTCOME RESEARCH[1]

THOMAS D. BORKOVEC AND GERALD T. O'BRIEN

Department of Psychology
University of Iowa
Iowa City, Iowa

I. INTRODUCTION

Psychotherapy outcome research has recently entered a scientific epoch (Paul, 1969a). The use of factorial designs, control groups, and objective behavioral measurement has greatly increased the researcher's ability to reach cause-and-effect conclusions regarding the effectiveness of behavior modification procedures and their components. An enormous number of studies evaluating the effectiveness and underlying theoretical mechanisms of systematic desensitization treatment for anxiety have been conducted in the last 10 years. This

[1] Several of the research studies cited in this paper were supported in part by Biomedical Sciences Support Grant FR-07035 from the Bureau of Health Professions, Education and Manpower Training, National Institutes of Health, made available in the form of a small grant awarded by the Graduate College of the University of Iowa and Grant MH-24603-01 from the National Institute of Mental Health.

has led writers in the area to claim that, *at last,* clinical psychology has demonstrated the efficacy of a psychotherapeutic technique.

Such claims have, however, been disputed. Lazarus (1971) has argued that enthusiasm over rapid symptomatic removal in clinical patients may be misplaced in light of his own long-term follow-up results. Additionally, since theoretical, procedural, and treatment component research require large numbers of subjects with homogeneous target problems, the majority of outcome studies have involved college samples displaying subclinical levels of distressing behavior. As a result, laboratory control has perhaps been purchased at the high price of clinical relevance. Serious questions have been raised regarding the external validity or generalizability of such analogue research to clinical populations (Cooper, Furst, & Bridger, 1969). Finally, even the internal validity (cf. Campbell & Stanley, 1963) of the presumably well-controlled analogue designs has been recently called into question. Criticisms of both the relevance and validity of the conclusions of analogue outcome research therefore threaten to remove the research base for claims of effectiveness.

On the basis of the above considerations, a programmatic approach to the analogue outcome area would ideally include four interrelated lines of research: (*a*) improvement of outcome methodology to allow more valid conclusions from outcome designs; (*b*) identification, measurement, and evaluation of clinically relevant target behaviors in analogue populations; (*c*) therapy outcome research utilizing what is learned in methodological and target behavior studies; (*d*) basic research on the origins, maintenance, and modification of fear. The purpose of the present chapter is to review what we have learned from studies in the first three of these areas and to discuss the implications of these findings for outcome research.[2] Concerns in the first area focus on the influence of extratherapeutic variables on outcome results. To the extent that treatment and control groups differ in improvement rates as a function of factors other than essential therapy ingredients, conclusions regarding the therapy procedure will be misleading. Demand characteristic effects have drawn the greatest amount of attention, while the adequacy of the principal control for their influence (the placebo condition) has only recently been scrutinized. The second area to be discussed is closely related to the first. Identification of target behaviors that are

---

[2] Our basic research efforts have focused on the role of physiological feedback, cognitive processes, and individual differences in the anxiety process. A review of these studies is presented elsewhere (cf. Borkovec, 1976).

both less susceptible to extratherapeutic influence and more relevant to clinically distressing behavior insures greater internal as well as external validity. Finally, we will discuss attempts to apply the suggestions emanating from the methodological studies to therapy outcome investigations of fear and of a different, possibly related target problem (that of sleep disturbance).

II. OUTCOME METHODOLOGY RESEARCH

In the behavior therapy literature over the past 10 years, it is obvious that small animal phobias have been the most frequently selected targets for outcome research. The trend was set by Lang and Lazovik's (1963) now classic investigation. Large numbers of subjects display various degrees of fear in response to snakes, thus providing an apparently limitless subject population. However, comparison of the strict selection criteria employed by Lang and Lazovik, on the one hand, and by subsequent investigators, on the other, reveals a rapid decline in the initial fear level of analogue subjects.

Bernstein (1973) has demonstrated that various procedural aspects of the pretesting for subject selection purposes may contribute to the amount of measured fear, independent of actual level of fear. Thus, for example, the demand characteristics implicit in a fear assessment study promote greater levels of measured anxiety than do the same testing procedures when represented to the subject as unrelated to fear. More directly relevant to outcome research are the demand characteristics inherent in the typical analogue therapy study itself. A subject is pretested, undergoes several sessions of some technique, and is subsequently presented with a behavioral posttest usually identical in procedure to the pretest. Regardless of the stated purpose of the experiment, the implicit demand in such a design is that the subject should display posttest behavior different from pretest behavior. In addition, the vast majority of outcome investigations are conducted under positive expectancy instructions and therefore include *explicit* demand for improved posttest behavior. Notice that the demand for treated subjects is quite different than the demand for subjects in the no-treatment condition. Since Bernstein's (1973) studies indicate the susceptibility of fear measures to general demand effects, and since outcome studies routinely employ positive expectancy instructions for treated subjects and not for untreated subjects, outcome differences between conditions may reflect primarily a demand effect or demand by treatment interaction, thus precluding valid conclusions regarding the active nature of the therapy conditions in and of themselves. The traditional control for demand as well as for client expectancy and suggestion effects has been the placebo condition. Our research program therefore began with investigations of the nature and extent of demand effects on fear and with evaluation of the adequacy of typical placebo conditions to control for those influences.

A. Demand Characteristics

Our earliest study (Borkovec, 1972, 1974) assessed the influence of desensitization, implosive therapy, an avoidance response placebo, and no treatment on snake phobic behavior. Half of the subjects received therapeutic instructions regarding the purpose of the therapy sessions, while half were given a nontherapeutic rationale. Desensitization and implosion subjects displayed a reduction in heart rate during therapy and in pulse rate at posttest regardless of whether they had been given positive or neutral "expectancy" instructions. Approach behavior, however, was dramatically influenced by the therapeutic instructions regardless of the type of treatment.

Thus, while autonomic indices reflected changes predictable from the theories underlying behavioral techniques, overt behavioral change was found to be primarily a function of the demand, inherent in the expectancy instructions, for display of improvement.

Numerous studies in addition to the above investigation have found that treatment administered under therapeutic instructions promotes greater behavioral change than treatment under nontherapeutic instructions. An equal number of studies, however, have shown no difference. Comparison of the selection methods employed in these two sets of studies reveals that more stringent criteria were used to identify phobics in the latter group of investigations (cf. Borkovec, 1973b). Two hypotheses were derived from these observations: (a) the conclusions based on studies employing weak selection criteria may have been confounded by the relatively powerful effect of demand characteristics; (b) the influence of such variables is lessened if strict selection criteria are used.

Support for these hypotheses was quickly found in two studies that evaluated the effects of repeated fear assessment with intervening suggestions of improvement (Borkovec, 1973a). In the first study, half of the female subjects were snake "phobics" (reports of much fear, very much fear, or terror on Geer's (1965) fear survey schedule), while half were nonphobic (no fear, a little fear, or some fear). Subsequent to a behavioral approach test, subjects were asked to repeat the test and were told that it was important for the success of the experiment that they approach as close as they could to the snake and that students in past research had been found to be much less fearful during the second exposure. Thus, the 60-sec tape-recorded message condensed the high demand and expectancy sets implicit or explicit in most analogue therapy studies. High and low fear groups were significantly different, as would be expected, in degree of approach, self-reported fear, and number of reported physiological arousal cues. A finding of importance for later discussion was the absence of pulse rate differences between the fear groups (pretest means equaled 87.2 beats/min for the high fear group and 90.0 beats/min for the low fear group). Separate analysis of the high fear subjects indicated significant increases in approach from pre- to posttest.

The second study assessed the differential influence of high versus low demand instructions on female snake phobics. Subsequent to the pretest, half of the subjects were instructed simply to repeat the behavioral test; these instructions were similar to the posttest instructions employed in the no-treatment conditions of most analogue therapy studies. The other half were presented with the high demand instructions of the first experiment. As expected, high demand produced significantly greater approach improvement than low demand.

Subjects in these studies were also categorized into high versus low physiological reaction groups, depending on the extent to which they displayed anticipatory pulse rate elevations. In general, the demand manipulation was less effective with high reactors than with low reactors, suggesting that demand effects are mitigated by the presence of strong physiological activity.

In both studies, demand characteristics in the form of suggested improvement resulted in significant increases in approach to the feared object, and the second study indicated that such effects are significantly greater than those produced by simple repeated exposure. It is clear, therefore, that demand may contribute to the absolute level of behavioral outcome improvement in therapy studies employing animal phobics and to the relative outcome in therapy groups as compared to no-therapy (simple repeated exposure) groups. The mean posttest approach step in both studies was just below actual physical contact with the feared object (touching the snake). It is important to note that: (a) failure to physically contact the feared object is the usual behavioral criterion for subject selection in most animal phobia studies; (b) the most improved treatment groups—in the majority of analogue studies reported in enough detail to determine absolute magnitude of approach improvement—have displayed average posttest approach just short of physical contact. Thus, a 60-sec demand tape was as effective in modifying approach behavior as the five to eight therapy sessions typically employed in analogue therapy research.

Several other investigators have documented the potential efficacy of simple demand manipulations in modifying avoidance of small animals (e.g., Bernstein, 1974; Bernstein & Nietzel, 1973, 1974; Kazdin, 1973; Smith, Diener, & Beaman, 1974). While numerous criticisms have been made concerning the relevance of studies on small animal phobias to clinical populations (Cooper et al., 1969), the demand research suggested that the internal validity of these investigations may also be limited.

Although the above data argue convincingly that past studies employing analogue snake phobics may not permit valid cause-and-effect conclusions regarding the effectiveness of the therapy procedures employed, it should be pointed out that these arguments do not preclude the valid use of such targets for the study of fear. Appropriate design methods to correct the problem are available. Bernstein and Paul (1971) have suggested two such methods: (a) High demand pretests can be employed to guarantee the selection of only truly fearful subjects. (b) In the absence of stringent selection criteria, additional control groups involving high demand "treatment" and posttesting procedures can be used. Unfortunately, application of either suggestion will directly or indirectly reduce the number of subjects available for therapy assignment.

Our own program has focused on two alternative methods. First, in nontherapeutic studies of fear employing snake phobics, selection can be based on usual pretest criteria while posttesting is conducted under very high demand. As long as the posttest demand is equally strong across all experimental and control conditions, any differential outcome among conditions can be viewed as a purer reflection of fear differences among conditions and not a function of differential demand. None of the three methods described above, however, is satisfactory for therapy outcome studies. While Bernstein and Paul's (1971) suggestions reduce the functional number of subjects, therapy versus no-therapy comparisons always involve differential demand, precluding the use of equivalently high demand posttests. Our second alternative, therefore, is to identify target behaviors which occur at high frequency in the analogue population but are not susceptible to demand influences. Therapy studies employing such targets completely circumvent the demand issue. Evaluation of these target behaviors will be described later.

Finally, the fact that demand influences can potentially contaminate therapy effects does not preclude the use of snake-fearful subjects, however selected, in studies of physiological process or outcome. Research demonstrating significant demand effects on behavioral or subjective fear indices have routinely failed to find such effects on autonomic measures. Although one can expect relatively low levels of physiological activity among typically selected snake phobics, if physiological outcome differences are found, they probably reflect the effect of factors other than demand (e.g., Borkovec, 1972, 1974; Lang, Melamed, & Hart, 1970).

B. Placebo Controls

Therapy outcome designs of the last decade have routinely employed placebo comparison conditions constructed to be theoretically inert in an effort to control for demand, suggestion, and client expectation of improvement. The notion of placebo controls was originally derived from medical research. Inert substances having no direct effect on the physical processes underlying medical disorders have been frequently found to promote symptom reduction. The placebo effect was conceptually translated into psychotherapeutic expectancy effects in the 1950's. Establishment in the client of belief and confidence in the psychotherapist and his techniques was proposed to be a powerful contributor to outcome improvement irrespective of the specific technique employed. Indeed, the effectiveness of placebo manipulations has received considerable support in traditional psychotherapeutic investigations (Shapiro, 1971) and is compelling evidence for the importance of cognition in behavioral disorders and their modification.

As pointed out earlier, a major component of the expectancy construct is best conceptualized in terms of posttest demand characteristics, since expectancy in the behavior therapy literature has been operationally defined by the presence or absence of therapeutic instructions. The potential cognitive component of expectancy implied in the general psychotherapy literature may perhaps be a distinct factor related to outcome. Research by Goldstein and others

(Friedman, 1963; Goldstein, 1960; Goldstein & Shipman, 1961) has supported this traditional view, despite recent criticism (e.g., Wilkins, 1973). For the present moment, regarding methodology, the question is whether typically used placebo conditions in behavior therapy outcome research do indeed control for either client expectation or experimental demand. Several authors (e.g., Baker & Kahn, 1972; Rosenthal & Frank, 1956) have noted that a placebo condition should be both theoretically inert and capable of generating a positive expectancy equivalent to its comparison treatment condition. Placebo conditions devised by individual investigators for particular studies may indeed be theoretically inactive in their procedural ingredients, although the reasoning behind their creation is rarely presented.

Even the weak assumption that the placebo condition is credible has rarely been questioned or empirically tested, and comparisons of placebo and therapy credibility are even rarer. Borkovec and Nau (1972) presented frequently used rationale and procedural descriptions to 450 introductory psychology students and asked them to rate the credibility and the amount of expectation for improvement generated by each treatment description. Systematic desensitization was found to be significantly superior to Davison's (1968) relaxation-recall control, Borkovec's (1972) avoidance response placebo, Paul's (1966) attention-placebo, and Marcia, Rubin, and Efran's (1969) tachistoscope placebo. Implosive therapy also was superior to the control conditions, significantly so in the case of attention and tachistoscope placeboes. In a subsequent unpublished replication with a separate sample, Nau found significant differences among the six prodecures, with desensitization and implosive therapy rationales again being rated higher than the control rationales. Finally, in a study with 120 psychiatric inpatients, Boudewyns and Borkovec (1974) found psychoanalytic and drug treatment rationales to be significantly more credible than the attention-placebo rationale, while psychoanalysis was also superior to the implosive therapy rationale. McGlynn and McDonell (1974) recently demonstrated that snake phobic college students exposed to excerpts from desensitization and a frequently employed pseudotherapy control procedure rated the former significantly more credible than the latter on the Borkovec and Nau scales. The results of these studies indicate that treatment conditions are not equivalent in credibility and generation of client expectation for improvement, that therapy conditions are more credible to college students than control conditions, and that inpatient psychiatric samples differ from college samples in their differential ratings of therapy and control procedures. It appears that highly familiar treatments are more credible to psychiatric patients than less familiar therapies.

The consistently poor credibility and expectancy in control conditions, combined with the evidence of powerful demand effects on measured fear in analogue populations, suggest that the behavioral outcomes of past therapy studies may have been confounded not only by general experimental demand differences between treatment and no-treatment conditions but also by the differential demand inherent in the therapy and placebo conditions themselves. Pursuit of additional ways to evaluate the demand present in different treatment conditions led to a series of three studies employing Orne's (1965) simulation procedure (Nau, Caputo, & Borkovec, 1974). Snake phobic subjects were pretested, exposed to tape-recorded rationale and procedural descriptions, and subsequently asked to simulate on the posttest the effects they would expect to occur had they undergone five therapy sessions of the described technique. Questionnaire data had indicated that college students had greater confidence in cognitively oriented therapy than in physiologically oriented therapy. Therefore, in one study the same treatment procedure (systematic desensitization) was presented with one group hearing a cognitive rationale for the treatment and the other group receiving a rationale which stressed a physiological interpretation. The former group displayed significantly greater simulated approach improvement than the latter. In a separate study, implosive therapy and desensitization rationales were found to generate greater simulated improvement than the relaxation-recall, attention-placebo, and tachistoscope placebo conditions, although the differences were not significant. The third study supplemented audio descriptions of the rationales with brief video-taped excerpts from respective treatment sessions. Implosive therapy, while producing (nonsignificantly) larger simulated improvement, resulted in significantly greater variance in improvement than the other treatment conditions. In all three studies, credibility ratings of the rationales correlated significantly with simulated outcome improvement. The results of the three investigations support the hypothesis that variability in self-reported confidence in different treatment conditions is related to differential demand characteristics for improvement inherent in the treatment procedures themselves; also, this variability in confidence may potentially be contributing to differential behavioral improvement among therapy and control conditions in analogue outcome studies. Notice that these arguments are specific to differential demand considerations and do not begin to address the potentially important cognitive component of expectation differences.

Two recommendations for future outcome studies have been drawn from this series of studies: (*a*) Credibility and expectancy for improvement should be assessed in any outcome study where demand characteristics may influence posttest behavior. (*b*) Constructions of placebo and other control conditions should be done with care. In addition to clear specification of the reasons for considering a particular placebo condition to be theoretically inert (and not deteriorating in effect), it would be desirable to match placebo procedural components as closely as possible to the active therapy condition. In the above rationale studies, control conditions procedurally similar to desensitization and implosion (avoidance-response placebo and relaxation-recall) resulted in credibility ratings and simulated outcome improvement more similar to those obtained in the active therapy conditions than did attention and tachistoscope placeboes.

III. RESEARCH ON THE IDENTIFICATION AND EVALUATION OF CLINICALLY RELEVANT TARGET BEHAVIORS

Based on demand studies of small animal phobias, the review of expectancy studies (Borkovec, 1973b), and suggestions by Bates (1970), Bernstein and Paul (1971), and Levis (1970) in their support of analogue therapy research with animal phobias, several criteria might be offered to increase the clinical relevance of target behaviors employed in analogue therapy studies and the validity of conclusions derived from their investigation.

In terms of the face validity of the target as a clinically relevant problem, two characteristics are desirable. *First*, the distressing behavior ought to occur at some reasonable frequency in the psychiatric population. In the first author's experience, snake phobia has been the presenting problem in only three voluntary clinical cases. Furthermore, Lawlis' (1971) factor analysis of psychiatric patient responses on Lang's fear survey schedule indicated that fears of small animals accounted for only 2.1% of the variance. *Second*, the problem behavior ought to be a source of concern to the subject and interfere with his daily functioning. As Cooper *et al.* (1969) have pointed out, snake-phobic individuals rarely have an opportunity to encounter snakes. Unless special circumstances force such exposures (e.g., the client is an avid camper), complete avoidance of the feared object is routine and has almost no implication for his/her daily living. In addition, analogue subjects should be motivated to participate in the therapy study not in order to fulfill course requirements but by the incentive of potential benefit that may result (Bernstein & Paul, 1971). Selection of analogue problems which do have implications for the individual's daily adjustment would better insure that motivation.

The three remaining criteria may ultimately be found to relate to the external validity or the clinical relevance issue, but for present discussion they are more important for the internal validity of conclusions based on current outcome designs:

First, pre- to posttest changes in the target behavior should be relatively uninfluenced by suggestion or demand effects. If extra-therapeutic stimuli have a strong effect on improvement scores, as documented for small animal phobics, assessment of therapeutic impact is either obscured or made impossible. (It is important to note that this criterion applies to the repeated testing situation typical of outcome designs and not to single testing. Thus, the demonstration that snake approach can be influenced by demand is less relevant to outcome concerns than the demonstration that demand increases approach from pretest to posttest.) While additional design considerations discussed previously do allow valid fear research with snake phobic populations, identification of target behaviors which occur frequently in college samples but are uninfluenced by simple demand effects would provide considerable advantages to the analogue therapy researcher.

Second, large increases in physiological activity should occur in anticipation of, and in response to, presentation of the feared situation. The physiological component has long been central in behavioral definitions of anxiety and theoretical statements regarding the underlying mechanisms of various behavior therapy techniques. Indeed, Bernstein and Paul (1971) have insisted that analogue subjects display significant increases in physiological arousal to qualify for an outcome study. Physiological response systems, however, have rarely been assessed in therapy research, either as screening or outcome measures. When autonomic assessment has taken place, there is little evidence in the analogue literature of dramatic autonomic increases upon presentation of the phobic stimulus. Part of the problem may derive from the typical use of discrete physiological measures taken some period of time after completion of the test. Under these circumstances, subjects are often no longer aroused. Thus, for example, mean pulse rate among analogue snake phobics upon completion of the approach test has been found to be no greater than 94.8 beats/min in the Borkovec and Craighead (1971) study and 87.2 beats/min in Borkovec's (1973a) study. Similarly, average pulse rates among speech-anxious subjects taken just prior and just after the speech (Blom & Craighead, 1974) and 1.5 min before the speech (Paul, 1966) were found to be no greater than 92.5 and 92.7 beats/min, respectively. Either the measurements are obtained at inappropriate times, suggesting the necessity of continuous autonomic monitoring, or the phobic subjects selected by self-report and behavioral criteria are not displaying clinically significant levels of physiological activity (or both). In the case of snake phobias, the second possibility appears to be the case. Craighead (1973), in a rare example of continuous heart rate recording during a behavioral approach test, found the greatest average heart rate arousal to be 96.08 beats/min. Thus, even the most ideal recording situation failed to provide evidence that analogue snake phobics, as they are typically selected, display large increases in autonomic activity in the presence of the feared object.

Another problem inherent in approach tests is that the subject can avoid close physical contact with the stimulus. Although level of fear as measured indirectly by degree of approach would be defined as high under such circumstances, physiological activity may be quite low due to the successful avoidance response itself. Three recommendations regarding subject selection can be made on the basis of these considerations: (a) Selection of phobic subjects should be based on physiological as well as behavioral and self-report criteria. (b) Continuous recording prior to and during phobic stimulus presentation should be included to insure valid assessment of anticipatory and reactive responses to the feared situation. (c) Subjects should not have an opportunity to avoid confrontation with the feared situation. While the latter suggestion may preclude the use of behavioral approach tests, the importance of selecting subjects who display significant levels of reported, behavioral, and physiological fear may override reasons for adherence to traditional assessment techniques. Numerous behavioral indicants of anxiety other than approach can be employed (Borkovec, Weerts, & Bernstein, in press). In the absence of a substantial physiological response, the severity of fear in selected subjects may be questionable. In addition, since both desensitization and implosive therapy depend in part on notions of classical conditioning of autonomic responses for their theoretical underpinnings, outcome assessment of those responses is at least desirable and may be essential if conclusions are intended to bear directly on those theoretical issues.

Finally, pre- to posttest exposures to the feared situation should not result in rapid habituation of physiological responses. Although repetitious CS exposure appears to be the necessary condition underlying the effectiveness of systematic desensitization and related techniques (Mathews, 1971; Wilkins, 1971; Wilson & Davison, 1971), test exposures should not, in and of themselves, produce such large decrements in autonomic anxiety measures that the effect of therapeutic intervention is unassessable. The problem of pre- to posttest habituation, due both to *in vivo* fear extinction as well as to reduction in the general novelty of the experimental test situation, presents interpretive difficulties similar to those arising from demand influences on behavioral and self-report measures. When much of the improvement variance is a function of such extratherapeutic variables, detection of differential therapy effects becomes virtually impossible.

In search of target behaviors which occur with high frequency in the normal population and yet satisfy the above criteria, our research program has focused on target behaviors involving fear of negative social evaluation (e.g., social, speech, and heterosexual anxiety). Presenting problems among psychiatric populations often involve difficulties in interpersonal situations. Indeed, social anxiety is so pervasive in clinical cases that when a therapist is considering the use of desensitization with a particular client, "it is imperative . . . also to identify the interpersonal factors which usually underlie situational fears" (Lazarus, 1971, p. 105). While fears of small animals emerged as a minor factor in Lawlis' (1971) analysis of patient responses to the fear survey schedule, a general social anxiety factor accounted for 87.3% of the variance. Furthermore, social anxiety among normal subjects would appear to be more disruptive to daily functioning and of greater concern to the individual than fear of small animals. Complete avoidance of social situations is impossible, and anxiety is maintained despite necessary and repeated exposure. The target thus appeared to have face validity as an appropriate analogue of clinical anxiety. However, evaluation of specific social anxiety target behaviors in terms of demand effects and physiological characteristics still had to be carried out.

Data collected from the introductory psychology class ($N = 553$) at the University of Iowa in 1970 indicated that 28% of the males and 29% of the females experienced much fear, very much fear, or terror when speaking before a group. One may conclude from these data that a large population is available in terms of the usual fear survey criterion. During the conduct of an investigation of false physiological feedback effects on speech anxiety (Borkovec, Wall, & Stone, 1974b), speech-anxious college students prepared and presented three consecutive speeches within a 30-min period. Heart rate was monitored continuously during the preparation and delivery phases; 10-sec heartbeat samples were drawn from several phases of each speech. For the total group of 60 subjects, average heart rate rose from a baseline of 87.0 beats/min to 118.2 beats/min at the onset of the first speech. The subsequent speeches continued to elicit strong arousal (88.8 to 111.0 beats/min during the second speech and 86.4 to 108.6 beats/min during the third speech). Similarly, in a recently completed study investigating the effects of attribution manipulations on anxiety (Singerman, Borkovec, & Baron, 1976), 60 speech-anxious students prepared and delivered two consecutive speeches. Average heart rate increased from 98.9 to 113.4 beats/min during the first speech and 90.6 to 109.2 beats/min during the second speech. In comparison to the absolute levels of heart rate cited earlier for snake phobics monitored continuously or discretely and for speech phobics measured discretely, heart rate change under the present conditions was substantial in response to the feared situation. Furthermore, although statistically significant habituation occurred from the first to the second speech in both studies, it is clear that repeated exposure to the speech situation, even within a single brief experimental session, continued to evoke clinically significant levels of heart activity.

Although Blom and Craighead (1974) have shown that speech anxiety can be influenced by demand in a single testing situation, a pre- to posttest evaluation was necessary. In a pilot study by Wall in our laboratory, speech phobic subjects gave two speeches with intervening high versus low demand instructions. Similar to the earlier demand studies with snake phobics, high demand subjects were told that it was important to display less fear and that college students had been found in past research to be much less anxious during the posttest speech. Low demand subjects were merely asked to present a second speech. As expected, high demand did not produce improvement greater than simple repeated exposure on either self-report or several behavioral measures of fear. The three speech anxiety studies, taken together, indicate that speech anxiety is an appropriate analogue target, uninfluenced by demand and suggestions of improvement, and involving a strong physiological component that fails to habituate rapidly.

Our most recent investigation of an anxiety target (Borkovec, Stone, O'Brien, & Kaloupek, 1974a) involved heterosexual social anxiety and is prototypic for the design to be employed in future evaluations of target behaviors. Fear survey data from 1971 and 1973 (N = 1000) indicated that 15.5% of males and 11.5% of females experience some or greater fear of being with a member of the opposite sex, while 32% of males and 38.5% of females feel some or greater fear of meeting someone for the first time. Male subjects scoring either high or low on both items were exposed to two brief interactions with a female research assistant. Pre- and posttests occurred 3 weeks apart. Posttest instructions for half of each anxiety group involved high demand, while half received low demand instructions. Heart rate was monitored continuously prior to and during the interaction task. The procedure validly discriminated high and low anxiety groups on one behavioral and several self-report measures. In contrast to the physiological data from snake analogue studies, high social anxiety subjects displayed significantly greater pretest heart rate than low anxiety subjects. Also in contrast to the demand results from the snake studies, demand-suggestion instructions had no positive improvement effect on any measure, thus removing the confounding influence of demand from the interpretation of the outcomes in future therapy studies employing this target. Similar to the speech anxiety results, physiological responses in anticipation of and reaction to the social interaction were substantial among high anxiety subjects (92.5 beats/min baseline to 114 beats/min after initiation of the interaction). No evidence of habituation was found on the posttest. These data suggest that physiological activity is indeed a relevant response system involved in analogue social anxiety. As Lader and Mathews (1968) have suggested, the high basal level of autonomic responding in socially anxious individuals may preclude the habituation of autonomic responses and their presumed motoric and cognitive concomitants. The degree of autonomic activity elicited and the absence of habituation of that activity indicate that assessment of the impact of therapeutic intervention in reducing the autonomic component of anxiety is feasible with both social and speech anxiety targets.

Why demand should be effective in modifying snake approach and ineffective with social/speech anxiety remains to be empirically established. Two obvious possibilities can be suggested. First, differential demand effects may be based on the different behaviors measures in each fear situation and presumed to reflect the level of fear. In the case of typical snake studies, the nature of improvement suggested by the high demand testing conditions is ordinarily clear to the subject, i.e., closer approach. The subject's interpretation of what is meant by improvement and the nature of the measures being taken are perhaps more ambiguous in the social and speech situations. The other explanation depends on the degree of physiological activity demonstrated to occur in different target tests. An hypothesis mentioned earlier and empirically supported with snake phobics suggested that the presence of substantial physiological activity may mitigate demand influences on subjective and behavioral fear responses. The differences in heart rate found between snake-fearful and social/speech-anxious subjects may account for the failure of demand to induce pre- to posttest improvement in the latter target group.

IV. ANALOGUE OUTCOME RESEARCH

The implications of the preceding sections may be far reaching. Analogue investigations of the effectiveness of various anxiety-reducing behavioral techniques, and particularly studies of the theoretical mechanisms underlying these techniques, may be less convincing than we have previously thought. If this conclusion is correct, then it implies that we may have to begin anew to address some basic issues in therapy research, using increasingly more valid experimental methods.

The remainder of this chapter will consider a few applications of what we have learned from the demand, placebo, and target evaluation research that we hope may lead in this direction. The outcome research focuses on progressive relaxation training. In the first part of this section, studies investigating a basic theoretical issue in systematic desensitization (the role of relaxation) will be briefly reviewed and evaluated, primarily in terms of the potential confounding influence of demand characteristics. A recently completed study investigating the same topic but attempting to preclude such confounding will also be reported. In addition, a series of studies on the effectiveness and possible mechanisms of progressive relaxation in the treatment of sleep disturbance will be examined. Finally, a methodological control to increase the validity of self-report measures will be described.

A. Role of Relaxation in Systematic Desensitization

Procedurally, progressive relaxation training involves the systematic tensing and releasing of various muscle groups throughout the body and learning to attend to the sensations that result (Bernstein & Borkovec, 1973). Originally developed by Jacobson in the early 1900's, the technique was designed to teach the individual a skill that could be used to reduce general tension, arousal, and anxiety. Currently, initial training sessions lasting some 45 min involve the sequential tensing and releasing of various muscle groups with interspersed indirect suggestions from the therapist of feelings of calmness, heaviness, warmth, and relaxation. The client is asked to practice the procedures daily between sessions. As he practices and becomes more successful in producing feelings of deep relaxation and attending to those feelings, muscle groups are gradually combined over subsequent sessions. After seven to ten sessions, tension release of muscles is eliminated altogether, and the client learns to relax himself by simply recalling the sensations that resulted from previous tension-release occurrences.

The popularity of the procedure in behavior therapy markedly increased when Wolpe (1958) included relaxation training in his systematic desensitization procedure. In that procedure, relaxation, presumably a response incompatible with the autonomic response of anxiety, is paired with hierarchical presentations of feared stimuli. Repeated presentations with anxiety thus suppressed hypothetically result in a reciprocal inhibition process that breaks the bond between the feared stimuli and the anxiety reaction. Competing learning theories which have been offered to explain desensitization effectiveness suggest that nonreinforced presentation of the conditioned aversive stimuli allows for simple extinction of the conditioned emotional response (Lomont, 1965), that relaxation produces low levels of physiological activity [Lader & Mathews' (1968) maximal habituation hypothesis], or increases functional CS exposure (Wilson & Davison, 1971), thereby facilitating the extinction process.

The first theoretical question concerned whether relaxation was a necessary component in desensitization; the later question, whether it was facilitative. It is now frequently concluded in the literature that CS exposure is the only essential procedural ingredient and that a variety of patient responses may facilitate the anxiety-reduction process and/or ability to cope with anxiety-provoking situations, relaxation being only one possibility. While this conclusion may be eminently reasonable, its basis resides in a proliferation of primarily analogue outcome investigations. In some of these studies the components of desensitization have been examined. In others, relaxation has been replaced by a variety of other responses (e.g., distracting responses, reinforcement for approach, participant modeling). In many of these studies a limited number (i.e., range) of dependent measures have been used. The conclusion itself may thus represent an oversimplification of the construct of anxiety and its process.

For our present purpose, we will focus on a brief review of some investigations examining specific desensitization components and contributing to the above conclusion. The results of these 22 studies have been equivocal. Table I summarizes critical characteristics of these investigations and their outcomes. With the exception of the Wolpin and Raines (1966) article, which did not include a desensitization condition, and the Laxer and Walker (1970), the Kondas (1967), and the Sue (1972) articles, which did not utilize an exposure-only group, every study listed in Table I compared a desensitization condition to a group exposed to the same hierarchy without relaxation ($N = 17$) and/or with noncontiguous relaxation ($N = 4$). Several designs included additional control conditions, e.g., relaxation-only, relaxation-plus-neutral-images, placebo, no-treatment. The three columns on the right summarize whether desensitization was found to be significantly superior, equivalent, or significantly inferior to exposure-only and noncontiguous relaxation conditions on each channel of anxiety measurement obtained. (Since the noncontiguous relaxation condition involves both hierarchy presentation and relaxation training, but presented in an unpaired fashion, the procedure provides a comparison condition superior to the exposure-only group. The outcomes of the two groups were similar, however, and were therefore combined.)

Various methodological problems arising from the studies listed in Table I have been highlighted by other investigators (e.g., Blanchard, 1971; Davison, 1969, 1971; Nawas, Mealiea, & Fishman, 1971), and these have prevented the drawing of unambiguous conclusions regarding the role of relaxation in desensitization. If we ignore these problems for the moment, some provocative trends can be found in the overall outcome. Table II presents a summary of the studies in terms of the self-report and behavioral outcome of de-

TABLE I

Studies Comparing Desensitization to Exposure-Only and/or Noncontiguous Relaxation

Author	Target	Treatment conditions[a]	Approximate number of sessions	Subject control over progress[b]	Outcome[c] Self-report	Outcome[c] Behavioral	Outcome[c] Physiological
1. Aponte & Aponte, 1971	Test anxiety	SD, NCR, R, NT	5	No	NCR > SD	SD = NCR	—
2. Calef & MacLean, 1970	Speech anxiety	SD, E, NT	5	No	SD = E	—	—
3. Cooke, 1968	Rat phobia	SD, E, R, P, NT	5	Yes	SD = E	SD = E	—
4. Craighead, 1973	Snake phobia	SD, E, R, NT	5	Yes	SD = E	SD = E	SD = E
5. Crowder & Thornton, 1970	Snake phobia	SD, E, P	4	No	SD = E	SD = E	—
6. Davison, 1968	Snake phobia	SD, E, R, NT	10	No	SD = E	SD > E	—
7. Freeling & Shemberg, 1970	Test anxiety	SD, E, R	6	No	SD > E	SD = E	—
8. Folkins, Lawson, Opton, & Lazarus, 1968	Reaction to stressful film	SD, E, R, P	3	No	E > SD	—	E > SD

(continued)

TABLE I (*contd.*)

Author	Target	Treatment conditions[a]	Approximate number of sessions	Subject control over progress[b]	Outcome[c] Self-report	Behavioral	Physiological
9. Gillian & Rachman, 1974	Multiple phobias in outpatients	SD, E, R, Psychotherapy	20–30	Yes	SD = E	SD = E	Pretherapy measures only
10. Hyman & Gale, 1973	Snake phobia	SD, E, R	6	No	SD > E	SD > E	Process measures only
11. Kondas, 1967	Stage fright	SD, E, R, NT	?	?	SD = E	—	No analysis
12. Laxer & Walker, 1970	Test anxiety	SD, E to *in vivo* tests with and without R, P, NT	20	?	?	SD = E	—
13. Lomont & Edwards, 1967	Snake phobia	SD, NCR	10	No	SD > NCR	SD > NCR	SD = NCR
14. Marshall, Strawbridge, & Keltner, 1972	Spider phobia	SD, E with "mental relaxation," combination, P	6	No	SD = E	SD = E	—
15. Nawas, Mealiea, & Fishman, 1971	Snake phobia	SD, NCR, E, R_1, R_2, NT	6	No	—	SD = NCR / SD > E	—
16. Nawas, Welsch, & Fishman, 1970	Snake phobia	SD, E, E + tension, R, NT	5	No	—	SD > E	—

17. Persely & Leventhal, 1972	Rat and mice phobia	SD, NCR, under therapeutic (+) and nontherapeutic instructions	6	Yes	—	SD$^+$ = NCR$^+$	—
18. Rachman, 1965	Spider phobia	SD, E, R, NT	10–11	No	SD > E^d	SD > E^e	—
19. Sue, 1972	Snake phobia	SD, E + tension, NT	6	No	SD = E + tension	SD = E + tension	—
20. Vodde & Gilner, 1971	Rat phobia	SD, E, E + money, E + tension, P	5	No	SD = E	SD = E	—
21. Waters, Mc-Donald, & Koresko, 1972	Rat phobia	SD, E	2	No	—	SD = E	Process measures only
22. Wolpin & Raines, 1966	Snake phobia	E, E + tension, E to top item only	4–5	No	—	No differences	—

^{a}SD, relaxation contiguous with hierarchy presentation; NCR, relaxation noncontiguous with hierarchy presentation; E, hierarchy presentation only; R, relaxation only or relaxation contiguous with irrelevant hierarchy presentation; P, a noncomponent placebo; NT, no treatment.

^{b}"Yes" indicates that subjects controlled progress through relaxation and/or item presentations in all hierarchy exposure conditions.

^{c}Indicates comparative improvement between SD and either E or NCR; the symbol ">" here indicates statistical superiority of one condition over the other, alone or in combination with the other conditions.

^{d}Three-month follow-up assessment.

^{e}Posttest and follow-up assessment.

TABLE II

Self-Report and Behavioral Outcomes of Desensitization (SD) Compared to
Exposure-Only (E) and Noncontiguous Relaxation (NCR) Conditions in Terms of Subject
Control Over Procedures and Number of Therapy Sessions[a]

	Self-Report			Behavioral		
	SD > E or NCR	SD = E or NCR	E or NCR >SD	SD > E or NCR	SD = E or NCR	E or NCR > SD
a. Subject control over relaxation and/or item presentation:						
Yes	—	3, 4, 9	—	—	3, 4, 9, 17	—
No	7, 10, 13, 18	2, 5, 6, 14, 20	1, 8	6, 10, 13, 15, 16, 18	1, 5, 7, 14,15,20, 21	—
b. Number of sessions:						
2	—	—	—	—	21	—
3	—	—	8	—	—	—
4	—	5	—	—	5	—
5	—	2, 3, 4, 20	1	16	1, 3, 4, 20	—
6	7, 10	14	—	10, 15	7, 14, 15, 17	—
10	13, 18	6	—	6, 13, 18	—	—
30	—	9	—	—	9	—

[a]Italic numbers refer to their respective entries in Table I.

sensitization relative to exposure-only and noncontiguous relaxation conditions. The investigations are further categorized according to: (*a*) the degree of subject control over progress in relaxation training and/or item presentation; (*b*) the number of therapy sessions administered.

The majority of investigators found no differences between desensitization and the other two conditions, and two studies (Aponte & Aponte, 1971; Folkins, Lawson, Opton, & Lazarus, 1968) demonstrated desensitization to be significantly inferior, a finding limited to self-report measures. In the absence of other information, such a box-score effect argues against relaxation's facilitative role. However, in every study where subject control was employed, exposure-only and noncontiguous relaxation produced outcome statistically equivalent to those yielded by desensitization. Where control over relaxation training and item presentation was solely in the hands of the therapist, 44% of the self-report outcomes and 46% of the behavioral outcomes found desensitization to be superior to the other two conditions. Generalization from this trend would suggest that the facilitative effect of relaxation is negligible for self-report and behavioral change, as long as the subject can determine his own rate of progress during therapy. In the absence of such control, contiguous relaxation often improves outcome. Finally, with very few sessions, equivalence among the groups is obtained or, in the case of self-report, there is a slight advantage for exposure or noncontiguous relaxation. As the number of sessions increases, so does the percentage of studies demonstrating desensitization superiority. On the basis of one study (Gillian & Rachman, 1974), it appears that the conditions may once again be equivalent after the administration of very many sessions. These data would suggest that with an increasing number of sessions, contiguous relaxation provides an increasing contribution to the self-report and behavioral effects of desensitization; if CS exposure is extensive, as in the Gillian and Rachman study, relaxation may no longer contribute to ultimate outcome.

We could speculate endlessly on the implications of these trends for determining relaxation's role and its mechanisms. Such speculation, however, would be somewhat fruitless. Most of the studies share two characteristics (suggested in the preceding sections of this chapter) that limit conclusions derived from analogue anxiety research: (a) a preponderance of animal-phobic subjects (15 of 22 studies); (b) a general absence of physiological outcome measurement. These two characteristics have separate as well as combined implications for any conclusions drawn from studies listed in Table I. Given the research documenting the effectiveness of demand on self-report and behavioral fear measures with animal phobia targets, the contribution of demand to outcome is potentially substantial. The absence of data supporting an equivalence of the expectancy and/or demand inherent in the comparison conditions utilized in these studies creates further ambiguity in interpretation of any differential treatment effects. Although the trends could well be used to support theoretical arguments regarding the contribution of relaxation and its mechanisms, such speculation would be premature.

Furthermore, the absence of physiological outcome measures restricts the range of theoretically relevant conclusions. Only seven studies obtained any physiological data at all: three involved pretherapy correlates (Gillian & Rachman, 1974) or process measures

(Hyman & Gale, 1973; Waters, McDonald, & Koresko, 1972); two employed nonstringently selected snake phobics (Craighead, 1973; Lomont & Edwards, 1967); one investigation employed a discrete palmar sweat measure without quantified analysis (Kondas, 1967); and one study evaluated continuous heart rate and skin conductance outcome in a posttest-only design involving a unique target [normal samples exposed to a stressful accident film (Folkins, Lawson, Opton, & Lazarus, 1968)].

Since anxiety is a multidimensional construct operationally defined by three measurement channels, conclusions regarding the influence of manipulations on "anxiety" should ideally be based on outcome assessments in all three channels; in the absence of one or more channels, conclusions should be restricted to the channel(s) obtained. We are not suggesting that the physiological channel is more important than the other two; only that the physiological component, of equal importance in past behavioral definitions of anxiety, has been relatively ignored in the behavior therapy literature. Its particular importance for theories of desensitization resides in the fact that the original theoretical underpinnings of the technique rest on notions of classically conditioned autonomic responses. The self-report, behavioral, and physiological fear components appear to be separate but interacting responses (Lang, 1968). We cannot, therefore, feel completely comfortable in generalizing our conclusions based on behavioral measures to the autonomic component so central to the issue being addressed. It must be kept in mind that there may be several different mechanisms by which hierarchy exposure or contiguous relaxation effect changes in each anxiety response component. In testing the reciprocal inhibition versus extinction mechanisms of desensitization, we are suggesting that the physiological component represents an important level of analysis. The apparent absence of that component in animal phobic subjects and the general absence of its measurement in studies listed in Table I greatly restrict our interpretation of the trends in Table II.

Finally, level of demand and level of physiological involvement appear to interact. Demand effects are behaviorally most efficacious when the physiological component is relatively weak or absent. Consequently, the use of small-animal phobics may guarantee both strong demand effects and relatively low levels of physiological activity. It may be the case, then, that conclusions specific to the *autonomic* theory of desensitization derived from these studies cannot legitimately depend either on behavioral and self-report measures or on physiological indices.

B. A Component Study of Desensitization with Social Anxiety

With these notions in mind, we recently attempted to readdress the question of relaxation's contribution to desensitization (O'Brien, 1975). Social anxiety, found earlier to be uninfluenced by demand and to involve substantial anticipatory and reactive physiological activity, was selected as the target behavior. Forty-three socially anxious female undergraduates were pretested in an analogue social situation, as outlined in Borkovec et al. (1974a), and randomly assigned to one of four conditions: desensitization, hierarchy exposure without relaxation, hierarchy exposure with noncontiguous relaxation, and no treatment. Two therapists treated half of the subjects in each therapy condition. The first session for treated subjects involved rationale presentation and construction of a 15-item hierarchy enumerating in temporal sequence the major situations involved in the pretest. Since treatment was conducted in small groups, average individual ranking of the items was used to create a group hierarchy. Following hierarchy construction, subjects practiced relaxation and/or visualization, depending on their treatment condition, and rated the credibility of the procedures. In these ratings, subjects from all three therapy conditions reported moderately high and equivalent expectations for improvement.

In desensitization and noncontiguous relaxation, subjects were trained in pleasant-image visualization and progressive relaxation for the remainder of the first session. Sessions 2 to 4 involved hierarchy presentation. Desensitization followed Wolpean procedures as outlined in Paul (1966). Noncontiguous relaxation subjects received hierarchy presentations alone during the first half of each session and relaxation training alone during the second half.

In the exposure-only condition, visualization of pleasant images and completion of a demographic questionnaire comprised of remainder of Session 1. Sessions 2 to 4 involved hierarchy presentation only. In all three conditions, subjects signaling of anxiety during item visualization resulted in scene termination and re-presentation via parameters outlined by Paul (1966).

No-treatment subjects returned 6 to 8 weeks after the pretest for posttesting, contemporaneous with the posttesting of treated subjects.

The most surprising outcome, given the specificity of the hierarchy to the restricted testing situation, was a general lack of impact of all three treatment conditions of a variety of self-report and behavioral measures; improvement was unsubstantial on eight of nine indices. On the frequently employed timed behavioral checklist measure, all three therapy groups combined (and noncontiguous relaxation separately) displayed improvement significantly greater than no-treatment. Also, they did not differ from each other, an outcome in accord with Table II for studies involving subject control over progress and the administration of four or fewer therapy sessions. The most interesting result for its theoretical relevance was found in the heart-rate data collected continuously prior to and during the social interaction test. The treatment by phase of interaction effect was significant ($F = 1.62$, $df = 23$, 311, $p < .05$). Table III presents the posttest heart-rate scores, adjusted for pretest levels, for the four treatment conditions.

All four groups still displayed high heart-rate activity at the initiation of the interaction, perhaps reflecting the cognitive-motor demands of the task itself (cf. Borkovec et al., in press). Both groups receiving relaxation training displayed similarly reduced anticipatory activity prior to the onset of the interaction, relative to the two groups in which relaxation training was absent. The desensitization procedure, however, resulted in rapidly diminishing heart rate subsequent to task initiation, while the other three procedures produced a more gradual decrease during the interaction.

Our conclusions, based strictly on this study, would be that when applied to a target behavior uninfluenced by demand and involving a substantial physiological component: (a) brief desensitization is less effective than previous research would suggest; (b) relaxation, either contiguous or noncontiguous with hierarchy presentations, has no immediate facilitative effect on cognitive or behavioral change; (c) brief relaxation training reduces anticipatory physiological activity, while relaxation contiguous with hierarchy presentations (desensitization) reduces reactive physiological activity.

There are, of course, several serious limitations in the above study (e.g., the small number of therapy sessions, failure to include a placebo condition, dependence on a single autonomic measure). We attempted to eliminate only the demand problem and to provide a more adequate assessment of physiological outcome than has been previously reported. It is hoped, however, that the assumed clinical and theoretical relevance of such studies will provide in the future more valid outcome data, uncontaminated by extratherapeutic variables. The arguments presented in earlier sections, the trends observed in Table II, and the outcomes of the present study suggest that determination of the role of relaxation (or any technique

TABLE III

Adjusted Posttest Heart Rate for the Four Treatment Conditions During
Anticipatory and Reactive Phases of an Analogue Social Interaction[a]

	Phase of interaction								
	Anticipatory period					Reactive period			
Condition	1	2	3	4	5	6[b]	7	8	9
Systematic desensitization	88.6	91.8	93.1	91.8	96.1	104.0	93.3	91.7	90.7
Noncontiguous relaxation	91.3	90.7	92.0	90.9	98.1	107.8	99.3	101.5	97.9
Exposure only	97.9	97.3	100.1	100.9	102.4	105.7	103.6	101.6	100.6
No treatment	96.4	97.2	95.5	95.6	102.2	106.0	99.5	95.9	95.0

[a]From O'Brien (1975).
[b]Initiation of interaction.

component) is likely to be a complex undertaking involving a series of studies. Such variables as the number of sessions, level of demand and physiological activity, credibility of the comparison conditions, and subject control over therapy progress may all interact, and they must therefore be controlled and/or entered into factorial designs. All three channels of anxiety measurement should be assessed, since component effects may be limited to one or two channels and may operate by different mechanisms in different channels. Like the oversimplified psychotherapy question ("Does therapy work?"), the component question of whether relaxation facilitates desensitization has been inappropriately broad. It must be restated to ask under what conditions, with what kinds of subjects, and for which anxiety response components does relaxation contribute to anxiety reduction, and which mechanism(s) account for each contribution.

C. Role of Relaxation in Treatment of Sleep-Onset Disturbance

In 1971 we decided to begin experimental evaluation of progressive relaxation effects on sleep-onset disturbance. The demand, placebo, and measurement studies were in progress, and it was clear that we were not prepared to initiate outcome research on fear. Too many problems, outlined earlier, remained to be solved until the

O'Brien (1975) study could be conducted. It seemed desirable, however, to have a concurrent outcome program in which to apply methodological and theoretical ideas emitting from the other lines of research. Choice of the sleep-onset disturbance target was based on two considerations. *First,* it possessed face validity as a clinically relevant problem. In addition, similar to social anxiety, sleep disturbance was more likely to interfere with the daily functioning of the analogue subject than were small-animal phobias. Thus, the probability of volunteer participation was high. *Second,* Monroe (1967) found poor sleepers to display higher levels of physiological activity prior to and during sleep than good sleepers, suggesting that the physiological component served as a maintainer of the disorder and that relaxation would be an effective intervention strategy.

From 1971 to 1975, six outcome investigations involving more than 230 mildly sleep-disturbed subjects have been conducted in our laboratory. In each study, subject selection criteria have included: (*a*) reports of average latency to sleep onset of more than 30 min, considered by the subject to represent a sleep problem; (*b*) current nonuse of drugs; (*c*) current noninvolvement with other professional services. Participating subjects were given a packet of daily sleep questionnaires during a pretherapy interview, with instructions to fill out a questionnaire upon awakening each morning until 1 week after the last therapy session. Initial data reduction involved calculation of average reported latency to sleep onset during pretherapy and posttherapy weeks.

An extensive review of behavioral treatments of sleep disturbance in general will be presented by Bootzin in a subsequent volume of this serial publication. In the present chapter, we focus only on four of our own studies in order to describe our attempts to isolate the active mechanism of relaxation effects on sleep-onset disturbance and the employment of counterdemand instructional strategies to aid us in that effort. As a summary reference for the outcomes of these four investigations, Table IV presents the mean latencies for treatment and control conditions at pretherapy, posttherapy, and follow-up periods.

Paul (1969b) has demonstrated that progressive relaxation training was significantly superior to hypnotic and self-relaxation conditions in reducing physiological activity. The first outcome study therefore assessed the effectiveness of these three techniques in reducing sleep-onset disturbance (Borkovec & Fowles, 1973). Forty female subjects were randomly assigned to one of the three relaxation conditions [all modeled after Paul (1969b)] or to a waiting-list

TABLE IV

Mean Self-Reported Latency to Sleep Onset (in Minutes) During Pretherapy, Counter-demand, and Positive Demand Periods and at 5-Month Follow-up for Therapy and Control Conditions from Four Outcome Investigations

Treatment condition	Pretherapy	Counter-demand	Positive demand	Follow-up
a. Progressive relaxation				
Relaxation alone				
Borkovec & Fowles, 1973	46	–	25	21
Borkovec, Steinmark, & Nau, 1973	38	–	24	–
Steinmark & Borkovec, 1974	39	28	27	18
Borkovec *et al.*, 1975	46	25	23	16
Relaxation plus desensitization				
Borkovec *et al.*, 1973	44	–	24	–
Borkovec *et al.*, 1973	40	–	27	–
Steinmark & Borkovec, 1974	36	26	24	18
Mean latency	41.3	26.3	24.9	18.2
b. Placebo				
Hypnotic relaxation (Borkovec & Fowles, 1973)	43	–	24	39
Self-relaxation (Borkovec & Fowles, 1973)	42	–	24	27
Quasi-desensitization (Steinmark & Borkovec, 1974)	42	40	24	29
Quasi-desensitization (Borkovec *et al.*, 1975)	43	35	24	32
No tension-release relaxation (Borkovec *et al.*, 1975)	38	28	26	23
Mean latency	41.6	34.3	24.4	30.0
c. No treatment				
Borkovec & Fowles, 1973	44	–	44	–
Steinmark & Borkovec, 1974	32	36	42	–
Borkovec *et al.*, 1975	35	32	33	–[a]
Mean latency	37.0	34.0	39.7	

[a]No-treatment subjects were treated by a variety of stimulus control and relaxation procedures immediately after the conclusion of therapy weeks for the treated subjects; thus, no follow-up data were collected.

no-treatment condition. Four male graduate students in clinical psychology served as therapists, each therapist administering individual treatment to subjects from each condition. Each subject received three 1-hr therapy sessions plus instructions to practice her respective relaxation techniques just prior to going to bed. Skin conductance, heart rate, respiration, and an electromyogram (EMG) were recorded during each treatment session.

All three treated groups reported significant improvement in latency of sleep onset from pretherapy to posttherapy weeks, while the no treatment group showed no change. Statistical comparisons revealed that progressive and hypnotic relaxation both produced significantly greater improvement than did no treatment, while self-relaxation did not differ from no treatment or the other two treatment procedures. During therapy, physiological reduction was uncorrelated with outcome improvement within or across treated groups. Four-month follow-up data, not reported in the original article, indicated that only the progressive relaxation group had further improved, while self-relaxation and hypnotic relaxation reported losses in improvement.

This first controlled study of sleep-onset disturbance provided supporting evidence for the immediate effectiveness of relaxation techniques in general and long-term effectiveness of progressive relaxation in particular, but the nearly equal improvement produced by the self-relaxation control procedure at the end of treatment and the lack of relationship between physiological process and outcome measures raised several interpretive problems. Specifically, three explanations of the data remained: (a) The subjects were responding on self-report measures solely to the demand characteristics of the experiment, and latency was not substantially modified. (b) Latency was reduced in all three treated groups, but the improvement was a function of suggestion, therapist contact, expectancy, and other nonspecific therapy components. (c) Latency was improved in all three groups, but the change was a function of some active component common to all three procedures. All treated subjects were instructed to relax, to focus on pleasant internal feelings, and to use that technique to get to sleep at night. Such attention-focusing training may have been incompatible with typical bed-time cognitive activity and thus effective in promoting actual improvement in each of the three treatment conditions.

Geer and Katkin (1966) have suggested that tension may become conditioned to the sleep situation itself and contribute to sleep disturbance. Monroe (1967) had found that poor sleepers reported greater ease in falling asleep in the laboratory situation than in their own home situation, while good sleepers felt their laboratory sleep was poorer than usual. Such results suggested that behavior which is incompatible with efficient sleep may become conditioned to the subject's typical sleeping environment. Consequently, desensitization procedures may be particularly appropriate. The second investigation evaluated whether additional treatment effectiveness might be gained by adding a systematic desensitization procedure to the basic progressive relaxation technique (Borkovec, Steinmark, & Nau, 1973). College and noncollege subjects were obtained through newspaper advertisements and leaflets requesting volunteers for sleep disturbance treatment. Initial interviews identified 24 appropriate subjects, who were randomly assigned to either relaxation or one of two desensitization procedures. The relaxation group received procedures identical to the progressive relaxation condition in the first study. One group of desensitization subjects was trained in relaxation and then desensitized to a single item [modeled after Geer & Katkin (1966)]. The item simply involved visualization of the subject lying in bed and attempting to fall asleep. The second desensitization group underwent the same therapy procedures, including relaxation training. They were not instructed to practice the relaxation technique just prior to going to sleep; this did not prevent them from doing so, however. Two graduate student therapists treated half of the subjects in each condition. Three therapy sessions were administered, and all therapy was given in groups of three to four subjects.

All three therapy groups reported improvement in latency to sleep onset from pretherapy to posttherapy weeks. The amount of change reported was very similar to that reported in the first study. While the group profile of the subjects was strikingly similar to that obtained in Monroe's (1967) poor sleeper group, individual Minnesota Multiphasic Personality Inventory (MMPI) scales were uncorrelated with outcome improvement. The absence of differential effects among treatment conditions and the potential influence of demand on self-report again mitigated the validity of cause-and-effect conclusions.

At this point, it was clear that we needed a method to eliminate the confounding influence of demand characteristics on the self-report sleep data. Our snake phobia studies indicated that subjects will show improvement as long as improvement is requested. The same effect could easily occur in the daily sleep questionnaires, despite Baker and Kahn's (1972) convincing arguments for the use of self-report in insomnia studies. We had previously concluded (Borkovec, 1973b) that a treatment procedure demonstrated to produce improvement greater than a placebo condition, regardless of whether therapeutic or nontherapeutic instructions were used, is indeed a powerful modification technique and includes active ingredients separate from demand and placebo effects. Extrapolating from this conclusion, we developed the notion of counterdemand and positive demand instructional manipulations. All treated subjects would be told not to expect improvement in sleep disturbance until after the last (fourth) therapy session. They were told that past research had indicated that it would take four sessions and conscientious practice on their part before the procedures would have an effect. They were assured that after four sessions, dramatic improvement in sleep disturbance would occur. Thus the demand characteristics were in opposition to reports of improvement during the first 3 weeks of therapy and in the direction of improvement during the last week. Critical statistical comparisons would, of course, be made at the end of the first 3 weeks (the counterdemand period).

Two further considerations arose due to the results of the credibility studies described earlier: (a) It was found necessary to create a placebo condition that was procedurally similar to the therapy conditions in order to insure equivalent credibility. (b) Participating subjects therefore were asked to rate the credibility of their respective procedures in order to assess the success of that attempt.

The third sleep disturbance study (Steinmark & Borkovec, 1974) was designed to incorporate these additional methodological aspects. Forty-eight volunteer college students meeting the usual criteria were randomly assigned to one of four conditions: relaxation, single-item desensitization, placebo, and waiting-list no-treatment. Relaxation and desensitization procedures were identical to those employed in the second study. Placebo involved the paired presentation of chronologically ordered bedtime behaviors and neutral imagery in a quasi-desensitization procedure. Relaxation training was not administered to this group. Two male graduate student therapists treated one half of the subjects in each condition. Four therapy sessions were given in groups of four to six subjects, and all treated subjects rated the credibility of their respective procedures on the Borkovec and Nau (1972) scales at the end of treatment.

Relaxation and desensitization produced significantly greater improvement in sleep-onset latency than did the placebo and no treatment during the counterdemand period, while the two active treatments did not differ from each other. After the fourth therapy session, all three treated groups reported significantly greater improvement than the untreated group. At the 5-month follow-up assessment, relaxation and desensitization subjects reported additional gains, while the placebo group reported an increase in latency. The three treatment groups did not differ on credibility ratings.

These results supported both the immediate and long-term effectiveness of relaxation therapy (common to both relaxation and desensitization) in the treatment of sleep-onset disturbance. Most importantly, the validity of this conclusion is strengthened by the use of a strategic demand manipulation. Despite demand instructions incompatible with reports of improvement, both relaxation and desensitization groups indicated reduction in sleep disturbance, while placebo reported no change.

The dramatic shift that was reported by the placebo group after the fourth therapy session raised two possibilities. *First,* these data may reflect the influence of demand on self-report outcome measures. In that case, prior insomnia studies cannot be clearly interpreted, since improvement by any treated group (placebo or active treatment) may reflect demand or demand by therapy interaction effects. *Second,* the change may reflect actual improvement. In that case, the "active" effect of placebo treatment might have resided in the client's expectation of improvement. If concern over falling asleep is a major maintaining factor in moderate insomnia, then elimination of that concern by placebo manipulation would be expected to facilitate actual improvement. In support of placebo effectiveness with moderate insomniacs, Nicolis and Silvestri (1967) reported that moderate insomniacs improved under both active and placebo medication, while severe insomniacs responded only to active drugs. In the present study, credibility ratings did not correlate significantly with outcome. All subjects rated the placebo procedure as highly credible with little variability, however, thus precluding a significant relationship.

The purpose of the fourth investigation (Borkovec, Kaloupek, & Slama, 1975) was to replicate the Steinmark and Borkovec study. At the end of the counterdemand period (prior to the fourth therapy session), progressive relaxation was again compared to the same quasi-desensitization placebo and no-treatment conditions. While the presence of some active ingredient in progressive relaxation procedure had been demonstrated in the earlier study, isolation of that active component remained. At least two possibly interacting causative factors may contribute to sleep disturbance (intrusive cognitions and high levels of physiological arousal). Training in progressive relaxation, however, involves both attention-focusing instructions as well as tension-release of gross muscle systems to reduce physiological arousal. Consequently, a third control group was added which involved only the attention-focusing component. Its procedures were identical to those of progressive relaxation with the single exception that tension-release of muscle groups was omitted. Finally, credibility ratings had been obtained after the last therapy session in the Steinmark and Borkovec study to preclude obtrusive questioning from influencing outcome reports; in the present study, ratings were obtained immediately after the first session. Two graduate students administered four group treatment sessions to half of the subjects in each therapy condition. Progressive relaxation with tension-release was found to be significantly superior in producing sleep-onset improvement than were both the placebo and control conditions during the counterdemand period. The occurrence of that difference despite instructional demand sets in opposition to reports of improvement again suggests that demand characteristics do not account for the reported gains among sleep-disturbed subjects receiving progressive relaxation training; this therefore supports the presence of an active ingredient independent of placebo effects in that technique. Furthermore, the statistically significant superiority of progressive relaxation over relaxation without tension-release suggests that attention focusing alone is not sufficient to promote sleep. Again, there were no credibility differences between treated conditions to account for the differential outcome.

As is usually true in research, the outcome of this study raised more questions than it answered. Specifically, while a combination of tension release with focused attention was found to be a critical procedural component in the relaxation treatment of sleep-onset disturbance, there remained three rival interpretations for why this is the case: (a) Progressive relaxation may have produced greater reductions in physiological arousal than the other procedures, and such reduction may be a necessary prerequisite for efficient sleep onset. The studies by Paul (1969b) and Monroe (1967) support this interpretation. (b) It may be, however, that arousal reduction produced by progressive relaxation interacted with attention focusing to facilitate sleep onset. In the absence of a control condition which results in physiological reductions but involves no attention-focusing component, this hypothesis remains tenable. (c) Finally, the tension release of gross muscle groups may have facilitated attention focusing by providing the focal stimuli, either directly or indirectly via the resulting internal sensations, regardless of their effect on the level of physiological arousal. This third interpretation raises some interesting possibilities. Inherent in progressive relaxation is the repetitive nature of the training procedure. The subject repeatedly presents monotonous stimulation to himself on a variable interval schedule. By so doing, he has established an environment which is conceptually similar to that produced by the monotonous stimulation paradigm. Bohlin (1971, 1972), for example, has found that subjects exposed to variable interval tones fell asleep more quickly than control subjects.

Our attempts to identify the active mechanism(s) of relaxation in ameliorating sleep-onset disturbance have only begun. A series of studies on monotonous stimulation effects with good and poor sleepers has been initiated and should provide informative data relevant to the third hypothesis. Further outcome studies are planned to test the simple and interactive effects of attention focusing and reduced physiological activity suggested by the first two hypotheses. The counterdemand strategy will greatly enhance our confidence that valid self-report data will be forthcoming.

V. SUMMARY AND CONCLUSIONS

Progress in science frequently involves a step backwards for every two steps forward. Such is the current status of analogue therapy outcome research. Vastly improved experimental designs initiated a decade ago heralded the advent of solid therapy outcome conclusions. In our opinion, the time has come for a reexamination of the adequacy of our outcome methods. The extensive use of animal phobics provided subjects for requisite factorial designs but at the same time introduced target characteristics (e.g., susceptibility to the effects of extratherapeutic variables, absence of a substantial physiological fear component, irrelevancy to typical clinical anxiety cases) that threaten the internal and external validity of the conclusions drawn from those powerful designs. The effects of demand characteristics on such targets and the failure of traditional placebo groups to control for those effects have been adequately demonstrated. Recognition of these factors now seriously limits our confidence in both effectiveness investigations and studies of underlying theoretical mechanisms of effect. The result is painfully reflected in the inconclusive nature of more than a score of studies assessing the contribution of relaxation to systematic desensitization.

Some initial recommendations in an effort to improve analogue research were presented. Social and speech anxiety targets, for example, appear to provide a useful alternative to small animal phobias. Demand effects appear to be minimal, and increased heart rate occurs in anticipation of and response to presentation of the feared situation. Placebo conditions can be created to match procedural elements of therapy conditions, and credibility of rationale and procedures can be rated to provide an assessment of their adequacy in controlling for client expectation of improvement. The use of counterdemand instructional sets allows for the acquisition of more valid self-report data.

Two attempts to apply these recommendations were presented: a component study of desensitization employing a social anxiety target, and a series of studies on the relaxation treatment of sleep-onset disturbance.

One year from now (two, if we are lucky) outcome investigators will once again point out the fatal flaws inherent in our current methodology and will recommend methods of correcting these errors. Perhaps the issues that have been addressed and some of the suggestions we have made will contribute to their insights in spite of our own myopic vision.

REFERENCES

Aponte, J. F., & Aponte, C. E. Group preprogrammed systematic desensitization without the simultaneous presentation of aversive scenes with relaxation training. *Behaviour Research and Therapy*, 1971, 9, 337–346.

Baker, B. L., & Kahn, M. A. A reply to "Critique of 'Treatment of insomnia by relaxation training': Relaxation training, Rogerian therapy, or demand characteristics." *Journal of Abnormal Psychology*, 1972, 79, 94–96.

Bates, H. D. Revelance of animal-avoidance analogue studies to the treatment of clinical phobias: A rejoinder to Cooper, Furst, and Bridger. *Journal of Abnormal Psychology*, 1970, 75, 12–14.

Bernstein, D. A. Behavioral fear assessment: Anxiety or artifact? In H. Adams & P. Unikel (Eds.), *Issues and trends in behavior therapy*. Springfield, Ill.: Thomas, 1973. Pp. 225–267.

Bernstein, D. A. Manipulation of avoidance behavior as a function of increased or decreased demand on repeated behavioral tests. *Journal of Consulting and Clinical Psychology*, 1974, 42, 896–900.

Bernstein, D. A., & Borkovec, T. D. *Progressive relaxation training*. Champaign, Ill.: Research Press, 1973.

Bernstein, D. A., & Nietzel, M. T. Procedural variation in behavioral avoidance tests. *Journal of Consulting and Clinical Psychology*, 1973, 41, 165–174.

Bernstein, D. A., & Nietzel, M. T. Behavioral avoidance tests: The effects of demand characteristics and repeated measures of two types of subject. *Behavior Therapy*, 1974, 5, 183–192.

Bernstein, D. A., & Paul, G. L. Some comments on therapy analogue research with small animal "phobias." *Journal of Behavior Therapy and Experimental Psychiatry*, 1971, 2, 225–237.

Blanchard, E. B. A comparison of reciprocal inhibition and reactive inhibition therapies in the treatment of speech anxiety: A methodological critique. *Behavior Therapy*, 1971, **2**, 103–106.

Blom, B. E., & Craighead, W. E. The effects of situational and instructional demand on indices of speech anxiety. *Journal of Abnormal Psychology*, 1974, **83**, 667–674.

Bohlin, G. Monotonous stimulus, sleep onset, and habituation of the orienting reaction. *Electroencephalography and Clinical Neurophysiology*, 1971, **31**, 593–601.

Bohlin, G. Susceptibility to sleep during a habituation procedure as related to individual differences. *Journal of Experimental Research in Personality*, 1972, **6**, 248–254.

Borkovec, T. D. Effects of expectancy on the outcome of systematic desensitization and implosive treatments for analogue anxiety. *Behavior Therapy*, 1972, **3**, 29–40.

Borkovec, T. D. The effects of instructional suggestion and physiological cues on analogue fear. *Behavior Therapy*, 1973, **4**, 185–192. (a)

Borkovec, T. D. The role of expectancy and physiological feedback in fear research: A review with special reference to subject characteristics. *Behavior Therapy*, 1973, **4**, 491–505. (b)

Borkovec, T. D. Heart-rate process during systematic desensitization and implosive therapy for analogue anxiety. *Behavior Therapy*, 1974, **5**, 636–641.

Borkovec, T. D. Physiological and cognitive processes in the regulation of anxiety. In G. Schwartz & D. Shapiro (Eds.), *Consciousness and self-regulation: Advances in research*. New York: Plenum, 1976, in press.

Borkovec, T. D., & Craighead, W. E. The comparison of two methods of assessing fear and avoidance behavior. *Behaviour Research and Therapy*, 1971, **9**, 285–291.

Borkovec, T. D., & Fowles, D. C. A controlled investigation of the effects of progressive and hypnotic relaxation on insomnia. *Journal of Abnormal Psychology*, 1973, **82**, 153–158.

Borkovec, T. D., Kaloupek, D. G., & Slama, K. The facilitative effect of muscle tension-release in the relaxation treatment of sleep disturbance. *Behavior Therapy*, 1975, **6**, 301–309.

Borkovec, T. D., & Nau, S. D. Credibility of analogue therapy rationales. *Journal of Behavior Therapy and Experimental Psychiatry*, 1972, **3**, 257–260.

Borkovec, T. D., Steinmark, S. W., & Nau, S. D. Relaxation training and single-item desensitization in the group treatment of insomnia. *Journal of Behavior Therapy and Experimental Psychiatry*, 1973, **4**, 401–403.

Borkovec, T. D., Stone, N. M., O'Brien, G. T., & Kaloupek, D. G. Evaluation of a clinically relevant target behavior for analogue outcome research. *Behavior Therapy*, 1974, **5**, 504–514. (a)

Borkovec, T. D., Wall, R. L., & Stone, N. M. False physiological feedback and the maintenance of speech anxiety. *Journal of Abnormal Psychology*, 1974, **83**, 164–168. (b)

Borkovec, T. D., Weerts, T. C., & Bernstein, D. A. Behavioral assessment of anxiety. In A. Ciminero, K. Calhoun, & H. E. Adams (Eds.), *Handbook of behavioral assessment*. New York: Wiley, in press.

Boudewyns, P. A., & Borkovec, T. D. Credibility of psychotherapy and placebo therapy rationales. *V.A. Newsletter For Research in Mental Health and Behavioral Sciences*, 1974, **16**, 15–18.

Calef, R. A., & MacLean, G. D. A comparison of reciprocal inhibition and reactive inhibition therapies in the treatment of speech anxiety. *Behavior Therapy*, 1970, **1**, 51–58.

Campbell, D. T., & Stanley, J. C. *Experimental and quasi-experimental designs for research*. Chicago: Rand McNally, 1963.

Cooke, G. Evaluation of the efficacy of the components of reciprocal inhibition psycho-therapy. *Journal of Abnormal Psychology*, 1968, 73, 464–467.

Cooper, A., Furst, J. B., & Bridger, W. H. A brief commentary on the usefulness of studying fear of snakes. *Journal of Abnormal Psychology*, 1969, 74, 413–414.

Craighead, W. E. The role of muscular relaxation in systematic desensitization. In R. D. Rubin, J. P. Brady, & J. D. Henderson (Eds.), *Advances in behavior therapy*. New York: Academic Press, 1973. Pp. 177–197.

Crowder, J. E., & Thornton, D. W. Effects of systematic desensitization, programmed fantasy and bibliotherapy on a specific fear. *Behaviour Research and Therapy*, 1970, 8, 35–41.

Davison, G. C. Systematic desensitization as a counterconditioning process. *Journal of Abnormal Psychology*, 1968, 73, 91–99.

Davison, G. C. A procedural critique of "Desensitization and the experimental reduction of threat." *Journal of Abnormal Psychology*, 1969, 74, 86–87.

Davison, G. C. Noncontiguous presence during treatment sessions of relaxation and imaginal aversive stimuli: A reply to Nawas, Mealiea, and Fishman. *Behavior Therapy*, 1971, 2, 357–360.

Folkins, C. H., Lawson, K. D., Opton, E. M., & Lazarus, R. S. Desensitization and the experimental reduction of threat. *Journal of Abnormal Psychology*, 1968, 73, 100–113.

Freeling, N. W., & Shemberg, K. M. The alleviation of test anxiety by systematic desensitiza-tion. *Behaviour Research and Therapy*, 1970, 8, 293–299.

Friedman, H. J. Patient-expectancy and symptom reduction. *Archives of General Psy-chiatry*, 1963, 8, 61–67.

Geer, J. H. The development of a scale to measure fear. *Behaviour Research and Therapy*, 1965, 3, 45–53.

Geer, J. H., & Katkin, E. S. Treatment of insomnia using a variant of systematic desensitiza-tion: A case report. *Journal of Abnormal Psychology*, 1966, 71, 161–164.

Gillian, P., & Rachman, S. An experimental investigation of desensitization in phobic patients. *British Journal of Psychiatry*, 1974, 124, 392–401.

Goldstein, A. P. Patient's expectancies and nonspecific therapy as a basis for (un)-spon-taneous remission. *Journal of Clinical Psychology*, 1960, 16, 399–403.

Goldstein, A. P., & Shipman, W. G. Patient expectancies, symptom reduction, and aspects of the initial psychotherapeutic interview. *Journal of Clinical Psychology*, 1961, 17, 129–133.

Hyman, E. T., & Gale, E. N. Galvanic skin response and reported anxiety during systematic desensitization. *Journal of Consulting and Clinical Psychology*, 1973, 40, 108–114.

Kazdin, A. The effect of suggestion and pretesting on avoidance reduction in fearful subjects. *Journal of Behavior Therapy and Experimental Psychiatry*, 1973, 4, 213–222.

Kondas, O. Reduction of examination anxiety and "stage-fright" by group desensitization and relaxation. *Behaviour Research and Therapy*, 1967, 5, 275–281.

Lader, M. H., & Mathews, A. M. A physiological model of phobic anxiety and desensitiza-tion. *Behaviour Research and Therapy*, 1968, 6, 411–421.

Lang, P. J. Fear reduction and fear behavior: Problems in treating a construction. In J. M. Shilien (Ed.), *Research in psychotherapy*. Washington, D.C.: American Psychological Association, 1968. Pp. 90–102.

Lang, P. J., & Lazovik, A. D. Experimental desensitization of a phobia. *Journal of Abnormal and Social Psychology*, 1963, 66, 519–525.

Lang, P. J., Melamed, B. G., & Hart, J. A psychophysiological analysis of fear modification using an automated desensitization procedure. *Journal of Abnormal Psychology*, 1970, 76, 220–234.

Lawlis, G. F. Response styles of a patient population on the Fear Survey Schedule. *Behaviour Research and Therapy,* 1971, **9**, 95–102.

Laxer, R. M., & Walker, K. Counterconditioning versus relaxation in the desensitization of test anxiety. *Journal of Counseling Psychology,* 1970, **17**, 431–436.

Lazarus, A. A. *Behavior therapy and beyond.* New York: McGraw-Hill, 1971.

Levis, D. J. The case for performing research on non-patient populations with fears of small animals: A reply to Cooper, Furst, and Bridger. *Journal of Abnormal Psychology,* 1970, **75**, 36–38.

Lomont, J. F. Reciprocal inhibition or extinction? *Behaviour Research and Therapy,* 1965, **3**, 209–219.

Lomont, J. F., & Edwards, J. E. The role of relaxation in systematic desensitization. *Behavior Research and Therapy,* 1967, **5**, 11–25.

Marcia, J. E., Rubin, B. M., & Efran, J. S. Systematic desensitization: Expectancy change or counterconditioning. *Journal of Abnormal Psychology,* 1969, **74**, 382–387.

Marshall, W. L., Strawbridge, H., & Keltner, A. The role of mental relaxation in experimental desensitization. *Behaviour Research and Therapy,* 1972, **10**, 355–366.

Mathews, A. M. Psychophysiological approaches to the investigation of desensitization and related procedures. *Psychological Bulletin,* 1971, **76**, 73–91.

McGlynn, F., & McDonell, R. Subjective ratings of credibility following brief exposure to desensitization and pseudotherapy. *Behaviour Research and Therapy,* 1974, **12**, 141–146.

Monroe, L. J. Psychological and physiological differences between good and poor sleepers. *Journal of Abnormal Psychology,* 1967, **72**, 255–264.

Nau, S. D., Caputo, J. A., & Borkovec, T. D. The relationship between credibility of therapy rationale and the reduction of simulated anxiety. *Journal of Behavior Therapy and Experimental Psychiatry,* 1974, **5**, 129–133.

Nawas, N. M., Mealiea, W. L., & Fishman, S. T. Systematic desensitization as counterconditioning: A retest with adequate controls. *Behavior Therapy,* 1971, **2**, 345–356.

Nawas, N. M., Welsch, W. V., & Fishman, S. T. The comparative effectiveness of pairing aversive imagery with relaxation, neutral tasks, and muscular tension in reducing snake phobia. *Behaviour Research and Therapy,* 1970, **8**, 63–68.

Nicolis, F. B., & Silvestri, L. C. Hypnotic activity of placebo in relation to severity of insomnia: A quantitative evaluation. *Clinical Pharmacology and Therapeutics,* 1967, **8**, 841–848.

O'Brien, G. T. The role of progressive relaxation in the systematic desensitization of analogue social anxiety. Unpublished master's thesis, University of Iowa, 1975.

Orne, M. T. Demand characteristics and their implications for real life: The importance of quasi-controls. Paper presented at the Symposium on Ethical and Methodological Problems in Social and Psychological Experiments at the meeting of the American Psychological Association, Chicago, September 1965.

Paul, G. L. *Insight vs. Desensitization in psychotherapy.* Stanford, Calif.: Stanford University Press, 1966.

Paul, G. L. Behavior modification research: Design and tactics. In C. M. Franks (Ed.), *Behavior therapy: Appraisal and status.* New York: McGraw-Hill, 1969. Pp. 29–62. (a)

Paul, G. L. Physiological effects of relaxation training and hypnotic suggestion. *Journal of Abnormal Psychology,* 1969, **74**, 425–437. (b)

Persely, G., & Leventhal, D. B. The effects of therapeutically oriented instructions and of the pairing of anxiety imagery and relaxation in systematic desenitization. *Behavior Therapy,* 1972, **3**, 417–424.

Rachman, S. Studies in desensitization. I. The separate effects of relaxation and desensitization. *Behaviour Research and Therapy,* 1965, **3**, 245–252.

Rosenthal, D., & Frank, J. D. Psychotherapy and the placebo effect. *Psychological Bulletin*, 1956, 53, 294–302.

Shapiro, A. K. Placebo effects in medicine, psychotherapy, and psychoanalysis. In A. E. Bergin & S. L. Garfield (Eds.), *Handbook of psychotherapy and behavior change*. New York: Wiley, 1971. Pp. 439–473.

Singerman, K., Borkovec, T. D., & Baron, R. S. Failure of a "misattribution therapy" manipulation with a clinically relevant target behavior. *Behavior Therapy*, 1976, 7, 306–313.

Smith, R. E., Diener, E., & Beaman, A. Demand characteristics and the behavioral avoidance measures of fear in behavior therapy analogue research. *Behavior Therapy*, 1974, 5, 172–182.

Steinmark, S. W., & Borkovec, T. D. Active and placebo treatment effects on moderate insomnia under counterdemand and positive demand instructions. *Journal of Abnormal Psychology*, 1974, 83, 157–163.

Sue, D. The role of relaxation in systematic desensitization. *Behaviour Research and Therapy*, 1972, 10, 153–158.

Vodde, T. W., & Gilner, F. H. The effects of exposure to fear stimuli on fear reduction. *Behaviour Research and Therapy*, 1971, 9, 169–175.

Waters, W. F., McDonald, D. G., & Koresko, R. L. Psychophysiological responses during analogue systematic desensitization and nonrelaxation control procedures. *Behavior Research and Therapy*, 1972, 10, 381–393.

Wilkins, W. Desensitization: Social and cognitive factors underlying the effectiveness of Wolpe's procedure. *Psychological Bulletin*, 1971, 76, 311–317.

Wilkins, W. Expectancy of therapeutic gain: An empirical and conceptual critique. *Journal of Consulting and Clinical Psychology*, 1973, 40, 69–77.

Wilson, G. T., & Davison, G. C. Process of fear reduction in systematic desensitization: Animal studies. *Psychological Bulletin*, 1971, 76, 1–14.

Wolpe, J. *Psychotherapy by reciprocal inhibition*. Stanford, Calif.: Stanford University Press, 1958.

Wolpin, M., & Raines, J. Visual imagery, expected roles, and extinction as possible factors in reducing fear and avoidance behavior. *Behaviour Research and Therapy*, 1966, 4, 25–37.

BEHAVIOR MODIFICATION WITH LEARNING DISABILITIES AND RELATED PROBLEMS

BENJAMIN B. LAHEY

Department of Psychology
University of Georgia
Athens, Georgia

I. DEFINITION OF LEARNING DISABILITIES

There has been a rapid growth of interest in recent years in the diagnostic category of *learning disabilities*. Newly available federal funding for public school systems has resulted in the wide-spread proliferation of special programs for children with such problems and of teacher-training programs in universities. While learning disabilities programs are nearly universal in public schools in the United States today, there were no such programs prior to 1960 (McCarthy & McCarthy, 1969). Concurrently, there has been a marked increase in research on this topic during the past 10 years. But, while the subject of learning disabilities has only recently attracted the attention of the general public and of a wide spectrum of researchers, it has long been a topic for speculation among a small group of educators, physicians, and psychologists. Interest in this topic is often traced to a paper presented to the American Medical Association by Orton (1937). He described a 16-year-old boy who was of normal intelligence, had no sensory deficits or obvious signs of neurological impairment, did not seem to be emotionally disturbed, but yet was not able to read whole words. Orton coined the term *strephosymbolia,* meaning "twisted symbols," to refer to this condition because of the child's tendency to reverse letters and sequences of letters when reading.

Currently, a child with the condition just described would be diagnosed as learning disabled. The National Advisory Committee on Handicapped Children has adopted the following definition:

Children with special learning disabilities exhibit a disorder in one or more of the basic psychological processes involved in understanding or in using spoken or written languages. These may be manifested in disorders of listening, thinking, talking, reading, writing, spelling, or arithmetic. They include conditions which have been referred to as perceptual handicaps, brain injury, minimal brain dysfunction, dyslexia, developmental aphasia, etc. They do not include learning problems which are due primarily to visual, hearing, or motor handicaps, to mental retardation, and emotional disturbance, or to environmental disadvantage. [National Advisory Committee on Handicapped Children, 1968]

A. Administrative and Diagnostic Use of Definition

In practice, this means that children are diagnosed as learning disabled if they have serious deficits in one or more academic areas, average IQ scores (usually 90 or above), no serious uncorrected sensory deficits, are not from economically deprived homes, and do not show marked amounts of deviant behavior. Recently, however, these guidelines have been broadened through usage to include children with IQ scores below 90 whose achievement is below the expectation for that IQ and age (such as a 10-year-old boy with an IQ of 75 who cannot read at all), disadvantaged children whose problems are primarily "linguistic" or "perceptual," and children with motor handicaps that do not interfere with school performance (Gearheart, 1973).

This diagnostic definition serves two purposes. *First,* school systems usually adopt definitions very similar to the one stated above for *administrative* purposes. The definition serves as a guideline for assigning children to special classes or programs for which federal reinbursement can be sought. *Second,* many clinicians also use this definition as the guideline for *differential diagnosis* in the medical model sense. Many professionals use the term learning disabilities to refer to a unitary psychological or psychophysiological syndrome, and therefore use differential diagnosis as a prelude to choice of treatment. Widely differing viewpoints exist, however, as to the nature of this syndrome (Gearheart, 1973). More will be said on this point later in the chapter.

B. Characteristics of the Learning Disabled Population

Although the category learning disabilities is apparently narrowly defined, the children who are assigned to it are extremely heterogeneous in their behavioral characteristics. However, there are few data upon which to base a description of such children. Perhaps the most useful information comes from a major survey conducted by Meier (1971). The teachers of 284 traditionally diagnosed learning disabled children were given a behavioral checklist describing 80 characteristics that were thought to differentiate learning disabled from normal children. These children were drawn from a cross-section of school systems in eight Rocky Mountain states. Table I lists the characteristics checked by at least one-third of the teachers of learning disabled children. The heterogeneity of this group can be seen both in the variety of behaviors that are ascribed to the children and in the fact that only a few behaviors come close to being checked by all of the teachers. Most of the characteristics were checked for only from two-thirds to one-half of the group.

Before data such as these can be seriously considered, however, a great deal of additional information will be needed. Studies similar to Meier (1971), for example, will need to be conducted in which more than one independent observer rates each child to assess inter-observer reliability. In addition, information on validity is needed. This could be obtained by comparing the ratings of both normal and learning disabled children to see if they in fact are rated differently on these behaviors. In addition, direct observations of the frequency of selected behaviors will need to be done for children who are rated

TABLE 1

Descriptions of Behavior Most Frequently Checked by Teachers for Second-Grade Children Meeting Diagnostic Guidelines for Learning Disabilities[a]

Description of behavior	Percentage of children for whom description checked	Description of behavior	Percentage of children for whom description checked
1. Substitutes words which distort meaning ("when" for "where")	70	16. Reverses and/or rotates letters, numbers or words (writes "p" for "q," "saw" for "was," "2" for "7," "16" for "91") far more frequently than peers	52
2. Reads silently or aloud far more slowly than peers (word by word while reading aloud)	68	17. Seems very bright in many ways but still does poorly in school	50
3. Unusually short attention span for daily work	67	18. Points at words while reading silently or aloud.	49
4. Easily distracted from school work (can't concentrate with even the slightest disturbances from other students moving around or talking quietly)	66	19. Reverses and/or rotates letters and numbers (reads "b" for "d," "u" for "n," "6" for "9") far more than most peers	47
5. Can't follow written directions, which most peers can follow, when read orally or silently	65	20. Difficulty with arithmetic (e.g., can't determine what number follows 8 or 16; may begin to add in the middle of a subtraction problem)	46
6. Does very poorly in written spelling tests compared with peers.	64		

#	Item	Score
7.	Can't sound out or "unlock" words	64
8.	Reading ability at least .75 of a year below most peers	63
9.	Has trouble telling time	62
10.	Doesn't seem to listen to daily classroom instructions or directions (often asks to have them repeated, whereas rest of class goes ahead)	61
11.	Is slow to finish work (doesn't apply self, daydreams a lot, falls asleep in school)	56
12.	Repeats the same behavior over and over	56
13.	Has trouble organizing written work (seems scatterbrained, confused)	56
14.	Can't correctly recall oral directions (e.g., item 10 above) when asked to repeat them	54
15.	Poor handwriting compared with peers' writing	52
21.	Poor drawing of crossing, wavy lines compared with peers' drawing	46
22.	Omits words while reading grade-level material aloud (omits more than one out of every ten)	44
23.	Poor drawing of a man compared with peers drawing	43
24.	Can read orally but does not comprehend the meaning or written grade-level words (word-caller)	43
25.	Excessive inconsistency in quality of performance from day to day or even hour to hour	43
26.	Seems quite immature (doesn't act his/her age)	43
27.	Unable to learn the sounds of letters (can't associate proper phoneme with its grapheme)	43
28.	Avoids work calling for concentrated visual attention	41
		39

(continued)

TABLE 1 (continued)

Description of behavior	Percentage of children for whom description checked	Description of behavior	Percentage of children for whom description checked
29. Mistakes own left from right (confuses left-hand side of paper)	39	33. Tense or disturbed (bites lip, needs to go to the bathroom often, twists hair, high strung)	36
30. Demands unusual amount of attention during regular classroom activities	39	34. Poor drawing of diamond compared with peer's drawing	36
31. Loses place more than once while reading aloud for more than a minute	38	35. Overactive (can't sit still in class-shakes or swings legs, fidgety)	34
32. Cannot apply the classroom or school regulations to own behavior, whereas peers can	37		

[a]Teachers rated 284 second-grade children diagnosed according to accepted criteria for learning disabilities. Children were selected from a total population of approximately 2400 second-grade children in the eight-state Rocky Mountain region from rural and urban areas. Only categories checked for more than one-third of the diagnosed learning disabled children were included from a list of 80 descriptions. Table based on Meier (1971).

as exhibiting or not exhibiting a given behavior. This will determine if the likelihood of checking the presence of a behavioral characteristic is systematically related to the frequency of its occurrence.

In addition, these ratings are simply needed on other populations from other parts of the country to control for the possibility that different school systems use significantly different selection criteria within the general guidelines for learning disabilities. In support of the validity of the descriptions provided by Meier (1971), however, is the fact that they are very consistent with traditional descriptions of the learning disabled child. These traditional descriptions have even made a point of emphasizing the heterogeneity of the population, stating that the learning disabled child may be overactive or underactive, he may have problems of visual perception or he may not, he may seem to be too concerned about his school work, or he may seem uninterested, etc.

Studies abound that compare learning disabled children on a variety of published and ad hoc tests of visual perception (such as the Frostig Developmental Test of Visual Perception and the Bender Visual-Motor Gestalt Test), gross motor coordination, auditory perception, and so on. Only two conclusions can be drawn from these studies, however: *First,* when it has been assessed, the reliability and validity of these measures has generally been shown to be low. *Second,* the inconsistent findings only confirm the view of this group as an extremely heterogenous population (Zach & Kaufman, 1972).

Another area in which opinions greatly outweigh data is the question of the incidence of learning disabilities. Unlike diagnostic categories such as retardation, which are restricted by definition to a specified proportion of the population, the learning disabilities category is relatively unrestricted. The number of children that are assigned to this category will depend on individual interpretation of the meaning of "normal intelligence," "significant deficits in academic areas," and decisions as to whether behavioral problems are a cause of academic deficits or a result of them. This problem is further complicated by the fact that many diagnosticians require the presence of special characteristics, such as high variability among the subtests of IQ test or problems of visual perception, before they will use the term learning disabilities. Estimates of incidence, therefore, are variable, ranging from 1 to 5%. Meier (1971), however, recently found that approximately 10% of the children in a large sample drawn from the Rocky Mountain area could be labeled as learning disabled in spite of the generally good school systems in that area.

This seems like an unrealistically high estimate, but the methodology of this part of the study seems to be rigorous and appropriate.

II. TRADITIONAL APPROACHES
TO LEARNING DISABILITIES

Learning disabled children are a paradox. They are "normal," but yet they have serious academic problems. Perhaps it is because these children do not fit in with the way the school systems traditionally categorized problem children—as either "retarded" or "emotionally disturbed"—that so little attention was paid to learning disabled children for such a long time. Inspite of, or perhaps because of, the absence of information on these children, theories as to why normal children should have such serious difficulties with school learning have been promulgated at a rapid rate. These theories generally fall into three categories, proposing that the underlying causes of learning problems stem from: (a) minor neurological impairments; (b) disorders of perceptual functioning; or (c) deficits in linguistic ability.

A. Brain Dysfunction Theories

Cruickshank (1967), Johnson and Myklebust (1967), Orton (1937), and Strauss and Lehtinen (1947) have variously suggested that learning disabilities stem from subclinical neurological impairments. They have suggested refinements in neurological assessment and have designed educational environments and procedures which are based on observations of patients with known brain damage. The model advanced by Strauss and Lehtinen (1947) and later developed by Cruickshank (1967) views learning disabilities as resulting from actual structural damage to the brain that is often too minor to be detected using current methods of neurological assessment. This damage is presumed to cause an impaired ability to focus on relevant stimuli while screening out irrelevant ones. As a result, the child who gives the impression of being inattentive is actually "overattentive" in that he is responding in rapid alternation to a variety of stimuli, most of which are extraneous. These extraneous stimuli include minor noises and movements that normal children would not even notice.

According to this theory, education can only be effective when competing stimuli are removed from the child's environment to the greatest extent possible. The prescription therefore is for a classroom without colors or decorations, soundproofed as much as possible, with partially opaqued windows, with individual cubicles for each child, and with a teacher who wears no distracting makeup or jewelry. In addition, because these theorists believe that the brain damage results in various problems of perception, special materials that emphasize combined visual, auditory, and tactile perception have been developed. However, virtually no data exist to show the degree of effectiveness of these programs.

Johnson and Myklebust (1967) and Orton (1937) view the cause of learning disabilities more in terms of disordered brain functions than damaged structures. Orton (1937) sees the fundamental problem to be one of improper cerebral dominance. When images of letters are stored in the dominant hemisphere, they are stored in reversed form in the nondominant hemisphere. The child with mixed dominance selects inconsistently from the hemispheres and thus is plagued by reversals in reading and handwriting. Orton's view is not very tenable in light of current theories of cerebral functioning, but yet it still influences thinking about learning disabled children today.

Johnson and Myklebust's (1967) approach is similar, except that they view the confusion as existing between the brain systems that control visual, auditory, and tactile perception. The educational recommendations of both Johnson and Myklebust (1967) and Orton (1937) are considerably less controversial than their theories, emphasizing structured practice in a phonics reading approach [as developed by Orton's colleagues Gillingham and Stillman (1965)], with recommendations to avoid reversible letters in beginning reading instruction and to use "multisensory" presentations of materials. Again, however, virtually no experimental tests of these methods have been conducted.

B. Perceptual and Perceptual-Motor Theories

Barsch (1967), Cratty (1969), Delacatto (1959), Fernald (1943), Frostig and Horne (1964), Getman and Kane (1964), and Kephart (1971) have suggested that disorders in a broadly conceived process of perception (in the Gestalt sense which treats perception as a virtual synonym for intelligence) underlie learning disabilities. Fernald (1943) and Frostig and Horne (1964) view disorders of perception as the primary causes of learning disabilities. Frostig emphasizes visual perception and has developed tests and training programs based on drawing abstract visual forms. Fernald (1943) sees the problem as involving the integration of visual, auditory, kinesthetic, and tactile perception. Based on this notion, she has developed procedures using textured cutout letters, drawing large blackboard letters, asking the child to pronounce words as he writes them, etc.

Barsch (1967), Cratty (1969), Delacatto (1959), Getman and Kane (1964), and Kephart (1971) have developed variants of this theory, viewing deficits of perceptual-motor integration as the primary cause of learning disabilities. Much like Piaget, they view early "sensorimotor" learning as the basis for later cognitive intelligence. Deficits in intellectual skills are seen as arising from inadequate sensorimotor experiences. Children who confuse and reverse letters, for example, did not properly learn the orientation of their own bodies in space. Based on this theory are educational prescriptions such as having children walk on balance beams in hopes of improving their reading skills.

Dalacatto's (1959) position is by far the most extreme. Although his basic theory is similar to those of other perceptual-motor theorists, his belief that children must often retrace their early motor development through such exercises as forced crawling as a means of locomotion ("patterning") has been widely criticized as potentially harmful and humiliating to the children. The efficacy of these programs will be discussed below.

C. Psycholinguistic Theories

Kirk and Kirk (1971) proposed a model of learning disabilities based on the Illinois Test of Psycholinguistic Ability (ITPA). This approach views learning disabilities as resulting from deficits in linguistic functioning (which are again defined in such a broad manner as to be almost synonymous with general intelligence). They have divided abilities into the three major categories of input, organization, and output. Emphasis is placed on identifying the specific problem areas of each child using the ITPA. Correspondingly, Kirk and Kirk (1971) have developed a series of excercises in which they attempt to train specific "linguistic processes." These exercises are quite varied depending on the "problem" at which they are aimed.

III. EFFECTIVENESS OF TRADITIONAL APPROACHES

Recent research, however, has questioned the effectiveness of these traditional approaches. Perceptual and perceptual-motor problems (confusing and reversing letters in letter sequences in reading and/or writing) are seen as particularly important diagnostic features by both the perceptual and brain dysfunction groups, as such problems are considered either to be "soft signs" of neurological impairment or symptoms of disorders of the global process of perception. For this reason, the bulk of research on the remediation of learning disabilities has focused on procedures which are designed to remediate basic processes of perception. Hammill (1972) recently reviewed the literature on "perceptual training" procedures:

Perceptual-motor training programs emanate from the overtly expressed or covertly implied assumption that perception (à la Frostig, Getman, Kephart, Barsch, etc.) can be developed or remediated. But this belief is by no means conclusively demonstrated by empirical research . . .

In fact, among 13 studies which employed at least 20 experimental subjects, control groups, and training for 15 or more weeks, 10 studies . . . reported no statistical differences between perceptually trained and nontrained subjects. Only three studies . . . found such training to be beneficial in developing perceptual processes, and in one of these . . . improvement was noted on one perceptual test and not another. [p. 556] . . . [Training] visual perceptual skills, using currently available programs, has no positive effect on reading and possibly none on visual perception. [p. 552]

Research published since this review generally confirms this conclusion, with one published study reporting significant improvement on tests of perceptual skills relative to a control group (Walsh & D'Angelo, 1971) and three studies reporting no significant improvement (Buckland & Balow, 1973; Church, 1974; Sabatino, Ysseldyke, & Woolston, 1973).

Goodman and Hammill (1973) have reviewed published studies on the effectiveness of the perceptual-motor training program of Kephart (1971) and Getman and Kane (1964). From among 42 published studies, 16 were selected as meeting minimal methodological criteria. In virtually all of these studies, no significant differences were found between treatment and control groups on measures of intellectual, academic, or even perceptual-motor skills.

Published studies on the effectiveness of psycholinguistic training methods based on the Illinois Test of Psycholinguistic Abilities (Kirk, McCarthy, & Kirk, 1968) and the Peabody Language Development Kit (Dunn & Smith, 1966) are no more encouraging. Hammill and Larsen (1974) reviewed 38 studies on this topic and found that the results generally did not support the utility of the training programs. Interpretation of these studies is next to impossible in any case, as the majority of them used the Illinois Test of Psycholinguistic Abilities as their sole dependent measure.

The consistent lack of evidence on effectiveness of these traditional training programs is not at all surprising when they are evaluated according to basic principles of learning. Individually, and as a group, these methods violate virtually everything that is known about the way behavior changes. They require children to practice drawing abstract visual forms, perform calisthenics, repeat sentences, and the like, in the absence of systematic feedback or reinforcement, and expect to find improvement in reading skills as a result. The fact that these training programs are extensively used in the United States in spite of glaring inadequacies of design and evaluative research is surprising only to those who still expect the world to be rational.

IV. SIGNIFICANCE OF SIGNS OF NEUROLOGICAL DYSFUNCTION

There has been a noticeable lack of evaluative research on educational approaches that consider learning disabilities to be a result of minor neurological impairment. This seems to be due to many factors, particularly the fact that educational recommendations of this group have not been translated into commercially marketed programs and have not, therefore, been adopted widely. Considerable research has been done, however, on the relationship between signs of minor neurological impairment and learning problems. This evidence, of course, bears directly on the adequacy of the brain dysfunction model. In general, these studies do not support the notion that learning disabilities result from minor neurological abnormalities.

Most studies have focused on the significance of abnormalities in electroencephalograph (EEG) recordings, apparently the most widely used procedure in the medical diagnosis of "minimal brain dysfunction." The correlation of EEG abnormalities and learning disabilities, or in fact behavior problems of any sort, is extremely low. Freeman (1967) has reported that estimates of the frequency of abnormal EEG recordings in the normal population range from 10 to 20%. In comparison, estimates of the frequency of EEG abnormalities in diagnosed learning disabled children range from 19% (Hughes & Parks, 1968) to 50% (Hughes, 1968). These data suggest three things, none of which represents a substantial conclusion: *First,* the definition of what constitutes an "abnormal" EEG record is apparently quite difficult. *Second,* learning disabled children may or may not have a higher frequency of abnormal EEG records. And *third,* if they do, many learning disabled children, if not most, have normal EEG recordings. This suggests a very weak relationship. In fact, Freeman (1967) has reported that correlations between EEG abnormalities and known neurological disorders are far from perfect. When strict criteria for interpretation of abnormalities of the EEG are used, approximately 45% of patients with known seizure disorders such as neoplasms and mechanical brain injury show normal EEG records. Children with severely abnormal EEG records are apparently more likely to show behavior and learning problems than children with normal EEG records, but even those with grossly abnormal records show the full range of variation of behavior from complete normalcy to total incapacitation (Freeman, 1967). In a review of the literature, Grossman (1966) concluded: "Thus far, there does not seem to be any specific electroencephalographic abnormality that correlates with any specific abberation in learning" (p. 64). Similarly, several investigators have concluded that little diagnostic emphasis should be placed on the EEG in the absence of supporting evidence of neurological dysfunction (Freeman, 1967; Paine, 1965; Schwalb, Blau, & Blau, 1969).

The relationship between neurological evaluations by physicians and patient histories of neurological insults, however, does not seem to be any better. Paine, Werry, and Quay (1968) found no significant correlation between EEG measures, neurological examinations by physicians, behavior ratings, intellectual testing, or patient history using factor analytic techniques. Perhaps the most informative study on this topic was conducted by Edwards, Alley, and Snider (1971). Using large groups of normal readers and children diagnosed as learning disabled, they found that there was no significant relationship among academic achievement, patient history, neurological examination by pediatricians, and performance on the Bender Visual-Motor Gestalt Test (often used to obtain "soft signs" of neurological impairment), or among any combination of the above.

Taken together, these studies indicate that there is very weak evidence for a neurological etiology of learning disabilities. It may be that a slightly greater proportion of children diagnosed as learning disabled have signs of minor neurological impairment, but this does not tell us whether these factors play a causative role in some children, nor does it give us any information regarding methods of treatment.

V. BEHAVIORAL APPROACHES

Compared to the perceptual, psycholinguistic, and brain dysfunction approaches, the behavioral approach to teaching learning disabled children has had relatively little impact in the public schools. This is perhaps due in part to a relative lack of research evaluating the effectiveness of behavioral techniques. The body of literature that does exist is very promising, but it is not extensive and has many gaps and weaknesses. The relative lack of impact of this approach is probably also due, however, to the fact that it has not been commercially marketed to teachers specializing in learning disabilities. Current research will be divided in this section into two types: (a) evaluations of full-scale reading programs that are based on behavior principles; (b) studies that have applied behavioral interventions to specific behavior problems of learning disabled children.

A. Behavioral Reading Programs

Wadsworth (1971) developed and evaluated a reading program that was used in a public school system. Ten third-grade boys (from middle-class suburban families) who had been diagnosed as learning disabled by a school psychologist served as subjects. They had been previously observed and tested while they were receiving traditional treatments for learning disabilities. For a 3-month period at the end of the second grade, a learning disabilities teacher consulted with their regular classroom teacher on teaching strategies. During the summer following the second grade, the children attended a reading clinic for 3 months. Test data gathered during these two treatments were used as the baseline phase of an AB experimental design. During the 9 months of the third-grade year, the children were first assigned to a self-contained classroom in which the behavioral reading program was implemented for 4 months, and were then gradually faded back into the regular classroom for increasing proportions of the school day.

General classroom organization included a posted list of class-room rules. Infractions of these rules were generally ignored, with major infractions resulting in brief periods of time-out. Compliance with rules was regularly reinforced with points. Points earned for good general classroom behavior and academic performance could be exchanged for a variety of tangible reinforcers. The academic program emphasized student responding on spelling, handwriting and reading worksheets, and individual work with the teacher on phonics and oral reading. Points were given contingent on correct performance during the tutoring sessions and for completion of pages in the workbooks. After 4 months of this type of program, the children were gradually reintegrated into regular classes. No points were given for behavior in the regular classrooms, but the children continued to spend some part of the day in the reinforcement program of the self-contained learning disabilities room. By January of the third-grade year, however, the children were spending only 80 min per day in the learning disabilities room. By the end of March, they all spent their entire day in their regular classrooms.

Figure 1 shows the results of this teaching program as measured by the Slossan Oral Reading Test. Data are presented on the achievement of the ten children in each phase of the experiment, their expected achievement as calculated from their previous performance, and the grade norms for children of their age. As can be seen, there was slight but nonsignificant improvement in reading achievement during the consultant and reading clinic stages, with large and statistically significant changes following the two stages of the treatment phase. During the treatment phase, the children rapidly approached grade level norms. Inspection of the data for individual subjects showed that nine of ten subjects exceeded their expected achievement level. Marked improvements in rated problem behaviors were also reported for all children.

In comparison to the effectiveness of traditional intervention programs in bringing learning disabled children up towards grade level in reading, these results are extremely encouraging. There are, however, many methodological problems with this experiment. *First,* it would be very helpful to have more information about the program itself. Information on the type of workbooks and on the specific nature of the contingencies and reinforcers would also be desirable. *Second,* the AB design used in this experiment is a very weak test of the effectiveness of the reading program. The extended baseline does give some information on the possibility of spurious test-retest improvement and other time-related confounds, but the experiment would have been greatly improved had it used better

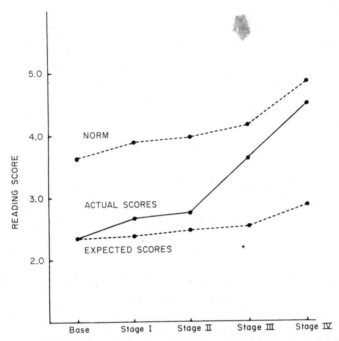

Fig. 1. *Performance of ten learning disabled boys on the Slossan Oral Reading Test during two baseline and three treatment phases. [From Wadsworth(1971).]*

within- or between-subjects control procedures and better measures of reading. Most desirable in this case would be a control group that was either untreated or received a traditional treatment program. The fact that there was very little improvement from one test administration to the next during the baseline administrations, however, makes a tentative conclusion that the behavioral program was in fact responsible for the large increases in test performance more tenable. This particularly true in view of the fact that several other studies that are similar in nature and design confirm these findings.

Haring and Hauck (1969) tested a behavioral reading program using four third- through sixth-grade learning disabled boys who were described as "severely disabled in reading." Three of the four children in this experiment could read only at the primer level. This means essentially that they could not read at all, in spite of the fact that they were in the third through fifth grades. Both the design and procedures of this experiment are similar to that of Wadsworth (1971). The primary difference is that the contingencies were much more precisely controlled in this procedure. The children were given points that could be exchanged for material reinforcers contingent on correct answers to specific items in a programmed reading text (Sullivan Programmed Reading Books). Their procedure was notable too in that it gradually brought the children from continuous reinforcement to a thin variable ratio schedule and then transfered the reinforcement contingencies to reading behavior from standard basal reading texts. The children were seated in a "language lab"–type situation in which the teacher could frequnetly communicate directly with the students through a microphone.

The results of this experiment showed that the four children showed improvement in reading achievement of from 1.5 to 4 years during the 5 months of the instructional program. At the end of the experiment, two of the children were reading at grade level in the programmed materials, while the other two were within 1 year of grade level. Again, while this experiment is subject to criticisms because of its weak design, limited academic measures, and small number of subjects, the results are encouraging.

Similar results were reported by Nolen, Kunzelmann, and Haring (1967) using older children. Ryback and Staats (1970) also had similar success in an AB design using parents of three learning disabled and one mildly retarded children as tutors. However, it is difficult to determine how many of the subjects used by Nolen and associates would be diagnosed as learning disabled according to current standards.

McKenzie, Clark, Wolf, Kothera, and Benson (1968) developed and tested a similar token reinforcement program using a well-defined group of learning disabled children. They found increases in the amount of attending to reading and arithmetic tasks but did not report substantial data on achievement.

B. Modification of Specific Academic Behaviors in Learning Disabled Children

Novy, Burnett, Powers, and Sulzer-Azaroff (1973) studied a 9-year-old male who had been diagnosed as learning disabled and described as distractable, hyperactive, and having poor study habits. After observing the child, a program was developed to increase the amount of time that he spent attending to school work. The study was conducted in the child's regular learning disabilities classroom, where observers could watch the child from behind a one-way mirror. During baseline observations, it was found that the child spent a high proportion of the time looking away from his work, walking around the room, and talking to other children, while he spent very little time attending to his work. The child was informed of a contingency in which he would be given a signal from a small light every time he had attended appropriately to his work for a full 5-min interval. One point was assigned to the child each instance the light went on, which could be exchanged later for inexpensive toys or free time to play with a tape recorder or padded chairs on rollers. In addition, the children in the class were also verbally praised when they met the criteria for reinforcement. Otherwise, the classroom continued as usual during all phases of the experiment.

The effects of this contingency were examined using an ABA design. Results are presented at Fig. 2. During the baseline phase, the child attended to his work in an average of 60% of the thirty minute observation. During reinforcement, his attending averaged 88% of the intervals. During the second baseline, his rate of attention dropped to an average of 67%.

Similar results were found in a large-scale study by Wagner and Guyer (1971). They implemented a token reinforcement procedure in nine classes of 11 to 12 learning disabled students each. Tokens

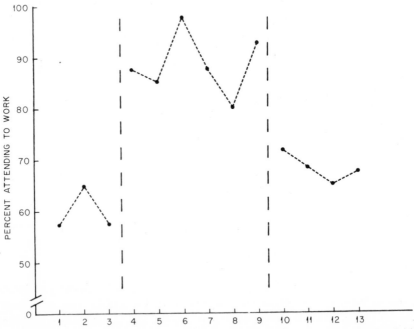

Fig. 2. Percent of intervals in which the child was attending to his work during an initial baseline phase, treatment, and second baseline. [From Novy et al. (1973).]

that could be exchanged for material backup reinforcers were given contingent on 15-min periods of consistent attending. The results showed marked increases in attending and decreases in rated behavior problems. Both of these recent studies confirm the results of an earlier investigation by Allen, Henke, Harris, Baer, and Reynolds (1967). Taken together, these three studies provide strong evidence that attending behavior can be controlled in learning disabled children using operant techniques. Furthermore, the behavior changes produced in these children differed in no significant way from those produced using similar techniques in children who have been given other traditional diagnostic labels.

In a recent study by Lahey, Busemeyer, and Dotts (1975), the "perceptual-motor" problems of two learning disabled children were analyzed and modified. Subjects were two second-grade children who made a high frequency of errors of orientation and sequence in their handwriting. The majority of their written words, in fact, were mirror images of the correct word. This behavior was studied using a multiple baseline across subjects design. During each session, the children were asked to copy their first name five times and also five simple words and five geometric forms that were similar to the forms used on standard tests of perceptual-motor functioning. The experiment was conducted each day during tutoring sessions that lasted a total of 30 to 60 min. During the treatment phase, the children were told "right" and given a token after each correct response, or were told "wrong" and given corrective feedback after each incorrect response. Corrective feedback consisted of a brief explanation of why the response was incorrect and shown an illustration of the correct response on a separate sheet of paper. Tokens were exchanged at the end of the daily sessions for pennies, at the rate of three tokens per penny. The contingency was applied to all three responses in the same way. Occasionally, during the baseline and treatment phases, probe trials were interspersed in which the children were asked to copy five words and five new geometric figures of a form similar to the original stimuli in addition to copying their first name five times. No consequences of any type were given during the probe trials, as they were being used as a test of generalization of the reinforced responses. Figure 3 shows handwriting samples taken from subject A during the last baseline session and the eighth treatment session. The stimuli that were presented to the subjects are shown on the left. Results of the experiment are shown in Fig. 4. When the contingency was introduced, the frequency of correct handwriting responses rapidly increased. Similarly, there were marked changes in

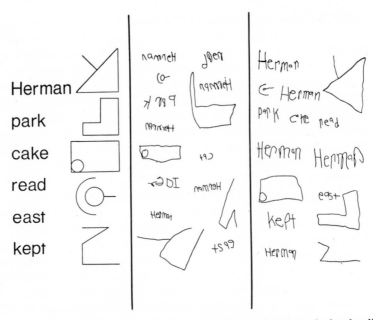

Fig. 3. *Handwriting samples from a learning disabled boy taken from the last baseline and eighth treatment session. Stimuli presented to the child are shown on the left.*

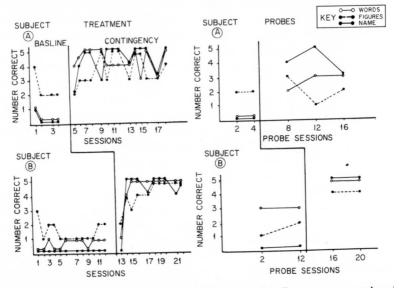

Fig. 4. *Frequency of correct handwriting responses during baseline, treatment, and probe trials for two learning disabled children who made a high frequency of errors of sequence and orientation in their handwriting.*

the number of correct responses from baseline to treatment on the probe trials, indicating a useful degree of generalization of the behavior change. The exception to these results was found with geometric forms. Because of a lack of corelation between baseline performance on geometric figures and writing actual words or names, no change can be seen for subject A when the contingency was introduced. A similar finding was reported by Lahey *et al.* (1975) for the disadvantaged child with "perceptual" problems. It is interesting that the one "maverick" behavior in this set is the behavior that was chosen by traditional perceptual theorists to appear on standard tests of perceptual-motor functioning.

The behavior problem of "mirror writing" was chosen for this study partly because it is a problem that appears to create academic difficulties for many children, but mostly because of the central role that perceptual-motor problems have played in the brain damage and perceptual theories of learning disabilities. As above, however, the importance of these results derives more from the fact that children who have been labeled learning disabled respond to reinforcement procedures in much the same way as do other children than from the fact that this particular behavior can be effectively modified.

Drass and Jones (1971) provide additional information that operant techniques can be used to teach specific skills to learning disabled children. In their study, learning disabled children of elementary and junior high school age were taught to use praise and material reinforcers in a one-to-one tutorial framework to teach other well-defined learning disabled children to engage in fewer off-task activities, to initiate and complete assignments more rapidly, and to identify letters more acurately. The study employed an AB design, but consistant findings following stable baselines were found for all behaviors. The tutors were reinforced by teachers for their teaching performance using praise and material backups.

C. Reinforcement of Terminal Behaviors

Perhaps the most provocative data that we now have on learning disabled children appeared in a recent study by Ayllon, Layman, and Kandel (1975). Three learning disabled children of elementary school age who were referred to as "hyperactive" served as subjects. The activity level of these children was controlled by a previously prescribed dosage of methylphenidate (Ritalin). The children were observed in their regular learning disabilities classroom, with data being recorded on activity levels and performance with reading and mathematics workbooks. Following a baseline phase in which activity level and academic performance were both at extremely low levels, medication was discontinued. All three children showed rapid and marked increases in activity, with no corresponding change in academic performance. After 3 days, a reinforcement contingency was introduced for correct responses in the mathematics workbook. The children were given one check mark on an index card carried by the teacher for each correct response in the workbook. Later in the day, the check marks could be exchanged for a variety of material and free-time backup reinforcers. Immediately after the initiation of this contingency, the amount of activity returned to medication levels during the math period but stayed at the high postmedication levels during the reading period. At the same time, the percentage of correct responses in the math workbook rose markedly during the reinforcement-of-mathematics response phase, while academic performance stayed at the low baseline levels during the reading period. After 9 days, the contingency was also introduced during the reading period, at which time academic performance rose sharply while activity levels fell to the baseline medication range.

These data are exciting for several reasons. *First,* as the authors point out, extreme degrees of activity can be effectively controlled in the classroom without the use of medication. *Second,* whereas medication controls activity without resulting in corresponding increases in academic performance, the method reported in this study produces beneficial effects in both areas. The results of this study have another implication that is perhaps more important to the broader field of learning disabilities. By reinforcing the terminal behavior in a complex sequence (the correct solution to problems in workbooks), other behaviors that are prerequisite to correct responding were also modified (sitting down, attending to the task, etc.). This finding offers a possible explanation for the success of the studies by Haring and Hauck (1969) and Wadsworth (1971), which rely primarily on the reinforcement of terminal academic responses. Apparently, they were able to treat the heterogeneous population of learning disabled children without dealing with their specific problems of perception, activity, and attending because these behaviors were indirectly modified when reinforcement was made contingent on the final behavior in the sequence (academic responses in the workbooks). This suggests a radically different conceptualization and approach to the remediation of learning disabilities. Results of Ayllon et al. (1975) were confirmed by similar studies using extremely disruptive normal children (Ayllon, Layman, & Burke, 1972; Ayllon & Roberts, 1974). Instead of using complex, individually prescribed treatment procedures, it may be possible to deal with the majority of problems that learning disabled children have by simply using good programmed textbooks with reinforcement for accurate responding. Should this not be effective with certain individuals, however, the literature described above strongly suggests that any behavior problem a learning disabled child might have would be amenable to behavior modification.

VI. RESEARCH ON OTHER CATEGORIES OF CHILDREN WITH ACADEMIC PROBLEMS

Because children who are classified as learning disabled appear to react to behavioral techniques the same way as do other children, the use of such programs might be extended to other populations of children with academic problems. Approaches that rely on programmed instruction, good classroom management procedures, and/ or reinforcement of academic behaviors have been shown to be effective with children who have been classified as retarded (Birnbrauer, Wolf, Kidder, & Tague, 1965; Brown & Perlmutter, 1971), emotionally disturbed (Drabman, Spitalnik, & O'Leary, 1973), or disadvantaged and underachieving children (Chadwick & Day, 1971; Miller & Schneider, 1970; Sulzer, Hunt, Ashby, Koniarski, & Krams, 1971; Wolf, Giles, & Hall, 1968) and as normal children (Harris & Sherman, 1972; Harris, Sherman, Henderson, & Harris, 1973; Winett, Richards, Krasner, & Krasner, 1971).

In addition, operant techniques have been used to modify a wide variety of specific academic problems, including reading rate (Whitlock & Bushell, 1967), reading comprehension (Lahey, McNees, & Brown, 1973a), basic arithmetic (Greenwood, Sloane, & Baskian, 1974; Johnson & Bailey, 1974), sight word vocabulary (Corey & Shamow, 1972; Lahey & Drabman, 1974), oral reading in deaf children (Wilson & McReynolds, 1973), phonic skills (Lahey, Weller, & Brown, 1973b), beginning handwriting instruction (Lahey et al., 1975), and spelling (Hopkins, Shutte, & Garton, 1971; Lovitt, Guppy, & Battner, 1969).

Studies by Lahey, McNees, and Brown (1973a) and Johnson and Bailey (1974) exemplify this literature. Lahey et al. (1973a) examined problems of reading for comprehension. The subjects were two sixth-grade black children from low-income families, one male and one female. They both showed a reading problem that is very common among children with deficits in school achievement. Their oral reading of connected prose passages was extremely good, but they did not accurately answer questions about the material they had just read. In the language of the schools, they decoded well from visual stimuli to sounds, but they did not "comprehend" what they read.

If reading is conceptualized as a composite of many. different skills, rather than as a single global skill, this is not a surprising finding. It does not seem unlikely that variations in reading instruction and other conditions could produce varying degrees of proficiency in different reading skills. It seems likely that teachers might emphasize the obvious skill of oral reading and neglect reading for comprehension. In any case, these children are quite numerous and present an enigma to their teachers. Although they appear to "read" quite well (orally), they have great difficulty with school subjects that require reading (for comprehension).

The subjects were selected on the basis of the discrepancy in grade levels between their oral reading (both at the 6–5 level) and reading for comprehension (both at the 4–5 level). Both subjects received poor grades but were placed in normal classes. They were seen together three times a week in a tutoring situation.

During baseline, the children alternated reading brief passages aloud and then answering factual questions about them. For example, a subject might be asked to read the following passage: "The dog chased the cat up a tree. The cat ran as fast as it could." After reading the passage, the subject would be asked, "The dog chased the cat up the what?" An answer of "tree," or a close synonym, was considered as correct. No feedback of any kind was given following the questions during baseline.

During the first treatment phase, the children were told "right" and were given a penny following each correct answer. Nothing was said or given following incorrect answers. Subsequent to this phase, a second baseline was carried out with conditions identical to the first baseline, followed by a second treatment phase.

The results of this study are shown in Fig. 5. During baseline the two subjects answered 65–85% of the questions correctly. When the contingency was introduced, accuracy rose immediately to 80–100%, with the last five sessions at or above 90% accuracy. The percentage of correct responses fell during the second baseline but rose again during the second treatment phase.

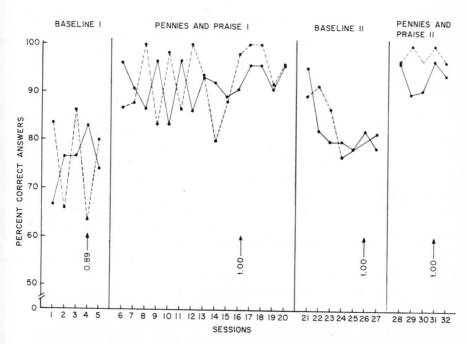

Fig. 5. Percent of correct answers to questions about previously read material by two children whose oral reading was on grade level but whose comprehension was 2 years below grade level. [From Lahey et al. (1973a).]

These data suggest a strong effect of reinforcement on a "complex" intellectual/academic behavior. In comparison with two children whose oral reading and reading for comprehension are both at grade level, the two experimental subjects answered questions at essentially grade level as soon as reinforcement was introduced. However, these results cannot be translated directly into clinical application at this time. Of particular concern is the rapid decrement in performance when reinforcement is discontinued. Research on methods of "fading" children from the contingency or on contingencies that will result in less rapid extinction will be needed.

A study by Johnson and Bailey (1974) on cross-age tutoring illustrates another dimension of this type of research. In this investigation, kindergarten children who were not proficient in preacademic skills were taught a variety of counting and number recognition skills by trained fifth-grade tutors.

The tutors were selected from the top 15% of their class in academic performance on the basis of their teacher's ratings on dependability. The kindergarten children were selected on the basis of their lack of number skills. The tutors were trained in teaching procedures and the use of social reinforcement during three 30-min sessions. Both verbal instruction and role playing were used in training the tutors.

The one-to-one tutoring sessions were held daily for $7\frac{1}{2}$ weeks. The sessions were 20 min in length, followed by a 10-min activity period. The activity period was contingent on appropriate social behavior of the kindergarten student but not on academic behavior.

Prior to tutoring, the five experimental subjects and five matched control subjects answered a mean of 26% questions on an informal test of number naming and counting. On tests given at 2-week intervals the experimental subjects scored 48% and 57% correct; they scored 66% correct on the final posttest. In comparison, the matched control subjects scored 28%, 31%, and 38% on the two midtests and posttest, respectively.

These data again show strong control over learning produced by academic instruction and reinforcement aimed directly at the target behavior. These procedures seem directly applicable to the classroom, both in their effectiveness and savings in time and effort for the teacher. This and many other investigations attest to the modifiability of academic behaviors.

A. Reinforcement of Work in Programmed Texts

A study with normal children by Holt (1971) deserves special attention because of its practical importance. It provides guidelines for the effective use of reinforcement with programmed materials and teaching machines. The subjects were 21 normal, average first-grade male and female children. This study was conducted during their reading and mathematics periods. The Sullivan Programmed Reading Books, Series I and II (published by McGraw-Hill), which are composed of a total of fourteen texts, were used as the reading material. The first seven books of the series are equivalent to an average first-grade program, with Books 8 to 14 being equivalent to an average second-grade reading program. The books contain programmed reading instruction that is designed in a linear format. The mathematics materials were produced by McGraw-Hill and were presented on the Min-Max III teaching machine marketed by Grolier Company. The contents of this program included introduction to numbers, addition, subtraction, and multiplication and division.

Following baseline phases in both classes, the children were placed on a schedule in which they could engage in 5 min of free time with a variety of attractive toys and activities after completing a fixed number of pages in the reading book or a fixed number of frames in the mathematics program. After finishing the assigned amount of work, the children were allowed to enter the reinforcement area and a timer was set for 5 min. At their choice, the children could also continue to work on their academic materials and skip any given reinforcement period. Initially, ten pages of reading materials were required to obtain 5 min of free-time activity, with the requirements being gradually increased to 40 pages. Following the reinforcement period, a second baseline was conducted during which no access to the reinforcement area was allowed, after which the 40 page requirement was reinstituted. The results for the reading class are shown in Fig. 6. Introduction of the reinforcement contingency resulted in an extremely high rate of responding. Due to the design of the experiment, it is not possible to separate the effects of reinforcement from the effects of changing the response requirement, but the over-all package was clearly successful in increasing the amount of work in the programmed text. The results for the mathematics program were very similar.

It is important to note that the contingency in this experiment was not placed on correct responses, but only on completing a specified number of pages. The results of this use of programmed materials, as measured by achievement tests, however, suggests that the program was very successful even when designed in this manner. Should the teacher note that the contingency is generating increases in the amount of responding with the deterioration of accuracy, the program could be modified with additional effort to place the contingency on correct responses.

The results of this study are extremely impressive. Due to the high rate of responding, the children finished all of the programmed reading text for the first and second grades in 7 weeks of instruction, with 8 hr per week devoted to reading, including baseline. At the end of 7 weeks, the median grade placement on the California Achievement Test was 2.5 years, with subtest scores of 3.0 years on comprehension and 2.25 years on vocabulary. Inspection of the instructional materials showed that 95% of the children performed at the 80% level of accuracy throughout the program. This study provides useful information on the programmed reading materials and gives further indication of the effectiveness of combining reinforcement with programmed instruction.

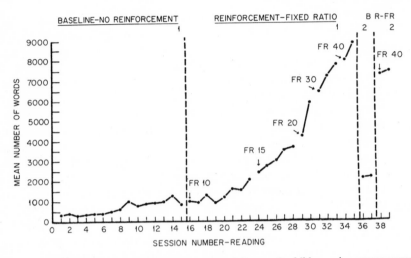

Fig. 6. Number of words read per session by normal first-grade children using a programmed text during baseline and reinforcement conditions. [From Holt (1971).]

B. Project Follow Through

The best data currently available on the effectiveness of behavioral approaches in the education of children who are difficult to teach comes from the large-scale federally sponsored "Follow Through" project. This project has enabled a variety of investigators to develop model educational programs for children who meet the federal guidelines for poverty (kindergarten through the third grade). The investigators were intentionally chosen to cover a wide range of theoretical orientations from Piagetian to behavioral. According to a recent interim evaluation (Cline, 1974), only the two behavioral models have shown significant promise for the education of disadvantaged children. These were developed by Don Bushell, at the University of Kansas, and Sigfried Engelmann and Wesley Becker, at the University of Oregon. The Oregon model is based on the DISTAR (Science Research Associates) instructional programs designed by Englemann, while the Kansas model is based on the Sullivan Reading Program. Both, however, augment their instructional programs with social or token reinforcement.

The results of the Kansas Follow Through model are presented in Fig. 7. Disadvantaged children in regular school programs gain an average of about one-half year of achievement per academic year, and therefore fall progressively farther below grade level over time.

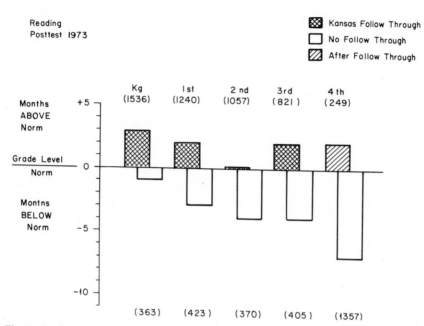

Fig. 7. *Reading achievement for disadvantaged children who were in the Kansas Follow Through program and a similar group who were in regular school programs. (The posttest used was the Wide Range Achievement Test.)*

The non-Follow Through disadvantaged children pictures in Fig. 7 show this cumulative deficit. In contrast, the children in the Kansas Follow Through programs have stayed consistently at or above grade level, even after they have been returned to regular fourth-grade classrooms. Similar results have been reported by Englemann and Becker (see Becker, Englemann, & Thomas, 1975) for the Oregon Follow Through model.

VII. CONCLUSIONS

When the experimental literature described above is viewed in an objective fashion, there are factors which argue in favor of a conclusion that learning disabled children can be effectively treated using behavioral techniques and also factors that argue against it. A variety of studies consistently suggested the effectiveness of behavioral techniques. On the other hand, the experimental designs and dependent measures used in these studies have been very weak in most instances, with a complete absence of investigations that compare behavioral techniques with alternative methods of remedial teaching. Positive evidence can also be derived, however, from the strong experimental literature supporting the use of behavioral intervention with a wide variety of children with academic problems who have been given other diagnostic labels. There is absolutely no reason at this point to believe that the nosological categories developed by medical-model psychologists, educators, and physicians determine in any significant way the effectiveness of any given treatment procedure. The most reasonable conclusion at this point, therefore, would be to support the clinical use of behavioral techniques with so-called learning disabled children and simultaneously to call for greatly expanded research efforts. Certainly, no other approach has shown as much clinical promise at this time.

REFERENCES

Allen, K. E., Henke, L. B., Harris, F. R., Baer, D. M., & Reynolds, N. J. Control of hyperactivity by social reinforcement of attending behavior. *Journal of Educational Psychology*, 1967, 58, 231–237.

Ayllon, T., Layman, D., & Burke, S. Disruptive behavior and reinforcement of academic performance. *Psychological Record*, 1972, 22, 315–323.

Ayllon, T., Layman, D., & Kandel, H. J. A behavioral-educational alternative to drug control of hyperactive children. *Journal of Applied Behavior Analysis*, 1975, 8, 137–146.

Ayllon, T., & Roberts, M. Eliminating discipline problems by strengthening academic performance. *Journal of Applied Behavior Analysis*, 1974, 7, 71–76.

Barsch, R. *Achieving perceptual-motor efficiency*. Seattle, Wash.: Special Child Publications, 1967.

Becker, W., Englemann, S., & Thomas, D. *Teaching: A course in applied psychology*. (Rev. ed.) Chicago: Science Research Associates, 1975.

Birnbrauer, J. S., Wolf, M. M., Kidder, J. D., & Tague, C. E. Classroom behavior of retarded pupils with token reinforcement. *Journal of Experimental Child Psychology*, 1965, 2, 219–235.

Brown, L., & Perlmutter, L. Teaching functional reading to trainable level retarded students. *Education and Training of the Mentally Retarded*, 1971, 6, 74–84.

Buckland, P., & Balow, B. Effect of visual perceptual training on reading achievement. *Exceptional Children*, 1973, 39, 299–304.

Chadwick, B. A., & Day, R. C. Systematic reinforcement: Academic performance of underachieving students. *Journal of Applied Behavior Analysis*, 1971, 4, 311–319.

Church, M. Does visual perception training help beginning readers? *Reading Teacher*, 1974, 27, 361–364.

Cline, M. G. Education as experimentation: Evaluation of the Follow Through planned variation model. (Final Report No. OEC-0-72-5221) U.S. Office of Education, Washington, D.C., 1974.

Corey, J. R., & Shamow, J. The effects of fading on the acquisition and retention of oral reading. *Journal of Applied Behavior Analysis,* 1972, 5, 311–313.

Cratty, B. *Perceptual-motor behavior and educational processes.* Springfield, Ill.: Thomas, 1969.

Cruickshank, W. *The brain-injured child in the home, school and community.* Syracuse, N.Y.: Syracuse University Press, 1967.

Delacatto, C. *Treatment and prevention of reading problems.* Springfield, Ill.: Thomas, 1959.

Drabman, R. S., Spitalnik, R., & O'Leary, K. D. Teaching self-control to disruptive children. *Journal of Abnormal Psychology,* 1973, 82, 10–16.

Drass, S. D., & Jones, R. L. Learning disabled children as behavior modifiers. *Journal of Learning Disabilities,* 1971, 4, 418–425.

Dunn, L. M., & Smith, J. O. *The Peabody language development kits.* Circle Pines, Minn.: American Guidance Service, 1966.

Edwards, R. P., Alley, G. R., & Snider, W. Academic achievement and minimal brain dysfunction. *Journal of Learning Disabilities,* 1971, 4, 134–142.

Fernald, G. *Remedial techniques in basic school subjects.* New York: McGraw-Hill, 1943.

Freeman, R. D. Special education and the electroencephalogram: Marriage of convenience. *Journal of Special Education,* 1967, 2, 61–73.

Frostig, M., & Horne, D. *The Frostig program for the development of visual perception:* Chicago: Follett Educational Corporation, 1964.

Gearheart, B. R. *Learning disabilities: Educational Strategies.* St. Louis, Mo.: Mosby, 1973.

Getman, G. N., & Kane, E. R. *The physiology of readiness: An action program for the development of perception for children.* Minneapolis, Minn.: Programs to Accelerate School Success, 1964.

Gillingham, A., & Stillman, B. *Remedial training for children with specific disability in reading, spelling and penmanship.* (7th ed.) Cambridge, Mass.: Educators Publishing Service, 1965.

Goodman, L., & Hammill, D. The effectiveness of Kephart-Getman activities in developing perceptual-motor and cognitive skills. *Focus on Exceptional Children,* 1973, 4, 1–9.

Greenwood, C. R., Sloane, H. N., & Baskian, A. Training elementary aged peer behavior managers to control small group programmed mathematics. *Journal of Applied Behavior Analysis,* 1974, 7, 103–114.

Grossman, H. J. The child, the teacher and the physician. In W. M. Cruickshank (Ed.), *The teacher of brain-injured children.* Syracuse, N.Y.: Syracuse University Press, 1966. Pp. 57–66.

Hammill, D. Training visual perceptual processes. *Journal of Learning Disabilities,* 1972, 5, 552–559.

Hammill, D., & Larsen, S. C. The effectiveness of psycholinguistic training. *Exceptional Children,* 1974, 41, 5–14.

Haring, N. G., & Hauck, M. A. Improved learning conditions in the establishment of reading skills with disabled readers. *Exceptional Children,* 1969, 35, 341–352.

Harris, V. W., & Sherman, J. A. Effects of homework assignments and consequences on classroom performance in social studies and mathematics. *Journal of Applied Behavior Analysis,* 1972, 7, 505–519.

Harris, V. W., Sherman, J. A., Henderson, D. G., & Harris, M. S. Effects of peer tutoring on the spelling performance of elementary classroom students. *A new direction for education: Behavior analysis.* Lawrence, Kans.: University of Kansas Support and Development Center for Follow Through, 1973.

Holt, G. L. Effect of reinforcement contingencies in increasing programmed reading and mathematics behaviors in first-grade children. *Journal of Experimental Child Psychology,* 1971, **12**, 362–369.

Hopkins, B. L., Schutte, R. C., & Garton, K. L. The effects of access to a playroom on the rate and quality of printing and writing of first and second-grade students. *Journal of Applied Behavior Analysis,* 1971, **4**, 77–87.

Hughes, J. Electroencephalography and learning. In H. Myklebust (Ed.), *Progress in learning disabilities.* New York: Grune & Stratton, 1968. Pp. 113–147.

Hughes, J., & Parks, G. EEG in dyslexic children. In H. Myklebust (Ed.), *Progress in Learning disabilities.* New York: Grune & Stratton, 1968. Pp. 132–133.

Johnson, D., & Myklebust, H. *Learning disabilities: Educational principles and practices.* New York: Grune & Stratton, 1967.

Johnson, M., & Bailey, J. S. Cross-age tutoring: Fifth graders as arithmetic tutors for kindergarten children. *Journal of Applied Behavior Analysis,* 1974, **7**, 223–232.

Kephart, N. *The slow learner in the classroom.* Columbus, Ohio: Merrill, 1971.

Kirk, S. A., & Kirk, W. D. *Psycholinguistic learning disabilities: Diagnosis and remediation.* Urbana: University of Illinois Press, 1971.

Kirk, S. A., McCarthy, J. J., & Kirk, W. D. *Illinois test of psycholinguistic abilities.* Urbana: University of Illinois Press, 1968.

Lahey, B. B., Busemeyer, M. K., & Dotts, J. Reduction of errors of orientation and sequence in the handwriting of "learning disabled" children. Unpublished manuscript, University of Georgia, 1975.

Lahey, B. B., & Drabman, R. S. Facilitation of the acquisition and retention of sight-word vocabulary through token reinforcement. *Journal of Applied Behavior Analysis,* 1974, **7**, 307–312.

Lahey, B. B., McNees, M. P., & Brown, C. C. Modification of deficits in reading for comprehension. *Journal of Applied Behavior Analysis,* 1973, **6**, 475–480. (a)

Lahey, B. B., Weller, D. R., & Brown, W. R. The behavior analysis approach to reading: Phonics discriminations. *Journal of Reading Behavior,* 1973, **5**, 200–206. (b)

Lovitt, T. C., Guppy, T. C., & Blattner, J. E. The use of a free-time contingency with fourth graders to increase spelling accuracy. *Behaviour Research and Therapy,* 1969, **7**, 151–156.

McCarthy, J. J., & McCarthy, J. F. *Learning disabilities.* Boston: Allyn and Bacon, 1969.

McKenzie, H., Clark, M., Wolf, M., Kothera, R., & Benson, C. Behavior modification of children with learning disabilities using grades as tokens and grades as back up reinforcers. *Exceptional Children,* 1968, **34**, 745–752.

Meier, J. H. Prevalence and characteristics of learning disabilities found in second grade children. *Journal of Learning Disabilities,* 1971, **4**, 1–16.

Miller, L. K., & Schneider, R. The use of a token system in project Head Start. *Journal of Applied Behavior Analysis,* 1970, **3**, 213–220.

Nolen, P. A., Kunzelmann, H. P., & Haring, N. G. Behavioral modification in a junior high learning disabilities classroom. *Exceptional Children,* 1967, **34**, 163–168.

Novy, P., Burnett, J., Powers, M., & Sulzer-Azaroff, B. Modifying attending-to-work behavior of a learning disabled child. *Journal of Learning Disabilities,* 1973, **6**, 217–221.

Orton, S. *Reading, writing and speech problems in children.* New York: Norton, 1937.

Paine, R. S. Organic neurological factors related to learning disorders. In J. Hellmuth (Ed.), *Learning disorders.* Vol. I. Seattle, Wash.: Special Child Publications, 1965. Pp. 32–73.

Paine, R. S., Werry, J. S., & Quay, H. C. A study of "minimal cerebral dysfunction." *Developmental Medicine and Child Neurology*, 1968, **10**, 505–520.

Ryback, D., & Staats, A. W. Parents as behavior therapy-technicians in treating reading deficits (dyslexia). *Journal of Behavior Therapy and Experimental Psychiatry*, 1970, **1**, 109–118.

Sabatino, D. A., Ysseldyke, J. E., & Woolston, J. Diagnostic-prescriptive perceptual training with mentally retarded children. *American Journal of Mental Deficiency*, 1973, **78**, 7–14.

Schwalb, E., Blau, H., & Blau, H. Child with brain dysfunction. *Journal of Learning Disabilities*, 1969, **2**, 182–188.

Strauss, A., & Lehtinen, L. *Psychopathology and education of the brain-injured child.* New York: Grune Stratton, 1947.

Sulzer, B., Hunt, S., Ashby, E., Koniarski, C., & Krams, M. Increasing the rate and percentage correct in reading and spelling in a fifth grade public school class of slow readers by means of a token system. In E. A. Ramp & B. L. Hopkins (Eds.), *A new direction for education: Behavior analysis.* Lawrence, Kans.: University of Kansas Support and Development Center for Follow Through, 1971. Pp. 5–25.

Wadsworth, H. G. A motivational approach toward the remediation of learning disabled boys. *Exceptional Children*, 1971, **37**, 33–42.

Wagner, R. F., & Guyer, B. P. Maintenance of discipline through increasing children's span of attention by means of a token economy. *Psychology in the Schools*, 1971, **8**, 285–289.

Walsh, J. F., & D'Angelo, R. Effectiveness of the Frostig program for visual perceptual training with Head Start children. *Perceptual and Motor Skills*, 1971, **32**, 944–946.

Whitlock, C., & Bushell, D. Some effects of "back-up" reinforcers on reading behavior. *Journal of Experimental Child Psychology*, 1967, **5**, 50–57.

Wilson, M. D., & McReynolds, L. V. A procedure for increasing oral reading rate in hard-of-hearing children. *Journal of Applied Behavior Analysis*, 1973, **6**, 231–240.

Winett, R. A., Richards, C. S., Krasner, L., & Krasner, M. Child-monitoring token reading program. *Psychology in the Schools*, 1971, **8**, 259–262.

Wolf, M. M., Giles, D. K., & Hall, R. V. Experiments with token reinforcement in a remedial classroom. *Behaviour Research and Therapy*, 1968, **6**, 51–64.

Zach, L., & Kaufman, J. How adequate is the concept of perceptual deficit for education? *Journal of Learning Disabilities*, 1972, **5**, 351–356.

ANIMAL ANALOGUES OF

BEHAVIORAL TREATMENT PROCEDURES:

A CRITICAL EVALUATION

HENRY E. ADAMS

Department of Psychology

University of Georgia

Athens, Georgia

AND

HOWARD H. HUGHES

Department of Psychology

North Texas State University

Denton, Texas

I. INTRODUCTION

If we modify the environment of an organism in order to assess, alter, or otherwise investigate the organism's behavior, the procedure can be labeled an analogue. The general purpose of all analogues is to enable us to predict and/or control behavior as it occurs in a more complex environment. This is the case whether the behavioral analogue consists of a behavior therapist administering systematic desensitization to phobic humans to eliminate their avoidance behavior in life situations, or an experimental psychologist administering various schedules of reinforcement in a Skinner box in order to determine the principles of learning of organisms. Whether a clinical researcher uses phobic individuals to investigate the parameters of phobic behavior or "subclinical" college student phobics, the procedure is an analogue since the nature of the environment has been altered by introduction of treatment procedures. Whether the former is a more appropriate analogue for the investigation of phobias than the latter remains to be determined, a point which has been recently ignored and misunderstood. Changing the type of subject is not always the solution for an inadequate analogue. In any case, the point is that all research and clinical activities are analogues of more complex situations. The science and technology of psychology, like other scientific fields, use analogues to generate knowledge.

In many analogues, the natural environment may not be the situation of interest. For example, the research clinician may be interested in developing an analogue of a clinical treatment procedure in order to investigate the parameters of the technique. While this is an analogue of a clinical treatment procedure rather than of the natural environment, the same principles governing the development of an analogue still operate. Only the focus of interest has changed. In one case, we are interested in parameters of the behavior in the environment, and, in the other case, we are interested in predicting the parameters of given treatment or assessment technique.

The particular analogue that is selected by an experimenter seems to be determined largely by two factors (i.e., the rigor of controls necessary and the availability of subjects). The purpose of the control factor is to isolate the principal ingredients in phenomena without altering their basic operation. The amount of control of error or systematic variance in any given analogue should ideally be determined a priori by the researcher, depending on the purposes and goals of the particular experiment. Since it is practically, if not theoretically, impossible to control all of the extrinsic as well as intrinsic factors that may interact with the variable under investigation, the absolutely controlled experiment is a myth. The greater the number and degree of control of the variables—both extrinsic (i.e., error) and intrinsic (i.e., other factors that influence the phenomenon under investigation in a meaningful fashion)—the simpler the analogue. It also follows that the greater the degree of control over intrinsic and extrinsic factors, the less likely is it that the data and principles generated from the analogue will be applicable to the situation the researcher has used the analogue to investigate. This could be labeled as the experimenter's "double-bind."

The second factor in selecting an analogue is the availability of subjects. The type of analogue used is determined by whether one can obtain the targeted population and whether the procedures to be used with the subjects are warranted. This becomes a particularly difficult problem with human subjects when the clinical researcher may be employing investigative procedures which could violate their human rights. Guidelines for these determinations can be found in the American Psychological Association (1973) publication on human rights of subjects. When a "patient" population is used, numerous questions arise, such as the justification for using placebo or noneffective control procedures with clients. It has often been assumed that university professors used college students and rats because they are easy to obtain. It has also been assumed by some individuals that use of college students or animal analogues was not justified since data or principles derived with these subjects can not be extrapolated to the target population. This has led to the suggestion that psychology journals interested in abnormal behavior should not publish student or animal analogue studies. While there may be elements of truth in these claims, the situation is not so simple, nor is the solution so obvious. Whether an analogue is adequate to investigate a particular problem or not is a decision that should be made based on a number of aspects of the situation. The type of subjects is not the only criterion. The crucial criterion for evaluation of analogue is whether the same principle(s) operate in the analogue and in the targeted situation (Bachrach, 1965).

Animal analogues of various types constitute a large part of the studies in the psychological literature. For our purposes, we will differentiate between analogues of psychological disorders and analogues of behavior treatment methods, with emphasis on the latter. Another factor in our coverage is whether the animal analogue is a planned evaluation (i.e., a priori) or a post hoc extrapolation of the results of animal experimentation to a particular treatment technique. This chapter will be interested primarily in the a priori analogues of behavior treatment methods that were designed to evaluate the effects of various components of the behavioral treatment methods.

Animal analogues have a number of limitations and difficulties. One of the most obvious is whether the behavior under investigation is species specific. While it is obvious that animal neurotic behavior is quite different in topology when compared to human abnormal behavior, the basic requirement is whether the same principles operate in both animal and human disorders (Bachrach, 1965). A good example of this difficulty has been discussed by Dmitruk (1974) in his evaluation of the phenomenon of "experimental neurosis," particularly with regard to the work of Masserman (1943) and Wolpe (1952). He notes that the behavior which these authors label as neurotic may be fairly characteristic of cats. A similar problem of this type is language behavior. When a behavioral technique depends heavily on the content of language (e.g., covert sensitization), it is difficult to investigate the procedure with animal analogues. A number of behavior treatment techniques based on speech and instructions do not lend themselves readily to investigation by animal analogues.

In the majority of investigations of behavioral treatment techniques, the animal analogue must also incorporate an analogue of the disorder with which the technique is assumed to be effective. If one is investigating the effects of various parameters of systematic desensitization in phobias with an animal analogue, then both the components of the treatment package and the analogue of the phobia are required. Consequently, the clinical researcher must address questions of what constitutes depression, anxiety, rituals, and similar disorders in lower organisms. For this reason, most of the animal analogues have been restricted to anxiety, phobias, or conflict where there is some face validity for the analogue. Animal analogues of schizophrenia, paranoia, and other complex disorders are rare or absent in the literature. This is due to the fact that, in humans, such classification categories are more vague and ambiguous than are phobias, anxiety, or rituals; and, consequently, it is more difficult to devise appropriate analogues. It may be that one index of the validity of a diagnostic category is whether one can devise an analogue of it.

Animal analogues of behavioral treatment methods are useful only if they are informative about the principles of operation of the particular treatment method, suggesting modification of a technique to improve precision and efficiency. As a matter of fact, since they imply a rigorous definition of terms and a scientific methodology, if behavioral treatment techniques can be investigated by animal analogues, then this is one indication of the scientific nature of the techniques. It must also be noted that the animal analogue is only one of the steps in the evaluation of a particular treatment method. Data derived from such analogues should be further evaluated with human analogues and/or treatment cases.

Table I shows the majority of animal analogues of behavioral disorders and behavioral modification procedures. In general, the majority of work has occurred with systematic desensitization, flooding, response prevention, and various extinction procedures. The rest of this chapter will discuss methodological problems, conduct a selective review of these studies, and suggest future research.

II. METHODOLOGICAL ISSUES

As an area of research, animal analogues of behavioral treatment procedures are relatively young and neglected. Operational definitions of the analogues of behavior disorders and behavioral procedures are by no means standardized. Consequently, it is desirable to review methodological issues and operational definitions before reviewing the research in this area.

The major behavioral procedures that may be collectively subsumed under the headings of behavior therapy and behavior modification for our purpose are systematic desensitization, flooding, response prevention, modeling, contingent reinforcement, and extinction.

All animal analogues of behavioral treatment procedures utilize an analogue of a behavioral disorder. This is usually some type of conditioned avoidance responses (CAR) which is essentially an analogue of human phobias. Conditioned emotional responses (CER) or passive avoidance are also used as an index of emotional disorders. The phobic responses essentially involve avoidance behavior associated with a set of conditioned stimuli (CS) but may also include anxiety responses (CER), depending upon the stage of development and success of the avoidance behavior. The various behavioral procedures are essentially different ways of exposing the subject to feared CS without allowing effective avoidance to continue. In other words, they are all ways to bring about nonreinforced functional exposure to the aversive fear/avoidance-eliciting CS (Delprato, 1973b; Wilson & Davison, 1971). In this manner new responses (various nonavoidance and nonanxiety behaviors) are conditioned to the previously anxiety/avoidance-eliciting CS. Systematic desensitization

TABLE I

Selected Animal Analogues

Animal analogues of behavioral disorders	Hypothesized human clinical referents
Conditioned avoidance responses	Anxiety, defense mechanisms, phobias
Conditioned emotional responses: urination, defecation, freezing, squealing, piloerection, recordings of physiological changes, etc.	Anxiety, emotional arousal, emotionality, fear, distress, tantrums, etc.
Deprivation, confinement, impossible learning tasks	Frustration, conflicts, etc.
Electric shock contingent upon presence of another animal, social dominance, overcrowding, food, deprivation, etc.	Aggression, fighting, rage, antagonistic behavior, etc.
Difficult discriminations, with confinement, approach-approach, approach-avoidance, and avoidance-avoidance paradigms, etc.	Conflict, fixation, stereotyped behavior, ambivalence, neurosis displacement, regression, behavioral disorganization
Conditioned ulcers	Psychosomatic disorders
Conditioned suppression	Disruption of goal-oriented behavior
Loss of positive reinforcement	Depression
Genetic selection	Alcoholism, emotionality, neuroticism
Infantile feeding frustration	Hoarding, overeating
Conditioned immobility	Catatonic behavior, psychoses
Tactile behavior	Affection, pleasure, love, etc.
Stimulus generalization, higher-order conditioning	Thinking disorder, loose associations
Courting, mating, and parental behaviors	Sexual deviations
Learned helplessness	Depression
Early sensory deprivation	Intelligence, affection
Series of conditioned stimuli varying along the dimension of aversiveness	CS hierarchy
Conditioned response that is incompatible to the target behavior	Competing responses
Presentation of conditioned stimuli in series from least to most aversive	Graded exposure to CS hierarchy
Organism may make a response that terminates the CS being presented	Response contingent CS termination

TABLE I (*continued*)

Animal analogues of behavioral procedures	Hypothesized human clinical referent
Graded exposure to CS hierarchy in the response contingent CS termination and conditioned competing responses	Systematic desensitization
Massed trials	Negative practice
Presentation of CS that is most aversive without allowing response contingent CS termination	Flooding
Prevention of avoidance response	Response prevention
Drugs	Drug therapy
Reinforcement for successive approximations	Shaping
Observational learning, social facilitation, mimicry, etc.	Modeling, imitation, vicarious learning
Acquisition, maintenance, and/or extinction	Contingent reinforcement
Learned autonomic control	Biofeedback

utilizes graded presentation of the CS, while a competing response inhibits the occurrence of anxiety. In flooding, the CS presentation is presented in such a manner as to elicit maximal anxiety regardless of motor behavior. In response prevention, avoidance responses are not allowed. Modeling and shaping are procedures that focus on establishing approach and/or nonavoidance responses which result in CS exposure. Other behavioral procedures involving different combinations of these variables or additional component procedures will also be considered.

Complete animal analogues of systematic desensitization (SD) should include the following components: (*a*) *Graded in vivo CS presentation*—begin with the least aversive and move toward the most aversive CS in the hierarchy. (*b*) *Presence of anxiety-avoidance response results in CS termination and decreased exposure on the next trial*—or return to a lower step in the hierarchy. The subject is able to terminate the CS temporarily and thus postpone continued exposure by making a response rather than receiving preprogrammed CS presentation. (*c*) *Responses which compete with anxiety and/or avoidance in the situation,* such as eating. Strictly speaking, these competing responses should be shaped or developed before the actual treatment procedure. (*d*) *Continuation of all CS in avoidance hier-*

archy until the last item without anxiety/avoidance occurs. Termination of CS occurs with CER or CAR. *(e) Presence of another nonanxious/avoiding organism*—analogous to a therapist. Other aspects of SD and other behavioral procedures with humans, such as positive instructional sets, imaginal CS presentation, and similar procedures based on language, are not easily established in animals.

An animal analogue of flooding (CSF) involves: *(a)* nongraded *in vivo* CS presentation—beginning with the most aversive CS in the anxiety-avoidance hierarchy; *(b)* avoidance responses not contingent with CS termination: CAR does not eliminate CER (in other words, the CS continues regardless of the animal's motor behavior); *(c)* competing responses for anxiety/avoidances are not presented; *(d)* continuation of CS until CER dissipates (duration of session should be determined by this factor); *(e)* presence of another nonanxious/ avoiding organism—analogous to a therapist. The goal of flooding is to maximize anxiety until habituation to the CS occurs.

Response prevention (RP) is a technique very similar to flooding and differs primarily because of the emphasis on the response rather than the CS. Animal analogues should include: *(a)* nongraded presentation of the CS *in vivo*; *(b)* prevention of CAR (except to determine if they do occur to the CS); *(c)* no deliberate introduction to the situation of responses which compete with anxiety or avoidances; *(d)* termination of CS when CAR does not occur (however, CER may continue to occur); *(e)* another nonfearful organism.

An analogue of modeling (M) does not specify: *(a)* graded or nongraded CS presentation; *(b)* response prevention; *(c)* competing responses, other than the presence of a nonfearful organism; or *(d)* criterion for termination of CS presentation. Rather, attempts are made to establish anxiety/avoidance competing responses utilizing the presense of another nonanxious/avoiding organism. This may be accomplished by: *(a)* placing the subject in the situation with another nonfearful organism; *(b)* having the subject observe the other organism in the situation; or *(c)* both in succession.

An animal analogue of shaping or contingent reinforcement (CR) is somewhat similar to M in that it does not specify: *(a)* graded versus nongraded CS presentation, or *(b)* response prevention. The emphasis is on *(c)* establishing anxiety/avoidance competing responses by shaping approach behavior using contingent reinforcement or feedback. Although *(d)* CS termination and *(e)* the presence of another nonanxious/avoiding organism may be utilized, they are not primary, as in modeling.

Extinction procedures are often used as baseline to evaluate other techniques, but it is a treatment procedure in its own right. Extinction involves exposing the organism to the situation without reinforcement. However, to be similar to behavior therapy with humans, a nonthreatened organism should be present.

There may be further procedural variations within each method that should be differentiated. For example, the terms implosion, response prevention, and flooding have been more or less used interchangeably when there are quite different procedures used. The following distinctions must be made in order to compare treatment methods. In *response prevention* (RP), the CAR is not allowed. For example, a clear plexiglass panel may prevent hurdling responses in a shuttle box (this procedure has also been referred to as blocking), or the safety ledge may be retracted in an automated avoidance apparatus. The *response prevention delay* (RPD) procedure utilizes similar methods, but the CAR is allowed to occur at some specified period after CS onset. In other words, response prevention occurs for a relatively brief period at the onset of each trial. *Punishment response prevention* (PRP) is another special type of response prevention. Prevention of CARs is achieved by making onset of an aversive stimulus contingent upon the occurrence of a CAR rather than by employing physical suppression. In *CS flooding* (CSF) procedure, the CAR is allowed, but it does not terminate the CS or the CS continues for a long period of time. The *CS flooding by delay* (CSFD) procedure delays termination of the CS for some specified period after the CAR has occurred (Kamin, 1957). This delay period is relatively short compared to the CSF procedure. Finally, in the massed trials (MT) procedure the CAR is allowed to occur but is no longer functionally effective because the intertrial interval is drastically shortened and the aversive CS reappear rapidly. In addition, it should be noted that RP, PRP, and CSF may be either a few massed long-duration trials or many spaced short-duration trials. RPD and CSFD are by definition spaced trials.

Animal analogues are possible for other combinations of the procedural components discussed and also as additional components. For example, D'Zurilla, Wilson, and Nelson (1973) have developed a treatment package, "graduated prolonged exposure," which involves: (a) graded CS presentation as in SD; (b) absence of anxiety/avoidance responses as a contingency for CS termination; and (c) prevention of avoidance without preestablished anxiety/avoidance competing responses.

III. SELECTIVE REVIEW OF
ANIMAL ANALOGUES

A question of major interest is which of these behavioral procedures are most efficient in eliminating anxiety and/or avoidance.
Unfortunately, the authors were unable to find animal studies
evaluating stimultaneously two or more behavioral procedures that
meet the criteria of a relatively complete analogue as previously
presented in this chapter. In particular, the presence of another
nonanxious/avoiding organism has seldom been utilized in animal
analogues. Davitz and Mason (1955), Hake and Laws (1967), and
Morrison and Hill (1967) all have demonstrated that the presence of
another nonanxious/avoiding animal during extinction reduces fear
responses. This phenomenon has been described as social facilitation.
Hall (1955) and Baum (1969a) found that the presence of other rats
during response prevention significantly reduced fear behavior and
also significantly reduced the number of CAR that occurred during
extinction. Baum's (1969b) study suggests that there is an interaction between social facilitation and duration of response prevention. He found that social facilitation was maximally effective with
short intervals (5 min) of response prevention when extinction of the
CAR was not completed, but did not enhance the efficiency of long
intervals (30 min) of response prevention when extinction of the
CAR was effectively completed. However, Hall (1955) found that
social facilitation reduced conditioned escape responses with four
15-min treatment sessions. Additional research is required to identify
the relevant parameters of social facilitation and how this variable
interacts with other procedural components. The social facilitation
variable may be viewed as a particular anxiety/avoidance competing
response procedure (the relationship variable?), suggesting that most
behavioral change procedures in humans include this component
whether explicitly stated or not. To complicate the issues further,
the social facilitation variable may also be viewed as modeling.

Although there have been few animal analogue studies that have
utilized the social facilitation component of behavior change procedures, the remaining procedural variables have, in various combinations, been extensively investigated. For this review, the authors have
chosen particular combinations of these variables as labeled in Table
I. Although these labels are arbitrary, they are descriptions of experimental treatments to be discussed in the review of the literature.

A. Extinction with Graded Conditioned Stimuli Presentation

Several studies have assessed the effects of adding the graded CS exposure component to the extinction procedure. Bankart (1972) utilized a one-way active CAR and demonstrated that a CSF procedure was more effective in reducing CARs and residual fear than graded extinction. Since a statistical comparison of graded extinction and regular extinction was not presented (this is often the case) we may assume they were not significantly different. In Wilson's (1972) factorial study the RP and SD procedures were significantly more effective than graded extinction. A statistical comparison of graded extinction and regular extinction was not presented, but the graphed data suggest that there was no difference across the 60 extinction test trials, except that in the last 12 trials the trend was in favor of the graded extinction procedure. Delprato (1973a) utilized a two-way (shuttle) active CAR, controlled for CS exposure by yoking, and found that graded extinction and regular extinction resulted in a lower percentage of CARs (approximately 47% and 30%, respectively) during extinction tests than in a SD-like procedure (approximately 75%, which was about the same as control subjects) where food pellets were presented and then the CS was presented 3 sec after the subject began eating. The fact that temporal placement of the competing response before the CS presentation may not be a valid analogue of SD is illustrated by Delprato's (1973b) later findings which clarify his previous results. Utilizing the same paradigm, he found that a SD procedure where the food was presented with the offset of the CS (no food was received if a CAR occurred—which is more similar to shaping) was significantly more effective than the SD-like procedures where the food is presented simultaneously or before CS onset. Since the latter procedure had previously (Delprato, 1973a) been shown not to differ significantly from regular extinction, one may with some reservations conclude that the SD procedure (food presented with CS offset) was more effective than regular extinction. In addition, graded extinction was found to be as effective as the SD procedure, both evidencing approximately 18% CAR during extinction tests.

These studies are somewhat conflicting and not conclusive; they suggest that graded extinction may be as effective as RP and SD procedures—possibly when the number of steps in the CS hierarchy is greater (approximately 15) and the criterion for progression in the

CS hierarchy is more strenuous [e.g., two or more consecutive CS presentations without a CAR, following Delprato's (1973b) procedure]. These techniques effectively increase the amount of CS exposure. With these techniques and sufficient time to conduct them, graded extinction would likely be more effective than regular extinction. However, where the number of steps in the CS hierarchy is few and the criteria for progression in the CS hierarchy are less strenuous, as in the Wilson (1972) and Bankart (1972) studies, graded extinction is likely to be less effective than RP and SD procedures and not different from regular extinction.

B. Extinction with Anxiety-Competing Responses

Nelson (1967) employed a one-way active conditioned escape response with a drug (chlorpromazine, abruptly withdrawn at the end of treatment). The fear test was conducted 1 day later to allow the drug effects to be eliminated. This procedure should cause competing response to anxiety. Nelson assessed residual fear utilizing the learning of an active CAR (placed in the fear compartment with door open so the animal could cross over into the safe compartment). Results indicated that extinction with competing responses was as effective as RP procedure and both were significantly more effective than regular extinction.

Nelson (1966) in an earlier experiment utilized a conditioned escape response. Trials 1–25 and 36–40 allowed immediate escape (i.e., the door was open). Trials 25–35 allowed a delayed escape where the door was opened 30 sec after shock onset. Extinction of the escape response was employed as a posttreatment measure of fear. Results suggested that extinction with competing responses (eating) was significantly more effective than regular extinction.

Sherman (1967), after establishing a lever press for food response, utilized a schedule wherein bar pressing was periodically followed by the immediate delivery of 2 sec shock. Under these conditions avoidance of bar pressing was established. He found that extinction with competing responses (amobarbital sodium abruptly withdrawn) was not significantly different from regular extinction (saline-injected control), and both were significantly less effective than a novel SD procedure. This SD-like procedure employed gradual withdrawal of the drug over 5 days. Gambrill (1967) utilized a Sidman avoidance procedure (there was no specific SC; shock occurred 15 to 20 sec after the last wheel-turning response) with food-reinforced bar lifting as a competing response. In comparison to a regular extinction procedure, the extinction with competing response procedure significantly reduced the number of CARs during the first extinction session. During the two subsequent extinction treatment sessions and the seven subsequent extinction test sessions there was no significant difference.

Wilson and Dinsmoor (1970) employed a sequence of conditioning trials involving both active and passive CARs and including acquisition, extinction, and retraining prior to treatment—and finally passive avoidance extinction. They found that extinction with competing responses (food) was significantly more effective than regular extinction. Extinction with competing responses was also more effective than an RP procedure. However, this finding is questionable as it appears the RP group was not matched with respect to initial level of fear as indicated by the number of hours required to reach the criterion during the initial extinction period before retraining, treatment, and the passive avoidance fear test. Of the subjects that took more than 30 hours to meet the criterion during the initial extinction period (high level of initial fear), a disproportionate number were in the RP group. In his 1972 study Wilson found that extinction with a competing response (food) was not different from regular extinction and was significantly less effective than either RP or SD procedures. Poppen (1970), utilizing conditioned suppression, found that in terms of suppression, extinction with competing responses (food) was significantly more effective than regular extinction but less effective than SD. The results of these studies are far from conclusive. On occasions (possibly where active avoidance conditioning is employed), extinction plus competing responses is not as effective as RP and SD and is no more effective than regular extinction.

C. Systematic Desensitization

There have also been a number of studies that purport to assess the efficiency of SD. Few of these studies have all of the essential procedural components. Sherman (1967) found that his novel SD procedure was significantly more effective than regular extinction. Delprato's (1973a, 1973b) studies also suggested that SD was significantly more effective than regular extinction. Wilson's (1973) factorial study (both Experiment 1 and Experiment 2) further indicated that SD was more effective than regular extinction. The initial studies addressing this question are consistent and point to the conclusion that SD is more effective in reducing CARs and CERs than regular extinction.

D. Systematic Desensitization versus Response Prevention

There have been a number of studies that attempted to compare the efficiency of SD and RP. Few have included all of the procedural components for both SD and RP conditions. Wilson (1972, 1973) found the RP procedure to be optimally effective in decreasing resistance to extinction of a one-way active CAR and residual fear, as assessed by approach toward food and the CS. The SD procedure was significantly more effective than regular extinction, but it did not differ significantly from the RP procedures. In a second experiment Wilson yoked the CS exposure of the RP procedure group to that of the SD procedure group to control for this variable. The RP procedure was significantly more effective in extinguishing the CAR than either the SD procedure or regular extinction. However, for residual fear the RP and SD procedures were both significantly better than regular extinction but did not differ significantly from each other. Tentatively, these findings suggest that RP and SD procedures are equally effective, although SD may require longer CS exposure and take longer. Differences in spontaneous recovery (relapse?) have not been evaluated.

E. Conditioned Stimulus Flooding and Response Prevention

There have been a large number of studies that have assessed the efficiency of flooding procedures. The major shortcoming of these studies has been failure to provide for termination of the CS when anxiety responses dissipate and are no longer present to any significant degree. Just as the duration of a given CS presentation has not been individualized, neither has the duration of a treatment session been individualized. The results that have been obtained usually allow for long, fixed durations of CS exposures (the same for each group member) controlled by the experimenter rather than by the subject's behavior. The great strength of the CSF procedure lies in the simplicity and the ease with which the procedures may be conducted—no competing responses, response prevention, or graded CS presentations are necessary. These facts may well forcast a future popularity of this procedure in the behavioral treatment of humans.

Poppen (1970), utilizing a condition suppression measure, found that with respect to the number of trials to extinction SD was significantly more effective than the CSF (ten or less 10-min trials), which was not significantly different from the regular extinction procedure. However, in terms of a suppression measure, SD was significantly better than CSF, which was significantly better than regular extinction. The results of this study are difficult to assess, since neither the duration or distribution of CS exposure was held constant across groups. All groups except those involving the CSF procedure had distributed trials. It should also be noted that when a conditioned suppression paradigm is employed, the CAR is not physically prevented, but CSF is difficult to differentiate from regular extinction. In general, regardless of the method of CS exposure, the greater the CS exposure, the greater is the fear reduction (Baum, 1969b; Baum & Oler, 1968; Schiff, Smith, & Prochaska, 1972). However, when CS exposure is controlled, there may be differences in these analogue procedures. For example, Polin (1959) utilized a two-way (shuttle) active CAR and demonstrated that massed CSF (MT) was significantly more effective in reducing conditioned avoidance responding than spaced RP and a no-treatment control procedure. However, the 5 sec of CS exposure by RP on each of 20 trials can be too brief a period to assess adequately the effects of the RP procedure (Baum, 1969b). Weinberger (1965) also employed a two-way active CAR and found that RPD was significantly better than CSF in facilitating extinction of CARs. Katzev (1967) also used a two-way active CAR and demonstrated that as CSFD increased (0, 2, 5, and 10 sec delay) the number of avoidance responses during extinction decreased significantly.

Baum and Oler (1968) used an automated (retractable ledge) avoidance apparatus to condition a one-way active CAR. Their results indicated that the MT procedure was significantly more effective than the RP procedure in reducing CARs—142.2 sec of CS exposure was utilized. However, a RP group receiving 15 min of CS exposure was as effective as the MT group. In addition, the results of 142.2-sec conditioning were confounded in that the duration of CS exposure was individualized for the MT group but not for the RP group, the latter being yoked to the former. For a more complete discussion of this issue of confounding that results from the use of the yoked control procedure, see Church (1964) and Holder (1974).

Coulter, Riccio, and Page (1969) conditioned a one-way active avoidance response. They found that an RP procedure was significantly more effective than an RPD or regular extinction procedure in facilitating the extinction of conditioned avoidance responding. On the other hand, they found that the reverse was the case with respect to a passive avoidance measure of residual fear or CER. The regular extinction and RPD groups evidenced significantly less residual fear than the RP group. However, the duration of CS exposure (2 sec for five trials) may have been too brief to assess adequately the effects of the RP procedure. Best and Baum (1969) utilized an automated one-way avoidance apparatus and demonstrated that as the duration (3, 9, and 12 sec) of the intertrial interval during treatment decreased, extinction was facilitated—supporting the efficacy of the MT procedure.

Sherman (1970) found no difference between RP and CSF procedures. Both of these procedures were significantly more effective than a no-treatment control procedure in eliminating active CARs in a two-way avoidance paradigm. Shipley, Mock, and Levis (1971) utilized a one-way active CAR, and their results indicated that an RP procedure was significantly more effective in facilitating the extinction of CARs than RPD or no-treatment control procedures. However, RP and RPD were equally effective in reducing residual fear. Bersh and Paynter (1972) utilized a one-way active avoidance conditioning paradigm. They found that RP and CSF were equally effective in reducing residual fear. Berman and Katzev (1972), in a two-way active CAR utilizing the elimination of conditioned avoidance responding as a measure, found that both massed and spaced RP were significantly more effective than regular extinction. Spaced CSF were in turn significantly more effective than massed CSF and no-treatment. Bankart (1972) also demonstrated that RP and PRP procedures were significantly more effective than CSF in facilitating the extinction of conditioned avoidance responding. Finally, Baum (1973a) used a one-way active avoidance response and found that CSF and RP procedures were equally effective in facilitating the extinction of conditioned avoidance responding.

These studies indicate that RP and PRP are effective treatment procedures. However, some minimal duration of CS exposure may be necessary when utilizing these methods. Tentatively, since there has as yet been no replication, it would appear that the MT procedure is an effective one. The results of studies evaluating CSF and RPD procedures are equally divided—pro and con. Nevertheless, CSF appear to be less effective than RP when direct comparisons are made.

The one study utilizing the CSFD procedure does not allow one to draw any conclusions concerning its relative effectiveness. In addition, these results suggest that flooding procedures and the RP and PRP methods are significantly more effective than regular extinction and no-treatment control procedures in eliminating conditioned avoidance responding. The flooding procedures also appear to be effective in reducing residual fear if the duration of DS exposure is not too brief.

F. Response Prevention versus Extinction

A number of studies have attempted to evaluate the effectiveness of RP without contrasting different types of analogues of the procedure. Since studies on RP are numerous, at this point only studies that have restricted the comparisons of RP to regular extinction and/or no-treatment control procedures will be considered. Studies that have incorporated additional procedures combining RP and/or CSF with graded CS presentation, anxiety-competing responses, or both of these components, will be reviewed in a later section.

Page and Hall (1953), utilizing a one-way active avoidance paradigm, found that RP was significantly more effective than regular extinction in reducing the number of trials to reach extinction. Page (1955), utilizing the same paradigm, also found RP to be significantly more effective than regular extinction in reducing conditioned avoidance responding. However, he also then tested for residual fear, utilizing passive avoidance of the shock compartment with food present (subjects were deprived of food for 24 hr) as an index. He found that the no-acquisition control procedure resulted in significantly less residual fear than the regular extinction procedure, which resulted in significantly less residual fear than RP. However, the duration of CS exposure during response prevention was relatively brief—five trials for 15 sec each or 75 sec. Carlson and Black (1959) employed a two-way active avoidance response with dogs and found RP significantly increased the mean response latency over that found during the regular extinction condition. Baum (1966) found that the RP significantly reduced the number of trials to extinction of a one-way active avoidance response in comparison to no-treatment control. Benline and Simmel (1967), in an active two-way CAR, found that the RP significantly reduced conditioned avoidance responding for the first 3 days (20 trials per day) of 5 days of extinction trials. This advantage in comparison of a no-treatment control group was temporary. Nelson (1969) conditioned an active one-way escape response and found that RP was significantly more effective than regular extinction and no-treatment control procedures which did not differ from each other in facilitating extinction. In a second part of this study, Nelson utilized a passive avoidance paradigm: entry into the second compartment resulted in electric shock. He found that the regular extinction procedure was significantly more effective in reducing residual fear (passive avoidance of the shock compartment with shock absent and food present) than the RP, which in turn was significantly more effective than the no-treatment control group. Linton, Riccio, Rohrbaugh, and Page (1970) with a one-way active CAR also demonstrated that the RP resulted in significantly fewer trials to extinction than regular extinction and no-treatment control procedures. However, residual fear (passive avoidance) was significantly greater than the nontreatment control procedure. The RP procedure resulted in an intermediate level of residual fear that was nevertheless significantly greater than the regular extinction and no-acquisition control procedures, which did not differ significantly. Again, it should be noted that the duration of CS exposure during response prevention was relatively brief—five trials for 15 sec each, or 75 sec. Finally, Baum (1971) conditioned a one-way active avoidance response and found that the RP was significantly more effective than the regular extinction procedure in facilitating extinction. A review of these studies further emphasizes the fact that RP is significantly more effective than regular extinction and no-treatment control procedures in facilitating extinction of CAR. However, a longer duration of the RP appears to be necessary before residual fear is effectively reduced.

G. Response Prevention and Conditioned Stimulus Flooding with Graded Conditioned Stimuli Presentation

A number of studies have assessed the effects of adding the graded CS exposure component to CSF or RP. These procedures with graded CS approximate the *graduated prolonged exposure* procedures (D'Zurilla *et al.*, 1973). Kimble and Kendall (1953) employed wheel turning as a CAR and found that CSF with graded CS presentation (seven 15-sec trials) was more effective than no-treatment control procedures in reducing conditioned avoidance responding. Gale, Sturmfels, and Gale (1966) utilized a classical conditioning paradigm to establish a CER. Mean weight of boli defecated was utilized as an index of fear. Although all comparisons were not reported, the authors appeared to indicate that the no-treatment control procedure was significantly less effective than the CSF procedure with graded CS presentation (30 1-min trials), which was significantly less effective than the CSF with both graded CS and competing responses. Goldstein (1969) used Cebus monkeys as subjects and their existing fear of a toy bear as the basis for avoidance response. Results indicated that over all 21 test trials the CSF (15 3-min trials), CSF with graded CS presentation, CSF with anxiety-competing responses, and CSF with graded CS presentation and anxiety-competing responses were not significantly different from one another, but were all significantly more effective than a no-treatment control procedure in reducing avoidance responding. In terms of the number of trials necessary to eliminate avoidance, the CSF with graded CS and competing responses was significantly more effective than the other treatment procedures. Bankart (1972) utilized a one-way active CAR and found that CSF with graded CS presentation resulted in slower extinction than the RP procedure and was not significantly different than the regular extinction procedure. In Wilson's (1973) study, previously cited, results indicated that CSF with graded CS presentation and the CSF procedure (15 30-sec trials) alone were both significantly more effective in reducing conditioned avoidance responding than the regular extinction procedure but not significantly different from each other. Hughes (1971) utilized one-way active avoidance responses and found no significant difference between RP (20 min of CS exposure) and RP with graded CS presentation procedures, both of which were significantly more effective than a no-treatment control procedure. Nelson (1971) employed a fear conditioning paradigm wherein each rat received eight acquisition trials. Each trial included exposure to 2 sec of inescapable shock, which was followed 30 sec later by an additional 2 sec of inescapable shock, after which time the door opened, allowing an escape response to occur as the grid remained charged. Posttreatment assessment of fear involved a measure of competing responses in the presence of the CS—amount of food eaten in the shock compartment with the door closed and shock off. Results indicated that RP with graded CS presentation was significantly less effective than RP procedures (18 2-min trials). A review of these studies suggests that CSF or RP with graded CS presentation is more effective than are no-treatment control and regular extinction but does not differ significantly from CSF or RP. The graded CS presentation component apparently adds nothing to CSF or RP.

H. Response Prevention and Conditioned Stimulus Flooding with Anxiety-Competing Responses

The anxiety-competing response component has received more attention than the graded CS presentation component, particularly with RP. Lane (1954) found that after one-way escape conditioning, RP with anxiety-competing responses (eating) was significantly more effective in facilitating extinction than RP (four 15-min trials), which was more effective than a no-treatment control procedure. Hall (1955) utilized a one-way conditioned fear and escape response. The competing responses were elicited by the presence of another animal which had not been shocked but had been habituated to and positively reinforced in the apparatus (social facilitation). Results indicated that RP with anxiety-competing responses was significantly more effective in reducing the strength of the escape response than RP (four 15-min trials) and the regular extinction procedures, which were not significantly different from each other. All three of these procedures were significantly more effective than the no-treatment control procedure. Sermat and Shephard (1959) utilized a one-way active avoidance response and reported that individualized RP with anxiety competing responses (eating) significantly increased the latency of the jumping responses relative to nonindividualized (yoked) RP (six trials of 1 min or less) and individualized regular extinction procedures. However, this effect was small (latency of jumping response increased, but the avoidance responses were made by every subject on every trial) and transient (significant effect was observed only on the first 20 trials and not on the last 30 trials of the extinction test procedure). Nelson (1966, 1971) in studies previously cited, found RP (three 10-min trials) were significantly more effective than RP with anxiety-competing responses (eating), which was significantly more effective than a no-treatment control procedure. In the second experiment, Nelson found that nonindividualized RP with anxiety-competing responses (eating) was more effective than nonindividualized RP (five 2-min trials), which was not significantly different from a regular extinction procedure in reducing the speed of escape responding. Unfortunately, a no-treatment control procedure was not included.

Nelson (1967) in another study utilized a one-way conditioned escape response and found that CSF with anxiety-competing responses (effects of chlorpromazine) was not significantly more effective than RP (four 5-min trials and eight 5-min trials) in reducing the speed of escape responding. These procedures were significantly more effective than a very brief (one 5-min trial) RP. Baum (1969a) found that for a relatively long period of CS exposure (one 30-min trial) there was no significant difference between RP with anxiety-competing responses (the effects of the presence of two naive rats—social facilitation) and RP. For a relatively brief period of CS exposure (one 5-min trial) RP with anxiety-competing responses was significantly more effective than RP in reducing conditioned avoidance responding. Gordon and Baum (1971) employed an automated apparatus to condition an active avoidance response. They found that RP with anxiety-competing responses (effect of positive intracranial stimulation) was significantly more effective in reducing the number of trials to extinction than either RP (one 5-min trial) or no-treatment control procedures, which did not differ significantly from each other.

Dickson (1972) used a passive avoidance paradigm and a licking (dipper) response. He found that RP with anxiety-competing responses (drinking) and RP were equally effective and significantly more effective than regular extinction and no-treatment control procedures. Kamano (1972) conditioned an active two-way (shuttle) avoidance response. He found that the RP (five 10-sec presentations) was significantly more effective than RP with anxiety-competing responses (effects of amobarbital or chlordiazepoxide) in reducing the number of trials to extinction of the CAR. Baum (1973b) conditioned an active CAR in an automated apparatus. Results indicated there was no difference between the RP (one 5-min trial) and RP with anxiety-competing responses (effects of chlorpromazine) with respect to the number of trials to extinction. However, during response prevention the addition of the anxiety-competing response significantly reduced the incidence of abortive avoidance activity while significantly increasing freezing responses. Leclerc, St. Laurent, and Baum (1973) also utilized an automated avoidance apparatus to condition an active CAR. They found no differences among RP (one 5-min trial), RP with anxiety-competing responses (effects of positive, aversive, or neutral intracranial stimulation), and no-treatment control procedures in reducing avoidance responding.

With regard to the role of competing responses in CSF, Goldstein (1969), as previously cited, found that CSF with competing responses was not significantly different from other procedures, but in terms of the number of trials necessary to eliminate avoidance the CSF with graded CS presentation and anxiety-competing responses was significantly more effective than the other treatment procedures. Poppen (1970) found that, in terms of a suppression measure, CSF with anxiety-competing responses was not different from CSF (ten or lass 10-min trials), but both were significantly more effective than regular extinction.

Moltz (1954) trained rats (40 trials with food reinforcement) to make a position choice in a T maze. On the subsequent 65 trials they were shocked just after the choice point. Shock was unavoidable in that it occurred after either alternative. After treatment procedures, extinction trials were run with shock absent and food present in the goal box. CSF with anxiety-competing responses (eating) was not significantly different from the CSF (two 5-min trials).

An overview of these studies suggests that both RP and RP with anxiety-competing responses are consistently more effective than regular extinction and no-treatment, particularly in cases of brief durations of RP. With longer durations of RP, the effects of the anxiety-competing response competence appear to be nil. In CSF, anxiety-competing responses contribute little to behavioral change. These results, taken together, support the suggestion of Nelson (1966) that the anxiety-competing response procedures exert their major influence by facilitating increased CS exposure.

I.   Conditioned Stimulus Flooding with Graded Conditioned Stimuli and Competing Responses

Another question is the effect of both graded CS and competing-response components added to CSF. This procedure is similar to SD, with the exception that CS termination is not contingent upon the occurrence of a CAR. Gale et al. (1966), in a study previously cited, indicate that CSF with graded CS and competing responses (eating) was significantly more effective than CSF (30 1-min trials) with graded CS presentation, which was significantly more effective than the no-treatment control procedure. Goldstein (1969), as previously cited, found that, with respect to the number of trials necessary to overcome avoidance, the CSF with graded CS and competing responses (eating) was significantly more effective than CSF (15 3-min trials), CSF with graded presentation, and CSF with anxiety-competing responses, which were all significantly more effective than the no-treatment control procedure. Heath (1968) employed an active

CAR and found that CSF with graded CS and competing responses (eating) and CSF (five 100-sec exposures) were both significantly more effective than the no-treatment control procedure but not significantly different from each other. Wilson's (1973) factorial studies demonstrated that CSF with graded CS and competing responses (eating), CSF with graded CS presentation, CSF with anxiety-competing responses, and RP (15 30-sec trials) were not significantly different from one another, and all were more effective than regular extinction.

An overview of these studies indicates that both CSF and CSF with graded CS and competing responses are more effective than regular extinction and no-treatment. Whether graded CS and competing responses add to CSF is questionable. The first two studies, which support this hypothesis, appear to have major shortcomings in experimental design. Gale et al. (1966) have been criticized methodologically for utilizing defecation as a dependent variable when food was given to one group and not to the other (Wilson & Davison, 1971). The major limitation of Goldstein's (1969) study was the small number (two) of subjects in each group. Consequently, the conclusion appears warranted that graded CS and competing-response components combined add little to CSF. As indicated by Wilson (1973), these components appear to exert their influence by increasing nonreinforced exposure to the CS. As a result, they likely facilitate extinction most effectively in conditions where the subject is free to emit the CAR, thereby controlling their own CS exposure, as in SD as opposed to CSF where CARs are not effective in terminating the CS.

J. Modeling

Animal studies of observational learning and modeling appear to be less numerous than human studies (Bandura, Blanchard, & Ritter, 1969; Bandura & Menlove, 1968). Most of the animal studies in this area focus on acquisition rather than on extinction. The social facilitation studies (Baum, 1969a; Davitz & Mason, 1955; Hake & Laws, 1967; Hall, 1955; Morrison & Hill, 1967) reviewed earlier can be considered to be a type of modeling. These studies suggest that in vivo modeling of nonfearful responses by an experimentally naive animal significantly facilitates the extinction of avoidance responding. Uno, Greer, and Goates (1973) utilized a one-way CAR and studied the effect of a subject's observing another subject undergo one 5-min trial of response prevention. With respect to mean latency of responding during extinction, this modeling procedure (36-sec latency) was intermediate to and not significantly different from the no-treatment control procedure (13 sec) or RP (64 sec). The bipolarity of the effects of the modeling procedure strongly indicated an individual differences effect and suggested that individualization of the duration of the modeling procedure would be an effective method. More research is needed.

K. Contingent Reinforcement

Hamilton (1972) has criticized the dichotomization of treatment based on hypothesized etiology of the behavior to be modified. He notes that operant conditioning procedures have been employed to build in desired instrumental behaviors or eliminate inappropriate instrumental behaviors, whereas systematic desensitization techniques have been directed at the modification of inappropriate behavior based on classically conditioned fear. Hamilton suggests that SD may involve a combination of classical anxiety extinction and instrumental conditioning of approach behavior. He further suggests that operant conditioning can be utilized to modify emotionally based maladaptive behavior. With human subjects, Hamilton has found support for these hypotheses. Leitenberg and Callahan (1973) also utilized human subjects and demonstrated that reinforced practice was significantly more effective than a no-treatment control procedure in reducing fear responses.

Unfortunately, neither human nor animal studies in this area have been numerous. Carlsmith, (1961), after establishing active avoidance responding, studied the effects of contingent punishment on CARs. He found that if the noxious stimulus utilized for contingent punishment were the same as the noxious stimulus utilized during acquisition of the avoidance response (shock–shock or loud horn–loud horn), the procedure resulted in increased resistance to extinction. However, if the noxious stimuli were different (shock–loud horn or loud horn–shock), the CR procedure resulted in decreased resistance to extinction. Overmier and Bull (1969) demonstrated that after conditioned avoidance responding had been established to a specific warning stimulus, a CR procedure could be utilized to alter the stimulus control component of the stimulus response sequence. In other words, the CAR now occurs in the presence of a new stimulus (tone) and not in the presence of the original warning stimulus (light off-set). Counterconditioning (Delprato, 1973b; Goldstein, 1969) essentially involves the other portion of the stimulus response chain; that is, a CR procedure is utilized so that the stimulus that originally elicited fear and/or avoidances now elicits competing responses such as relaxation and approach. Extinction is more or less an intermediate step whereby the original fear stimulus after a CR procedure no longer elicits fear and/or avoidance responses, but neither altered stimulus control or counterconditioning has been explicitly achieved. Wells (1971) employed one-way active CAR and found that SD and CR procedures were equally effective in reducing conditioned avoidance responding. The SD procedure involved simultaneous presentation of the CS and food, whereas the CR procedure stressed presentation of the CS before the food. It would appear that CR is an effective procedure for reducing maladaptive fear and/or avoidance responding and this procedure may be increasingly used with clinical cases in the future.

IV. IMPLICATIONS FOR BEHAVIORAL TREATMENT OF HUMANS

An overview of research involving animal analogues of behavioral procedures and their effect on the elimination of fear and avoidance responding suggests that relatively complete analogues are infrequent. In particular, the presence of another nonanxious/avoiding organism has been a seldom-utilized component in analogue studies in spite of the fact that studies uniformly demonstrate the effectiveness of social facilitation, which may be considered either as a type of modeling or as a competing-response procedure.

There are numerous analogue studies evaluating the presence or absence of other major procedural components: response contingent CS termination; graded CS presentation; and the establishment of anxiety-competing responses. Studies have concentrated on the investigation of particular combinations of these procedural components on regular extinction (CS termination being contingent upon a CAR), SD (extinction with graded CS and competing responses), RP (CS termination contingent upon the absence of a CAR), and CSF (CS termination not contingent upon CAR but absence of CER). A major problem is that most studies confuse RP and CSF although these two procedures are operationally, clinically, and theoretically different. It is strongly suggested that future studies make this distinction.

Within these limits the following tentative conclusions are offered. SD, RP, and CSF are more effective than regular extinction and no-treatment control procedures. SD may require longer CS exposure and more treatment time than the other procedures. No behavioral procedure is effective without some minimum duration of CS exposure that varies with the individual subject. CSF and RP may be more stressful than other behavioral procedures. There are a number of different analogues of these procedures. Prevention of the CAR (by physical means or by contingent punishment) and massed trials (CAR is allowed but is no longer functionally effective as the intertrial-interval is drastically shortened, allowing the feared CS to reappear rapidly) are both effective in eliminating CAR but may be less effective with CER. Flooding (CAR is allowed but no longer terminates the CS contingently) has not been as effective with CAR but may be more effective with CER. These results are not surprising in view of the emphasis of each technique.

Optimal grading of CS requires an adequate number of steps (approximately 15 in rats) and an individualized, relatively strenuous criterion (two presentations of each graded CS without the occurrence of the CAR) for progression up the CS hierarchy. Intracranial stimulation and social facilitation appear to be more effective competing responses than drugs, food, and water. With this in mind, extinction with graded CS and extinction with competing responses appear to be as effective as SD (extinction with graded CS and competing responses), and all of these procedures significantly more effective than regular extinction and no-treatment control procedures. Each of these components add significantly to the regular extinction procedure, but there is no additive effect of both. With adequate durations of CS exposure, CSF and RP with graded CS, CSF and RP with competing responses, and CSF with graded CS and competing responses are also as effective as SD and RP. All are significantly more effective than regular extinction and no-treatment control procedures. In other words, these components add little significant effect to either RP or CSF. As Nelson (1966) and Wilson (1973) have stated, these components exerted their influence by increasing nonreinforced exposure to the CS; they are likely to facilitate effective elimination of avoidance responding in conditions where the subject is free to emit the CAR, thereby controlling his own CS exposure (extinction procedure), as opposed to conditions where the CAR is not effective in terminating the CS, as in CSF or RP. Generalization decrements resulting from the presence of these components, which were not present during acquisition, are offset by increased exposure to the CS in the free-exposure conditions of CSF or RP. Nevertheless, with very brief durations of CS exposure these components, when added to RP, may prove to be more effective than RP alone—which, under these conditions, is no more effective than regular extinction. It also appears that when these components are added to CSF, the procedure becomes less stressful to the subject, as indicated by behavioral observation of a reduction of abortive avoidance responses.

Modeling with the subjects in the same situation (social facilitation) or with one subject observing another subject undergo treatment (providing that duration of exposure is individualized) appears to be a powerful procedure. Contingent reinforcement involving either positive reinforcement or a punishment contingency also appears to be an effective technique. Behavioral procedures, contingent reinforcement in particular, may be utilized in such a manner as to alter independently the stimulus control of the CAR or response control of the feared CS. When stimulus control is emphasized, the CAR is intact but is elicited by a new CS other than the original CS. A specified new response is not conditioned to the original CS. For example, the sight of a mouse (original CS) no longer results in an avoidance or an approach response, but the avoidance response occurs at the sight of snakes (new CS). When response control is emphasized, a new response is conditioned to the original CS. A specified new stimulus is not conditioned to elicit the original CAR. For example, the sight of a mouse now results in an approach response rather than an avoidance response. The avoidance response does not occur at the sight of a snake. Conceptually, a combination of stimulus and response contorl could be utilized simultaneously.

A number of implications for the behavioral treatment of humans can be derived from these studies. Of course, the level of confidence varies from hypothesis to hypothesis and direct testing with both human analogues and in clinical settings is necessary. The most important variable appears to be duration of nonreinforced exposure to the aversive CS. For optimal effects the duration of CS exposure needs to be tailored to each individual, as noted by McCutcheon and Adams (1975) with CSF with humans. An investigation of the parameters of duration of CS exposure may be fruitful in establishing the lower limits of temporal exposure. For example, a minimum of 25 to 30 sec of CS exposure may be necessary before conditioned relaxation can occur in rats (Denny & Ratner, 1970). Since this still varies on an individual basis, individualization is still imperative. Duration of CS exposure is a multidetermined variable involving the number and duration of treatment sessions and the type, number, and duration of CS. In order to individualize treatment it is frequently necessary to monitor multiple indices of fear and avoidance responses. The following methods may be utilized in monitoring subjects: physiological recording; behavioral observation (approach, avoidance relaxation, etc.); and subjective report of the experience or anticipation of fear (McCutcheon & Adams, 1975). Such an ongoing data system within a multiple baseline framework would provide a basis for the decision making and evaluation required for individualized treatment. This approach would allow for the reorganization of the procedural components in multiple and unique ways to meet the requirements of a particular individual at a particular time.

Since all of the procedures may be conceptualized as different ways of facilitating CS exposure, any single component or any of the possible combinations of components could be utilized at a given time. For example, it may be that early in the treatment process, when the CS elicit anxiety beyond that which is optimal for learning, the graded CS and/or competing response components could be utilized with extinction or RP procedures. Then, as soon as possible, these components would be faded out, thus facilitating rapid treatment without excessive stress. In particular, the CSF and RP need to be standardized. As has been noted clinically, RP is effective in eliminating avoidance, but CSF may be required to eliminate the residual fear (Mills, Agras, Barlow, & Mills, 1973). The indices monitored should be utilized to define operationally CS termination and treatment termination contingencies.

Clinical analogues of the massed trials and punishment response prevention procedures could be profitably developed and evaluated for use with clinical cases. A comparison of the effects of stimulus control, response control, and a combination of both seems to be in order. Certainly, social facilitation, modeling, and contigent reinforcement need to be utilized more frequently in the elimination of anxiety and avoidance responses. Cost effectiveness in terms of treatment time required and rate of premature termination of treatment need to be considered in evaluating the relative merits of SD, CSF, RP, and other procedural combinations.

The factor of individualization must be assessed and/or held constant when assessing other variables in both analogue and clinical procedures. Simple yoked control procedures are not adequate. Factorial design where yoking is included as an independent variable may be necessary along with repeated-measures designs, including N-of-one and N-of-two designs (Gottman, 1973). With an appropriate experimental design it may be possible to demonstrate that the refined individualization methods are the important components of the CS grading procedure. Animal analogue studies would be then able to increase their predictive power by shifting emphasis from the normal population of animals to those whose CARs are extremely resistant to the regular extinction procedure.

It would seem desirable to employ the CS grading and/or competing-response components and possibly the modeling and/or contingent reinforcement procedures when the subject is allowed to control his own CS exposure. These components may not be necessary when the subject is not allowed to control his exposure to the CS, as in RP and CSF. In cases where an adequate duration of CS exposure is not guaranteed (for example, when sufficient time is lacking, or when the client's motivation for treatment is minimal), the CSF or RP procedure may be ruled out or at least combined with some other components.

In conclusion, one should be cautioned that in making a transition from animals to humans a number of additional factors such as subject expectancies, demand characteristics, and experimenter bias (Morganstern, 1973) must be considered. The role of these variables in animal analogues is not clear. It is hoped, and expected, that in future research with animal analogues of behavioral treatment methods, other analogues of behavioral disorders such as rituals, addictions, and similar disorders will receive more attention.

REFERENCES

American Psychological Association. *Ethical principles in the conduct of research with human participants.* (2nd ed.) Washington, D.C.: American Psychological Association, 1973.

Bachrach, A. J. *Psychological research: An introduction.* New York: Random House, 1965.

Bandura, A., Blanchard, E. B., & Ritter, B. Relative efficacy of desensitization and modeling approaches for inducing behavioral, affective, and attitudinal changes. *Journal of Personality and Social Psychology,* 1969, 13, 173–199.

Bandura, A., & Menlove, F. L. Factors determining vicarious extinction of avoidance behavior through symbolic modeling. *Journal of Personality and Social Psychology,* 1968, 8, 99–108.

Bankart, B. M. Behavior therapy for phobias (extinction of avoidance) in rats: Effects associated with certain stimulus and response parameters. *Dissertation Abstract International B*, 1972, 32(7-B), 4238.

Baum, M. Rapid extinction of an avoidance response following a period of response prevention in the avoidance apparatus. *Psychological Reports*, 1966, 18, 59–64.

Baum, M. Extinction of an avoidance response motivated by intense feat: Social facilitation of the action of response prevention (flooding) in rats. *Behaviour Research and Therapy*, 1969, 6, 57–62. (a)

Baum, M. Extinction of an avoidance response following response prevention: Some parametric investigations. *Canadian Journal of Psychology*, 1969, 23, 1–10. (b)

Baum, M. Extinction of an avoidance response in rats via response prevention (flooding): A test for residual fear. *Psychological Reports*, 1971, 28, 203–208.

Baum, M. Extinction of avoidance behavior: Comparison of various flooding procedures in rats. *Psychonomic Science*, 1973, 1, 22–24. (a)

Baum, M. Extinction of avoidance in rats: The effects of chlorpromazine and methylphenidate administered in conjunction with flooding (response prevention). *Behaviour Research and Therapy*, 1973, 11, 165–169. (b)

Baum, M., & Oler, I. D. Comparison of two techniques for hastening extinction of avoidance responding in rats. *Psychological Reports*, 1968, 23, 807–813.

Benline, T. A., & Simmel, E. C. Effects of blocking of the avoidance response on the elimination of the conditioned fear response. *Psychonomic Science*, 1967, 8, 357–358.

Berman, J. S., & Katzev, R. D. Factors involved in the rapid elimination of avoidance behavior. *Behaviour Research and Therapy*, 1972, 10, 247–256.

Bersh, P. J., & Paynter, W. E. Pavlovian extinction in rats during avoidance response prevention. *Journal of Comparative and Psychological Psychology*, 1972, 78, 255–259.

Best, J. K., & Baum, M. Studies of the extinction of avoidance responding through the massing of trials. *Canadian Journal of Psychology*, 1969, 23, 438–444.

Carlsmith, J. M. The effect of punishment on avoidance responses: The use of different stimuli for training and punishment. Paper presented at the meeting of the Eastern Psychological Association, Philadelphia, April 1961.

Carlson, N. J., & Black, A. H. Traumatic avoidance learning: Note on the effect of response prevention during extinction. *Psychological Reports*, 1959, 5, 409–412.

Church, R. M. Systematic effect of random error in the yoked control design. *Psychological Bulletin*, 1964, 62, 122–131.

Coulter, X., Riccio, D. C., & Page, H. A. Effects of blocking an instrumental avoidance response: Facilitated extinction but persistence of "fear." *Journal of Comparative and Physiological Psychology*, 1969, 68, 377–381.

Davitz, J. R., & Mason, D. J. Socially facilitated reduction of a fear response in rats. *Journal of Comparative and Physiological Psychology*, 1955, 48, 149–151.

Delprato, D. J. An animal analogue to systematic desensitization and elimination of avoidance. *Behaviour Research and Therapy*, 1973, 11, 49–55. (a)

Delprato, D. J. Exposure to the aversive stimulus in an animal analogue to systematic desensitization. *Behaviour Research and Therapy*, 1973, 11, 187–192. (b)

Denny, M. R., & Ratner, S. C. *Comparative Psychology*. Homewood, Ill.: Dorsey Press, 1970.

Dickson, A. L. An analysis of Wolpe's reciprocal inhibition principle. *Dissertation Abstracts International*, 1972, 32, 6675.

Dmitruk, V. M. "Experimental neurosis" in cats: Fact or artifact? *Journal of Abnormal Psychology*, 1974, 83, 97–105.

D'Zurilla, T. J., Wilson, G. T., & Nelson, R. A preliminary study of the effectiveness of graduate prolonged exposure in the treatment of irrational fear. *Behavior Therapy*, 1973, 4, 672–685.

Gale, D. S., Sturmfels, G., & Gale, E. N. A comparison of reciprocal inhibition and experimental extinction in the psychotherapeutic process. *Behaviour Research and Therapy*, 1966, 4, 149–155.

Gambrill, E. Effectiveness of the counterconditioning procedure in eliminating avoidance behavior. *Behaviour Research and Therapy*, 1967, 5, 263–274.

Goldstein, A. J. Separate effects of extinction, counter-conditioning and progressive approach in overcoming fear. *Behaviour Research and Therapy*, 1969, 7, 47–56.

Gordon, A., & Baum, M. Increased efficacy of flooding (response prevention) in rats through positive intracranial stimulation. *Journal of Comparative and Physiological Psychology*, 1971, 75, 68–72.

Gottman, J. M. N-of-one and N-of-two research in psychotherapy. *Psychological Bulletin*, 1973, 80, 93–105.

Hake, D. F., & Laws, D. R. Social facilitation of responses during a stimulus paired with electric shock. *Journal of the Experimental Analysis of Behavior*, 1967, 10, 387–392.

Hall, J. C. Some conditions of anxiety extinction. *Journal of Abnormal and Social Psychology*, 1955, 51, 126–132.

Hamilton, M. G. A comparison of systematic desensitization and operant conditioning techniques in the reduction of fear behavior. *Dissertation Abstracts International B*, 1972, 32,(9-B), 5440–5441.

Heath, G. H. A comparison of reciprocal inhibition and flooding in decreasing the strength of a conditioned avoidance response. *Dissertation Abstracts*, 1968, 29, 1842B–1843B.

Holder, R. One session of flooding as treatment for conditioned avoidance responding in humans: The effect of individualization of treatment duration. Unpublished master's thesis, North Texas State University, 1974.

Hughes, H. H., An investigation of the assumptions of implosive therapy and systematic desensitization using an animal analogue. *Dissertation Abstracts International*, 1971, 31, 4996–4997.

Kamano, D. K. Using drugs to modify the effects of response prevention on avoidance extinction. *Behaviour Research and Therapy*, 1972, 10, 367–370.

Kamin, L. J. The gradient of delay of secondary reward in avoidance learning tested on avoidance trials only. *Journal of Comparative and Physiological Psychology*, 1957, 50, 450–456.

Katzev, R. Extinguishing avoidance responses as a function of delayed warning signal termination. *Journal of Experimental Psychology*, 1967, 75, 339–344.

Kimble, G. A., & Kendall, J. W. A comparison of two methods of producing experimental extinction. *Journal of Experimental Psychology*, 1953, 45, 87–89.

Lane, B. The reduction of anxiety under three experimental conditions. *Dissertation Abstracts International*, 1954, 14, 1460–1461.

Leclerc, R., St. Laurent, J., & Baum, M. Effects of rewarding, aversive, and neutral intracranial stimulation administered during flooding (response prevention) in rats. *Physiological Psychology*, 1973, 1, 24–28.

Leitenberg, H., & Callahan, E. J. Reinforced practice and reduction of different kinds of fears in adults and children. *Behaviour Research and Therapy*, 1973, 11, 19–30.

Linton, J., Riccio, D. C., Rohrbaugh, M., & Page, H. A. The effects of blocking an instrumental avoidance response: Fear reduction or enhancement? *Behaviour Research and Therapy*, 1970, 8, 267–272.

Masserman, J. *Behavior and neurosis.* Chicago: University of Chicago Press, 1943.

McCutcheon, B. A., & Adams, H. E. The physiological basis of implosive therapy. *Behaviour Research and Therapy,* 1975, 13, 93–100.

Mills, H. L., Agras, S., Barlow, D. H., & Mills, J. R. Compulsive rituals treated by response prevention. *Archives of General Psychiatry,* 1973, 28, 524–529.

Moltz, H. Resistance to extinction as a function of variations in the stimuli associated with shock. *Journal of Experimental Psychology,* 1954, 47, 418–425.

Morganstern, K. P. Implosive therapy and flooding procedures: A critical review. *Psychological Bulletin,* 1973, 79, 318–334.

Morrison, B. J., & Hill, W. F. Socially facilitated reduction of the fear response in rats raised in groups or in isolation. *Journal of Comparative and Physiological Psychology,* 1967, 63, 71–76.

Nelson, F. Effects of two counterconditioning procedures on the extinction of fear. *Journal of Comparative and Physiological Psychology,* 1966, 62, 208–213.

Nelson, F. Effects of chlorpromazine on fear extinction. *Journal of Comparative and Physiological Psychology,* 1967, 64, 496–498.

Nelson, F. Free versus forced exposure with two procedures for conditioning and measuring fear in the rat. *Journal of Comparative and Physiological Psychology,* 1969, 69, 682–687.

Nelson, F. Fear-reducing effect of graduated versus nongraduated forced exposure. *Psychological Reports,* 1971, 28, 907–910.

Overmier, J. B., & Bull, J. A. On the independence of stimulus control of avoidance. *Journal of Experimental Psychology,* 1969, 79, 464–467.

Page, H. A. The facilitation of experimental extinction by response prevention as a function of the acquisition of a new response. *Journal of Comparative and Physiological Psychology,* 1955, 48, 14–16.

Page, H. A., & Hall, J. F. Experimental extinction as a function of the prevention of a response. *Journal of Comparative and Physiological Psychology,* 1953, 46, 33–34.

Polin, A. T. The effect of flooding and physical suppression as extinction techniques on an anxiety-motivated avoidance locomotor response. *Journal of Psychology,* 1959, 47, 235–245.

Poppen, R. Counterconditioning of conditioned suppression in rats. *Psychological Reports,* 1970, 27, 659–671.

Schiff, R., Smith, N., & Prochaska, J. Extinction of avoidance in rats as a function of duration and number of blocked trials. *Journal of Comparative and Physiological Psychology,* 1972, 81, 356–359.

Sermat, V., & Shephard, A. H. The effect of a feeding procedure on persistent avoidance response. *Journal of Comparative and Physiological Psychology,* 1953, 46, 33–34. 206–211.

Sherman, A. R. Therapy of maladaptive fear-motivated behavior in the rat by the systematic gradual withdrawal of a fear-reducing drug. *Behaviour Research and Therapy,* 1967, 5, 121–129.

Sherman, R. W. Response-contingent CS termination in the extinction of avoidance learning. *Behaviour Research and Therapy,* 1970, 8, 227–239.

Shipley, R. H., Mock, L. A., & Levis, D. J. Effects of several response prevention procedures on activity, avoidance responding, and conditioned fear in rats. *Journal of Comparative and Physiological Psychology,* 1971, 77, 256–270.

Uno, T., Geer, S., & Goates, L. Observational facilitation of response prevention. *Behaviour Research and Therapy,* 1973, 11, 207–212.

Weinberger, N. M. Effect of detainment on extinction of avoidance responses. *Journal of Comparative and Physiological Psychology*, 1965, **60**, 135–138.

Wells, A. M. An investigation of operant elements in desensitization: A comparison of differential reinforcement of other behaviors and desensitization in the reduction of phobic responses in rats. *Dissertation Abstracts International B*, 1971, **31**(7-B), 4350.

Wilson, E. H., & Dinsmoor, J. A. Effect of feeding on "fear" as measured by passive avoidance in rats. *Journal of Comparative and Physiological Psychology*, 1970, **70**, 431–436.

Wilson, G. T. A comparison of different methods of extinction of the conditioned avoidance response in rats. *Dissertation Abstracts International B*, 1972, **32**,(8-B), 4873.

Wilson, G. T. Counterconditioning versus forced exposure in extinction of avoidance responding and conditioned fear in rats. *Journal of Comparative and Physiological Psychology*, 1973, **82**, 105–114.

Wilson, G. T., & Davison, G. C. Process of fear reduction in systematic desensitization: Animal studies. *Psychological Bulletin*, 1971, **76**, 1–14.

Wolpe, J. Experimental neurosis as learned behavior. *British Journal of Psychology*, 1952, **43**, 243–268.

BEHAVIORAL CONSIDERATIONS IN THE TREATMENT OF SEXUAL DYSFUNCTION

L. MICHAEL ASCHER

Behavior Therapy Unit
Department of Psychiatry
Temple University
Philadelphia, Pennsylvania

AND

RUTH E. CLIFFORD

Department of Psychology
Temple University
Philadelphia, Pennsylvania

I. INTRODUCTORY CONSIDERATIONS

For several decades, the body of literature related to sexual dysfunction was largely stagnating under the influence of psychoanalysis. Since Freud's initial work, few who followed his orientation had done more than to shadow his word with only the slightest elaboration. In the late 1950's Wolpe (1958) revolutionized the course of thinking as to the etiology and treatment of sexual dysfunction. He viewed sexual dysfunction as a maladaptive behavior which could be influenced by experimentally validated principles of learning. To test this hypothesis he applied his *in vivo* desensitization model to several dysfunctional complaints and successfully corrected the difficulties. Between 1958 and 1970 a small number of behaviorally oriented mental health workers followed through with Wolpe's initial work, both by developing additional techniques and by utilizing the behavioral orientation with variations of sexual dysfunction. Subsequently, Masters and Johnson (1970) produced a second major contribution, a systematic program for the treatment of sexual dysfunction. From these two major innovations a literature has developed which is markedly different from that which existed prior to 1958, both in conceptions of the problem and its treatment and in the effectiveness of the procedures utilized.

This review takes as its point of departure the work of Wolpe (1958) and that of Masters and Johnson (1966, 1970, 1975) and follows the development of the related behavioral literature to the present. It would seem appropriate at this juncture to state definitions of several terms important to our subject.

It was a bit difficult to select a working definition of behavior therapy in the present case, because significant conponents of the relevant literature are not typically presented under the aegis of behavior therapy (e.g., Kaplan, 1974; Masters & Johnson, 1970). A broad definition of behavior therapy must, therefore, be selected in order to avoid dismissing potentially beneficial programs prematurely. In a recent article, Begelman (1975) surveyed various widely accepted definitions of behavior therapy and chose the following: "the development of techniques of behavior change whose effectiveness can be explained in terms of learning theory or experimentally derived psychological principles." Despite its shortcomings, this definition would seem to be broad enough for the purpose of the present review.

We will define *sexual dysfunction* as a notably diminished or unsatisfying sexual response in the presence of appropriate sexual stimuli. Such complaints are most commonly reported in the context of a heterosexual relationship (and less often within a homosexual relationship). In contrast, *sexual deviation* may be defined as a satisfying sexual response in the presence of inappropriate sexual stimuli (e.g., children, animals, pieces of clothing, unwilling adults). Considerations in the present review will be restricted to sexual dysfunction.

A wide variety of factors have been implicated in the etiology of sexual dysfunction; the interested reader is referred to Cooper (1969b), Masters and Johnson (1970), and Kaplan (1974) for detailed reviews on the topic. Because there is general agreement that psychological factors play a role in the vast majority of sexual dysfunctional complaints, this chapter is devoted to behavioral techniques which have been applied to these psychological factors. It should be noted that even in the relatively few cases in which physical pathology (e.g., the effects of drugs, diabetes) plays a decisive role, psychological reactions (particularly performance anxiety) probably develop as secondary factors. The longer the individual experiences the dysfunction, the greater the significance of the hypothesized role of anxiety. Thus, alleviation of the physical basis of the dysfunction does not guarantee resumption of normal sexual behavior. Only when the psychological components of the problem are directly dealt with can one expect complete and reliable reversal of the dysfunction. Therefore, programs which are totally physically oriented or drug oriented are probably doomed to failure for the majority of patients.

In an area which is speculative at best, considerations of the etiology of sexual dysfunctions stand out as little more than fiction. Therefore, we will give little attention to etiology in this chapter, beyond the brief statement here.

From the point of view of the researcher, this chapter is perhaps 5 years premature. There is, to date, little controlled experimentation; the majority of supporting data are derived from case studies. The reader who expects to find firm conclusions with a solid experimental basis in the area of sexual dysfunction will no doubt be disappointed. In our presentation we are forced by the inadquacies of the literature into speculation and methodological criticism. Perhaps the chapter can best be described as a critical review of the state of the art of sex therapy. Parenthetically, this may not turn out to be the liability which it at first appears since, because of the nature of the behavioral complaint, research will most probably emanate from clinical settings. Our hope is that this chapter will serve to forestall

premature conclusions based on weak evidence and to encourage
more rigorous work in the area of sex therapy.

II. MALE SEXUAL DYSFUNCTION

A. Definitions

In the past, it had been the convention to label all male sexual
dysfunctions under the rubric of "impotence." Recent understanding
permits the discrimination of various consistent dysfunctional syndromes and, consequently, the specific behavioral interventions effective for each dysfunction. The nosological system, of course,
varies with the conception of the behavioral difficulty and/or the
proposed treatment. For example, Masters and Johnson (1970) indicate three major categories of dysfunction, each having different
hypothesized etiologies and behaviors; yet their treatment is basically
the same for each syndrome, with the addition of various ancillary
techniques for specific problems. They define *impotence* as the
inability to achieve or maintain an erection of sufficient quality to
accomplish successful coital connection. They arbitrarily differentiate between *primary* and *secondary* impotence: the former signifies
that successful intercourse has never occurred, while the latter does
specify the occurrence of successful intercourse at least once. Again,
however, there are no differential treatment implications resulting
from this dichotomy.

In their attempt to define *premature ejaculation*, Masters and
Johnson (1970) criticize definitions based on duration as being
arbitrary and without consideration of the partner's needs or societal
conventions. They label as premature ejaculation "the inability to
control the ejaculatory process for a sufficient length of time during
intravaginal containment to satisfy one's partner in at least fifty
percent of their coital connections." It would seem that this definition of premature ejaculation could, with some individuals, produce
performance anxiety, and thus become iatrogenic, particularly
among men not in therapy or those in the hands of inept therapists.
Furthermore, the stringency of this definition would result in classi-
fying many more males as premature ejaculators.

Perhaps a better definition was proposed by Schapiro (1943),
who suggested that premature ejaculation was that condition wherein
orgasm and ejaculation persistently occur before or immediately

after entering the female during coitus. With respect to distinctive groups within the class of premature ejaculation, Schapiro described two types: type A, in which premature ejaculation was associated with erectile insufficiency; and type B, in which it was associated with abnormally high sexual tension. Cooper (1969a) used a tripartite system: type 1 was similar to Schapiro's "type B"; type 2 referred to acute onset of premature ejaculation; and type 3 was similar to Schapiro's "type A." Both in the system of Schapiro and of Cooper, discriminations within the class of premature ejaculation were based on developmental data and had implications for differential treatment approaches.

Masters and Johnson (1970) define *retarded ejaculation* as the inability to ejaculate intravaginally and view it as a syndrome opposite to that of premature ejaculation; no additional descriptive details are given, however. A more refined definition was provided by Johnson (1965). He referred to retarded ejaculation as the persistent inability to experience orgasm or to ejaculate in the presence of normal erection and sexual desire.

In contrast to Masters and Johnson's schema (1970), Kaplan (1974) conceives of two classes of male dysfunction, i.e., *erectile* (or arousal) *dysfunction* and *ejaculatory dysfunction;* the latter class is subdivided into *premature ejaculation* and *retarded ejaculation.* Based upon her differential treatment directives, one finds more justification for Kaplan's classification system than for that of Masters and Johnson.

B. Wolpe's (1958) Behavioral Approach

Although behavior therapy has directed itself to all of the male dysfunctional syndromes, much of the work has concerned erective dysfunction. It is hypothesized (Wolpe, 1958) that the basis of erectile failure lies in anxiety related to performance concerns, which dysfunctional males have learned to associate with the sexual situation. In the normally functioning male, several sources of stimulation interact to produce sexual arousal: observation of the sexually aroused female, erotic fantasy, and the direct ministrations of the female to arouse the male. In contrast, the dysfunctional male attends to other aspects of the sexual situation that produce stimulation incompatible with sexual arousal. The initial source of incompatible stimulation, often anxiety, develops and gains strength as the male realizes sexual activity is imminent. Other arousal-inhibiting emotions, such as anger at or disgust towards the partner, have also been reported in connection with erectile failure. Since the role of sex therapy in such cases may be supplanted by marital counseling, we have chosen to concentrate on anxiety as a primary factor. This performance anxiety is related to concerns about the male's ability to satisfactorily perform intercourse and the possible contingencies of failure: rejection or, at least, disappointment from the frustrated female. Once involved in sexual activity, an additional source of anxiety seems to result from the tendency of the dysfunctional male to monitor his level of arousal, especially the degree of penile tumescence (Masters & Johnson, 1970). In addition to producing anxiety, such cognitive activity distracts the male from attending to those stimuli which could contribute to his arousal. Thus, it is hypothesized that the normally functioning male attends to stimuli in the sexual situation which can serve to arouse him, while the dysfunctional male attends to stimuli which are nonarousing, distracting him from arousal stimuli and producing anxiety which is incompatible with sexual arousal.

The behavioral program is designed to reduce performance anxiety related to the sexual situation and to enhance the effectiveness of erotic components of the interaction. The prototype of such an approach was first described by Wolpe (1958), who utilized *in vivo* desensitization as the major component of the treatment program. After conducting a behavioral analysis, the therapist typically instructs the patient in deep muscle relaxation (Jacobson, 1938; Wolpe, 1973), determines the availability of a cooperative female partner, and assigns the patient graded homework assignments. In the case of married males, obtaining the cooperation of their wives is often possible as long as the relationship remains viable. Most difficulty at this point is encountered with single males. Frequently, the dysfunctional single male has so great a level of performance anxiety that he will avoid any type of interaction with females which could possibly lead to intimate contact and consequent failure. A long-term pattern of avoidance may leave such individuals without the necessary skills required to develop such interpersonal relationships. Before therapy can be conducted for the dysfunctional behavior, a program must be undertaken to teach the patient how to relate appropriately to females.

Homework assignments of graded types of stimulation are based on two principles: (1) the patient should never progress past the point at which he begins to feel anxiety; (2) intercourse is strictly prohibited. The patient is instructed to lie in bed nude with his partner and to progress as far as he wishes, stopping at the initial point of discomfort. The therapist may give specific assignments past which the patient may not venture, and may coordinate these *in vivo* tasks with imaginal desensitization conducted during the therapy session. In most cases the therapist does not have to "instruct" the patient to attempt intercourse; as Masters and Johnson (1970) have pointed out, this would probably engender renewed performance anxiety. Typically, as the patient gains confidence he violates the prohibition. In the frequent situations where the patient continues to abide strictly by the therapist's rules, the female partner may be given *sub rosa* instructions to proceed to female superior position.

The sequence described above represents the ideal situation. Unfortunately, various difficulties may arise which impede the patient's progress (cf. Lobitz, LoPiccolo, Lobitz, & Brockway, 1975). Such problems may be dealt with by the behavioral clinician with the aid of a number of techniques in addition to systematic desensitization. For example, performance anxiety, which has been hypothesized to be a basic etiological factor in erective failure, seems to be related to responses that are goal oriented. That is, the dysfunctional male may set up behavioral goals or criteria which may have deleterious effects on therapeutic progress. This being the case, the therapist should be careful to avoid emphasizing the patient's erection after the intake interview; such reference might inadvertently suggest a goal for the patient. Thus, the couple may be given a homework assignment restricted to the initial level of their particular *in vivo* hierarchy. Upon returning for the next session the man may report that they engaged in four home sessions during the week and that he had a strong erection throughout each session. A wise therapist would comment in passing that he/she is pleased that this made the patient happy. However, as they are far from the point at which the patient will need an erection, the patient's report is of little consequence now.

The question has been raised as to whether *in vivo* or imaginal desensitization is more effective. Unfortunately, no systematic evidence concerning sexual dysfunctions in relation to this question is available. Most behavior therapists currently rely to a great extent on *in vivo* procedures, perhaps turning to imaginal desensitization in extremely severe cases where even very gradual approximations to intimate contact are highly anxiety arousing (see Annon, 1971). Actually, there is no evidence that *in vivo* procedures are superior in effectiveness to imaginal desensitization, and some workers note that either one seems equally successful (Laughren & Kass, 1975) in dealing with sexual dysfunctions. One study with snake phobics did find that for high-anxiety clients imaginal procedures were more effective than *in vivo* techniques (Cooke, 1966).

Since Wolpe's (1958) original statement on the subject, numerous clinicians have reported successful use of a treatment program organized around desensitization (*in vivo* or in imagination) to alleviate male sexual dysfunction (e.g., Cooper, 1968, 1969a, 1969b, 1969e; Dengrove, 1967, 1971b; Friedman, 1968; Friedman & Lipsedge, 1971; Garfield, McBrearty, & Dichter, 1969; Laughren & Kass, 1975; Lazarus, 1961, 1965; Lobitz *et al.*, 1975; LoPiccolo, Stewart, & Watkins, 1972; Razani, 1972). In addition, reviews of published and unpublished data regarding the effectiveness of systematic desensitization with sexual dysfunction have appeared in the literature (e.g., Ince, 1973; Laughren & Kass, 1975; Rachman, 1961; Shusterman, 1973).

Recently, there have been several attempts to test the effectiveness of systematic desensitization (usually applied with ancillary behavioral techniques such as assertive training) in treating sexual dysfunctions. (Studies which considered only female sexual dysfunction will be described in a later section.)

Cooper (1969e), following some initial pilot work, conducted a study assessing the effects of a short-term therapeutic program that resembled a behavioral approach. He studied two types of male sexual dysfunctions: impotence, which he defined as the persistent inability to obtain an erection sufficient to allow orgasm during heterosexual coitus; and retarded ejaculation, "the persistent inability to experience orgasm or ejaculate in the presence of normal erection and sexual desire." A four-part treatment was employed: deep muscle relaxation as outlined by Wolpe (1958); instructions on ways in which the couple could increase the level of sexual stimulation for the man; sexual education; and a superficial, supportive psychotherapy, which was used particularly when the couple became discouraged. Of the 57 patients who satisfied the selection criteria, 44 completed treatment (at least 20 biweekly sessions). The results were classified in the following terms: (1) *recovered*—the difficulty had completely subsided, and the male could engage in all aspects of heterosexual intercourse to his satisfaction whenever he desired (8 patients, or 18%, fell into this category); (2) *improved*—performance in all phases of coitus improved, but with difficulties still present (11 patients, or 25%); (3) *unchanged* (11 patients, or 25%); and (4) *worse* (14 patients, or 32%).

In a partial replication of the above work, Cooper (1969b) again studied the effectiveness of a short-term therapy program. In addition to impotence and retarded ejaculation, he included premature ejaculation. Impotence was classified in terms of acute onset (Hastings, 1963) or insidious onset. Forty-nine patients completed treatment, of whom 7 (14%) were rated as recovered, 12 (25%) as improved, 21 (43%) as unchanged, and 9 (18%) as worse.

A third study (Cooper, 1969b) focused on treatment of premature ejaculation. Cooper classified his sample into three groups based on the developmental history of their dysfunction: type 1, "premature ejaculation with good erections since adolescence" [similar to the "type B" premature ejaculation of Schapiro (1943)]; type 2, "acute onset of premature ejaculation with erectional insufficiency" [similar to the uncomplicated premature ejaculation of Tuthill (1955)]; and type 3, "premature ejaculation with insidious-onset impotence or retarded ejaculation (similar to Schapiro's "type A" premature ejaculation). Cooper's treatment program consisted of the four components employed in the abovementioned studies, and included a fifth procedure which was based on Semans' (1956) work. The five components played varying roles in the three different treatment programs developed, on an *ad hoc* basis, for each of the three syndromes. The 30 clients attended a minimum of 20 therapeutic sessions. They were classified as "improved" if they could delay ejaculation for a period twice as long as that prior to the therapeutic intervention and if the male reported an increase in satisfaction. Forty-three percent of the patients improved, 50% remained unchanged, and 7% regressed. The type 2, acute-onset patients improved the greatest amount and most rapidly (mean number of sessions to maximum improvement was 4), whereas those reporting to have experienced premature ejaculation continuously throughout adolescence (i.e., type 1) had the worst results and remained in therapy longest (only one case improved after ten sessions). There was a statistically significant difference between these two groups.

The experimental design used in Cooper's studies preclude the data from providing more than tangential support for the efficacy of the treatment which he utilized. For example, his design includes a single group which is not exposed to adequate pretreatment or follow-up testing. His samples are neither representative of the dysfunctional male population nor are they randomly drawn from that population. Nevertheless, Cooper's work is of importance because he attempted to study a rudimentary behavioral treatment of sexual dysfunction in a relatively objective manner; the studies represented the most systematic approach to the topic until that time.

Obler (1973) compared a group receiving desensitization with one receiving dynamically oriented group therapy. The two experimental groups were composed of 13 males and 9 females, and 11 males and 9 females, respectively. In addition, 13 males and 9 females were assigned to a no-treatment condition. Individuals complaining of various sexual dysfunctions were included in the study. Desensitization subjects were seen individually, by the author, for 15 sessions. The major technique employed was systematic desensitization in imagination, conducted during the session, with *in vivo* homework assignments. Assertive training was included in the sessions. Subjects assigned to the dynamically oriented group received an equivalent amount of therapeutic time in a group context. This condition was administered by two therapists skilled in an analytic orientation. Data indicated that subjects receiving the desensitization program improved significantly compared with subjects receiving the dynamic program or those receiving no therapy. According to the author, more than 80% of the desensitization subjects became sexually functional and remained so after a $1\frac{1}{2}$ year follow-up (details regarding the follow-up procedure and, to some extent, the criteria of "sexual functioning" were rather sketchy). On the other hand, those subjects exposed to the dynamic therapeutic approach yielded results more like the no-treatment control subjects. The many methodological shortcomings of Obler's study somewhat reduce the significance of the data; however, data yielded by this study provide more substantial information than those resulting from the voluminous case studies (Paul, 1969).

Goldstein, Ascher, Munjack, and Phillips (1975) conducted an outcome study of the effectiveness of a behavioral approach in treating secondary impotence. Seven couples were assigned to the treatment group and seven were assigned to a no-treatment control group. The level of sexual functioning was assessed both by an independent assessor and by self-report; these ratings were made at pretreatment, posttreatment, and follow-up sessions. The mean number of therapy sessions completed was 12.7. Ten measures were chosen as dependent variables, and all differentiated between the two groups at the posttreatment session. Posttreatment improvement was maintained by the experimental group at follow-up testing, 2 years later. However, because the control couples spontaneously improved during this period, differences between the two groups were diminished in follow-up tests.

C. Recent Developments in Sex Therapy

1. MASTERS AND JOHNSON

Wolpe's (1958) *in vivo* approach to sexual dysfunction represented a significant departure from the manner in which these maladaptive behavioral syndromes had been treated in the past. A second major advance in the behavioral treatment of dysfunction was developed by Masters and Johnson (1970). They described a systematic procedure whereby couples complaining of any type of dysfunction participate in an intensive 2-week therapeutic program. Most of these couples are carefully selected by the referring professionals: each person chosen must be relatively free of gross neurotic or psychotic disturbances, must have a good relationship with the partner, who is willing to cooperate in therapy, and in general must be highly motivated. During the initial period a very detailed examination of the couple's sexual behavior is conducted, within the context of a conventional life history, as well as a physical examination and laboratory evaluations. From this information the therapists formulate a therapeutic plan for the couple, which is presented to them at a "round table" discussion. Following this presentation the couple is ready to begin the actual therapy.

Although the Masters and Johnson program is not self-styled as behavioral, it is considered, by numerous authorities, to be essentially behavioral in nature (e.g., Annon, 1974; Dengrove, 1971c; Knox, 1971; Laughren & Kass, 1975; Murphy & Mikulas, 1974; O'Leary & Wilson, 1975). Therefore we will take the liberty of briefly describing Masters and Johnson's therapeutic approach as we conceive it, in terms of the desensitization model.[1]

A principle which is basic to Masters and Johnson's treatment of sexual dysfunction is the nondemand character of their therapeutic approach. They point out that many therapists dealing with erective failure, and most patients themselves, eventually attempt to take direct measures to produce an erection and maintain a high level of

---

[1] The authors recognize that sexual dysfunctions are probably common results of a multitude of factors: individual, interpersonal, and physiological. No one therapeutic approach is being advocated. Ultimately, multiple interventions tailored to the individual case will probably be most effective, particularly in cases of erectile failure and secondary orgasmic dysfunction. We view the *in vivo* desensitization paradigm as a useful unifying framework around which existing sex therapy procedures may be described, recognizing that any explanation of the processes involved in successful sex therapy still requires a great deal of additional study.

sexual performance. In contrast Masters and Johnson make no direct suggestions which involve responses not under the voluntary control of the patient. Further, there is never a criterion of performance which the patient must reach at a particular time; good performance is not overly praised. Indeed, the value of failure for therapeutic progress is constantly emphasized.

An example of a case treated by one of the authors (Ascher) illustrates the measures a therapist must sometimes take to counter the performance demands of a dysfunctional client. A couple being treated for erective failure was progressing smoothly until the therapist suggested that sensate focus could extend to the genitals. The couple was instructed only to touch the partner's genitals when specifically invited to do so. At the following session both were quite glum, the male reporting that he was unable to become even mildly aroused during their home sessions. After some questioning it became evident that the male did not want his partner to touch his genitals unless he had an erection. When an erection developed during the first home session he quickly put her hand on it and wondered how long he could maintain the erection or what would happen if it subsided while her hand was on it. Consequently, he had a new task for which he needed an erection, developing a behavioral goal and related performance anxiety. In this case, the therapist questioned the female in the presence of the male concerning her feelings about touching a flaccid penis; she expressed no objections to this. The therapist then sent the couple home with the instructions that the male should only invite his partner to touch his penis when it was flaccid and that she was to remove her hand when he developed an erection. This seemed to improve the situation, and progress was continued during subsequent sessions.

One of Masters and Johnson's most important concepts with respect to erective failure concerns the maladaptive response of "spectatoring." They hypothesize that the dysfunctional male shifts his attention away from active participation in the sexual interaction and becomes an outside observer, i.e., a spectator of his own sexual performance. In so doing, he attends to stimuli which distract him from more appropriate sources of sexual stimulation while creating anxiety that is incompatible with arousal. Much of this program aims at a reduction of the spectator role and a return of the dysfunctional male to active sexual participation.

The basic procedure in their approach to the treatment of all sexual dysfunctions is "sensate focus." The initial step involves each partner alternately stimulating the other by massaging, kissing, caressing, and touching the entire body except for the genitals and the female's nipples. Intercourse is not permitted. The active partner is instructed to concentrate on the signals (both verbal and nonverbal) of the passive partner in order to learn how to maximize his or her pleasure. In this way, when the male is the active partner, he begins to shift his attention from himself to his partner and her erotic responses. The passive partner is instructed to attend to the erotic feelings produced by such stimulation and to signal to the active partner how to increase the pleasure. When the male is the passive partner, his attention should be moving toward the pleasure which he derives from the direct stimulation of his partner.

The prohibition against intercourse is intended to obviate the concern over erections, thus facilitating a shift of attention from the distracting spectator stimuli to the more appropriate arousal stimuli. The nondemand nature of the program is emaphsized in several ways: *First,* the couple is told that intercourse is prohibited because some of the responses required for its successful conclusion are not under voluntary control (e.g., erection, orgasm). *Second,* genital contact is excluded to remove sexual aspects from what is intended to be initially a sensual experience. *Third,* there are no goals and no criteria for performance; the partners are simply to passively experience sensual stimulation and enjoy themselves. Thus, as Wolpe (1958) suggests, the low-demand *in vivo* desensitization situation serves to reduce performance anxiety and increase erotic feelings.

Masters and Johnson (1970) ask the couple to remain at this level until they are comfortable with the prescribed activity (an unspecified criterion which perhaps reflect the way they describe their expectations to their clients). On the second level of the *in vivo* hierarchy the couple is permitted to engage in genital stimulation within the range of behaviors already included in sensate focus. The sensual aspect of the home practice sessions now takes on a more sexual tone. However, the nondemand complexion is still emphasized. The stimulation applied to the genitals is teasing, brushing, gentle—not the hard rhythmic type often used to force erection and orgasm. The "give-to-get" aspect of the Masters and Johnson approach become evident here as the active partner begins to experience feelings of arousal resulting from attention to the signals of pleasure emitted by the passive partner (cf. Stuart, 1969).

At this point, Masters and Johnson begin to differentiate among the three male sexual disorders by including specific techniques relevant to the different dysfunctions.

a. Erectile Failure Once an erection reliably results from sensate focus, the "stop-start" method is employed. On the third level of the hierarchy the female stimulates the male until an erection develops, at which point stimulation ceases and does not begin until the erection has completely disappeared. This exercise demonstrates to the couple that the erection can subside and yet not be permanently lost, thus reducing anxiety concerning erective return.

Success at this level leads to further sex play, with the female astride the supine male in order that she may introduce his penis into her vagina if she wishes. In this position, she is in control of intromission, which may be accomplished without change of position or any other preparation. This reduces anxiety on the man's part related to finding the vaginal opening, touching his erection and finding it to be less firm than he would like, or the possible diminution of his erection during a change in position. It also reduces the time between extravaginal and intravaginal stimulation of the penis. Anxiety regarding maintenance of the erection during vaginal containment may be approached by having the female introduce the penis into her vagina and remain motionless until the erection subsides. Of course, the male is informed that with this cessation of stimulation the erection should normally be expected to diminish. The female then stimulates the penis directly until the erection returns and again introduces it into her vagina.

The development of increasing confidence then permits the couple to move to the fifth level. During vaginal containment of the penis, the woman is instructed to move gently back and forth in a slow, nondemand fashion. The reduction of anxiety associated with this behavior enables the man to begin gentle thrusting. Again, if the erection is lost, the woman stimulates the penis extravaginally until an erection is obtained and intromission is repeated. Intromission is not a signal for any goal to be achieved. Pelvic nondemand pleasuring is the object, and goal-oriented behaviors (i.e., those designed to produce orgasm), with the associated anxiety and distraction, are strictly prohibited. If orgasm should occur it should not be the result of directed activity.

b. Premature Ejaculation Treatment for premature ejaculation (Masters & Johnson, 1970) begins with sensate focus, but if erective difficulties have not developed as a complication, the woman is immediately instructed to stimulate the penis directly in order to produce a strong erection. From here the couple follows a program based on procedures developed by Semans (1956). Masters and Johnson (1970) suggest that the woman should bring the man to a high level of sexual excitement and then, just prior to the point of ejaculatory inevitability, "squeeze" the penis (in a manner in which they carefully instruct the couple). This action has the effect both of an immediate loss in ejaculatory urgency and a significant reduction of erective strength. The goal of the procedure is to develop discrimination of those stimuli premonitory to ejaculation and to delay ejaculatory release during sexual activity. This initial level of the premature ejaculation hierarchy is completed when the male can delay his ejaculation for 15 to 20 min of extravaginal stimulation.

Once performance anxiety has been reduced, female-superior intromission may be attempted. At this second level, the woman remains motionless until her partner becomes accustomed to vaginal containment in a nondemand context. If he feels the need to ejaculate, the husband communicates this to his partner and she applies the "squeeze" procedure. When confidence and satisfactory delay are achieved in vaginal containment, the man is encouraged to engage in gentle thrusting. The woman remains motionless in order that the male can stop and start as he requires and can maintain full control over his sensations. Succeeding levels bring the couple to female thrusting, then to lateral position, and finally to male-superior position.

c. *Retarded Ejaculation* Sensate focus again forms the initial level of responding in the case of the male suffering from retarded ejaculation (Masters & Johnson, 1970). Once the couple reports sexual arousal as the results of sensate focus including genital stimulation (i.e., when erective difficulties are not present), the woman stimulates the penile shaft, manually or orally, in a demanding fashion in order to produce ejaculation. Masters and Johnson suggest that ejaculation in the presence of the woman is quite important, since the man will begin to associate her with sexual arousal and pleasure rather than with anxiety and other arousal-inhibiting emotions. At the next level the female stimulates the male to a point just short of ejaculation and then inserts the penis into her vagina; in this way, ejaculation can occur intravaginally. Stimulation should be maintained throughout the process of intromission. If ejaculation fails to occur, the woman should resume manual or oral stimulation and again attempt intravaginal ejaculation after her partner's level of arousal has regained sufficient strength. Eventually, a decreasing amount of preliminary stimulation will be required prior to intravaginal ejaculation.

d. *Results* Masters and Johnson report their findings in terms of total number of couples treated and number of treatment failures within each dysfunctional syndrome. In the case of primary impotence, Masters and Johnson have worked with 32 couples (including single males with surrogate partners), with 13 failures (yielding a success rate of 59.4%). Their success with secondary impotence is somewhat better; of 213 couples treated, 56 failed to respond to treatment (here the success ratio was 73.7%). They treated 186 premature ejaculators and failed with 4 (success was 97.8%), while 17 males complaining of retarded ejaculation were treated, with 3 failing to improve (resulting in a success ratio of 82.4%). Although they present carefully detailed definitions of the sexual dysfunctions in discussing their treatment, Masters and Johnson are rather obscure regarding the details of their results, never actually apprising their readers of their criteria for success or failure. Thus, what ostensibly appear to be objectively quantified data, turn out to be nothing more than the subjective description of the outcome of multiple uncontrolled case studies. As Paul (1969) points out, multiple case studies produce a product only slightly more useful than do single case studies. Such studies may serve to demonstrate new therapy techniques but can in no way provide evidence to support the therapeutic value of the technique.

2. KAPLAN'S PROGRAM

Kaplan's program (1974) is largely a restatement of Masters and Johnson's (1970), to which she has added some improvements and compounded some errors. The improvements consist largely of her clear, step-by-step, detailed descriptions of the behavioral techniques that she employs in her practice (but, as in the case of Masters and Johnson, does not credit appropriately to behavior therapy). Kaplan has included verbatim instructions for the couple who embarks on sensate focus. Her descriptions of the levels in the *in vivo* hierarchies for treatment of ejaculatory dysfunctions are most helpful, particularly for the therapist with little experience in behavioral treatment of sexual dysfunction (cf. Lobitz *et al.*, 1975).

On the other hand, her attempt to integrate three schools of therapy (behavioral, dyadic, and psychoanalytic) for the purpose of providing a context for the explanation and development of a therapeutic approach to sexual dysfunctions serves only to protract the book and obscure her message (Ascher & Phillips, 1975; Eysenck, 1975; LoPiccolo, 1975). Though even from a novice's viewpoint the analytic and interpersonal components are misrepresented and shortchanged, we are in a position where we can best comment on the behavioral component. We feel that Kaplan's treatment of behavioral principles as they are applied to sexual dysfunction is distorted and misleading (Ascher & Phillips, 1975). From Kaplan's presentation

(1974) it would not be difficult for the behaviorally uninitiated to see behavior therapy as an approach which treats only the individual, perceives the dysfunction as a phobia, and exclusively employs imaginal techniques in the therapist's office (e.g., Kaplan, 1974, p. 329).

III. FEMALE SEXUAL DYSFUNCTIONS

Female sexual dysfunctions were historically labeled under the generic term, "frigidity." Today our greater sophistication has led to the abandonment of this highly pejorative label and to the use of more precise categories (Kaplan, 1974).

Masters and Johnson (1970) list four basic types of dysfunction: (1) *primary orgasmic dysfunction,* in which orgasm has never occurred; (2) *situational orgasmic dysfunction,* in which orgasm occurs only during masturbation (coital type), only during intercourse (masturbatory type), or rarely in various situations (random type); (3) *low sexual tension,* or lack of arousal in general; (4) *vaginismus,* spasm of the vagina preventing penetration. Treatment is designed either for the orgasmic dysfunctions or for vaginismus, with no attention to greater specificity of application.

Wolpe (1973) divides female sex dysfunctions into two general types: *essential frigidity,* or lack of response to males in general; and *situational frigidity,* lack of response to a particular male. The former may either be *absolute,* a complete absence of arousal, or *relative,* in which some arousal occurs. Clearly, these subtypes may also apply in situational frigidity.

Vaginismus is included within these general categories, although it demands additional therapeutic procedures and hence probably deserves a separate category. While we do not favor Wolpe's retention of the term "frigidity," his typology recognizes one dimension which may be crucial for treatment decisions: the relationship of the dysfunction to the partner or to males in general. Decisions about treating nonsexual aspects of the relationship may hinge on this factor.

Kaplan's (1974) nosology, like that of Masters and Johnson (1970), is only loosely related to treatment plans. She lists four types of disorders: (1) *general sexual dysfunction,* in which the arousal system is disordered although orgasm ability may exist; (2) *orgastic dysfunctions;* (3) *vaginismus;* (4) *sexual anesthesia,* which, unlike the others, is a neurotic conversion symptom rather than a psychosomatic disorder. According to Kaplan sexual anesthesia is best treated using in-depth psychotherapy rather than sex therapy. Behavioral approaches such as aversion relief, discrimination training, or Kegel exercises might be alternatives in treating this syndrome. Kaplan's separation of general and orgastic dysfunction is theoretically appealing, since the male dysfunctions also are divided along the same dimension. However, few differences in treatment are currently available for the two conditions in women.

Since treatment approaches have not typically been related to specific subtypes (although the technology exists in behavior therapy to individualize programs for specific disorders), the discussion of sex therapy for females will be organized according to general treatment paradigms, with a separate section on vaginismus.

A. Systematic Desensitization

The application of behavior therapy to problems of women's responsivity began with Wolpe's use of systematic desensitization. The principles are similar to those discussed with regard to erective failure. The reader may wish to refer to several brief case descriptions in Wolpe's (1958) writings. Two entries appear in Wolpe's (1958) earliest book, in a table of cases treated with behavior therapy. In dealing with one woman whose problem was "partial frigidity" (presumably situational), the outcome as subjectively assessed by Wolpe was "much improved," meaning 80% freedom from symptoms. Treatment continued for 19 sessions over a 5-month period. The second case involved "sexual anxiety," among other problems, and after 57 sessions was judged by Wolpe as "moderately improved" (he considered failure as only 50% reduction in symptomatology). Neither of these reports specified the effectiveness of the therapy for the sexual problem separate from other target problems.

More recently, Wolpe (1973) described several cases of female sexual disorders. In one, a case of vaginismus, imaginal and *in vivo* desensitization were combined. In another, the woman's revulsion toward sex was treated with imaginal desensitization alone. In a third case, imaginal desensitization and assertive training were combined. All were apparently successful. However, with the limitations of the therapist's subjective report as the only criterion for success and the vagueness of the problem descriptions, these reports must be viewed as only suggestive of the potential of systematic desensitization for dealing with the sexual problems of women.

More recent work with systematic desensitization lends stronger support to claims of effectiveness with sexual dysfunctions. Numerous variations on Wolpe's basic paradigm have been introduced by subsequent behavior therapists. Those reports which include imaginal desensitization alone or along with *in vivo* methods will be discussed first.

Madsen and Ullmann (1967) presented a successful case in which the husband was asked to participate in the hierarchy construction and worked with his wife at home, describing the scenes to her while she relaxed. This innovation was based on the rationale that the husband's participation should reduce worries that he might have about his wife's therapy, enhance generalization of relaxation to the situation of his presence, and teach him principles of gradual progression of activities.

In a series of seven cases (male and female) reported by Hussain (1964), relaxation during desensitization was induced through hypnosis. Unfortunately the results of treatment for these cases were not presented separately from those of the entire multisymptomatic sample.

Brady (1966) injected intravenous Brevital (methohexital sodium) during desensitization to facilitate relaxation in five cases of severe aversion to intercourse. Imaginal desensitization was conducted in the therapist's office. Four of these women were "greatly improved" after 10 to 14 sessions, meaning that they entered freely into sexual activity with their husbands, experienced no pain or anxiety, and reach orgasm at least some of the time.

The duration of therapy was considerably shorter in Brady's series of cases than that in a group of 16 clients treated by Lazarus (1963), where the average number of sessions was 28. However, the latter women had all been in therapy previously for their sex problems without improvement, suggesting that they may have been a group more highly selected for the severity of their problems than those in Brady's study. Hierarchies ranged in content from watching animals copulate, hearing distracting noises during sex, varying the degree of darkness during the sex act, and graded intimacy of contacts. Of the 16 women, nine were "sexually adjusted" after therapy; those who completed at least 15 sessions all had successful outcomes, meaning that they looked forward to intercourse, initiated sex on occasion, and were nearly always orgasmic. Follow-ups were rather sketchy and involved an inadequate sample: only four clients were contacted, of whom two continued to improve and two relapsed after 15 months.

In his more recent book (1971), Lazarus mentioned that desensitization hierarchies may be particularly useful if they include social anxieties such as fear of criticism, rejection, disapproval, and ridicule. Geisinger (1969) provided a detailed example of a woman complaining of painful intercourse, guilt accompanying orgasm, and anxiety about sex. The patient was treated successfully using desensitization to sexual situations, with the addition of assertive training. Other case studies using imaginal desensitization have been presented, with varying claims of success, by Kraft and Al-Issa (1967), Goldstein (1971), and Wincze (1971).

Munjack, Cristol, Goldstein, Phillips, Goldberg, Whipple, Staples, and Kanno (1975) conducted an outcome study of the effectiveness of systematic desensitization, graduated tasks, and other behavior therapy techniques for primary and secondary orgasmic dysfunction. Twenty-two couples were randomly assigned to a treatment group or placed on a waiting list for 10 weeks. Sexual functioning and general personality variables were assessed before treatment, immediately after treatment, and at follow-ups 6 and 12 months later. All women had been nonorgasmic with their partners for at least a year before therapy. After 20 sessions, about 30% of the treated group was orgasmic in at least 50% of their sexual relations, while there was no change in orgasmic ability for the controls. Although this rate of improvement seems significantly lower than those reported by other programs, the failure of other programs to define their criteria precludes any meaningful comparison. More improvement was apparent concerning satisfaction from sex relations: the treated groups increased from satisfaction 15% of the time to about 70%, whereas the control group improved slightly, to about 30% of the time. Reductions in anxiety and depression were also noted for both groups combined.

One interesting finding was a difference between primary orgasmic dysfunctional women and those who were secondarily dysfunctional. Although both showed equal improvement during treatment, the primary group tended to decline by the time of the follow-up session, whereas the secondary group continued to improve. This finding suggests that additional steps may have been advisable in the treatment of the primary dysfunctional women. Unfortunately, the individualized nature of the treatment procedure and the combination of techniques compound the difficulty of pinpointing the deficiency of this particular program. This study deserves mention for its rare specification of outcome criteria and therapeutic method. The reliance on independent assessors for determining outcome is a significant improvement over the usual therapist judgments used.

B. Masters and Johnson's Method

Masters and Johnson's (1970) method of sensate focus has been described in detail in the previous section on male dysfunctions. The same steps are applied for women with all kinds of dysfunctions. When the woman is the receiver, she is told to assume a position which will maximize her comfort and accessibility: sitting between her partner's legs, with her back to him, and her legs draped over his. Masters and Johnson refer to this position as "back-protected," presumably because it provides the woman with a sense of security. It is unclear why this position should be viewed by Masters and Johnson as the only way in which a sense of protection can be conveyed, if such is necessary. Other workers (e.g., Kaplan, 1974) suggest that the couple adopt a position which is comfortable and convenient for the exercise, but leave the exact position to the couple's ingenuity and individual preference. To the extent that variety needs to be injected into the couple's sexual routine, choosing positions may be an early stage where creativity can be encouraged.

Given that sensate focus is a reciprocal procedure, an interesting question may be raised: Does it matter which spouse gives or receives first? Virtually no attention has been directed to this question in the literature, although couples often ask about this when they are first instructed about the technique. Kaplan (1974) recommends that when the woman is dysfunctional, she should be the giver first. The man, being satisfied first, will be more likely to caress her in a relaxed, nondemanding fashion, while she may feel relieved from any pressure to minister to him. Both partners can, therefore, devote themselves to carrying out the exercise in an undistracted fashion. Another advantage of this manner of proceeding, given Masters and Johnson's framework, is that it emphasizes even further that the target is primarily the dysfunctional system of the couple's interaction, not the individual. Finally, there may be benefit for the man, who sometimes learns for the first time through sensate focus to enjoy receiving relaxed, sensual, diffuse stimulation. At the same time the woman is asked to take a more active role sexually, which may be new to her. One interesting speculation is that such new assertiveness generalizes to greater assertion when she is in the receiving role, in directing her partner to stimulate her most effectively.

In discussing sensate focus, Kaplan describes a process in females analogous to the male's "spectatoring," which she calls "orgasm watching." This tension-mediating response is a cognitive event, a desperate overvaluation of orgasm that triggers arousal-inhibiting physiological mechanisms. In order to change the physiological response, an intervention directly at the cognitive level may be useful as a component of a total program. Kaplan suggests that fantasy, apart from its directly arousing qualities, may serve the function of distracting the client from orgasm watching so that the process of arousal is allowed to progress without inhibition. Other methods of stopping orgasm watching have been suggested. Murphy and Mikulas (1974) advocate use of the thought-stopping technique discussed by Taylor (1963). Instead of anticipating, hoping for, or fearing the occurrence or nonoccurrence of an orgasm, the client turns her attention to her immediately perceived pleasurable feelings. Similarly, Ellis (1968) emphasizes that the primary target for sex therapy is the fear of failure. Rather than fully perceiving and enjoying her sensations, the dysfunctional woman focuses on her hatred of herself because she is less than perfect. These irrational ideas become the "behaviors" that are changed during rational-emotive therapy, with or without adjunct procedures. Certainly rational-emotive therapy would fit comfortably into a sensate focus program for modifying distracting, self-denigrating thoughts.

For women who are orgasmic in some situations but not during intercourse, the task of therapy becomes the generalization of responsivity to a new stimulus, the experience of penile penetration. To accomplish this transfer, the effective stimulus, usually manual clitoral stimulation, is paired with intercourse, and gradually faded out (e.g., Annon, 1971; Hastings, 1963; Kaplan, 1974; LoPiccolo & Lobitz, 1972). Other stimuli which already bring the client to a climax may also be included such as oral stimulation, erotic fantasies or pornography, breast fondling, or use of a vibrator. Pairing may involve stimulation simultaneous with intercourse or just preceding it. At the moment when the stimulus is removed and intercourse begins, the woman should be on the verge of a climax, close enough so that intercourse alone will carry her over the threshold. Orgasm will then act as a reinforcer, and intercourse will gradually become a conditioned stimulus for orgasm.

Just as they prescribed the specific position for sensate focus, Masters and Johnson strongly recommend one position for intercourse, the lateral coital position with the female superior. In this position women are reported to obtain maximal vaginal and clitoral stimulation, while the man is able to easily control ejaculation. Both partners are relatively free to move, since their bodies are lying at a 30° angle rather than directly on top of each other. The same objection raised with regard to the pleasuring position applies here as well: Are there not other positions that would be equally suitable? The value of variety, experimentation, and individual preference is neglected in the Masters and Johnson discussion.

Success rates as reported by Masters and Johnson vary with the type of dysfunction. Primary orgasmic dysfunction, in which the woman has never reached orgasm, was treated successfully (presumably with the occurrence of orgasm at least once) in 83% of 193 cases. Several types of situational orgasmic dysfunction were considered. In masturbatory orgasmic dysfunction, a relatively rare disorder in which the woman was orgasmic except in masturbation, 91% of 11 cases were successful. A somewhat lower figure was obtained in 106 cases of coital orgasmic dysfunction, with 80% success. The worst prognosis held in cases of random orgasmic dysfunction, in which the ability to have orgasm was sometimes absent in various situations. In these cases only 63% were successful. Since the treatment was similar for all woman, rather than tailored to specific maintaining factors, and since diagnosis in these cases apparently failed to isolate these factors, the poor results in this group are not surprising.

C. Other Approaches to Situational Orgasmic Dysfunctions

Kaplan adds one modification which is particularly relevant in cases of coital orgasmic dysfunction. The goal is to increase clitoral stimulation without interfering with thrusting. Kaplan recommends that manual caresses with slow thrusting be alternated with more active thrusting without concurrent clitoral massage. Transfer of orgasmic response to penile thrusting should be expedited by this method. In addition, clitoral stimulation should be used to maximize arousal before penetration occurs, not in a heavy-handed or mechanical fashion, but teasingly, stopping and starting.

LoPiccolo and Lobitz (1972) stand out in the sophistication of their technology for transferring responsibility from masturbation to intercourse. Other possible strategies exist which may be useful in difficult cases. For instance, D'Zurilla (personal communication, 1971) uses a method similar to Marquis's (1970) orgasmic reconditioning. One form of stimulation is gradually substituted for another, moving backwards in the time sequence. Thus, either the woman or her partner may use a vibrator to arouse her almost to the point of orgasm, at which time the man switches to digital, oral, or penile stimulation. D'Zurilla recommends random alternation among these modes to increase generalization to the widest possible range of stimuli.

Although cases have been reported where orgasm during intercourse alone was established by such methods, more reliable results have been achieved by establishing the ability to have orgasm during some form of clitoral sex play (LoPiccolo & Lobitz, 1972). In most cases the couple has learned to continue direct manipulation of the clitoris during intercourse so that orgasm occurs in the context of intercourse, although additional manual stimulation is still required.

A few sex therapists apply the work of Kegel (1952, 1953, 1956) in cases where there is very little sensation in the vagina or where pain accompanies intercourse. Kegel found that women with urinary incontinence following childbirth often suffered from weakness of the pubococcygeus muscle, a band of tissue which normally supports the pelvic floor. Contracting this muscle many times each day caused an increase in its tone that improved the woman's continence and, incidentally, resulted in a new-found ability to climax during intercourse in some cases. When Kegel investigated this serendipitous finding, he discovered that vaginal sensitivity depended on the condition of the pubococcygeous muscle around the vaginal barrel. A well-toned muscle formed a tight channel which would grip the penis and obtain maximal stimulation, whereas in cases of poor tonus the vagina was loose and would be insufficiently stimulated during intercourse. Kegel believed that vaginal feelings was produced not by friction as much as by stretching of this muscle, which would create proprioceptive sensations resulting in orgasm. In addition, he reported that in most women the vagina was most sensitive at the four and eight o'clock position on its circumference.

Although his work is not widely accepted among medical practitioners, some sex therapists are applying Kegel's findings with their clients. Hartman and Fithian (1974) routinely measure the tonus of the pubococcygeous with a device called a perineometer (Riedman, 1957; pictured in Dengrove, 1971a) and prescribe strengthening exercises for women who can only weakly contract their vaginas. They estimate that 10% of their clients are unable to voluntarily contract their vaginal muscles at all at the outset of therapy, suggesting that the condition of the pubococcygeous may be one, but not the only, factor in sexual dysfunction. Kaplan (1974) recommends that the couple attempt to maximize stimulation of the four and eight o'clock positions of the vagina by adjusting the angle of penetration during intercourse.

Unfortunately, no controlled test has been done to validate the utility of Kegel's (1952, 1953) exercises. Although he claimed that 60% of his patients became more sexually responsive as a result of his treatment, no independent evaluation has been undertaken. In cases where the exercises have been used, they have been adjuncts to other procedures, so that evaluation has been impossible. Additionally, no information has been collected from a nonclinical sample to test the correlation of pubococcygeous muscle tonus and sexual responsivity. Weakness in the muscle may be secondary to anorgasmia rather than a causal variable.

D. Masturbation Programs

Behavior therapists like LoPiccolo and Lobitz (1972) recommend masturbation as a preliminary step to partner stimulation. For the purpose of inducing orgasm, masturbation appears to be the optimal method. Masturbation was the most reliable method of reaching orgasm observed by Masters and Johnson (1966) in their laboratory subjects. Further, it resulted in orgasms that were subjectively and physiologically more intense than orgasms during other activities. In applying masturbation in a sex therapy regimen, the assumption is made that once orgasmic ability is established through this easier route, it can then be gradually transferred to the partner situation, which requires more assertiveness, concentration, and cooperation. In the program there are nine graduated steps for *in vivo* desensitization incorporating masturbation. In the *first* step, the woman studies her genital area with a mirror, identifying anatomical features with the aid of a diagram. Kegel exercises may be prescribed at this point. *Second,* she explores her genitals tactually. In the *third* phase, she identifies the areas which are most sensitive. *Fourth,* she stimulates these areas using a lubricating lotion.

If orgasm does not occur, the next two steps are included. The *fifth* stage involves prolonging stimulation until something happens or the woman becomes fatigued. If this fails, the *sixth* step is introduced: the use of an electric vibrator for self-stimulation. LoPiccolo and Lobitz (1972) report that eventually the vibrator has brought about a climax in all cases in which it was used. In the *seventh* step the husband observes his wife masturbating to orgasm, which should disinhibit her further and also demonstrates to the husband exactly what kind of stimulation she finds optimal. Step *eight* involves the husband stimulating his wife by hand or with a vibrator until he learns to bring her to orgasm. In the *last* phase, intercourse is allowed, with clitoral massage by hand or with a vibrator until he learns to bring her to orgasm. The program runs for fifteen sessions.

LoPiccolo and Lobitz (1972) present several innovations in their treatment of sexual dysfunction that cast the Masters and Johnson (1970) approach, as modified, in a more behavioristic light. LoPiccolo and Lobitz emphasize data collection, in the form of a daily record specifying the sexual behaviors in which the couple engaged, their duration, and the level of arousal of each partner. Clients who might ordinarily skip record keeping, miss appointments, or fail to follow instructions are motivated by a refundable deposit, part of which is forfeited upon any violation of the therapist's rules. Six violations result automatically in termination (no such case has been reported yet by the authors, however). Special techniques for enhancing interpersonal skills in the sexual domain are used. When appropriate, the therapists engage in self-disclosure to reduce the clients' anxieties, increase rapport, and model effective responses. Finally, the problem of maintenance of change is dealt with by devoting the final sessions to planning assignments and future behaviors. The gains of therapy are reviewed, and plans are made for countermeasures in the event of a recurrence of the dysfunction.

Using this program, LoPiccolo and Lobitz (1972) obtained a rate of 100% success with primary orgasmic dysfunction in 13 cases. "Success" was defined as satisfaction during one-half of all coital encounters. The addition of the masturbation treatment and other innovations to Masters and Johnson's (1970) basic program seems to yield a higher rate of success. However, the difficulty here lies in the fact that the approaches differ in numerous respects. A much lower rate (33%) was obtained by LoPiccolo and Lobitz (1972) in nine cases of secondary orgasmic dysfunction. Overall, the Sex Interaction Inventory developed by these clinicians showed significant improvement after sex therapy.

Together with other case studies, these results suggest that masturbation is a useful technique in cases which might otherwise not respond to sensate focus. Of particular relevance is a series of three cases of primary orgasmic dysfunction treated by Kohlenberg (1974). All had failed to reach orgasm from sensate focus procedures carried out for 2 to 6 months. Masturbation began while sensate focus, with intercourse if desired, was continued. Within 3, 4, and 6 weeks, respectively, each client became orgasmic in masturbation, followed in every case by orgasm in intercourse. Although this report does not validate the effectiveness of masturbation, it is the strongest data available relative to this question.

Other case studies by Annon (1971), Lehman (1974), and Reisinger (1974) reported success using masturbation programs. The Reisinger case is particularly interesting, since masturbation was conducted in the therapist's office, the client viewing erotic films while she stimulated herself. Self-report and heart-rate measures indicated that orgasm occurred for the first time during the second session of film watching. Unfortunately, since the client was not in a sexual relationship, generalization of orgasmic ability could not be assessed. However, generalization did occur to erotic fantasies.

One elaboration on the use of masturbation for dysfunctional women has been the recommendation that the partner also masturbate (Miller & Brockway, 1972). This seems like a good idea for several reasons: *First,* because she knows her husband is also masturbating, the woman is reassured that what she is doing is harmless and acceptable. *Second,* the husband may model neutral or positive attitudes to masturbation which she may imitate. *Finally,* the man is explicitly provided with masturbation as an outlet during a phase of therapy when his wife is perhaps less available to satisfy him sexually.

Use of a vibrator for masturbation has been a matter of considerable controversy. While its effectiveness in producing orgasm is universally acknowledged, concern has arisen over the possibility that women will become "addicted" to the vibrator (Dengrove, 1971a; Ellis, 1966; Kaplan, 1974). "Addiction" refers variously to preferring the vibrator to intercourse or, more generally, to the woman's partner (note here the common fallacy of equating the penis with the whole man). In spite of these fears, most authors concede they have never observed such a situation, and in fact none has been reported in the literature to the knowledge of the present authors. Engrossment with the vibrator may occur for a short period, but at least among women in sex therapy the goal is still to be satisfied by a live male partner.

Normative data have been collected (Clifford, 1975) indicating that women not in sex therapy engage in a number of strategies to transfer orgasm ability from masturbation to intercourse. Most commonly, the woman directs her partner to stimulate her in a manner similar to the way she stimulates herself. She may also fantasize during intercourse using content from her masturbatory fantasies.

Annon (1971) believes that transfer of responsivity will be most likely to occur if masturbation fantasies include activities in which the client normally engages with her partner. Some support for this contention may be found in one of Annon's studies. The woman was orgasmic only during masturbation, using fantasies of being gang raped. Therapy consisted of sensate focus augmented by masturbatory conditioning, a technique based on Davison's (1968) and Marquis's (1970) work with "orgasmic reconditioning."[2] In this case, the woman gradually reduced the violence and the number of men in her fantasy until finally she was imagining loving sex with her husband. Changes in fantasy were associated with learning to have orgasms from manual stimulation by her husband. The simultaneous practice of sensate focus, however, makes it difficult to attribute this change to one specific procedure.

Masters and Johnson do not include masturbation in their program. The reader may gain a sense of their attitude about the subject from their third book, *The pleasure bond* (Masters & Johnson, 1975). Although protesting their freedom from value biases, they handle the issue of masturbation tentatively and with ambivalence. Note, for instance, this comment about the use of a vibrator (made incidentally in a discussion of a husband who recommends it to his "suggestible" wife so she can become multiply orgasmic):

The fact that the husband wants his wife to experiment with a mechanical device appropriately symbolizes what the two of them are doing to their sexual relationship. Instead of seeing it as an extension of their marriage, reflecting how they feel about themselves and each other and expressing their particular needs on any given day, they are turning it into a performance. [p. 47]

Unfortunately the reader has difficulty in sorting out the referent of the objection. Is it the husband making a suggestion, the fact that the wife is already orgasmic, the use of a mechanical device or some combination?

At another point, Johnson speaks of masturbation as follows:

Here is a way of satisfying extraneous sexual need without making excessive demands on the relationship. It enables a woman to cope with her tensions at a time when, because of special concerns, she feels she cannot involve her husband, or she chooses not to. [p. 65]

---

[2] In the earlier method, the established fantasy was used during the masturbation sequence until the point of inevitability of orgasm, at which point the new fantasy was substituted. Once this procedure was learned, the client gradually introduced the new fantasy earlier in the sequence, always followed by orgasm as a reinforcer. Annon (1971) modified the technique, fearing that although the new fantasy was becoming eroticized, the old fantasy remained part of the pattern until the very end of treatment. Instead, he recommended gradual alteration of the fantasy content throughout the sequence. This approach may be particularly helpful in cases where the client loses involvement with the fantasy upon switching it suddenly.

Masters qualifies her remark:

Keep in mind that we are talking about occasional incidents. If we find an established masturbatory pattern of some significance, we then look into the relationship itself. [pp. 65–66].

Barbach (1975) conducts a group therapy program for non-orgasmic women, consisting of 10 hour-and-a-half sessions over a 5-week period. Six clients meet with two female therapists, a situation which is expected to "capitalize on the supportive features of women's consciousness-raising groups."

A discussion of attitudes is followed by "homeplay" assignments, a modified LoPiccolo masturbation program. The women watch a movie of a woman masturbating. Then they are instructed to masturbate at home but not to orgasm. Prohibiting orgasm may actually facilitate reaching it by relaxing the women's self-expectations.

Barbach's approach is focused on changing the behavior of the individual woman rather than of the couple. Although in the later steps of the masturbation program, the partner, if one is available, is involved in the treatment, the woman remains the primary agent for pleasing herself. When penile insertion is undertaken, the woman is encouraged to stimulate herself during intromission in order to reach orgasm. And, since intercourse is never prohibited, the necessity of involving the partner throughout the treatment is reduced. These features of Barbach's program seen to derive from an implicit philosophy that women should be primarily responsible for their sexual satisfaction and can learn orgasmic ability largely on their own initiative. As a corollary, becomming orgasmic from self-stimulation is seen as a legitimate goal of sex therapy in its own right. The male partners of those participating were reportedly initially threatened by the program but later became more enthusiastic when their partners grew more sexually responsive. Most of the women in Barbach's sample had applied to the program on the basis of a radio advertisement, although some were referred by physicians. One suspects that this group differs in significant ways from the Masters and Johnson clientele. The program is less expensive and might therefore be expected to attract a less affluent client population. Although no data are available on Masters and Johnson's clients, Barbach's women reportedly came from "all economic brackets, educational and work backgrounds." One is tempted also to speculate that this group, because of its location in San Francisco and the program's orientation, is less conservative sexually than the women in the Masters and Johnson sample. Barbach notes that no practicing Catholics were among those treated, in contrast to cases discussed by Masters and Johnson, and that not all women were married. Matching clients and programs in terms of sexual attitudes may be an important factor in successful outcome.

Results were presented, based on a sample of 83 "preorgasmic" women (the term *preorgasmic* is intended to suggest a less accusatory and more optimistic attitude than *nonorgasmic*); 91.6% reached orgasm with masturbation during the program. Seventeen clients who became orgasmic during masturbation were followed up 8 months later (Wallace & Barbach, 1974). Of the 16 who had available partners at the time of the follow-up assessments 14 (87%) were orgasmic in interactions with their partners at least sometimes. The report does not state whether orgasm generalized from self-stimulation in the partner's presence to any form of stimulation by the partner. Thus, the author's argument that "fixation" did not occur is somewhat weakly supported. Further, the basis for selecting these few clients out of the entire sample is unspecified, making evaluation of the result difficult.

E. *In Vivo* Desensitization and the Treatment of Vaginismus

A specific method of *in vivo* desensitization has been developed for the treatment of vaginismus, i.e., an involuntary spasm of the sphincter vaginae and leviter ani muscles at the entrance to the vagina that prevents or renders extremely painful the entry of any object into the vagina. At the same time the woman often avoids pelvic examination, withdrawing upon any attempted insertion by the gynecologist. Vaginismus is not always accompanied by aversion to sexual stimulation or anorgasmia; some of these women enjoy clitoral stimulation and reach orgasm by methods not involving vaginal penetration. Most behavior therapists regard vaginismus as a phobic response specific to vaginal penetration. Often the presenting complaint is an unconsummated marriage. Actually, one problem with the literature in this area is that writers often fail to distinguish vaginismus from other difficulties preventing consummation, including the couple's ignorance about the mechanics of sexual intercourse, the woman's avoidance of the husband, or the man's erectile failure. For example, Dawkins and Taylor (1961) remark that in some instances when a woman presents herself for treatment of nonconsummation she has been found to be covering up the contribution of her husband's sexual inadequacy to the problem.

In cases of vaginismus, specific exercises to enable vaginal insertion have been used by therapists of diverse theoretical persuasions. Although they vary to some extent, all of the treatment modalities have a common basis. The muscle spasm which makes entry painful or impossible is alleviated by introducing graduated dilators into the vagina under conditions that minimize anxiety. The dilators are typically of glass or rubber, although Kaplan objects to the "rape-like" quality of these mechanical devices and relies simply on finger dilation.

In order to create this nonthreatening situation, Haslam (1965) and Dawkins and Taylor (1961) use exercises focused on the client's learning voluntary tension and relaxation of the pelvic musculature while the dilators are in place. Other workers emphasize the woman's voluntary control of the dilator rather than, or in addition to, her own muscular response (Abraham, 1956; Cooper, 1969c). She is instructed to perform the insertions herself, progressing at her own pace, perhaps with encouragement from the therapist or her husband. An additional embellishment on the same theme is Dawkins and Taylor's use of self-examination, the woman exploring the vagina with her own fingers. By familiarizing herself with the interior of her vagina, the client learns about her body in a unique way. Perhaps she discovers the angle of her vagina for the first time, a piece of information that will help her in future efforts at insertion. When vague, perhaps unarticulated fears about the interior of the vagina exist, such as the presence of a hymen deep inside (reported by these authors as a common occurrence in their sample of cases), self-exploration may correct the idea and dispel the accompanying anxiety.

Besides the helpful features noted by Dawkins and Taylor, self-exploration shares some of the advantages of masturbation in general. Whatever mechanism may be operating, women report a number of positive effects of masturbation on other aspects of their sexuality. Some of these include learning more positive attitudes about their bodies, especially the genitals, knowing the kinds of stimulation they like, and being better able to express their desires (Clifford, 1975).

In extreme cases where even the smallest dilator cannot be tolerated, behavior therapists might use systematic desensitization to prepare the client for *in vivo* penetration. Kaplan (1974), however, discounts the necessity for imaginal desensitization in such cases. Instead, she recommends that the therapist confront the client about her hesitation, stressing that using the dilators is necessary if she truly wishes to have intercourse. The woman is encouraged to "stay with her feelings," try to tolerate her fear and pain, until she discovers that she can indeed allow the insertion. Such a procedure is suggestive of implosion (Hogan & Kirschner, 1967; Stampfl & Levis, 1967), a method in which high levels of anxiety are deliberately evoked, which will subside through extinction during a single session. It is possible that implosion could be a more rapid approach to the problem of vaginismus than imaginal desensitization, but there are no formal tests of the relative merits of the two formats. A case report by Wincze (1971), however, favors the use of systematic desensitization over a "vicarious extinction" procedure. The client in this instance was generally averse to sexual contact but not specifically vaginismic.

The role of the husband is variously construed by therapists treating vaginismus. Masters and Johnson (1970) state that this dysfunction, like all those they treat, is attributable to the couple rather than the individual. They emphasize the frequent incidence of dysfunctions in the male partners of vaginismic women. Before treatment begins, they ask that the husband be present at the pelvic examination of the wife in order that he observe the vaginal spasm when the examiner's finger is inserted. Presumably the husband will feel relief from any feelings of rejection or personal inadequacy when he sees the reflexive response in this situation. The feelings of the wife are not discussed. One might imagine that for some women the experience might be more humiliating than comforting. Why the point could not be made verbally or with a simple model is not clear.

Abraham (1956) suggested that if the therapist does not examine the client himself, he should at least be present at the examination. Ostensibly the woman's transference will be heightened, constituting an advantage for the outcome of therapy. A behavior therapist might view this maneuver as beneficial if the therapist can aid in relaxation through instructions and/or the relaxing effect of his or her presence for the client. The examination thus would become not only a diagnostic demonstration but a therapeutic experience. Any improvement at this early stage should increase motivation and facilitate later stages of therapy. In addition, if gynecological contributing factors such as vaginal infections or lesions are to be checked, the examination will proceed more smoothly if the woman can relax. In severe cases, relaxation training might even be conducted in advance so that women who are extremely anxious about pelvic examinations are not thrust into this situation totally unprepared.

Generally, the husband is instructed not to initiate sexual intercourse until the woman can easily insert the largest dilator or several fingers and comfortably stroke in and out. At this point most cases are reported to proceed smoothly with intercourse. In one case

(Cooper, 1969c) the husband balked at his wife's request for intercourse. He was brought to the therapist's office, where he observed her easily tolerating the largest dilator. Consummation followed rapidly. This demonstration seems to be a somewhat insensitive handling of the situation, although the desired goal was certainly achieved with dispatch.

Results of these methods of therapy for vaginismus are impossible to judge adequately. Masters and Johnson (1970) reported that after 5 years, 100% of 29 clients with vaginismus were "successfully" treated, using 3 to 5 days of dilation, with no relapses. Whether this figure represents those who accomplished penile insertion or those who reached a particular level of pleasure during intercourse cannot be determined. Cooper's (1969b) report is the only one specifying the outcome clearly. The client consummated her marriage after six sessions of therapy and continued to reach climax through clitoral manipulation, although she was not orgasmic in intercourse at the time of termination. For the two cases treated by Haslam (1965), at a 1-month follow-up, both reported having intercourse "satisfactorily." Interestingly, the duration of therapy was consistent with the "personality" of each woman: the "anxious introvert" responded rapidly (in three sessions), whereas the "nonanxious extravert" required 16 sessions of therapy. Although Haslam did not specify the information, it seems likely that the therapist knew the personality information at the onset of therapy and may have been influenced in his expectations, which were subtly communicated to the clients. Finally, it is unfortunate that Abraham (1956), who treated 50 cases of nonconsummation, and Dawkins and Taylor (1961), with 70 cases, both neglected to report rate of improvement on any criterion. The duration of therapy was reported to be 2 to 3 weeks by Abraham (1956), while Dawkins and Taylor (1961) did not specify the length of therapy.

In sum, treatment of vaginismus appears to be rapid and effective in leading to consummation, i.e., penile penetration. The further progress of these clients is less certain.

THE "SEXUALLY SUCCESSFUL" FEMALE

Having discussed special treatment programs, a statement regarding criteria for judging dysfunction and therapeutic effectiveness seems in order.

The success of sex therapy for women usually is heavily or exclusively determined by the ability to reach orgasm. Several questions must be raised concerning the usefulness of this criterion, centering around one major issue: What *is* normal female sexual response? First there is a question about what "orgasm ability" means. Only a minority of women climax on every sexual occasion, according to Kinsey. Reports that clients "became orgasmic" oversimplify, since orgasm ability is seldom an all-or-none situation. The same fact holds true whether one considers sexual intercourse, noncoital interactions with partners, or masturbation. Maximal information is conveyed by reports of the *rate* of orgasm with a given type of stimulation.

A second point concerns the focus of some therapists on orgasm ability during intercourse as the primary gaol of sex therapy. A substantial number of women in normative surveys report that some direct clitoral stimulation is necessary for orgasm to occur (Fisher, 1973; Kinsey *et al.*, 1953). While in some cases sex therapy has led to orgasm ability during intercourse for some women, there may be as yet unknown biological reasons why others must rely on additional clitoral manipulation. The wisest approach probably encourages each couple to develop a pattern of stimulation suited to their particular needs.

Finally, most nonclinical surveys identify a minority of women who claim that although they do not have an orgasm, they do feel satisfied after sex. It is possible that they do have physiological orgasms without labeling them as such. However, it is equally likely that there are a variety of physical states that may be labeled pleasurable or even satisfying. The discrete, pulsating event labeled "orgasm" by Masters and Johnson (1970) may be only one of these.

In the face of these definitional problems, sex therapists should be wary of making assumptions about the kinds of responses women *should* experience to be satisfied sexually. Assessment devices should reflect a broad definition of sexual satisfaction based on a realistic appraisal of women's subjective experience of sexual feelings (a good example is LoPiccolo's Sex Interaction Inventory). In addition, male partners will sometimes require reeducation concerning goals for their female partners.

Occasionally clients are seen who report that they are *unsure* whether to label their responses "orgasm" or not. Masters and Johnson (1966) have summarized the subjective feelings during orgasms of their research subjects in one overall description. Additional descriptions reflecting greater individual variation in feelings may be found in Bunzl and Mullen (1974), Clifford, (1975), Hardenberg (1953), and Singer and Singer (1972). In answering questions concerning labeling of feelings, the wisest course for the clinician is probably to emphasize to the client the *range* of experiences labeled orgasm rather than to confine himself to one definition.

IV. DISCUSSION

A. Critique of Masters and Johnson

It is fair to note that Masters and Johnson (1970) have made a substantial contribution to the treatment of sexual dysfunction. It seems unnecessary to add to their laurels at this late date. We do, however, recognize the need to comment upon Masters and Johnson (1970), mainly because warranted criticism of various aspects of their approach has not as yet appeared in the literature.

We feel that the most serious handicap of their program results from Masters and Johnson's failure to recognize the vital contribution of behavior therapy to their approach; they have ignored the behavioral context from which their program has developed and within which it can be most successfully applied. As we suggested earlier, a conception of Masters and Johnson's therapeutic approach in terms of an *in vivo* desensitization model provides a logical overall system for their procedures. The alternative is to view their program as a conglomeration of loosely-fitting treatment principles and techniques. The advantages of utilizing a conceptual scheme are most significant for the less experienced therapist who wishes to employ Masters and Johnson (1970) as a therapeutic manual. Such individuals have no choice but to follow the procedures in the exact manner that Masters and Johnson have reported them. Unfortunately, not all patients are precisely suited to this program. For example, suppose that a therapist with little experience treating sexual dysfunctions were confronted by a male complaining of erective failure. Further, suppose that in attempting to apply the first level of the Masters and Johnson *in vivo* hierarchy, the therapist encounters difficulty. To simplify the example, we will assume that the difficulty is clearly due to anxiety which the patient experiences in attempting to carry out the therapist's initial instructions. If the therapist were an experienced behaviorist, perhaps he would successfully deal with this situation by stepping back several levels in the hierarchy (e.g., attempting sensate focus with both partners fully dressed lying in bed, or fully dressed sitting on the living-room couch); this could be coordinated with imaginal desensitization keyed to homework assignments. Unfortunately, the therapist who attempts to apply Masters and Johnson without these additional behavior skills may be faced with a therapeutic *cul-de-sac* (cf. Lobitz *et al.*, 1975). A comparison can be made with Wolpe's (1958) didactic approach, in which he details the major principles of systematic desensitization and then gives illustrative examples. In this way, the therapist can provide a flexible program for each patient, even when they vary significantly from those described by Wolpe. Because Masters and Johnson offer no theoretical context within which to provide flexibility, the inexperienced therapist has no choice but to follow their rigidly detailed program. This factor has significantly fostered the tendency toward dogma which seems to exist within the field of therapy for sexual dysfunction.

Masters and Johnson base their treatment of sexual dysfunctions on several principles. They suggest that all couples be treated by a dual-sex therapy team. Underlying this practice is the assumption that only a member of the same sex can understand and empathize with a client's experience. Certainly, if the client specifically desires a same-sex therapist, he or she should be provided with one when possible, if for no other reason than to use the client's expectations of help to his or her benefit. However, when a dual-sex team is involved, the expense and inefficiency of the procedure warrants serious consideration of the underlying assumptions.

In sex therapy, empathy with the same sex is often considered essential when questions arise as to the nature of normality of the client's subjective experience of sexual arousal. It is assumed that if the therapist is of the same sex, he or she will be able to rely on his or her own subjective experience in answering such questions. But there are a number of problems with this premise. Informal discussion with a few members of his or her sex will convince the reader that subjective experience of arousal varies widely among individuals. Whether this variation is greater across the sexes, across individuals within the same sex, or across experiences of any one individual is by no means clear. The labels attached to physiological events vary widely, or may be absent altogether (Clifford, 1975). The self-experience of any individual therapist of either sex is insufficient for assisting the client in labeling or evaluating the deviance of his or her particular pattern of response. Only solid normative data can fulfill this requirement.

In general, one may ask whether empathy depends on the sharing of specific experiences or of basic human emotions? If one seriously applied the idea of shared experiences to the sex therapy situation, he/she might justifiably insist that all sex therapists ought to have been dysfunctional at one time. One could argue that such shared experience might increase the therapist's general feeling that dysfunctions are painful and important influences in client's lives. But this understanding may be reached through many other avenues. In sum, if dual-sex therapy teams are to be recommended, there will have to be some other rationale to support the practice. Further doubt arises from reports by other workers (e.g., Kaplan, 1974; McCarthy, 1973; Prochaska & Marzilli, 1973) indicating that results with one therapist are as successful as with two. Probably when larger issues concerning sex roles are being confronted, an empathic same-sexed therapist for each client is most desirable. But for many straightforward sex therapy cases, the dual-sex team is a luxury rather than a necessity.

Masters and Johnson (1970) suggest that there is no uninvolved partner, either in the etiology or in the treatment of sexual dysfunctions. Thus, another basic principle suggests that the couple be treated as a unit, with neither partner singled out for special attention. Both spouses are usually told to take turns pleasuring each other, whatever the particular complaint of the couple. If the spouse is cooperative, making sensate focus a reciprocal exercise would seem to be a desirable arrangement, the responsibility for the problem and its treatment being extended from the individual to the couple. Additionally, if intercourse is forbidden for a period of time when the couple has been having sex with some frequency, the therapy recommendations will more likely be carried out if alternative sources of mutual satisfaction are available. Masters and Johnson were not the first clinicians to suggest that intercourse be forbidden as part of sex therapy. Even before Wolpe, Kraines (1948) suggested the idea. Finally, one goal of sensate focus is to alter the entire pattern of sexual interaction, not just the method of stimulating one partner or the other. The exercise should obviously be reciprocal if this goal is to be achieved.

Although there are many good reasons for reciprocal sensate focus, situations may arise that require a different approach. Sex therapists should be prepared to deal with cases where the partner is unavailable or uncooperative. Barbach's (1975) use of group therapy for dysfunctional women is an example of an apparently successful program which does not rely on partner involvement throughout therapy.

Part of the rationale for reciprocal sensate focus is based on the prohibition of intercourse, another maxim of Masters and Johnson's program. However, it may be possible to introduce some features of sensate focus into the couple's loveplay while allowing intercourse to occur as usual. The most important factor in the decision to permit intercourse, from a therapeutic perspective, is whether it can occur without anxiety (Madsen & Ullmann, 1967). If not, the prohibition would be necessary until the feared event can be approached gradually (Ullmann & Krasner, 1975). If no anxiety is present, the couple might proceed with intercourse, perhaps modifying the man's behavior by training the woman to be more assertive in guiding him (Wolpe, 1958). Alternatively, removal of the *demand* for response from the sexual situation may be accomplished without necessarily banning intercourse altogether. Compromise arrangements might also be considered, permitting intercourse at reduced frequency on occasions separate from sensate focus sessions. These measures should probably be regarded at this stage as less preferable than complete prohibition of intercourse, since reports by clinicians such as Chapman (1968) suggest that the prognosis is less favorable when husbands insist on continuing intercourse. However, one should bear in mind that "prognosis" in this instance can only be viewed within the context of a particular therapy program. Similarly, one cannot judge whether the prognostic factor in Chapman's study was continuing to have intercourse or acting against the therapist's recommendations in general.

Not all sex therapists begin sensate focus with the same format as do Masters and Johnson. Hartman and Fithian (1974) have independently developed a series of "caress" exercises which progress through more gradual steps at the outset than sensate focus. First, the spouses engage in relatively neutral utilitarian activities together, such as brushing each other's hair and bathing together. There follows a series of sensual massage assignments, caressing each others' feet and faces, and finally, a nude body caress which resembles Masters and Johnson's first step. A unique feature of Hartman and Fithian's program is the therapist's presence during all of these exercises. Although the ethics of such a practice may be questioned, one important advantage is that obvious misunderstandings or difficulties in carrying out the assignments are caught early in therapy and corrected. Reliance on verbal reports of the clients sometimes causes the therapists to overlook or misunderstand some crucial aspect of the couple's interaction that much later can emerge as a major obstacle to the therapy. For example, one partner may be caressing the other too hastily or roughly. One might have difficulty initiating the encounter, remaining in the receiving role, or expressing his or her desires. Particularly when therapy sessions are spaced a week or more apart, early detection of such difficulties would be most helpful (see Annon, 1971; Kaplan, 1974, for detailed examples). Alternatively, perhaps the therapist could observe only a facial caress, thereby retaining some of the advantages of direct observation while largely circumventing the ethical problems involved in observing clients' nude sex play.

A further requirement of Masters and Johnson that demands examination suggests that the couple be on vacation for 2 weeks and maintain daily contact with their therapists. The vacation provides the couple with an atmosphere free from day-to-day stresses and responsibilities and permits them to focus entirely on their relationship and sexual behavior. Daily conferences provide the opportunity for immediate feedback, particularly directed at misapplications and disappointments which the couple may experience. The therapists can present explanations and support before the couple's concern over the error develops into more intense anxiety. In addition, program modification can be arranged quickly to enhance therapeutic efficiency. In spite of these advantages of the intensive 2-week format, most sex clinicians see the couple weekly or twice weekly while they are living at home and engaging in routine daily schedules (see McCarthy, 1973). According to Kass (cited in Laughren & Kass, 1975), the results obtained through this less disruptive procedure are equal in effectiveness to those in Masters and Johnson's program and may in fact be longer lasting, since improvement occurs in the situation in which it will have to be maintained (Laughren & Kass, 1975; Murphy & Mikulas, 1974). Preliminary results with 16 couples with assorted sexual dysfunctions indicated that 14 of these, or 88% improved, a rate which is certainly comparable to that of Masters and Johnson.

A larger sample of 74 dysfunctional women was treated by Chapman (1968) in a program which expanded on Wolpe (1958, 1973). No intercourse was allowed; in fact, the husband was to conceal any sign of his arousal from his wife. Nondemand pleasuring was prescribed. After three to eight weekly sessions, 80% of these women were improved or recovered. In a rare 5-year follow-up, Chapman (1968) located 48 of his clients, of whom 94% were improved compared to their pretherapy responsivity. This improvement rate actually exceeds Masters and Johnson's success rate, although it is impossible to interpret these figures since neither measure was defined. The data do serve to cast doubt upon the necessity of the intensive 2-week therapy format.

B. Ancillary Techniques

Although we have emphasized desensitization as the primary paradigm for sex therapy, other approaches are used as adjuncts to desensitization. A few of these will now be considered.

Several behavior therapists have addressed the need for facilitating the maintenance of behaviors. Such a situation might arise when the couple has avoided sex for a long time and has had difficulty initiating sensate focus. Again, there may be strong behavioral preferences on the part of one person that are neutral or perhaps aversive to the partner; this would necessitate some mechanism for behavior maintenance for this latter partner. Stuart (1969), Knox (1971), and Annon (1971) have suggested that couples can negotiate contracts exchanging sexual behaviors for other reinforcers. All noted in particular the usefulness of the Premack Principle: reinforcers can be behaviors which have a high probability of occurring. In one example, Stuart (1969) counseled a couple to engage in conversation, a high-frequency behavior, immediately after sex, which had been infrequent. Of course, such maneuvers will only be effective if the couple is truly committed to increasing the priority of sexual activity in their daily lives. That increased frequency may lead to greater satisfaction was demonstrated by Stuart with four couples at a 48-week follow-up assessment of seven sessions of this treatment.

Another significant trend in brief sex therapy is the increased attention to interpersonal factors that are presumed to influence the sexual interaction. As unsuccessful cases are reviewed, communication difficulties have often been noted. In addition, communication training alone has been reported to improve sexual functioning in certain cases (e.g., Prochaska & Marzilli, 1973). Most therapists now incorporate some interpersonal exercise, at least in select cases where the problem is extreme and obvious. A number of examples will be listed briefly here to illustrate the variety of conceptual approaches to establishing "good communication."

Laughren and Kass (1975) simply exhort couples to fight at any time except during sexual encounters. In Stuart's (1969) "operant-interpersonal" method, spouses learn to reinforce each other rather than engaging in mutually destructive behaviors. Rappaport and Harrell (1972) carry Stuart's program a step further, training couples to negotiate "behavioral exchanges" in future conflicts. Ellis (1966) and Barbach (1975) emphasize reducing dependency in the marital relationship by a consciousness-raising process that establishes the woman's responsibility for her own sexual response. Greater physical expressivity and disinhibition are the aims of LoPiccolo and Lobitz's (1972) recommendation that the woman role-play orgasm in front of her husband in an exaggerated form. Increasing general assertiveness is the rationale for numerous therapeutic maneuvers: Annon (1971) asks couples to share their sexual anxieties and desires verbally in his presence; LoPiccolo and Lobitz (1972) use an initiation and refusal exercise where couples role-play sexual approaches and the partner's response; Hartman and Fithian (1974) have developed a "sensitivity" exercise involving emotional expression with hand gestures; and Wells, Figurel, and McNee (1975) report the success of "group facilitative training" in increasing communication of feelings between spouses. Chapman (1968) and Knox (1971) recast the man in a role of sexual restraint, rather than insatiability, by having him refuse his wife's advances on occasion. Finally, Hartman and Fithian (1974) use role-playing of permanent separation and unexpected reunion as a motivation exercise early in treatment. The usefulness of these procedures and their appropriateness for certain types of clients deserves systematic evaluation.

Finally, a therapeutic approach which seems to compare favorably with behavior therapy, at least at the case study level, is hypnosis. Interestingly it has been applied almost exclusively with women clients rather than with men. Some workers such as Hartman and Fithian (1974) use hypnosis as an auxiliary procedure, but many successful outcomes have been reported when hypnosis was used alone. Two paradigms involving hypnosis have been used: suggestion and hypnoanalysis.

In the first paradigm, the woman is hypnotized and given the suggestion that her enjoyment of sex will increase. Rubin (1972) reported that of nine cases of dysfunction (sex unspecified), four obtained "complete relief," two showed "marked improvement," and three showed "some improvement." His method was to describe sexual scenes, dwelling on their non-anxiety-arousing aspects. Clients practiced visualization and relaxation at home. Thus, the procedure was quite similar to imaginal desensitization.

August (1959) described a case illustrating the importance of correct phrasing of posthypnotic suggestions. The woman complained that intercourse was too infrequent and that her orgasm rate was too low (about 10% for coital encounters). The first suggestion was that she would "make up for lost time." Her orgasm rate increased to 100%, with intercourse six or eight times a week. Since this was too frequent for her husband, she returned to the therapist. This time the suggestion was that she would experience so much pleasure that in the future sex would pale in enjoyment by comparison. However, the woman followed this suggestion so well that her desire virtually disappeared. Finally, the therapist suggested that she would adjust to her husband's desired frequency, climaxing each time. (The authors, while acknowledging the happy ending from an old-fashioned point of view, cannot help but note the sexist solution to this woman's problem.)

When "hypnoanalysis" is the paradigm, typically the therapist uses age regression to locate the historical onset of the disorder. "Reliving" the experience has been reported to cause increased sexual responsivity. Coulton (1960) reported two successful cases using this approach. Of 12 cases seen by Kroger (1946), nine were "permanently relieved" of their symptom (coital orgasmic dysfunction).

To date, the largest study using hypnosis, again a multiple-case report, is by Richardson (1963). Seventy-six women with varying degrees of sexual dissatisfaction were seen for an average of 1.5 sessions (with a maximum of eight sessions). Of these, 61 received posthypnotic suggestions of increased responsivity, while 15 were treated with hypnoanalysis. Seventy-two, or 95%, were "dramatically improved." Four women, those with primary orgasmic dysfunction, were orgasmic after a follow-up period (of unspecified duration) in 72% of their coitus. Another group, eight women with secondary orgasmic dysfunction, were orgasmic 74% of the time during intercourse following treatment. While only three women climaxed 81% of the time or more initially, after therapy 63 women were in this category. Unfortunately, no breakdown of the results was presented for suggestion and hypnoanalysis separately, so that the two approaches cannot be compared.

Such a high success rate in so short time deserves our attention. No other treatment method has made such claims. A controlled test of the effectiveness of hypnosis compared to or in addition to other methods of sex therapy seems important, given these reports.

C. In-Depth Approaches

While none of the workers discussed in this paper advocate long-term depth therapy in all cases of sexual dysfunction, at least two acknowledge that it may be necessary at times. Each of them, Kaplan (1974) and Annon (1974) will be explored in turn.

Kaplan (1974) styles herself as an eclectic therapist. Although she may begin working with a couple in a brief therapy format using her version of sensate focus, she allows herself flexibility if any problems arise; at such a point she may move toward some form of psychotherapy. While she asserts in the theoretical portion of her book that this therapy might be behavioral, transactional, or psychoanalytic, in fact her case examples almost invariably illustrate the latter orientation. The therapist focuses on one individual, analyzing the underlying resistance to sexual response, commitment to the marriage, etc., often bringing in childhood reminiscences and dreams. The authors of this chapter feel that a more efficient and relevant intervention would use a behavioral orientation. Slow progress, for instance, may be due to reinforcers in the current situation that may be maintaining the dysfunction. What role does the dysfunction play in the marital relationship? How might these factors be modified? Alternatively, are there anxiety-provoking stimuli in the marital situation that have not been carefully assessed? Perhaps imaginal desensitization is necessary before progressing to sensate focus. A case illustrating such a transition in the treatment plan appears in Annon's dissertation (1971).

ANNON'S PLISSIT MODEL

Annon (1974) proposes a treatment approach called the PLISSIT model, in which existing techniques are organized on four levels: (1) permission; (2) limited information; (3) specific suggestions; (4) intensive therapy. Each level requires more professional skill or experience and more time (with respect to number of sessions and duration of each session) than the preceding level. The more serious the concern, the more advanced the level on which appropriate techniques would be classified.

"Permission," Annon's first level, deals with the concern that individuals may have about behaviors which they currently enjoy. Such individuals, Annon hypothesizes, seek authoritative permission. Permission-giving sometimes borders on paradoxical intention when the patient complains of some anxiety-provoking behavior which is maladaptive only in its anxiety component. In these cases, Annon suggests that patients should not only be given permission to perform the behavior but should be encouraged to increase the rate of such performance. In one example, a woman was in great discomfort regarding her sexual fantasies involving men other than her husband. Annon informed her that this was normal behavior and instructed her to increase the frequency with which she engaged in these fantasies. By allowing the behavior to occur rather than resisting it, the fantasy lost its significance and ceased to be a source of disturbance.

"Limited information," the second level, involves the presentation of factual data directly related to the patient's sexual concern. Information may be transmitted directly or in the form of reading material ("bibliotherapy"). The male who believes his penis is embarassingly small, for example, is given relevant information concerning the mean length and normal range of erections, the relation of the flaccid to the erect penis, and the relative unimportance of penis size for satisfying a women. In many cases, the client's hearing this will alleviate the problem, and the male who has been avoiding females for fear of "being found out" can assume a normal social life.

In a case seen by one of the authors (Clifford), a divorced 39-year-old man was suffering from impotence. His sex life was a mad whirl of activity, often including as many as six or seven episodes of intercourse a day with various partners. In explaining this behavior, he noted that he believed his potency would disappear with age if he did not exercise it fully, just as an unused muscle atrophies over time. It was pointed out that his experiences of erectile failure were not the result of aging, although in old age erections may develop more slowly. Instead, his high expectations of his ability to perform were suggested as the causal factor in his dysfunctions. As expected, when he began to reduce his sexual activity to one or two encounters a day, his "impotence" disappeared.

"Specific suggestions" (Annon's third level), unlike previous levels, which were aimed at helping the individual to become comfortable with existing behavior, is employed to modify maladaptive behavior. Most of the techniques which Annon describes are either commonly used "counseling" procedures or components of the Masters and Johnson program.

Thus, Annon attempts to classify sexual problems with respect to the type of technique that would have a high probability of effectively alleviating the concern; the techniques are, in turn, classified in terms of the amount of therapeutic expertise each requires of the professional, as well as the amount of time that is necessary for the most effective employment of each technique. If this classification is valid, then two conclusions may be drawn: *First,* all sexual problems do not require conventional therapy (i.e., ten to thirty 50-min sessions, once per week). Annon suggests the possibility that sexual dysfunctions could, in many cases, be treated in one to five sessions, each requiring 10 to 30 min. *Second,* once the appropriate technique is selected, it becomes obvious that an experienced clinician will not always be required to treat the problem. Thus, Annon points out that there is a wide range of professionals (e.g., family physicians, social workers, nurses, clergymen) whose time constraints, training, and experience do not permit the conduct of conventional sex therapy but who could adequately treat many common sexual concerns. In keeping with his goal of providing information to a wide range of professionals having varying degrees of knowledge about and experience in treating sexual problems, Annon includes details of initial interviews as well as suggested reading lists in a number of related topics. His manual is, therefore, most helpful to those lacking expertise in the treatment of sexual behaviors, but it can also be useful for the more experienced therapist who wishes to complement his therapeutic approach. Annon's explication of the fourth level, intensive therapy, is in press and thus not available at this time.

One disappointment is that, notwithstanding the inclusion of many behavioral aspects in Annon's book (e.g., the title, the detailed description of the behavioral approach to sexual deviation and dysfunction, rudimentary behavioral principles), he nevertheless fails adequately to relate the behavioral techniques which he describes to a general behavioral context. Thus, the book presents a fairly thorough, if basic, introduction to a behavioral approach to maladaptive behavior, in general, and sexual behavior, in particular; however, it also contains an isolated description of techniques. For example, Annon appears to be guilty of the same omission as that of Masters and Johnson (1970) in not recognizing the *in vivo* hierarchical organization underlying most treatment programs for sexual dysfunctions. Thus, those who are behaviorally naïve will, once again, be provided with a rigid program rather than a therapeutic format and a detailed example of a typical program. Finally, Annon reports his results exclusively in terms of individual case studies.

D. Sex Therapy and the Women's Liberation Movement

No discussion such as ours would be complete without mention of the women's liberation movement and its relationship to sex therapy. Do sex therapists advocate a realignment of sex roles as a prerequisite for sexual functioning, or should they? Some features of the *in vivo* desensitization paradigm seem inherently to restructure traditional sex roles within the sexual situation, while further modification of roles in that context or in other areas of functioning seems more dependent upon the politics of the individual program and practitioners.

Traditional sex roles (Gagnon & Simon, 1973) place the male in a more "active" and superordinate position in the sexual encounter. He initiates sex, fondles his partner more than she caresses him, focuses on her breasts and genital area, usually determines when to insert his penis as soon as she is lubricated sufficiently, and assumes the superior position during intercourse. In most sex therapy, all these features of the sexual "script" are violated. The woman is encouraged to initiate sex herself, sometimes exclusively during part of the therapy. She is instructed to pleasure her partner more actively during sensate focus. Both partners are advised to explore nongenital parts of their bodies in search of pleasurable sensations. When intercourse is undertaken, the woman determines the timing of intromission according to her building desire for penetration. Frequently, intercourse itself will be performed in the female-superior position. Throughout sex therapy, the emphasis shifts from the traditional role of the male knowing what his partner wants to active communication and guidance by the woman, who knows best what she wants.

Depending on the biases and politicosexual philosophy of the therapists, additional impetus to modify sex roles may occur within the context of sex therapy. Intercourse as the sole means of sexual consummation may be recast as one alternative source of gratification. Other forms of stimulation traditionally relegated to "foreplay," including manual, oral, and anal techniques, may become main events in the sexual encounter. In LoPiccolo's program, women are increasingly asked to set their own goals for sex therapy, which may or may not include transfer of responsivity to intercourse. Even more radical is the stance of Barbach's (1974) program, which presents masturbation primarily as a source of enjoyment and independent sexuality for women, and only secondarily as a means to greater responsivity with a man.

V. CONCLUSION

This chapter was initiated because the area of therapy for sexual dysfunction had grown quite rapidly in a relatively short period of time. Under these circumstances it seemed appropriate critically to review what had been accomplished and what remains to be undertaken. With this as the prime objective a selected review of the major programs of therapy for sexual dysfunction composed the first portion of the paper. The final portion of the chapter was devoted to a critique designed not so much to attack what exists as to point out where research seems most necessary.

The Masters and Johnson (1970) program received a great deal of attention in this chapter due to its overwhelming popularity among sex therapists and to the danger that these therapists might be less critical in their application of this program than would be consistent with their responsibilities to their patients. It is not suggested that the comments and criticisms directed toward any program mentioned here exhaust the possible concerns that one might have regarding these various approaches to sex therapy; rather, the critique was meant to illustrate the need to offer the practitioner procedures whose efficacy is based on sound experimental support rather than on faith or orthodoxy.

REFERENCES

Abraham, H. C. Therapeutic and psychological approach to cases of unconsummated marriage. *British Medical Journal,* 1956, **1,** 837–839.

Annon, J. S. The extension of learning principles to the analysis and treatment of sexual problems. Ph.D. dissertation, University of Hawaii, 1971.

Annon, J. S. *Behavioral treatment of sexual problems.* Vol. 1. *Brief therapy.* Honolulu: Kapiolani Health Services Press, 1974.

Ascher, L. M., & Phillips, D. Review of *The new sex therapy* by H. S. Kaplan. *Journal of Behavior Therapy and Experimental Psychiatry,* 1975, **6,** 175–177.

August, R. V. Libido altered with the aid of hypnosis: A case report. *American Journal of Clinical Hypnosis,* 1959, **2,** 88.

Barbach, L. G. Group treatment of preorgasmic women. *Journal of Sex and Marital Therapy*, 1974, **1**, 139–145.

Barbach, L. G. *For yourself: The fulfillment of female sexuality.* Garden City, N.Y.: Doubleday, 1975.

Begelman, D. A. Ethical and legal issues of behavior modification. In M. Hersen, R. M. Eisler, & P. M. Miller (Eds.), *Progress in behavior modification.* Vol. 1. New York: Academic Press, 1975. Pp. 159–190.

Brady, J. P. Brevital-relaxation treatment of frigidity. *Behaviour Research and Therapy*, 1966, **4**, 71–77.

Bunzl, M., & Mullen, K. A self-report investigation of two types of myotonic response during sexual orgasm. *Journal of Sex Research*, 1974, **10**, 10–20.

Chapman, J. D. Frigidity: Rapid treatment by reciprocal inhibition. *Journal of the American Osteopathic Association*, 1968, **67**, 871–878.

Clifford, R. E. Female masturbation in sexual development and clinical application. Ph.D. dissertation, State University of New York at Stony Brook, 1975.

Cooke, G. The efficacy of two desensitization procedures: An analogue study. *Behaviour Research and Therapy*, 1966, **4**, 17–24.

Cooper, A. J. A factual study of male potency disorders. *British Journal of Psychiatry*, 1968, **114**, 719–731.

Cooper, A. J. Clinical and therapeutic studies in premature ejaculation. *Comprehensive Psychiatry*, 1969, **10**, 285–295. (a)

Cooper, A. J. Disorders of sexual potency in the male: A clinical and statistical study of some factors related to short-term prognosis. *British Journal of Psychiatry*, 1969, **115**, 709–719. (b)

Cooper, A. J. An innovation in the "behavioral" treatment of a case of non-consummation due to vaginismus. *British Journal of Psychiatry*, 1969, **115**, 721–722. (c)

Cooper, A. J. Factors in male sexual inadequacy: A review. *Journal of Nervous and Mental Disease*, 1969, **149**, 337–359. (d)

Cooper, A. J. Outpatient treatment of impotence. *Journal of Nervous and Mental Disease*, 1969, **149**, 360–371. (e)

Coulton, D. C. Hypnotherapy in gynecological problems. *American Journal of Clinical Hypnosis*, 1960, **3**, 95–100.

Davison, G. C. Case report: Elimination of a sadistic fantasy by a client-controlled counter-conditioning technique. *Journal of Abnormal Psychology*, 1968, **73**, 84–90.

Dawkins, S., & Taylor, R. Non-consummation of marriage. *Lancet*, 1961, **2**, 1029–1033.

Dengrove, E. Behavior therapy of the sexual disorders. *Journal of Sex Research*, 1967, **3**, 49–61.

Dengrove, E. The mechanotherapy of sexual disorders. *Journal of Sex Research*, 1971, **7**, 1–12. (a)

Dengrove, E. Behavior therapy of impotence. *Journal of Sex Research*, 1971, **7**, 177–183. (b)

Dengrove, E. Review of *Human sexual inadequacy. Behavior Therapy*, 1971, **2**, 112–113. (c)

Ellis, A. *The art and science of love.* New York: Lyle, Stuart, 1968.

Eysenck, H. J. Review of *The new sex therapy* by H. S. Kaplan. *Behaviour Research and Therapy*, 1975, **13**, 69.

Fisher, S. *The female orgasm.* New York: Basic Books, 1973.

Friedman, D. E. The treatment of impotence by brietal relaxation therapy. *Behaviour Research and Therapy*, 1968, **6**, 257–261.

Friedman, D. E., & Lipsedge, M. S. Treatment of phobic anxiety and psychogenic impotence by systematic desensitization employing methohexitone-induced relaxation. *British Journal of Psychiatry*, 1971, **118**, 87–90.

Gagnon, J., & Simon, W. *Sexual conduct: The social sources of human sexuality.* Chicago: Aldine Press, 1973.

Garfield, Z. H., McBrearty, J. F., & Dichter, M. A case of impotence successfully treated with desensitization combined with an in vivo operant training and thought substitution. In R. D. Rubin & C. M. Franks (Eds.), *Advances in behavior therapy 1968.* New York: Academic Press, 1969. Pp. 97–103.

Geisinger, D. L. Controlling sexual and interpersonal anxieties. In J. D. Krumboltz & C. E. Thoresen (Eds.), *Behavioral counseling: Cases and techniques.* New York: Holt, 1969. Pp. 454–469.

Goldstein, A. Case conference: Conflict in a case of frigidity. *Journal of Behavior Therapy and Experimental Psychiatry*, 1971, **2**, 51–59.

Goldstein, A., Ascher, L. M., Munjack, D., Phillips, D. Outcome study of behavior therapy in the treatment of secondary erective dysfunction. Temple University, 1975.

Hardenberg, E. W. The psychology of feminine sex experience. In A. P. Pillay & A. Ellis (Eds.), *Sex, society and the individual.* Bombay, India: International Journal of Sexology, 1953.

Hartman, W. E., & Fithian, M. A. *Treatment of sexual dysfunction.* New York: Jason Aronson, 1974.

Haslam, M. T. The treatment of psychogenic dyspareunia by reciprocal inhibition. *British Journal of Psychiatry*, 1965, **111**, 280–282.

Hastings, D. W. *Impotence and frigidity.* Boston: Little, Brown, 1963.

Hogan, R. A., & Kirschner, J. H. Preliminary report of the extinction of learned fears via short term implosive therapy. *Journal of Abnormal Psychology*, 1967, **72**, 106–109.

Hussain, A. Behavior therapy using hypnosis. In J. Wolpe, A. Salter, & L. Reyna (Eds.), *Conditioning Therapies: The challenge in Psychotherapy.* New York: Holt, 1964. Pp. 54–61.

Ince, L. P. Behavior modification of sexual disorders. *American Journal of Psychotherapy*, 1973, **3**, 446–451.

Jacobson, E. *Progressive relaxation.* Chicago: University of Chicago Press, 1938.

Johnson, J. Prognosis of disorders of sexual potency in the male. *Journal of Psychosomatic Research*, 1965, **9**, 195–200.

Kaplan, H. *The new sex therapy.* New York: Bruner/Mazel, 1974.

Kegel, A. H. Sexual functions of the pubococcygus muscle. *Western Journal of Surgery, Obstetrics and Gynecology*, 1952, **60**, 521.

Kegel, A. H. A letter to the editor. *Journal of the American Medical Association*, 1953, **153**, 1303–1304.

Kegel, A. H. Early genital relaxation: A new technique of diagnosis and non-surgical treatment. *Obstetrics and Gynecology*, 1956, **8**, 545–550.

Kinsey, A., Pomeroy, W., Martin, C., & Gebhard, P. *Sexual behavior in the human female.* Philadelphia: Saunders, 1953.

Knox, D. *Marriage happiness: A behavioral approach to counseling.* Champaign, Ill.: Research Press, 1971.

Kohlenberg, R. J. Directed masturbation and the treatment of primary orgasmic dysfunction. *Archives of Sexual Behavior*, 1974, **3**, 349–356.

Kraft, T., & Al-Issa, I. Behavior therapy and the treatment of frigidity. *American Journal of Psychotherapy*, 1967, **2**, 116–120.

Kraines, S. H. *Therapy of the neuroses and psychoses.* Philadelphia: Lea & Febiger, 1948.

Kroger, W. S. The treatment of psychogenic disorders: Hypnoanalysis. *American Journal of Obstetrics and Gynecology*, 1946, 52, 409–418.

Laughren, T. P., & Kass, D. J. Desensitization of sexual dysfunction: The present status. In A. S. Gurman & D. G. Rice (Eds.), *Couples in conflict*. New York: Jason Aronson, 1975. Pp. 281–302.

Lazarus, A. A. Group therapy in phobic disorders by systematic desensitization. *Journal of Abnormal and Social Psychology*, 1961, 63, 504–510.

Lazarus, A. A. The treatment of chronic frigidity by systematic desensitization. *Journal of Nervous and Mental Disease*, 1963, 136, 272–278.

Lazarus, A. A. The treatment of a sexually inadequate man. In L. P. Ullmann & L. Krasner (Eds.), *Case studies in behavior modification*. New York: Holt, 1965. Pp. 243–245.

Lazarus, A. A. *Behavior therapy and beyond*. New York: McGraw-Hill, 1971.

Lehman, R. E. The disinhibiting effects of visual material in treating orgasmically dysfunctional women. *Behavioral Engineering*, 1974, 1, 1–3.

Lobitz, W. C., LoPiccolo, J., Lobitz, G., & Brockway, J. A closer look at simplistic behavior therapy for sexual dysfunction: Two case studies. In H. J. Eysenck (Ed.), *Case studies in behavior therapy*. London: Routledge & Kegan Paul, 1975.

LoPiccolo, J. Review of *The new sex therapy* by H. S. Kaplan. *Behavior Therapy*, 1975, 6, 136–138.

LoPiccolo, J., & Lobitz, W. C. The role of masturbation in the treatment of orgasmic dysfunction. *Archives of Sexual Behavior*, 1972, 2, 163–171.

LoPiccolo, J., Stewart, R., & Watkins, B. Treatment of erectile failure and ejaculatory incompetence of homosexual etiology. *Journal of Behavior Therapy and Experimental Psychiatry*, 1972, 3, 233–236.

Madsen, C. H., & Ullmann, L. P. Innovations in the desensitization of frigidity. *Behaviour Research and Therapy*, 1967, 5, 67–68.

Marquis, J. Orgasmic conditioning: Changing sexual object choice through controlling masturbation fantasies. *Journal of Behavior Therapy and Experimental Psychiatry*, 1970, 1, 263–271.

Masters, W. H., & Johnson, V. *Human sexual response*. Boston: Little, Brown, 1966.

Masters, W. H., & Johnson, V. *Human sexual inadequacy*. Boston: Little, Brown, 1970.

Masters, W. H., & Johnson, V. *The pleasure bond*. Boston: Little, Brown, 1975.

McCarthy, B. W. A modification of Masters and Johnson sex therapy model in a clinical setting. *Psychotherapy: Theory, Research and Practice*, 1973, 10, 290–293.

Miller, V., & Brockway, J. Commonalities and differences in the treatment of primary orgasmic dysfunction. Unpublished manuscript, University of Oregon, 1972.

Munjack, D. M., Cristol, A., Goldstein, A., Phillips, D., Goldberg, A., Whipple, K., Staples, F., & Kanno, P. Behavioral treatment of frigidity: A controlled study. Unpublished manuscript, Temple University, 1975.

Murphy, C. V., & Mikulas, W. L. Behavioral features and deficiences of the Masters and Johnson program. *Psychological Record*, 1974, 24, 221–227.

Obler, M. Systematic desensitization in sexual disorders. *Journal of Behavior Therapy and Experimental Psychiatry*, 1973, 4, 93–101.

O'Leary, K. D., & Wilson, G. T. *Behavior therapy: Application and outcome*. Englewood Cliffs, N.J.: Prentice-Hall, 1975.

Paul, G. Behavior modification research: Design and tactics. In C. M. Franks (Ed.), *Behavior therapy: Appraisal and status*. New York: McGraw-Hill, 1969. Pp. 29–62.

Prochaska, J. O., & Marzilli, R. Modifications of the Masters and Johnson approach to sex problems. *Psychotherapy: Theory, Research and Practice*, 1973, 10, 294–296.

Rachman, S. Sexual disorders and behavior therapy. *American Journal of Psychiatry*, 1961, 118, 235–240.

Rappaport, A. F., & Harrell, J. A behavioral exchange model for marital counseling. *Family Coordinator*, 1972, 21, 203–212.

Razani, J. Ejaculatory incompetence treated by deconditioning anxiety. *Journal of Behavior Therapy and Experimental Psychiatry*, 1972, 3, 65–67.

Reisinger, J. J. Masturbatory training in the treatment of primary orgasmic dysfunction. *Journal of Behavior Therapy and Experimental Psychiatry*, 1974, 5, 179–183.

Richardson, T. A. Hypnotherapy in frigidity. *American Journal of Clinical Hypnosis*, 1963, 5, 194–199.

Riedman, S. R. Heightening sexual satisfaction. *Sexology*, 1957, 13, 768–773.

Rubin, M. Verbally suggested responses for reciprocal inhibition of anxiety. *Journal of Behavior Therapy and Experimental Psychiatry*, 1972, 3, 273–277.

Schapiro, B. Premature ejaculation: Review of 1130 cases. *Journal of Urology*, 1943, 50, 374–379.

Semans, J. H. Premature ejaculation: A new approach. *Journal of Urology*, 1956, 40, 836–846.

Shusterman, L. R. The treatment of impotence by behavior modification techniques. *Journal of Sex Research*, 1973, 9, 226–240.

Singer, J., & Singer, I. Types of female orgasm. *Journal of Sex Research*, 1972, 8, 255–267.

Stampfl, T. G., & Levis, D. J. Essentials of implosive therapy: A learning theory based psychodynamic behavioral therapy. *Journal of Abnormal Psychology*, 1967, 72, 496–503.

Stuart, R. B. Operant-interpersonal treatment for marital discord. *Journal of Consulting and Clinical Psychology*, 1969, 33, 675–682.

Taylor, J. G. A behavioral interpretation of obsessive-compulsive neurosis. *Behaviour Research and Therapy*, 1963, 1, 237–244.

Tuthill, J. F. Impotence. *Lancet*, 1955, 1, 124–128.

Ullmann, L. P., & Krasner, L. *A psychological approach to abnormal behavior*. (2nd ed.) Englewood Cliffs, N.J.: Prentice-Hall, 1975.

Wallace, D. H., & Barbach, L. G. Preorgasmic group treatment. *Journal of Sex and Marital Therapy*, 1974, 1, 146–154.

Wells, R. A., Figurel, J. A., & McNee, P. Group facilitative training with conflicted marital couples. In A. Gurman & D. Rice (Eds.), *Couples in conflict*. New York: Jason Aronson, 1975. Pp. 315–326.

Wincze, J. P. A comparison of systematic desensitization and "vicarious extinction" in a case of frigidity. *Journal of Behavior Therapy and Experimental Psychiatry*, 1971, 2, 285–289.

Wolpe, J. *Psychotherapy by reciprocal inhibition*. Palo Alto, Calif.: Stanford University Press, 1958.

Wolpe, J. *The practice of behavior therapy*. (2nd ed.) Oxford: Pergamon, 1973.

TREATMENT AND TRANSFER:
A SEARCH FOR EMPIRICAL PROCEDURES[1]

DAVID MARHOLIN II

Department of Special Education
Boston University
Boston, Massachusetts

LAWRENCE J. SIEGEL[2]

Department of Psychology
Case Western Reserve University
Cleveland, Ohio

AND

DAVID PHILLIPS

Department of Psychology
University of Illinois at Urbana-Champaign
Champaign, Illinois

[1] The authors wish to express their appreciation to Larry G. Grimm, Tom B. Heads, Frederick H. Kanfer, and William H. Redd for their helpful comments on the manuscript.

[2] *Present address:* Mid-Missouri Mental Health Center and University of Missouri Medical School, Columbia, Missouri.

I. INTRODUCTION

The proliferation of learning-based treatment techniques in the past decade has provided a variety of clearly defined methods of effective child therapy (for reviews, cf. Bijou, 1976; Bijou & Redd, 1975; Gelfand & Hartmann, 1968; O'Leary & Wilson, 1975; Ross, 1974; Yates, 1970). There is little doubt of the efficacy of behavioral approaches for the treatment of a wide range of behavior problems in children when the proper contingencies are present in the treatment setting. However, a number of authors have questioned the evidence for the generalizability of behavioral changes due to a lack of empirical evidence supporting the transfer of newly learned behaviors to extra-therapy environments (Bandura, 1969; Davidson & Seidman, 1974; Marholin, Plienis, Harris, & Marholin, 1975a; Marholin & Siegel, 1976). In fact, available evidence suggests that effective transfer and maintenance of behavior change do not occur automatically when the treatment procedures are withdrawn (e.g., Ayllon & Azrin, 1968; Burchard, 1971). It is for this reason that Baer, Wolf, and Risley (1968) have admonished, "Generalization should be programmed rather than expected or lamented" [p. 97]. Despite the early recognition of this issue, recent reviews (e.g., Bijou & Redd, 1975; Kazdin, 1975; Reiss, 1973) have concluded that little data are available with respect to variables affecting transfer of training. In addition, few programs have been designed specifically to obtain or systematically study transfer of treatment effects.

The terms *stimulus generalization* and *transfer of training* have frequently been used interchangeably and perhaps confused in the applied literature (e.g., Kazdin, 1975; Kazdin & Bootzin, 1972; O'Leary & Drabman, 1971). While transfer relates to the "carrying over of an act or way of acting from one performance to another" (Woodworth & Schlosberg, 1954, p. 734), generalization refers to "the finding that a response conditioned in the presence of one stimulus also occurs in the presence of other physically different, although related stimuli" (Nevin, 1973, pp. 116–117). It seems that transfer of training is a preferable phrase when used to describe treatment effects in extra-training environments. In this sense, transfer is more properly considered a descriptive term rather than one implying a process explanation. In the applied behavior analysis and behavior therapy literatures the term generalization is frequently used, but in most cases it is not being investigated directly. In those instances in which transfer was found there are usually insufficient data to explain its occurrence, since the study was not designed to control the variables that might conceivably have produced transfer. Transfer of training is created in an ad hoc fashion in most studies; that is, in a probe following treatment a determination of whether or not the target behavior is occurring in other settings is made. In this fashion the conditions that promoted transfer are dealt with descriptively rather than experimentally.

When any treatment approach is utilized, three assumptions are commonly made concerning the generalizability of newly acquired behaviors. One of these assumptions is that changes in behavior effected in the treatment environment will automatically generalize to extra-therapy settings. For example, a child whose stuttering has been eliminated in the clinic is also expected to speak fluently at home and in the classroom. Second, it is expected that when a child is reinforced for a new behavior, similar behaviors will also occur more frequently in the training setting (i.e., response generalization). For example, a child who is being reinforced for a limited repertoire of social interaction skills in a preschool setting is expected to develop a much larger set of similar social skills without being directly reinforced for these behaviors. Finally, the maintenance of behavior change following formal treatment is often taken for granted. For instance, a delinquent youth whose car-stealing behavior has once been eliminated is expected to maintain a record of no car thefts thereafter in spite of any incompatible contingencies in the natural environment. Therapeutic or educational behaviors taught in the clinic, school, or office *must* occur in at least one other setting if they are to have any utility at all for the individual. In other words, appropriate social behavior learned in therapy is of little or no value to the individual if it does not occur in the natural social environment. In a similar manner, increased attention to task demonstrated in a special contingency management class is of no merit unless these behaviors carry over to the regular classroom.

On the other hand, it is well established that much human learning is situationally specific (e.g., Redd, 1969; Redd & Birnbrauer, 1969). Therefore, the specific stimuli in a training environment will come to set the occasion for the occurrence of the behavior being learned. This phenomenon is referred to as stimulus control. The learner discriminates that the behavior being reinforced is reinforced under the training conditions and not reinforced elsewhere, and therefore he does not emit the behavior in other settings. This concept emphasizes a major thesis of this review: Learned behavior is controlled by both antecedent and current environmental contingencies and is a joint function of the physical specifications of the stimuli and the subject's past history. In fact, one would expect this to be true for any behavioral change program. The discrimination literature suggests that changes in behavior brought about in one setting should usually remain specific to that setting (e.g., Wahler, 1969b).

The situation-specific aspect of behavior is reflected in the designs employed in single-subject research. A procedure frequently employed in operant methodology is to return to pretreatment conditions (baseline) following a period in which treatment contingencies have been in effect in order to demonstrate a functional relationship between the behavior change and the particular operant techniques used (i.e., ABA design). When the treatment condition is withdrawn, the frequency of the target behavior typically returns to its pretreatment level. With evidence for the situation-specific dependence upon existing contingencies of reinforcement (Bijou & Baer, 1961), it is not surprising to find behavioral changes specific to the treatment environment or the contingencies in effect. Multiple-baseline designs across settings also reflect the contingency-specific nature of behavior (Kazdin, 1975). In this particular type of multiple-baseline strategy a contingency is introduced to control a particular behavior within a specific setting. In introducing the contingency to various settings at different points in time, the design relies upon the failure of behavior change in one setting to transfer to other settings (Baer et al., 1968; Sidman, 1960).

Nevertheless, one of the frequent criticisms leveled at behavior therapies is that the behavior altered in one setting does not generalize to all situations in which it would be desirable. While this criticism is true of behavioral approaches, it is also true of all therapeutic and educational approaches. It is simply more apparent in behavioral treatment because the behaviors are specified more clearly and thus are more open to scrutiny.

Two important considerations are (1) the utility of transfer of training effects and (2) stimulus control; these present the therapist or educator with a very real dilemma. In other words, while it is known that treatment effects must occur outside of the training setting to have any lasting value, it is also clear that this is not inevitable. The principles of stimulus generalization derived from the animal laboratory have previously been applied to predict the occurrence of this phenomenon. Given that stimuli in the environment evoke or set the occasion for behavior as a result of their presence in the training situation, generalization will be limited to those situations which share stimuli similar to those in the training environment and will occur only as long as contingencies reinforce the behavior.

While the results from work conducted in laboratory settings with animal subjects have often been extrapolated to applied settings (Johnston, 1972), a certain amount of caution should be exercised in directly extending laboratory findings to clinical practice (Kazdin, 1973b). Therefore, at the present time it may be somewhat premature to suggest that the principles of generalization have wide generality (Blough, 1966; Nevin, 1973; Terrace, 1966). This is an especially salient point when comparing responses by an animal to stimuli varying on one specific physical dimension to a human responding to one stimulus in a vast stimulus complex with untold mediational processes in effect.

Although several researchers (e.g., Atthowe, 1973; Kazdin & Bootzin, 1972; O'Leary & Drabman, 1971) have noted that the availability of techniques which derive from a behavioral (Skinner, 1953; Terrace, 1966), mediational (Bandura, 1969; Kanfer, 1971), or cognitive-personality (Crandall, 1969; Rotter, 1966) framework *should* enhance transfer of treatment effects (Redd, 1974a), the literature on applied strategies reveals a paucity of research on the effectiveness of these approaches. Despite the availability of a number of studies in which transfer has been assessed, only a limited number of studies in the applied behavioral literature have focused directly on the question of variables affecting transfer (Redd, 1970; Reiss, 1973; Schroeder & Baer, 1972) or on treatment programs designed to enhance transfer (Barrett & McCormack, 1973; Emshoff, Redd, & Davidson, 1976; Garcia, 1974; Johnston & Johnston, 1972; Kale, Kaye, Whelan, & Hopkins, 1968; Koegel & Rincover, 1974; Marholin & Steinman, in press; Marholin, Steinman, McInnis, & Heads, 1975b; Reiss & Redd, 1970; Walker & Buckley, 1972).

This chapter evaluates the research in the area of transfer of training of operant treatment effects with children by reviewing the literature relevant to applied settings. The studies selected for review have a number of common characteristics. All discuss applications of positive reinforcement and/or punishment techniques to human operant behavior in laboratory or field settings, and all include a quantitative evaluation of the degree of transfer of training. The studies are analyzed in terms of stimulus control, parameters of reinforcement, intrasubject variables, and subject response characteristics. Strategies are suggested to increase the probability of transfer and maintenance of behaviors acquired during treatment. Finally, future directions for research are explored.

II. CONTINGENCIES OF REINFORCEMENT

The effect of reinforcement contingencies across environments is the parameter that has received the most attention in the applied literature as a variable responsible for the transfer of treatment effects. Reversal designs or multiple-baseline designs across settings are used in order to demonstrate a functional relationship between the contingencies of reinforcement and the frequency of occurrence of the behavior, reflecting the notion that behavior is presumed to be a function of the contingencies in effect in a specific situation.

Taken together, data support the situation-specific dependence of behavior upon the treatment contingencies in a given setting (Becker, Madsen, Arnold, & Thomas, 1967; Broden, Hall, Dunlap, & Clark, 1970; McArthur & Hawkins, 1975). For example, the disruptive behavior of second-grade children was investigated by O'Leary, Becker, Evans, and Saudargas (1969). A token program with backup reinforcers was demonstrated to be effective in reducing disruptive behaviors during afternoon class periods when the token program was in effect. When the token program was initially instituted in the afternoon, the frequency of disruptive behavior decreased in the morning for the first several days. A subsequent rapid increase to earlier levels suggested that the children had now learned to discriminate that appropriate behavior was reinforced only in the afternoon. In addition, careful observations indicated that in the afternoon period, during the token program, the teacher delivered a high frequency of contingent social reinforcement for appropriate behavior, whereas in the morning there was little contingent social reinforcement delivered. The failure of afternoon behavior to transfer to the morning sessions would appear to be the result of different contingencies of reinforcement. Meichenbaum, Bowers, and Ross (1968) present data consistent with O'Leary et al. (1969) showing that the inappropriate classroom behavior of institutionalized delinquent females decreased only during the class period in which reinforcement contingencies were in effect.

Wahler (1969b), in an investigation of setting generality, provides further support for the notion that a child's behavior conforms to the stimulus contingencies present in a specific setting. Two response classes of behavior for two children were simultaneously investigated in the home and school. The results indicated that each child's behavior was a function of the short-term consequences provided by the parents and teachers. Observations of the attention-giving behavior of the parents and teachers indicated a point-to-point correspondence between the frequencies of appropriate behavior and the parental and teacher attention provided for appropriate behavior. It is interesting to note that appropriate behavior at home increased briefly at school when reinforcement was being provided only in the home. However, with no contingencies to maintain the behavior at school, rapid extinction occurred. Similar short-lived transfer of treatment effects is reported by Herman and Tramontana (1971) and McArthur and Hawkins (1975). Other research corroborates these findings. Unless the transfer settings possess contingencies similar to those of the treatment environment, discrimination rather than generalization will occur (e.g., Hingtgen & Trost, 1966; Skindrud, 1972).

While changes in behavior appear to be specific to the setting in which the contingencies are present, transfer across time and setting has been reported in several instances (Hewett, Taylor, & Artuso, 1969; Kazdin, 1973a; O'Leary & Becker, 1967; Walker, Mattson, & Buckley, 1969). Kazdin (1973a), for example, found that task-oriented behavior that was reinforced in a token program during morning classes also improved in the afternoon although no token reinforcement was delivered at that time. In addition, during a 3-week extinction period, on-task behavior decreased only slightly from the level of the treatment condition. One interpretation of these results is that the teachers became conditioned reinforcers maintaining appropriate behavior acquired in the token condition. No data are provided, however, to assess the conditioned reinforcing properties of the teachers during the various conditions. In addition, with no control for the frequency of verbal reinforcement delivered in either the afternoon generalization sessions or the extinction period, it is possible that teacher-delivered social reinforcement was responsible for the observed transfer of effects. Walker *et al.* (1969) also report transfer to regular classes from a token classroom. Follow-up data taken 3 months after termination of the token program indicated that appropriate classroom behavior was maintained at near treatment levels and that task-oriented behaviors had increased from pretreatment levels. A number of factors may have accounted for this transfer effect. At the conclusion of the major treatment program, individual programs were written for the regular classroom teachers in order to maintain task-oriented behavior acquired in the token classroom. Walker *et al.* (1969) suggest that another factor that may have been responsible for the maintenance of appropriate classroom behavior was the increase in academic skills that resulted from the token program. It is not possible to reconcile the differences between those studies which report transfer of treatment effects and those which do not, since studies that report transfer lack sufficient controls and data to account for those variables which may have been responsible for its occurrence.

Most of the studies demonstrating the effects of various contingencies of reinforcement have utilized within-subject designs. Following a baseline or preexperimental period, the reinforcement procedure is applied, withdrawn, and reapplied. The ABAB design or its variations (Baer, 1975; Sidman, 1960) provide an additional opportunity to assess transfer of treatment effects. The return-to-baseline condition is actually a transfer probe. The matter is somewhat complicated by the impracticality of a precise return to baseline due to the requirements of the therapy setting. For example, while tokens may be withdrawn, contingent positive verbal feedback may remain; or while positive verbal reinforcement may be withdrawn, other forms of social reinforcement may still be provided by the environment. Bijou, Peterson, Harris, Allen, and Johnston (1969) cautioned researchers using a reversal design not to wait too long before returning to baseline, lest the behavior come under control of new conditioned reinforcers that maintain it during an attempt to return to baseline conditions. All too frequently, a return to baseline is not carefully monitored to control for additional reinforcement contingencies that were absent during the original baseline condition. Wahler (1969a) provided an exception, with careful monitoring of the behavior of the reinforcing agent during nonreinforcement (baseline and reversal) as well as reinforcement conditions. His data clearly indicated that the amount of reinforcement delivered during the return-to-baseline condition was equal to that delivered in the preexperimental baseline. In essence, the return-to-baseline period may be more appropriately termed an extinction period. Under such conditions, maintenance of treatment levels of behavior would not be expected. Whether behavior acquired during treatment conditions comes under the control of additional conditioned reinforcers and is maintained over time or whether the behavior is rapidly extinguished is dependent upon many variables. Among them may be the length of treatment conditions, programming of natural contingencies such as peer reinforcement, response generalization, and a number of setting factors.

It is suggested that in many experimental demonstrations treatment is not necessarily programmed in such a fashion as to favor maintenance of behavior in the return-to-baseline condition (Broden et al., 1970; Herman & Tramontana, 1971; Kuypers, Becker, &

O'Leary, 1968; O'Leary *et al.*, 1969). These results would appear to have clear implications for the specific planning of the transfer of contingencies from treatment to nontreatment settings; that is, if the goal of treatment is to have the behavior occur in another setting, one must establish the contingencies in that setting.

III. MANIPULATION OF REINFORCING AGENTS

Since the earliest stages of the development of behavior modification techniques, there has been an implied commitment to the efficacy of training "significant others" (e.g., parents, teachers, siblings, peers) as behavior change agents (Williams, 1959). Training of these individuals in behavior modification techniques has received a considerable amount of research attention (for reviews, cf. O'Dell, 1974; Patterson, 1971). Although the primary focus of these studies has not been the issue of transfer of treatment effects, the data suggest that programming of significant others in the treatment environment serves to enhance the probability of the maintenance of behavior change once the treatment program has been terminated.

Many investigators have reported that children placed in regular classrooms following residence in a token classroom soon revert to their deviant behavior. Walker and Buckley (1971) and Hall, Lund, and Jackson (1968) emphasize that in the average classroom, inappropriate behavior receives at least as much reinforcement from the teacher as appropriate behavior. In an observational study, Walker and Buckley (1971) showed that the teacher attended to inappropriate behavior 74% of the time and to appropriate behavior only 26% of the time. Thus, in order for a child to conform to the contingencies present in the classroom, he would have to engage in inappropriate behavior. In an effort to overcome posttreatment contingencies incompatible with the treatment goals, Walker and Buckley (1972) employed a strategy of direct posttreatment intervention into the regular classroom. One of the most successful procedures included the careful monitoring of teacher-administered social and token reinforcement after returning the child to the regular classroom. By providing an environment with contingencies sensitive to appropriate behavior rather than inappropriate behavior, maintenance of appropriate behavior can be expected.

Walker, Hops, and Johnson (1975) employed course credit to motivate teachers in a regular classroom to employ contingencies to maintain behaviors acquired during a systematic treatment phase. The credit was made contingent upon: (1) teachers mastering the material in a programmed behavior modification text and attending weekly feedback meetings with the investigators; and (2) students maintaining levels of appropriate behavior acquired earlier in the study in a special contingency management classroom. Results indicated that the procedures designed to facilitate maintenance of treatment-produced behavior changes were successfully implemented for one group of subjects in their regular classrooms, whereas a control group, exposed only to the experimental classroom procedures, failed to maintain treatment levels of appropriate behavior when returned to regular classrooms. These results are consistent with those of Lovaas, Koegel, Simmons, and Long (1973), whose follow-up measures, taken from 1 to 4 years after intensive treatment of the behavior of 20 autistic children, showed that significant differences existed between groups of children whose parents were trained in behavior modification techniques as compared to another group of children who were institutionalized. It is noted by these authors that the institutional environments failed to reinforce newly acquired behavior (e.g., free play, appropriate speech, social nonverbal behavior) while providing intermittent reinforcement for inappropriate behavior (e.g., self-injury, echolalia). In contrast, the parents trained in behavioral techniques provided sufficient contingent positive reinforcement to maintain appropriate behaviors while consistently extinguishing inappropriate behavior.

Tharp and Wetzel (1969) present a model of therapeutic intervention in which the significant members of a target subject's social environment are instructed in behavior change techniques. This model is based on the assumption that significant others are sources of positive reinforcement for the target subject. A number of researchers have shown that parents (Hawkins, Peterson, Schweid, & Bijou, 1966; Patterson, McNeal, Hawkins, & Phelps, 1967), teachers (Madsen, Becker, & Thomas, 1968; Phillips, 1974), and peers (Bailey, Timbers, Phillips, & Wolf, 1971; Siegel & Steinman, 1975; Solomon & Wahler, 1973) can successfully modify the behavior of deviant children. Following the training of these individuals in the use of contingent reinforcement of appropriate behavior and the punishment of inappropriate behavior, new behavioral patterns were maintained. Wahler (1972) further suggests that members of the child's environment may begin to apply reinforcement techniques to behaviors other than those they were trained to modify, thus producing additional prosocial behaviors. Changes in any one deviant response might also affect similar deviant responses in the behavioral repertoire of the target child.

It appears that whenever possible the ultimate answer to the problem of transfer of training is to modify the child's behavior in the natural environment using the significant others in that environment to manage the contingencies. As an example of achieving lasting behavior changes through manipulation of the social environment in which a deviant child resides, Patterson *et al.* (1967) employed a set of procedures to change the schedules of reinforcement used by two parents with their 6-year-old son, who displayed isolative and negativistic behaviors. Both parents frequently employed punishment to terminate various bizarre behaviors (e.g., head banging, violent outbursts) to the exclusion of positive reinforcement for appropriate behavior. The parents were taught to reinforce their son first for initiating contact with them and later for cooperation. As the child became more cooperative and approached his parents more often, the parents and child became increasingly more reinforcing for each other, thus increasing the probability of maintenance of positive child and parent behaviors. Patterson and Brodsky (1966) employed parents, teachers, and peers in extinguishing inappropriate behaviors (tantrums, negativism) and conditioning incompatible prosocial behaviors (cooperation). Measures obtained at a 3-month follow-up indicated that reprogramming of the social environment had succeeded in maintaining appropriate behaviors at a very high level.

The behavior modifier's contingency management behaviors may also transfer to other subjects. Lavigueur, Peterson, Sheese, and Peterson (1973) investigated changes in the behavior of a nontarget child as a result of training the mother in change techniques aimed at a sibling. While the nontarget child was not considered a behavior problem by the mother, it is interesting to note that observations in the home indicated improvements in the behavior of both the treated and untreated sibling. Improved behavior in the home was maintained for both children at a 10-month follow-up. Although it is not possible to determine the variables responsible for changes observed in the nontarget child, it might be suggested that the mother had learned to provide contingent reinforcement for appropriate behavior not only for the target child, with whom training had taken place, but also for the nontarget sibling. Arnold, Levine, and Patterson (1975) further report systematic changes in the behavior of the siblings of 27 treated predelinquents. The parents of the predelinquent target subjects had been trained in social learning techniques of child management. Follow-up results indicated that noted reductions in deviant behavior and concurrent increases in prosocial behavior were maintained over a 6-month period. Another study by Rinn, Vernon, and Wise (1975) indicated that behavior-problem children whose parents had participated in a class emphasizing the principles of applied behavior analysis were much less likely to reach the attention of mental health delivery systems than those children whose parents had been placed in a no-training control group. Taken together these studies strongly suggest that systematic training in behavior analysis generalizes to the behavior of the parents producing concurrent desirable changes in their children that are maintained over time.

Patterson, Cobb, and Ray (1972) describe a direct classroom intervention program for a deviant child. Additional time at recess for the entire class was made contingent upon the total number of points earned by a target subject. The contingencies were initially tailored in such a manner that on the first trial the child would obtain the requisite points to earn extra recess time for his classmates. Gradually, the contingencies were altered to require greater amounts of appropriate behavior from the target subjects. Results showed a dramatic increase in appropriate classroom behavior that was maintained at a follow-up. Similar procedures making reinforcement for a group contingent upon the performance of a single child in the group (e.g., Barrish, Saunders, & Wolf, 1969; Walker & Buckley, 1972), part of the group (e.g., Harris & Sherman, 1973), or the entire group (e.g., Packard, 1970) have been successfully employed. In such a situation each member of the group is likely to encourage the desired response of the target child or children in order to obtain reinforcers, thereby effecting a desired change in the stimulus function of the peer group; that is, peers become discriminative for appropriate rather than inappropriate behavior (Marholin *et al.*, 1975a). Given the subsequent likelihood of members of a child's peer group being present outside of the treatment setting, the probability of transfer is similarly enhanced. This notion gains some support from a comparison of group rewards and individual rewards for individual behavior during a 4-week treatment and a 4-week maintenance period with two groups of hyperactive elementary school children (Rosenbaum, O'Leary, & Jacob, 1975). Results indicated that subjects in the group-reward condition showed slightly better maintenance than those in the individual-reward condition.

IV. STIMULUS CONTROL

While direct intervention in the community remains a powerful tool in avoiding the transfer of treatment problem, it is useful to look at parameters within the treatment process itself that may provide at least short-term transfer to the community. One such parameter, the discriminative stimulus (S^D), has received some attention. Research with animals has clearly demonstrated that an S^D (i.e., a stimulus that sets the occasion for the occurrence of a conditioned operant) may acquire very strong positive stimulus control (Keller & Schoenfeld, 1950; Skinner, 1938).

Redd (1970) conducted a study with four severely retarded boys in which two subjects received both contingent and noncontingent reinforcement from two experimenters for cooperative play with other boys. For two other subjects only contingent reinforcement was given. In probes following this procedure, the subjects who had received both contingent and noncontingent reinforcement training failed to transfer their cooperative behavior to three novel adults in a free-play situation, whereas the subjects having only contingent reinforcement showed transfer to the novel adults in the new situation. For the subjects who received only contingent reinforcement, any adult entering the room was discriminative for reinforcement, since training did not teach any other discrimination. Those subjects who received contingent and noncontingent reinforcement training came to respond to each adult as a different S^D, which accounts for the lack of transfer to a novel stimulus that had not previously been paired with reinforcement.

To achieve transfer beyond the treatment environment, stimulus control must shift to stimuli in the extra-therapy environment. However, more often than not there is no systematic effort made to effect a shift of stimulus control beyond the training setting. All too frequently the trainer or behavior modifier is inadvertently programmed as the sole or major S^D for desired behavior. When the client is subsequently returned to the natural environment, leaving behind his trainer and principle S^D for appropriate behavior, it is not surprising to find a rapid decrease in the frequency of appropriate behaviors learned in the treatment setting (Redd, 1970; Redd & Birnbrauer, 1969; Risley, 1968).

Risley (1968) investigated the transfer effects of shock delivered to an autistic child contingent upon climbing and rocking. Immediate control was established over both of these behaviors in an experimental setting. However, the control was restricted to the specific stimulus condition of the experimenter being present in the laboratory setting. Climbing and rocking continued at home when the experimenter was present, in the laboratory when the experimenter was absent, but not in the experimental setting when the experimenter was present. These findings are consistent with the results of several similar studies involving punishment of autistic-type behaviors of children (Browning & Stover, 1971; Hamilton & Standahl, 1969; Lovaas, Schaeffer, & Simmons, 1965; Lovaas & Simmons, 1969; Tate & Baroff, 1966). Lovaas and Simmons (1969) suggest that for punishment of specific behaviors (e.g., self-destructive behavior) to be more enduring in its therapeutic effects it should be delivered by more than one person in a wide variety of settings in order to minimize discriminations.

Reiss and Redd (1970) reported that after a therapist had eliminated a 9-year-old girl's self-injurious behavior through time-out and reinforcement of incompatible behaviors, the girl resumed her self-injurious behavior with a novel therapist. The new therapist acquired subject control only after reinstating the treatment contingencies used by therapist I. Upon replacement of therapist II by therapist III in the same treatment setting, self-injurious behavior reappeared. After the third therapist again reinstated the treatment program with the subsequent reappearance of desired behavior, a fourth and fifth therapist were introduced without any recurrence of self-injurious behavior. This suggests that discrimination between adults had been minimized and transfer facilitated. A similar technique used with retarded children employing multiple tutors was more successful in reducing disruptive behavior in a classroom than was a technique using only one tutor (Barrett & McCormack, 1973). Consistent with the studies investigating transfer of punishment effects, it is suggested that for reinforcement to effectively promote transfer it should be delivered by more than one person.

As a further technique to minimize discrimination and maximize transfer, varying of stimulus conditions for appropriate behavior in the form of distractions (Goocher & Ebner, 1968) and physical setting (Lent, 1968; Rubin & Stolz, 1974) have been reported with encouraging results. Transfer of training as a function of multiple training settings was investigated in an operant speech therapy program aimed at correcting the misarticulation of a retarded woman in an institutional setting (Griffiths & Craighead, 1972). Transfer from the therapy setting (speech therapy room) to a nontherapy setting (cottage) did not occur until contingent reinforcement for correct articulation was provided in the cottage. However, reinforcement in a second setting facilitated transfer of appropriate speech to a non-training environment (classroom). Emshoff *et al.* (1976) simultaneously varied trainer, activity, time, and setting in a systematic attempt to program generalization of praise comments delivered to peers by delinquent adolescents. Generalization probes immediately following training and in the subjects' homes indicated a higher frequency of the trained response for two subjects receiving generalization training than for two other subjects who received their training by the same therapist, at the same time, in the same activity, and at the same place. These data are consistent with those of Callantine and Warren (1955), Duncan (1958), and Shore and Sechrest (1961), who have demonstrated that positive transfer is greatest when a variety of training stimuli are employed. Goldstein (1973) and Goldstein, Heller, and Sechrest (1966) proposed that this approach to transfer facilitation might be implemented in psychotherapy by having each patient interact with more than one psychotherapist.

Data demonstrating presence of a generalization gradient resulting from a differential reinforcement history with the test stimuli are provided by Craighead, O'Leary, and Allen (1973). An autistic child who exhibited a low frequency of compliance was trained to follow instructions using food and praise as reinforcers. During a test for generalization to stimuli not specifically used in the training sessions, a gradient of responding to novel stimuli was observed. The child followed 90% of the "trained" instructions (i.e., those directly reinforced), 85% of "similar" instructions to those trained, and 77% of "different" instructions. In addition, training sessions were interspersed with generalization probes in which the effects of different persons giving instructions were assessed. The child followed 70% of instructions given by a novel experimenter with whom there was no prior history of reinforcement for the target response. While contingent reinforcement for careful following of instructions was not provided by the child's parents, generalization sessions indicated that the subjects followed 64% of the instructions provided by his father and 84% of his mother's instructions. Thus, not only did the target response generalize outside the specific response class that was originally reinforced, but generalization occurred along a gradient of stimuli that resembled the training stimuli with various degrees of similarity. These results are consistent with Osgood's (1953) contention that the greater the similarity between practice and test stimuli, the greater the amount of positive transfer. His conclusion rests on a particularly solid base of experimental support, involving both motor (Crafts, 1935; Duncan, 1953; Gagne, Baker, & Foster, 1950) and verbal (Osgood, 1949, 1953; Underwood, 1951; Young & Underwood, 1954) behaviors. Implicit awareness of this principle of transfer enhancement has been utilized by Jones (1960) and Marlatt (1968), who enhanced the "real-lifeness" of certain stimuli in the training setting itself in an effort to facilitate transfer from an office to the "real world."

Another way of facilitating transfer of training is to program specific S^D s during treatment that have a high probability of appearing in the posttreatment environment. In an attempt to program generalization through the systematic use of a preprogrammed S^D, Johnston and Johnston (1972) demonstrated a high degree of control over responding in the presence of a peer who had become discriminative for peer-delivered reinforcement during training. In an initial treatment phase, two children were trained to monitor and subsequently differentially reinforce correct and incorrect speech of each other. Each child became discriminative for occasion-appropriate responding and reinforcement for the other. After training, each child responded appropriately only in the presence of the other child, indicating the specificity with which stimulus control can occur. Stokes and Baer (1975) present data replicating Johnston and Johnston's findings. The studies described above in which multiple trainers were employed in the treatment program suggest that had Johnston and Johnston (1972) or Stokes and Baer (1975) used additional children during the training phase, transfer of the target response might have been observed.

Marholin et al. (1975b) investigated the discriminative control exercised by a teacher's presence and absence on the task-oriented and disruptive classroom behavior of six conduct-problem children. They assessed the effect of the teacher's presence and absence under three sets of contingencies: (1) when reinforcement was delivered noncontingently by the teacher; (2) when the teacher specifically reinforced the children for being on-task and nondisruptive; (3) when the teacher only reinforced academic rate and accuracy. The teacher's programmed absences from the classroom served as transfer probes. The data indicated clear discriminative control by the teacher's presence during on-task reinforcement, with dramatic increases in disruptive behaviors and concurrent decreases in on-task behavior during the teacher's absence. It was predicted that an additional S^D, the academic materials, would be established when accuracy and rate of responding were reinforced. Presence of the academic materials during the transfer probes might then be expected to exert control over appropriate social behaviors. The results suggested this to be the case, as there was less deterioration of social behavior observed from teacher-present to teacher-absent condition (i.e., more positive transfer). These conclusions were further supported by data from a follow-up study employing eight fifth- and sixth-grade behavior-problem children in one public elementary school classroom. They performed various academic tasks during baseline and two reinforcement conditions: (1) reinforcement for being on task and nondisruptive; and (2) reinforcement for the accuracy and rate of their academic work itself (Marholin & Steinman, in press). Each child was sequentially exposed to a baseline period (A) followed by a series of on-task (B) and academic reinforcement (C) conditions in the ABCBC-type design. Following each of these conditions, the teacher was absent for a portion of each session (transfer probes) for 3 successive days. In the teacher's absence, on-task behavior was markedly reduced and disruptive and neutral behaviors were markedly increased, regardless of the reinforcement condition in operation. In addition, the teacher's absence resulted in a marked reduction in academic accuracy and rate during baseline and both reinforcement conditions. Of particular interest was that the extent to which the children became disruptive was reduced and the extent to which they remained on task was increased in the teacher's absence when reinforcement was contingent upon academic accuracy and rate, instead of being contingent upon being on task. In a similar manner, a greater number of problems were attempted in the teacher's absence during both conditions in which accuracy and rate of academic performance were being reinforced than the two conditions in which on-task behavior alone was being reinforced.

The use of a preprogrammed S^D to initiate behavior of sufficient strength in the posttreatment environment allows for the reinforcement of the desired behavior and thus further maintenance of that behavior. Without the S^D, the target behavior may never occur in the natural environment regardless of the contingencies of reinforcement that are present. This fact was nicely demonstrated in a study by Rincover and Koegel (1975). In the first phase, each of 10 autistic children were systematically taught a new behavior in a treatment room, and transfer to a novel extra-therapy setting was assessed. Four of the 10 children showed no transfer to the new setting. Therefore, in a second phase, each of the four children who failed to transfer their newly learned behavior to an extra-therapy setting participated in an analysis of stimulus control. Each of the four children was shown to be selectively responding to an incidental stimulus during the original training in the treatment room. Subsequently each of the four children responded correctly in the extra-therapy setting when the stimulus that was exerting functional control during training was identified and introduced into the extra-therapy setting. Clearly, the utility of preprogrammed S^Ds as a means of facilitating positive transfer requires further investigation.

Steinman (1970a, 1970b, 1971, 1973) and Hill (1973) have suggested that in many situations the presence and continued surveillance of an adult can strongly influence the behavior emitted by a child. Because of a past and/or current relationship with reinforcement contingencies, presence of an adult may interact with the specific contingencies in effect and either facilitate or inhibit a child's performance on a given task. Due to the adult's past or present role as a reinforcing and/or punishing agent, the adult can develop discriminative stimulus properties for classes of behavior that may or may not be related to the particular response requirements of the current situation. Thus, mere presence or absence of an adult can have a profound or negligible effect on a child's behavior depending upon the particular behavior in question and its relationship to the response class for which the adult's presence or absence has become discriminative.

Several studies have shown that mere presence or absence of an adult can exert strong control over children's behavior (Meddock, Parsons, & Hill, 1971; Peterson, Merwin, Moyer, & Whitehurst, 1971; Peterson & Whitehurst, 1971; Redd & Wheeler, 1973). Redd (1973, 1974b, 1976) has found that presence of an adult who has expressed a preference for a particular response can interact with, and even counteract, the specific contingencies available for the child's responses. The child will emit responses producing a lower magnitude of reinforcement rather than another response which is simultaneously available to him that produces higher magnitude reinforcement, if an adult has expressed a preference for the former response and is present to observe the child's behavior. In the adult's absence, the child will return to the response producing the higher magnitude of reinforcement. These studies would seem to indicate that presence of an adult in a treatment condition becomes discriminative for the particular response class reinforced during treatment. While the presence of an adult might clearly be considered as an S^D for certain consequences, the subtle interaction of the adult's presence with various contingencies of reinforcement requires special emphases

(Marholin & Steinman, in press; Marholin *et al.*, 1975b; Steinman, 1976a, 1976b)..

If the therapist or behavior modifier has reinforced "appropriate behavior" in a therapy setting and has become discriminative for these behaviors, then the presence of the therapist in the extra-therapy setting could potentially be advantageous in terms of promoting transfer. Of course, this problem of presence or absence of the individual who controls the contingencies is greatly reduced when the training or therapy takes place in the natural setting and is conducted by significant others (Tharp & Wetzel, 1969).

V. INSTRUCTIONAL CONTROL

A subtle yet potentially relevant variable in facilitating transfer and maintenance is that of instructions presented to the child during or just before treatment. Skinner (1966, 1969) and Marholin and Gray (1976) have emphasized a distinction between contingency controlled behavior and behavior under the discriminative control of instructions. Steinman (1970a, 1970b) and Wilcox, Meddock, and Steinman (1973) have further indicated that instructions play an important role in generalized imitation as well as in comparable nonimitative tasks. They suggest that initial priming procedures such as adult-delivered instructions or observing a model engaged in task-specific behavior may create an extremely durable pattern of responding during training. This pattern of responding has been shown to be particularly resistant to extinction. In fact, when subjects were differentially reinforced for literally hundreds of trials following initial priming procedures, responding to "nonreinforced" stimuli *never* extinguished.

The type of instructions given, either positive (e.g., "Do this") or negative (e.g., "Do not do this"), as well as their timing of presentation (i.e., early or late in training) have been shown to have a differential effect on the child's subsequent behavior. Negative instructions appear to exert more control than positive ones. For example, in a two-choice discrimination task, Redd and Winston (1974) demonstrated that compliance was greater following antecedant negative preference statements (e.g., "I don't like it; he chose Y") than following antecedent positive comments (e.g., "I like it; he chose W"). In an investigation of the potential overriding effects of adult-delivered negative instructions, Redd, Amen, Meddock, and Winston (1974) simply instructed a child not to make a particular response in a marble-drop game, thereby effectively blocking that particular response even though the payoff was greater than for a simultaneously available response. Wilcox *et al.* (1973) have also shown that while instructions (either positive or negative) delivered early in training may have a profound effect, similar instructions delivered late in training may have little or no effect upon subsequent responding.

These studies taken together suggest that when delivered early in training, comments or instructions (especially negative ones) made by an adult to a child may exert sufficient control over a response so that it would be maintained in a posttreatment setting where the contingencies may mitigate against it. The observed resistance to extinction following simple instructions is especially relevant to transfer situations in which reinforcement for new behavior may be lacking, at least initially. If instructions render some behaviors very resistant to extinction during a period following treatment, the probability of the behavior being reinforced and maintained is greatly enhanced.

VI. ESTABLISHMENT OF SOCIAL STIMULI AS FUNCTIONAL REINFORCERS

One variable frequently overlooked in behavioral treatment programs that may be critical to the transfer of treatment effects is the establishment of social stimuli as functional reinforcers. However, we may not assume that all social stimuli, such as praise, are reinforcing for everyone (Browning & Stover, 1971; Marholin & Bijou, 1976). For example, praise was not found to be an effective reinforcer with delinquents (Quay & Hunt, 1965), oppositional children (Wahler, 1969a), retarded children (Locke, 1969), and psychotic children (Lovaas, Freitag, Kinder, Rubenstein, Schaeffer, & Simmons, 1966). Before a change program employing praise is instituted, it is often necessary to establish or increase the reinforcing value of verbal statements and praise. Wahler (1969a) established praise as a reinforcer by pairing verbal praise with tokens after praise alone had failed to modify the uncooperative behavior of oppositional children. Lovaas *et al.* (1966) and Locke (1969) paired verbal praise and food when praise was ineffective in increasing the prosocial behavior of schizophrenic and retarded children, respectively. In each of these studies, the target behavior was finally maintained by praise alone after the tokens or food were gradually withdrawn. It is possible that the pairing of verbal praise with token or primary reinforcement during treatment is a key variable in achieving transfer. Evidence to support this view is presented by Nolan, Mattis, and Holliday (1970), who present follow-up data for six children with learning disabilities who had been treated with operant procedures to eliminate undesirable behavior and develop new appropriate classroom behaviors. The effects of treatment were maintained for all children at the 12-month follow-up assessment, based on behavioral observations and interviews with their teachers. Moreover, those children who had been gradually faded from food to social reinforcers were found to exhibit additional improvements in behavior, beyond the changes in target behaviors, compared to children who had not been graduated to social reinforcement at the termination of the treatment period.

A study by Blanchard and Johnson (1973) assessed the differential effectiveness of several frequently used operant classroom procedures in facilitating transfer to a nontreatment setting. During a 12-week program, two teachers provided various consequences to the behavior of five disruptive seventh-grade students. The experimental conditions, which included teacher attention variables (e.g., ignoring, praising, scolding) and tangible rewards and punishments (administered on an individual and group basis) for appropriate classroom behavior were interspersed with baseline periods to assess the maintenance of the treatment effects. In addition, transfer of the target responses was measured in a second classroom in which the experimental contingencies were not in effect. Contingent tangible rewards and punishments were demonstrated to be effective in improving classroom behavior for all subjects. Contingent manipulation of the teacher attention variables produced desirable behavior changes in only some of the students and appeared to be dependent on the specific teacher who delivered the social consequences. More important to the present discussion were the data obtained in the nonexperimental classroom. While an improvement was observed in the regular classroom under the conditions in which contingent rewards and punishments were provided, no transfer of treatment effects were obtained in the second classroom during the same period. Further observation of teacher behavior during experimental and transfer conditions showed a functional relationship between the teacher's behavior and changes in the students' behavior. The use of teacher attention variables was found to be highest during the experimental conditions when the contingencies were in effect. However, almost 100% ignoring of undesirable behavior during the transfer condition was observed. One caution that the authors themselves note in interpreting these results is that each experimental condition was in effect for only 1 week. It is possible that the results may have been different, particularly with regard to the findings for the transfer of social reinforcement treatment effects, had the contingencies been in effect for a longer period of time.

Ayllon and Azrin's (1968) *relevance of behavior rule,* "Teach only those behaviors that will continue to be reinforced after training" [p. 56], implies that only behavior that will come under the control of naturally occurring reinforcers should be taught. A corollary to this rule certainly requires that the person's environment possess reinforcers of sufficient strength and frequency to maintain the target behavior. In the studies cited, the development of praise as a functional reinforcer adds an additional reinforcer to the subject's total environment. Such a potential reinforcer, together with more subtle conditioned social reinforcers (e.g., eye contact, facial expression), will greatly increase the probability of reinforcement maintaining behaviors acquired in treatment (Chadwick & Day, 1971; Marholin & Siegel, 1976; Reisinger, 1972).

VII. SELF-MANAGEMENT

One potential strategy for enhancing response maintenance and transfer of training involves the client's learning to control his own behavior regardless of the setting environment (Cautela, 1969; Thoresen & Mahoney, 1974). Self-control or self-management (SM) techniques employing self-evaluation, self-monitoring, and self-reinforcement (Goldiamond, 1965; Goldfried & Merbaum, 1973; Kanfer, 1971, 1975) have been differentiated from external control procedures traditionally employed in most behavioral intervention programs (Kanfer, 1970; Kanfer & Karoly, 1972). Specifically, proponents of SM techniques suggest that a client can be taught to control the consequences of his own behavior (i.e., self-reinforcement or self-punishment) as well as the antecedents (i.e., self-instructions). Unfortunately, while some clinical techniques using self-control and self-reinforcement (SR) procedures have already shown some success (Kanfer, 1975; Masters & Mokros, 1974), the theoretical foundation for these techniques remains incomplete (Kanfer & Grimm, 1976).

While it has been concluded that behaviors acquired during treatment often will not be maintained because posttreatment environments fail to provide appropriate reinforcement contingencies, this *does not* suggest that the environment itself lacks sufficient reinforcers to maintain target behaviors. Instead, it is the arrangement of the available environmental stimuli which is absent (Bijou, 1970). However, it is possible for the client himself to exert control over available reinforcers in such a manner as to make them contingent upon his own behavior. This has been termed self-reward or self-reinforcement. Skinner (1953) has defined one property of SR by stating that it "presupposes that the individual has it in his power to obtain reinforcement but does not do so until a particular response has been emitted" [pp. 237–238]. SR may be in the form of: (1) a self-administered consequence, such as going to a movie at the completion of a homework assignment; or (2) verbal-symbolic SR, such as self-praise for a completed speech. Laboratory research with children and adults has demonstrated that SR procedures show the two characteristic properties of reinforcing stimuli, i.e., they alter the probability of occurrence of the response that preceded them, and they motivate new learning (Bandura & Perloff, 1967; Kanfer & Duerfelt, 1967; Montgomery & Parton, 1970).

In a frequently cited study, Bandura and Perloff (1967) taught children to determine the performance requirements for reinforcement, monitor their own behavior, and reinforce themselves during a mechanical game played under different reinforcement conditions. Children in a self-control group selected their own performance criteria and reinforced themselves whenever the criteria were met. Each subject in the self-control group was yoked to another child in an externally imposed group where reinforcers were automatically delivered according to the same performance criteria as in the self-control group. Control groups included either externally delivered noncontingent reinforcement or nonreinforcement. Both externally imposed and self-control procedures yielded significantly more responding than did either control procedure. While the self-control procedure itself produced high levels of performance, the process involved is unclear. Bandura (1969) has theorized that self-monitoring leads to the child's covert self-evaluation. If the child's performance falls below his own standard, negative self-evaluation results (i.e., punishment); if his performance is above his current standard, positive self-evaluation (i.e., reinforcement) occurs. Johnson and Martin (1974) have further suggested that the process of self-evaluation followed by SR becomes a conditioned reinforcer by virtue of prior pairings with primary reinforcement. Such arguments offer a possible explanation for the maintenance of children's behavior in the absence of immediate external reinforcement.

Several applied studies have attempted to compare self-imposed contingencies (SR) to reinforcement administered by another person (e.g., Felixbrod & O'Leary, 1973; Johnson & Martin, 1974; Lovitt & Curtiss, 1969). Most of the comparisons reveal SR to be equal or slightly superior to externally delivered reinforcement (ER). Although the SR procedures are often confounded with possible ER, they do provide a rather convincing argument for the further investigation of the effectiveness of SR.

Recent studies have employed various aspects of SM procedures in a therapy situation with apparent control of target behaviors (Bolstad & Johnson, 1972; Drabman, Spitalnik, & O'Leary, 1973; Fixsen, Phillips, & Wolf, 1973; Glynn, 1970; Glynn, Thomas, & Shee, 1973; Kaufman & O'Leary, 1972; Seymour & Stokes, 1975). Glynn *et al.* (1973) employed SM techniques with second-grade children in an attempt to maintain high levels of appropriate social behaviors in a behavior modification program. Each child assessed his own behavior to determine if he had met an on-task criterion, recorded his own behavior, and selected a reinforcer contingent on his performance. Follow-up at 5 and 7 weeks indicated that the procedure was very successful in maintaining target behaviors at a level equal to that obtained when the externally monitored behavior management program was in effect. Turkewitz, O'Leary, and Ironsmith (1975) demonstrated transfer and maintenance of academic and social behaviors of eight disruptive school children participating in an afterschool reading tutorial program. A token economy was modified to include the following self-control procedures: (*a*) points and backup reinforcers were made contingent upon accurate self-ratings; (*b*) the requirement of accurately matching teacher ratings was faded until the children had complete control over point distribution; and (*c*) backup reinforcers were also faded and eliminated. Transfer to a 15-min control period was observed, and maintenance was demonstrated in the final week of the program after all backup reinforcers were withdrawn. Unfortunately, these studies, as well as others like them, used ER procedures prior to institution of SR. Due to possible confounding of variables such as conditioned reinforcers (e.g., teacher attention, work completed) resulting from ER procedures, it is impossible to evaluate the effects of SR alone. Other serious methodological problems in isolating effects due to SR procedures have been discussed by Jeffrey (1975), Kanfer and Karoly (1972), and Mahoney (1972). These include dubious reliability of self-recorded behavior (Mahoney, Thoresen, & Danaher, 1972), problems in separating the effects of self-monitoring from other components of SM, susceptibility to demand characteristics (Orne, 1962, 1969), evaluation apprehension (Weber & Cook, 1972), outright instructional control versus contingency control (Marholin & Gray, 1976), and subject expectations. In addition, from a careful analysis of several SR studies (e.g., Glynn, 1970; Lovitt & Curtiss, 1969), it appears that the subjects knew they were being monitored and evaluated by the experimenter. The fact that the experimenter evaluated the subjects and that the subjects knew they were being monitored may have affected their behavior in an attempt to meet the experimenter's expectations (Steinman, 1976a, 1976b).

Another approach to SM involves developing verbal self-commands as controlling responses which may affect the probability of the occurrence of undesirable or desirable (controlled) responses. On the basis of work with children, several investigators have demonstrated verbal self-control of voluntary motor behaviors (Bem, 1967; Meichenbaum & Goodman, 1969) as well as more complex social behaviors (Giebink, Stover, & Fahl, 1968; Hartig & Kanfer, 1973; Meichenbaum & Goodman, 1971; O'Leary, 1968; Palkes, Stewart, & Kahana, 1968). For example, Palkes et al. (1968) trained hyperactive children to inhibit their behavior by repeating commands to "slow down" while completing a specific task. In a similar study "impulsive" children, who were trained to administer instructions directing themselves to perform various tasks methodically, showed significant improvement in performance over baseline at the 1-month follow-up (Meichenbaum & Goodman, 1971). While it may be argued that teaching a child to make increasing use of self-instructions will enable him to increase self-control, questions remain as to the degree to which self-instructions transfer across situations and become enhanced by ER and eventually SR for their execution.

One of the fundamental assumptions and purported advantages of SR and self-instructional training is that the probability of transfer and long-term response maintenance is increased; however, there is a paucity of data to substantiate this claim (Kazdin, 1975). While methodological problems exist in investigations of SM, preliminary research and practical considerations certainly justify continued efforts in this area.

VIII. RESPONSE CHARACTERISTICS

Response characteristics may be an important variable altering the probability of transfer; that is, if the response that is strengthened in treatment increases the probability that other related behaviors in the natural or nontreatment environment are reinforced (Marholin, McInnis, & Heads, 1974; Snyder, Lovitt, & Smith, 1975), then the initial target response characteristics are very important. Baer and Wolf (1970) have proposed the concept of "behavioral trap." They suggest that given a particular entry response, elements in the natural environment may combine to facilitate further behavioral change beyond that specifically programmed by the therapist. The implications of this concept for transfer or broadening of training efforts deserve further elaboration.

A typical example of a behavioral trap is a response allowing entry into one's peer group. In a preschool setting, a child's peer group will teach him new words, to share, to wait his turn, and a variety of other behaviors. "A preschool teacher would consider programming reinforcement for all of those behaviors, of course, but it is obviously a massive assignment. She will do better to trap him into those developments" (Baer & Wolf, 1970, p. 321). In one demonstration, a child was trapped into her peer group by extinguishing her crawling behavior which had kept her from the fast-moving games of her peers (Harris, Johnston, Kelley, & Wolf, 1964). Subsequent interaction was shaped by the peer group. In a similar example, a young girl was reinforced for being within 3 feet of another child. Within 6 days she was observed in novel interactions not previously observed (Allen, Hart, Buell, Harris, & Wolf, 1964). These examples are consistent with Whitman, Mercurio, and Caponigri (1970) as well as Altman (1971) in that a child's entry behavior was reinforced, thus allowing more socially skilled children to shape responses closely associated with the trained target response. Of course, one cannot be assured that the behaviors shaped by the peer group will always be those desired by the adult.

A discussion of behavioral traps suggests that the characteristics of a target response are functionally related to the development of other behaviors. This, in turn, affects the probability of transfer to new environments. More specifically, if a response acquired during treatment increases the probability of the subject's later acquiring related behaviors, it is also likely that the environment will support the particular target response. Studies in which children acquired an entry response in training, e.g., mutual cooperation and physical contact with concurrent verbalizations (Altman, 1971; Hauserman, Walen, & Behling, 1973; Hingtgen & Trost, 1966), indicate that the subjects engaged in certain social interactions that shaped additional behaviors (e.g., novel game playing, smiling). By virtue of their continued presence in the developing social milieu which apparently reinforced the behaviors, newly acquired patterns of behavior were maintained.

The language community is an obvious example of a community of reinforcement that evokes, consequates, and maintains general behavioral changes in anyone who develops an entry response (Baer & Wolf, 1970). Since Drennen's (1963) expressed concern with the problem of response or stimulus generalization of verbal conditioning, several demonstrations of generalization of trained language responses to nontrained responses have occurred (Schumaker & Sherman, 1970; Wheeler & Sulzer, 1970). Wheeler and Sulzer (1970) taught a child who formerly spoke in "telegraphic" English, omitting most articles and auxiliary verbs, to use a correct sentence form to describe certain test stimuli. When novel stimuli were substituted, the subject used the correct sentence form. In a similar demonstration, Schumaker and Sherman (1970) trained three retarded children to produce four separate classes of verb inflections (past and present tense). As past and present tense forms of verbs were trained, the subjects correctly produced past tense forms of untrained verbs within this class. Others (Baer & Guess, 1973; Guess, Sailor, Rutherford, & Baer, 1968; Garcia, Guess, & Byrnes, 1973; Gray & Fygetakis, 1968; Martin, 1975) report transfer of improved speech as a result of reinforcement training programs, not only to new responses not directly trained, but also to several extra-therapy settings. These results are in agreement with the concept of a social-emotional or language learning set (Harlow, 1949; Simon & Newell, 1962).

In an interesting demonstration of both response generalization and transfer, Meichenbaum (1969) employed healthy talk (as defined by Ullmann, Foresman, Kenney, McInnis, Unikel, & Zeisset, 1965) and appropriate high-level abstractions to proverbs (as defined by Meichenbaum, 1966) as the dependent variables in a study of schizophrenics. After baseline measures were taken of healthy talk and abstract responses to a verbal proverbs test, subjects were either reinforced for healthy talk or abstract responses to proverbs while baseline continued for the nonreinforced response class. The results indicated that response generalization occurred (i.e., improved proverb performance occurred for those subjects who were trained to give healthy talk and vice-versa). Furthermore, improvements in language transferred to a novel adult as assessed by pre- and posttreatment probes. Behavioral gains were maintained for at least 1 week after termination of training, the only follow-up data that are reported.

While frequencies of particular behaviors and the stimulus conditions under which they occur have been the major concern of behavior therapists to date, the topography of the behavior has often been overlooked. Teaching a nonambulatory child to walk or a nonverbal child to talk most certainly will radically alter his immediate environment (Bijou, 1966). The social setting conditions provided by his newly acquired entry behaviors allows for reinforcement of closely related behaviors. These behaviors are then likely to be maintained by virtue of their ability to acquire reinforcement. The fact that response generalization has been observed following the acquisition of an entry behavior can be viewed as evidence of the increased availability of reinforcers as a function of the appropriateness of the behavior to the environment. Moreover, the increased opportunities for contingent reinforcement will enhance the probability of transfer and maintenance of the original target response as well as related behaviors.

IX. INCOMPATIBLE BEHAVIOR

There is some evidence to suggest that training of incompatible behaviors represents a viable technique to facilitate transfer or enhance treatment effects in nontrained response areas. In the strictest sense, incompatible behavior is defined as any behavior that is physically impossible to emit at the same time as another response. Several studies report a decrease in disruptive behaviors that were not under direct contingency control (Ayllon & Roberts, 1974; Burchard & Tyler, 1965; Marholin et al., 1975b; Winett & Roach, 1973; Winkler, 1970). Winkler (1970) reports reduction of noise and violence in an adult psychotic population after institution of a token program, although these behaviors were not involved in the reinforcement procedures. Both Ayllon and Roberts (1974) and Marholin et *al.* (1975b) found that disruptive classroom behaviors decreased as a function of reinforcing academic quality alone. Several contrary findings have been reported by Corte, Wolf, and Locke (1971) and Young and Wincze (1974), who found that response contingent shocks were more effective in eliminating self-injurious behavior than was the reinforcement of alternative behaviors. These results suggest that the reinforcement of incompatible behavior *may* eliminate undesirable behavior and thus expand the settings in which the appropriate behaviors are emitted. However, if the posttreatment environments fail to support the newly acquired behavior, undesirable behavior may reappear.

X. COGNITIVE-PERSONALITY FACTORS

Another approach to the problem of transfer of training emphasizes cognitive-personality variables surrounding the client's attribution of his role in attaining success (i.e., reinforcement responsibility and locus of control). Given that a person is behaving in a particular manner, will the consequences be different if the cause of his behavior is attributed to himself as opposed to behavior change that is attributed to an external agent (Crandall, Katkovsky, & Crandall, 1965; Rotter, 1966; Weiner, 1970)? One area of research clearly related to this issue is discussed by Miller (1966), who found weak transfer of drug-induced patient improvements to nondrug states. Davison and Valins (1969) further report that subjects who had been told they had ingested a placebo attributed their behavior change to themselves and subsequently tolerated significantly more shock-induced pain stimuli than yoked subjects also receiving a placebo who attributed their behavior change to a drug (i.e., external agent). Taking note of the transfer problem, Davison and Valins suggest that maintaining drug-produced changes in behavior might be facilitated by allowing individuals to think that at least part of their behavior change is due to their own efforts.

In an analogous manner, a child may attribute the outcome of his efforts as being either under his own control or under the control of external factors. As demonstrated by Dweck and Reppucci (1973), two children may receive exactly the same number and sequence of success and failure trials yet react quite differently as a function of whether they are instructed to interpret the failure to mean that the situation is beyond their control (i.e., external control) or within it (internal control). In the former case the child gives up without trying after the first experience of failure because it is suggested he believes that he is helpless to affect outcomes (Hiroto & Seligman, 1975; Seligman, Maier, & Solomon, 1971). While many behavior modifiers advocate a success-only procedure (e.g., Bigelow, 1972; Hart & Risley, 1968; Meacham & Wiesen, 1969; Skinner, 1968), clients may fail to benefit to the extent that they believe behavior changes during treatment are due merely to the circumstances present in the training environment (Valins & Nisbett, 1972).

Individuals who employ errorless (success only) learning procedures with children often base their rationale on Terrace's (1963a) work on errorless discrimination. Terrace demonstrated that pigeons making unreinforced responses to a negative stimulus (i.e., errors) during discrimination training briefly showed gross emotional responses to that stimulus, and the same stimulus remained neutral when discriminations were trained using an errorless procedure (i.e., no responses to negative stimulus). Terrace (1969) states that in some cases "errorless discrimination is not an unmixed blessing" [p. 581]. For example, when an errorless discrimination was followed by a different discrimination trained with errors, the originally perfect discrimination was disrupted (Terrace, 1963b). Also, when a continuously reinforced errorless discrimination was followed by extinction, there was interference with the previous errorless performance (Terrace, 1969). While errorless learning led to superior performance, it seemed to render the subjects less able to deal with subsequent errors.

One might predict from Terrace's work that a child taught a particular skill through an error-free procedure in one setting may subsequently fail when faced with failures or errors in a second setting: he may have attributed his success in the first setting to external factors (e.g., therapist allowing him to succeed). Such children may need reattribution training; that is, they may have to be taught to view success as being a result of their own effort and thus under their control. The goal of reattribution training would be to teach the child to try harder in the face of failure rather than giving up, so that he persists when frustration is experienced (Redd, 1974a). Such attribution procedures have been studied with children identified as "helpless," i.e., children who gave up on academic tasks in the face of failure (Dweck, 1976a, 1976b). Half of the children received traditional success training on math problems taken from their classroom workbooks (problems that they could clearly master with low time requirements, thus assuring reinforcement). The other children received attribution retraining involving failure experiences on 20% of their problems (unattainable criteria employed). Following failure the adult would show the child that he had almost reached the criteria and stated he should try harder. Thus, the child was being given the attribution that failure was a result of insufficient effort (internal control) rather than lack of skill (external control). Both groups of children showed significant improvement in the rate and accuracy of the work. However, when faced with failure, subjects who had received success training alone showed severe deterioration in performance, while those subjects in the retraining group maintained or improved their performance following failure.

While sufficient data are lacking (e.g., applications to social behaviors in less controlled settings), the results suggest that behavioral intervention programs employing success-only training might be shortsighted. This is not to deny that an error-free learning situation would be most efficient during an acquisition phase. However, periodically programmed nonreinforcement trials might be capitalized upon following acquisition as a vehicle for teaching the child how to handle failure, thereby increasing the probability of persistence in an extra-therapy setting where immediate success is unlikely. Such increased persistence would increase the probability that behavior acquired during training would eventually be reinforced and hence maintained in the natural environment.

XI. SCHEDULES OF REINFORCEMENT

The notion of error-free versus error learning is conceptually tied to another principle, namely, increased resistance to extinction as a function of increasingly intermittent schedules of reinforcement in the training situation. Assuming that the extra-therapy setting contains appropriate contingencies to maintain desired behavior acquired during therapy, employment of progressively thinner schedules of reinforcement during training should increase the probability of the response occurring in the natural environment, allow the opportunity for contingent reinforcement to occur, and maintain the behavior.

Although animal research provides an abundant literature on the effect of various schedules of reinforcement on extinction,[3] their effect on the extinction of newly acquired responses during training

---

[3] See *Journal of the Experimental Analysis of Behavior*, 1957 to present.

with human subjects has not been adequately investigated. The several applied studies that have attempted to systematically study the effects of various schedules of reinforcement on resistance to extinction have obtained inconclusive results (Haring & Hauck, 1969; Meichenbaum et al., 1968). If the human data are at all consistent with those observed in animal studies, the use of variable schedules of reinforcement would be expected to produce very strong resistance to extinction (Ferster & Skinner, 1957; Orlando & Bijou, 1960). Since in even the most consistent behavioral programs some appropriate behavior goes unreinforced, it becomes extremely important that the function of various schedules of reinforcement and their effectiveness in resisting extinction be more thoroughly understood.

Kazdin and Polster (1973) studied the effects of intermittent and continuous schedules of token reinforcement on the maintenance of social interaction in two retarded subjects (S_1 and S_2). A high frequency of social interaction with peers was established using continuous reinforcement. Following an extinction period, there was a substantial decrease in social interaction for both subjects. In the second phase of the program S_1 was reinforced on a gradually increased variable-ratio schedule, while S_2 was again reinforced on a continuous schedule. During the second reversal period, S_1's social interaction was maintained at a level similar to that of the period when contingent reinforcement was in effect. There was a decrease in the target behavior to near baseline levels for S_2, who had received continuous reinforcement. While only a 5-week follow-up period is reported, observations indicated that intermittent reinforcement was more effective in maintaining the trained response than was continuous reinforcement.

Primary reinforcement and social praise delivered contingently upon the social responses of two severely retarded withdrawn children in a training situation resulted in a progressive increase of social interaction in a nontraining setting (Whitman et al., 1970). For 6 weeks following an initial baseline period, the subjects were taught a mutual block-passing and ball-rolling task in daily 1-hr sessions. For the first 20 training days, praise and food were administered on a schedule of reinforcement that was gradually increased to a fixed ratio of 30. During training and for 2 weeks following training (final baseline), two 15-min observations of the subjects' cooperative behavior were recorded each day in a free-play nontraining period. Data from these observations revealed greatly increased amounts of time spent in social interaction during the 15-min nonreinforced periods while training was in progress. Compared to the initial baseline, the final baseline period showed considerably more social interaction, although a decrease in the target behavior from the training period was observed. While several factors might account for the observed transfer, including peer modeling and the addition of other children to the training task, it is also quite possible that the systematic fading of reinforcement during the training sessions was responsible for the strong resistance to extinction. The confounding of these variables does not permit an adequate evaluation of the effect of the reinforcement schedules alone. Similar studies including systematic thinning of reinforcement schedules are confounded with other variables manipulated in the training programs (e.g., Hingtgen & Trost, 1966; Kale *et al.*, 1968; Kazdin, 1973a; Phillips, Phillips, Fixsen, & Wolf, 1971). This further limits conclusive statements regarding the efficacy of any particular schedule of reinforcement in maintaining treatment effects beyond the therapy setting.

XII.   DELAYED REINFORCEMENT

Given that numerous rewards in the natural environment are delayed (e.g., wages, grades), it would seem desirable to train subjects on a schedule of reinforcement that approximates more closely the delays in the extra-therapy environment. If a child comes to expect rewards in a delayed rather than immediate fashion, extinction should be retarded. Two types of delay procedures have been used. The first increases the delay between the response and contingent feedback. Schwartz and Hawkins (1970), using a videotape delayed feedback system, successfully modified face touching, posture, and voice loudness of a sixth-grade child. Appropriate behavior was maintained during other periods of the day. The second delay technique involves a progressive increase in time between token reinforcement and the exchange of tokens for backup reinforcers (O'Leary & Becker, 1967). Laboratory findings suggest that the delay between delivery of a conditioned reinforcer and the backup event contributes to the strength of the conditioned reinforcer (Bersh, 1951). In a classroom study, a delay between token acquisition and exchange was progressively extended to 4 days with little decline in reinforced target behaviors (Cotler, Applegate, King, & Kristal, 1972). While delays between responding and reinforcement (e.g., Nay & Legum, 1976) as well as between token delivery and exchange (e.g., Jones & Kazdin, 1975) have been employed in programs designed to develop response maintenance, the delay procedures are confounded with other techniques aimed at enhancing transfer. Although the delay of reinforcement procedures may very well be responsible for the maintenance of behavior change, such procedures alone require further systematic experimental investigation of their relationship, if any, to the maintenance of treatment effects.

XIII. SUMMARY AND FUTURE PERSPECTIVES

Consistent effort has been applied throughout this chapter to make distinctions among the terms *transfer, response maintenance,* and *generalization* (both stimulus and response). However, the phenomena of transfer and maintenance of behavior change may be viewed as continuities (Kantor, 1959; Skinner, 1953, 1963), differing only in the arbitrary dimensions of time and space, with occurrence or nonoccurrence of these phenomena depending upon contingencies of reinforcement in the extra-therapy setting. If the posttreatment contingencies are comparable with those present during training, the desired behavior will transfer; and it will be maintained as long as the supporting contingencies remain. On the other hand, should the transfer environment lack the necessary contingencies to support the desired behavior, ultimately it will extinguish if it occurs at all.

Stimulus control has been emphasized as a factor which must be carefully evaluated in any treatment program where transfer and maintenance are required. To the degree that the client differentiates between those stimuli present in the treatment setting and those in the transfer setting, discrimination rather than transfer will occur. There are a number of techniques that have been touched upon to overcome this obvious dilemma, including employment of S^Ds during treatment that are likely to occur in the posttreatment environment, decreasing discriminations by utilizing multiple therapists, and providing instructions regarding future desired behaviors. While these suggested procedures may facilitate positive transfer from a treatment setting to the natural environment, it is clear that the extra-therapy setting must contain the contingencies to maintain the newly acquired behaviors, lest they too will extinguish.

One of the strategies for overcoming the unfortunate dilemma posed by strict stimulus control exerted by untold stimuli in the treatment environment, namely, utilizing S^Ds during training that are likely to be present in posttreatment settings, deserves further elaboration. The results of a series of related studies (Johnston & Johnston, 1972; Marholin *et al.*, 1975b; Marholin & Steinman, in press; Rincover & Koegel, 1975; Stokes & Baer, 1975) strongly suggest at least two possible predictors of the occurrence or nonoccurrence of transfer of training. A lack of transfer may be due in part to very precise stimulus control developed during training by a particular stimulus or set of stimuli not present in the transfer environment. On the contrary, the observation of transfer from one setting to another may be a function of stimuli present in the posttreatment setting that became discriminative for reinforcing consequences during treatment. These conclusions provide sufficient evidence for future research emphasis on the use of preprogrammed discriminative stimuli during treatment to initiate behavior of notable strength in the posttreatment environment. Therefore, the occurrence of behavior in the posttreatment environment may allow for the reinforcement of desirable behavior and, thus, further maintenance of that behavior.

A set of variables has been suggested as being related to the initial occurrence and persistence of a target response in the transfer setting. These include response characteristics, the teaching of incompatible behaviors, reinforcement variables such as the schedule and delay parameters employed during treatment, and whether the client attributes behavior change during therapy to his own effort or to some external factor. While all of these variables have been discussed in light of their potential for facilitating the initial occurrences of treatment-acquired behaviors in an extra-therapy environment, they merely allow for the reinforcement and subsequent maintenance of these behaviors by significant others or by the client's personal management of the contingencies in the transfer environment.

The concept of stimulus generalization as discussed by Nevin (1973) and others may describe the occurrence in an extra-therapy setting of behaviors acquired during a treatment phase. However, available data from applied research do not clearly support the distinct occurrence of this phenomenon. In fact, it seems more appropriate at this juncture to suggest that stimulus generalization may infrequently occur; and if it does occur, its effects are likely to be transitory.

The central theme of this chapter has been that therapeutic behavior change is of little or no value to the client unless it occurs in the natural environment following formal intervention. The crux of all therapeutic learning situations, whether in school or a residential institution, is the requirement that newly acquired skills or behaviors have some functional utility beyond the confines of the learning setting in order to be maintained. To maximize the probability of therapeutic maintenance in the "real world," behavior therapists must continue to develop, test, and refine strategies aimed at training significant others in the target child's natural social environment to administer the contingencies of reinforcement that may subsequently maintain desired behaviors. Many of the studies discussed utilized training of significant others, but usually it followed treatment in a post hoc fashion. In other words, training those individuals most likely to come in direct contact with the client in basic behavioral principles for modifying behavior has typically been used to promote transfer of treatment effects across settings.

An alternate approach suggests "deprofessionalizing" treatment to the degree that parents, teachers, and siblings are trained and counseled in techniques to alter the problem behavior in the setting in which it is a problem as well as to maintain resulting desirable behavioral changes. If the problem behavior is successfully modified in the natural environment, the problem of transfer of treatment across settings is avoided. It has been amply demonstrated that significant others in the child's environment generally have at their command a variety of powerful reinforcers for the target child. By utilization of these reinforcers in a systematic and contingent fashion, a target child's behavior may be altered *and* maintained in the very environment in which he resides (Marholin *et al.*, 1975a; Wolf, Phillips, & Fixsen, 1972). Thus, in practice, two approaches are complementary: (1) use of significant others as change agents, and (2) work within the natural environment.

There are two other primary considerations involved in providing a treatment program in the child's natural life setting. *First*, while it has been suggested that the treatment setting should provide stimulus properties which are comparable with those found in the posttreatment setting to which the child will eventually return, the selection of such pertinent stimulus variables requires that a sophisticated clinical judgement be made for which there is currently little or no empirical base. Training in the natural environment, therefore, eliminates the complex and difficult assessment process involved in determining whether the stimulus characteristics of the treatment setting are compatible with those found in the natural environment of the individual. *Second*, working to change behavior in the natural environment provides an immediate source of feedback to the therapist regarding the potential resources available to promote the maintenance of the treatment effects following the treatment program. If it is discovered that insufficient reinforcers are present in the individual's natural environment to maintain any portion of the target behaviors, the therapist must decide: (1) whether the target of intervention should be the parents rather than the child; (2) if an alternate placement to the child's natural home should be considered; or (3) whether his professional involvement should realistically and ethically continue.

Obviously, the clinician is occasionally faced with some behavior problems which, at least initially, are not amenable to treatment in the client's natural environment, as in the case of a seriously disturbed or self-destructive child (Browning & Stover, 1971; Lovaas *et al.*, 1973) or where significant others are resistant to participating in the treatment program (Marholin & Hall, 1976). By temporary removal of the child from the natural setting, it may be easier to select, test, and implement treatment strategies which may later be used by the child's parents, siblings, and teachers upon his return to the community. With extremely complex behavior problems it is often necessary to foster initial behavior changes in an extremely controlled and structured environment employing systematic, data-based therapeutic techniques. Temporary removal of the child from his home environment may, in fact, lessen the generality of change; but the use of significant others as change agents upon return may reach long-range objectives more reliably than an attempt to lay all the responsibility for initial, intermediate, and final maintenance of behavioral change upon those in the child's natural environment who are possibly unable or unwilling to accept this responsibility. In such cases it becomes necessary to provide a treatment environment that will facilitate at least the temporary transfer of behavior change when the individual returns to his natural life setting. This might be accomplished, for example, by providing multiple therapists and/or multiple treatment settings. In addition, the child's repertoire of adaptive behaviors should be expanded by teaching him initial behaviors enabling him to enter environments that reinforce and otherwise support the acquisition of further positive behavioral changes. Finally, gains obtained in treatment environments might be maintained by teaching the individual to persist in the face of nonreinforced responses which often occur when contingencies in the natural environment are not always sensitive to the treatment-acquired behaviors.

If parents or teachers are taught differentially to reinforce the appropriate behavior of a child in the home or classroom, will the adults begin to use this technique on behaviors other than those they were initially trained to change? Also, will they continue to employ those recently acquired behavioral techniques after the consulting professional withdraws from the situation? These questions focus on the issue of whether or not the child's altered behavior is in itself sufficiently reinforcing to maintain the use of the new procedures. While at present this seems to be an open question, the literature tends to suggest that improved child behavior will not provide sufficient reinforcement for significant others to maintain their new behavior change techniques (Kazdin, 1975). Hence, it may be that a new research focus is needed in the area of nonprofessional training, with an emphasis on those variables which contribute to or promote the use of sound behavior modification techniques by significant others in natural settings.

The durability of behavior change continues to be of particular concern to behavior modifiers as well as more traditionally oriented therapists interested in permanent behavior change. Unfortunately, research directed at providing techniques to assure transfer and maintenance has lagged significantly behind efforts to demonstrate the functional relationships between behavior change and the manipulation of pertinent variables in the treatment setting. Follow-up data on the permanence of a behavior change seems only meaningful in terms of providing feedback on the extra-training contingencies. In most studies, only the short-range effects of operant techniques are reported after the termination of treatment, and these are often in the form of a post hoc anecdotal analysis. The fact that repeated experimental demonstrations of treatment techniques derived from applied behavior analysis have adhered closely to acknowledged principles of intrasubject experimental design (Baer *et al.*, 1968; Sidman, 1960) leads one to believe that the same rigor might be employed in the investigation of variables systematically related to the transfer and maintenance of behavior following formal treatment.

The studies reviewed seem consistent enough to warrant several conclusions: *First,* true generalization may occur briefly in an extra-training setting. *Second,* maintenance of target responses in the extra-training setting is totally dependent on the contingencies in effect in that environment. *Finally,* while this chapter has identified a number of crucial variables which *should* maximize the probability of transfer, response generalization, and behavioral maintenance, such therapeutic principles must be supported by both basic and applied research efforts before they are adopted as empirically tested techniques in the clinic, home, or school.

REFERENCES

Allen, K. E., Hart, B. M., Buell, J. S., Harris, F. R., & Wolf, M. M. Effects of social reinforcement on isolate behavior of a nursery school child. *Child Development,* 1964, **35**, 511–518.

Altman, K. Effects of cooperative response acquisition on social behavior during free play. *Journal of Experimental Child Psychology,* 1971, **12**, 387–395.

Arnold, J. E., Levine, A. G., & Patterson, G. R. Changes in sibling behavior following family intervention. *Journal of Consulting and Clinical Psychology,* 1975, **43**, 683–688.

Atthowe, J. M. Behavior innovation and persistence. *American Psychologist,* 1973, **28**, 34–41.

Ayllon, T., & Azrin, N. H. *The token economy: A motivational system for therapy and rehabilitation.* New York: Appleton, 1968.

Ayllon, T., & Roberts, M. D. Eliminating discipline problems by strengthening academic performance. *Journal of Applied Behavior Analysis,* 1974, **7**, 71–76.

Baer, D. M. In the beginning there was the response. In E. Ramp & G. Semb (Eds.), *Behavior analysis: Areas of research and application.* Englewood Cliffs, N.J.: Prentice Hall, 1975. Pp. 16–30.

Baer, D. M., & Guess, D. Teaching productive noun suffixes to severely retarded children. *American Journal of Mental Deficiency,* 1973, **77**, 498–505.

Baer, D. M., & Wolf, M. M. The entry into natural communities of reinforcement. In R. Ulrich, T. Stachnik, & J. Mabry (Eds.), *Control of human behavior from cure to prevention.* Vol. II. Glenview, Ill.: Scott, Foresman & Co., 1970. Pp. 319–324.

Baer, D. M., Wolf, M. M., & Risley, T. R. Some current dimensions of applied behavior analysis. *Journal of Applied Behavior Analysis,* 1968, **1**, 91–97.

Bailey, J. S., Timbers, G. D., Phillips, E. L., & Wolf, M. M. Modification of articulation errors of predelinquents by their peers. *Journal of Applied Behavior Analysis,* 1971, **2**, 265–281.

Bandura, A. *Principles of behavior modification.* New York: Holt, 1969.

Bandura, A., & Perloff, B. Relative efficacy of self-monitored and externally imposed reinforcement systems. *Journal of Personality and Social Psychology,* 1967, **7**, 111–116.

Barrett, B. H., & McCormack, J. E. Varied-teacher tutorials: A tactic for generating credible skills in severely retarded boys. *Mental Retardation,* 1973, **11**, 14–19.

Barrish, H. H., Saunders, M., & Wolf, M. M. Good behavior game: Effects of individual contingencies for group consequences on disruptive behavior in a classroom. *Journal of Applied Behavior Analysis,* 1969, **2**, 119–124.

Becker, W. C., Madsen, C. H., Arnold, C. R., & Thomas, D. R. The contingent use of teacher attention and praising in reducing classroom behavior problems. *Journal of Special Education,* 1967, **1**, 287–307.

Bem, S. L. Verbal self-control: The establishment of effective self-instruction. *Journal of Experimental Psychology,* 1967, **74**, 485–491.

Bersh, P. J. The influence of two variables upon the establishment of a secondary reinforcer for operant responses. *Journal of Experimental Psychology,* 1951, **41**, 62–73.

Bigelow, G. The behavioral approach to retardation. In T. Thompson & J. Garbowski (Eds.), *Behavior modification of the mentally retarded.* London & New York: Oxford University Press, 1972. Pp. 17–48.

Bijou, S. W. A functional analysis of retarded development. In N. R. Ellis (Ed.), *Inter-*

national Review of Research in Mental Retardation. Vol. 1. New York: Academic Press, 1966. Pp. 1–18.

Bijou, S. W. What psychology has to offer education—now. Journal of Applied Behavior Analysis, 1970, 3, 65–71.

Bijou, S. W. The basic stage of early childhood development. Englewood Cliffs, N.J.: Prentice-Hall, 1976.

Bijou, S. W., & Baer, D. M. Child development: A systematic and empirical therory. Vol. I. New York: Appleton, 1961.

Bijou, S. W., Peterson, R. F., Harris, F. R., Allen, K. E., & Johnston, M. S. Methodology for experimental studies of young children in natural settings. Psychological Record, 1969, 19, 177–210.

Bijou, S. W., & Redd, W. H. Child behavior therapy. In S. Arieti (Ed.), American handbook of psychiatry, Vol. 7. New York: Basic Books, 1975.

Blanchard, E. B., & Johnson, R. A. Generalization of operant classroom control procedures. Behavior Therapy, 1973, 4, 219–229.

Blough, D. S. The study of animal sensory process by operant methods. In W. K. Honig (Ed.), Operant behavior: Areas of research and application. New York: Appleton, 1966. Pp. 345–379.

Bolstad, O. D., & Johnson, S. M. Self-regulation in the modification of disruptive behavior. Journal of Applied Behavior Analysis, 1972, 5, 443–454.

Broden, M., Hall, R. V., Dunlap, A., & Clark, R. Effects of teacher attention and a token reinforcement system in a junior high school class. Exceptional Children, 1970, 36, 341–349.

Browning, R. M., & Stover, D. O. Behavior modification in child treatment. Chicago: Aldine (Atherton), 1971.

Burchard, J. D. Behavior modification with delinquents: Some unforeseen contingencies. Paper presented at the meeting of the American Orthopsychiatric Association, New York, April 1971.

Burchard, J. D., & Tyler, V. O. The modification of delinquent behavior through operant conditioning. Behaviour Research and Therapy, 1965, 2, 245–250.

Callantine, M. F., & Warren, J. M. Learning sets in human concept formation. Psychological Reports, 1955, 1, 363–367.

Cautela, J. R. Behavior therapy and self-control: Techniques and implications. In C. M. Franks (Ed.), Behavior therapy: Appraisal and status. New York: McGraw-Hill, 1969. Pp. 323–340.

Chadwick, B. A., & Day, R. C. Systematic reinforcement: Academic performance of underachieving students. Journal of Applied Behavior Analysis, 1971, 4, 311–319.

Corte, H. E., Wolf, M. M., & Locke, B. J. A comparison of procedures for eliminating self-injurious behavior of retarded adolescents. Journal of Applied Behavior Analysis, 1971, 4, 201–213.

Cotler, S. B., Applegate, G., King, L. W., & Kristal, S. Establishing a token economy program in a state hospital classroom: A lesson in training student and teacher. Behavior Therapy, 1972, 3, 209–222.

Crafts, L. W. Transfer as related to number of related elements. Journal of General Psychology, 1935, 13, 147–158.

Craighead, W. E., O'Leary, K. D., & Allen, J. D. Teaching and generalization of instruction following in an "autistic" child. Journal of Behavior Therapy and Experimental Psychiatry, 1973, 4, 171–176.

Crandall, V. C. Sex differences in expectancy of intellectual and academic reinforcement. In C. P. Smith (Ed.), Achievement related motives in children. New York: Russell Sage Foundation, 1969.

Crandall, V. C., Katkovsky, W., & Crandall, V. J. Children's beliefs in their own control of reinforcement in intellectual-academic achievement situations. *Child Development*, 1965, 36, 91–109.

Davidson, W. S., II, & Seidman, E. Studies of behavior modification and juvenile delinquency: A review, methodological critique, and social perspective. *Psychological Bulletin*, 1974, 8, , 998–1011.

Davison, G. C., & Valins, S. Maintenance of self-attributed and drug-attributed behavior change. *Journal of Personality and Social Psychology*, 1969, 11, 25–33.

Drabman, R. S., Spitalnik, R., & O'Leary, K. D. Teaching self-control to disruptive children. *Journal of Abnormal Psychology*, 1973, 82, 10–16.

Drennen, W. T. Transfer of the effects of verbal conditioning. *Journal of Abnormal and Social Psychology*, 1963, 66, 619–622.

Duncan, C. P. Transfer in motor learning as a function of degree of first-task learning and inter-task similarity. *Journal of Experimental Psychology*, 1953, 45, 1–11.

Duncan, C. P. Transfer after training with single versus multiple tasks. *Journal of Experimental Psychology*, 1958, 55, 63–72.

Dweck, C. S. The role of expectations and attributions in the alleviation of learned helplessness. *Journal of Personality and Social Psychology*, 1976, in press. (a)

Dweck, C. S. Children's interpretation of evaluative feedback: The effect of social cues on learned helplessness. *Merrill-Palmer Quarterly*, 1976, in press. (b)

Dweck, C. S., & Reppucci, N. D. Learned helplessness and reinforcement responsibility in children. *Journal of Personality and Social Psychology*, 1973, 25, 109–116.

Emshoff, J. G., Redd, W. T., & Davidson, W. S., II. Generalization training and the transfer of treatment effects with delinquent adolescents. *Journal of Applied Behavior Analysis*, 1976, 9, in press.

Felixbrod, J. J., & O'Leary, K. D. Effects of reinforcement on children's academic behavior as a function of self-determined and externally imposed contingencies. *Journal of Applied Behavioral Analysis*, 1973, 6, 241–250.

Ferster, C. B., & Skinner, B. F. *Schedules of reinforcement.* New York: Appleton, 1957.

Fixsen, D. L., Phillips, E. L., & Wolf, M. M. Achievement place: Experiments in self-government with predelinquents. *Journal of Applied Behavior Analysis*, 1973, 6, 31–47.

Gagne, R. M., Baker, K. E., & Foster, H. On the relation between similarity and transfer of training in the learning of discriminative motor tasks. *Psychological Review*, 1950, 57, 67–79.

Garcia, E. The training and generalization of a conversational speech form in nonverbal retardates. *Journal of Applied Behavior Analysis*, 1974, 1, 137–149.

Garcia, E., Guess, D., & Byrnes, J. Development of syntax in a retarded girl by using procedures of imitation and modeling. *Journal of Applied Behavior Analysis*, 1973, 6, 299–310.

Gelfand, D. M., & Hartmann, D. P. Behavior therapy with children: A review and evaluation of research methodology. *Psychological Bulletin*, 1968, 69, 204–215.

Giebink, J. W., Stover, D. O., & Fahl, M. A. Teaching adaptive responses to frustration to emotionally disturbed boys. *Journal of Consulting and Clinical Psychology*, 1968, 32, 366–368.

Glynn, E. L. Classroom applications of self-determined reinforcement. *Journal of Applied Behavior Anlaysis*, 1970, 3, 123–132.

Glynn, E. L., Thomas, J. D., & Shee, S. M. Behavioral self-control of on-task behavior in an elementary classroom. *Journal of Applied Behavior Analysis*, 1973, 6, 105–113.

Goldfried, M. R., & Merbaum, M. A perspective on self-control. In M. Goldfried & M. Merbaum (Eds.), *Behavior change through self-control.* New York: Holt, 1973. Pp. 3–36.

Goldiamond, I. Self-control procedures in personal behavior problems. *Psychological Reports*, 1965, 17, 851–868.

Goldstein, A. P. *Structured learning therapy: Toward a psychotherapy for the poor*. New York: Academic Press, 1973.

Goldstein, A. P., Heller, K., & Sechrest, L. B. *Psychotherapy and the psychology of behavior change*. New York: Wiley, 1966.

Goocher, B. E., & Ebner, M. A behavior modification approach utilizing sequential response targets in multiple settings. Paper presented at the meeting of the Midwestern Psychological Association, Chicago, May 1968.

Gray, B., & Fygetakis, L. The development of language as a function of programmed conditioning. *Behaviour Research and Therapy*, 1968, 6, 445–460.

Griffiths, H., & Craighead, W. E. Generalization in operant speech therapy for misarticulation. *Journal of Speech and Hearing Disorders*, 1972, 37, 485–494.

Guess, D., Sailor, W., Rutherford, D., & Baer, D. An experimental analysis of linguistic development: The productive use of the plural morpheme. *Journal of Applied Behavior Analysis*, 1968, 1, 297–306.

Hall, R. V., Lund, D., & Jackson, D. Effects of teacher attention on study behavior. *Journal of Applied Behavior Analysis*, 1968, 1, 1–12.

Hamilton, J., & Standahl, J. Suppression of stereotyped screaming behavior in a profoundly retarded institutionalized female. *Journal of Experimental Child Psychology*, 1969, 7, 114–121.

Haring, N. G., & Hauck, M. A. Improved learning conditions in the establishment of reading skills with disabled readers. *Exceptional Children*, 1969, 35, 341–352.

Harlow, H. F. The formation of learning sets. *Psychological Review*, 1949, 56, 51–65.

Harris, F. R., Johnston, M. K., Kelley, C. S., & Wolf, M. M. Effects of positive social reinforcement on regressed crawling of a nursery school child. *Journal of Educational Psychology*, 1964, 55, 35–41.

Harris, V. W., & Sherman, J. A. Effects of peer tutoring and consequences on the math performance of elementary classroom students. *Journal of Applied Behavior Analysis*, 1973, 6, 587–598.

Hart, B. M., & Risley, T. R. Establishing use of descriptive adjectives in the spontaneous speech of disadvantaged children. *Journal of Applied Behavior Analysis*, 1968, 1, 109–120.

Hartig, M., & Kanfer, F. H. The role of verbal self-instructions in children's resistance to temptation. *Journal of Personality and Social Psychology*, 1973, 25, 259–267.

Hauserman, N., Walen, S. R., & Behling, M. Reinforced racial integration in the first grade: A study in generalization. *Journal of Applied Behavior Analysis*, 1973, 6, 193–200.

Hawkins, R. P., Peterson, R. F., Schweid, E., & Bijou, S. W. Behavior therapy in the home: Amelioration of problem-parent child relations with the parent in a therapeutic role. *Journal of Experimental Child Psychology*, 1966, 4, 99–107.

Herman, S. H., & Tramontana, J. Instructions and group versus individual reinforcement in modifying disruptive group behavior. *Journal of Applied Behavior Analysis*, 1971, 4, 113–119.

Hewett, F. M., Taylor, F. D., & Artuso, A. A. The Santa Monica Project: Evaluation of an engineered classroom design with emotionally disturbed children. *Exceptional Children*, 1969, 35, 523–529.

Hill, K. T. Individual differences in children's response to adult presence and evaluation reactions. Symposium paper presented at the biennial meetings of the Society for Research in Child Development, Philadelphia, March, 1973.

Hingtgen, J. N., & Trost, F. C. Shaping cooperative responses in early childhood schizophrenics. In R. Ulrich, T. Stachnik, & J. Mabry (Eds.), *Control of human behavior from cure to prevention.* Vol. II. Glenview, Ill.: Scott, Foresman, & Co., 1966. Pp. 110–113.

Hiroto, D. S., & Seligman, M. E. P. Generality of learned helplessness in man. *Journal of Personality and Social Psychology,* 1975, 31, 311–317.

Jeffrey, D. B. Self-control: Methodological issues and research trends. In M. J. Mahoney & C. E. Thoresen (Eds.), *Self-control: Power to the person.* Monterey, California: Brooks/Cole, 1975. Pp. 166–199.

Johnson, S. M., & Martin, S. Developing self-evaluation as a conditioned reinforcer. In B. Ashem & E. Poser (Eds.), *Behavior modification with children.* Oxford: Pergamon, 1974.

Johnston, J. M. Punishment of human behavior. *American Psychologist,* 1972, 27, 1033–1054.

Johnston, J. M., & Johnston, G. T. Modification of consonant speech-sound articulation in young children. *Journal of Applied Behavior Analysis,* 1972, 5, 233–246.

Jones, M. C. A laboratory study of fear: The case of Peter. In H. J. Eysenck (Ed.), *Behaviour therapy and the neuroses.* Oxford: Pergamon, 1960. Pp. 45–51.

Jones, R. T., & Kazdin, A. E. Programming response maintenance after withdrawing token reinforcement. *Behavior Therapy,* 1975, 6, 153–164.

Kale, R. J., Kaye, J. H., Whelan, D. A., & Hopkins, B. L. The effects of reinforcement on the modification, maintenance, and generalization of social responses of mental patients. *Journal of Applied Behavior Analysis,* 1968, 1, 307–314.

Kanfer, F. H. Self-regulation: Research, issues, and speculations. In C. Neuringer & J. L. Michael (Eds.), *Behavior modification in clinical psychology.* New York: Appleton, 1970. Pp. 178–220.

Kanfer, F. H. The maintenance of behavior by self-generated stimuli and reinforcement. In A. Jacobs & L. B. Sachs (Eds.), *The psychology of private events.* New York: Academic Press, 1971. Pp. 39–59.

Kanfer, F. H. Self-management methods. In F. H. Kanfer & A. P. Goldstein (Eds.), *Helping people change: A textbook of methods.* Oxford: Pergamon, 1975. Pp. 309–356.

Kanfer, F. H., & Duerfeldt, P. H. Motivational properties of S-R. *Perceptual and Motor Skills,* 1967, 25, 237–246.

Kanfer, F. H., & Grimm, L. G. Promising trends toward the future development of behavior modification: Ten related areas in need of exploration. In W. E. Craighead, A. E. Kazdin, & M. J. Mahoney (Eds.), *Behavior modification: Principles, issues, and applications.* Boston: Houghton, 1976.

Kanfer, F. H., & Karoly, P. Self-control: A behavioristic excursion into the lion's den. *Behavior Therapy,* 1972, 3, 398–416.

Kantor, J. R. *Interbehavioral psychology.* (2nd rev. ed.) Bloomington, Ind.: Principia Press, 1959.

Kaufman, E. F., & O'Leary, K. D. Reward, cost, and self-evaluation procedures for disruptive adolescents in a psychiatric hospital school. *Journal of Applied Behavior Analysis,* 1972, 5, 293–309.

Kazdin, A. E. Role of instructions and reinforcement in behavior changes in token reinforcement programs. *Journal of Educational Psychology,* 1973, 64, 63–71. (a)

Kazdin, A. E. Time out for some considerations on punishment. *American Psychologist,* 1973, 28, 939–941. (b)

Kazdin, A. E. *Behavior modification in applied settings.* Homewood, Ill.: Dorsey Press, 1975.

Kazdin, A. E., & Bootzin, R. B. The token economy: An evaluative review. *Journal of Applied Behavior Analysis*, 1972, 5, 343–372.

Kazdin, A. E., & Polster, R. Intermittent token reinforcement and response maintenance in extinction. *Behavior Therapy*, 1973, 4, 386–391.

Keller, R. T., & Schoenfeld, W. N. *Principles of psychology*. New York: Appleton, 1950.

Koegel, R. L., & Rincover, A. Treatment of psychotic children in a classroom environment. 1. Learning in a large group. *Journal of Applied Behavior Analysis*, 1974, 7, 45–59.

Kuypers, D. S., Becker, W. C., & O'Leary, K. D. How to make a token economy fail. *Exceptional Children*, 1968, 11, 101–108.

Lavigueur, H., Peterson, R. F., Sheese, J. G., & Peterson, L. W. Behavioral treatment in the home: Effects of an untreated sibling and long-term follow-up. *Behavior Therapy*, 1973, 4, 431–441.

Lent, J. R. Mimosa Cottage: Experiment in hope. *Psychology Today*, 1968, 2, 50–58.

Locke, B. Verbal conditioning with retarded subjects: Establishment or reinstatement of effective reinforcing consequences. *American Journal of Mental Deficiency*, 1969, 73, 621–626.

Lovaas, O. I., Freitag, G., Kinder, M. I., Rubenstein, B., Schaeffer, B., & Simmons, J. Q. Establishment of social reinforcers in schizophrenic children using food. *Journal of Experimental Child Psychology*, 1966, 4, 109–125.

Lovaas, O. I., Koegel, R., Simmons, J. Q., & Long, J. S. Some generalization and follow-up measures on autistic children in behavior therapy. *Journal of Applied Behavior Analysis*, 1973, 6, 131–165.

Lovaas, O. I., Schaeffer, B., & Simmons, J. Q. Experimental studies in childhood schizophrenia: Building social behaviors by use of electric shock. *Journal of Experimental Studies in Personality*, 1965, 1, 99–109.

Lovaas, O. I., & Simmons, J. Q. Manipulation of self-destruction in three retarded children. *Journal of Applied Behavior Analysis*, 1969, 2, 143–157.

Lovitt, T. C., & Curtiss, K. A. Academic response rate as a function of teacher and self-imposed contingencies. *Journal of Applied Behavior Analysis*, 1969, 2, 49–53.

Madsen, C. H., Becker, W., & Thomas, D. R. Rules, praise and ignoring: Elements of elementary classroom control. *Journal of Applied Behavior Analysis*, 1968, 1, 139–151.

Mahoney, M. J. Research issues in self-management. *Behavior Therapy*, 1972, 3, 45–63.

Mahoney, M. J., Thoresen, C. E., & Danaher, B. G. Covert behavior modification: An experiment analogue. *Journal of Behavior Therapy and Experimental Psychiatry*, 1972, 3, 7–14.

Marholin, D., II, & Bijou, S. W. A behavioral approach to the assessment of children. *Child Welfare*, 1976, 55, in press.

Marholin, D., II, & Gray, D. Effects of group response-cost procedures on cash shortages in a small business setting. *Journal of Applied Behavior Analysis*, 1976, 9, 25–30.

Marholin, D., II, & Hall, K. From institution to community: A behavioral approach to contracting, advocacy, and staff training. *Adolescence*, 1976, in press.

Marholin, D., II, McInnis, E. T., & Heads, T. B. Effect of two free-time reinforcement procedures in a class of behavior-problem children. *Journal of Educational Psychology*, 1974, 66, 872–879.

Marholin, D., II, Plienis, A. J., Harris, S. D., & Marholin, B. L. Mobilization of the community through a behavioral approach: A school program for adjudicated females. *Criminal Justice and Behavior*, 1975, 2, 130–145. (a)

Marholin, D., II, & Siegel, L. J. Beyond the law of effect: Programming for behavioral maintenance. In D. Marholin (Ed.), *Child behavior therapy*. New York: Gardner Press, 1976, in press.

Marholin, D., II, & Steinman, W. M. Stimulus control in the classroom as a function of the behavior reinforced. *Journal of Applied Behavior Analysis*, in press.

Marholin, D., II, Steinman, W. M., McInnis, E. T., & Heads, T. B. The effect of a teacher's presence on the classroom behavior of conduct-problem children. *Journal of Abnormal Child Psychology*, 1975, 3, 11–25. (b)

Marlatt, G. A. Vicarious and direct reinforcement control of verbal behavior in an interview setting. Unpublished doctoral dissertation, Indiana University, 1968.

Martin, J. A. Generalizing the use of descriptive adjectives through modelling. *Journal of Applied Behavior Analysis*, 1975, 8, 203–210.

Masters, W. H., & Mokros, J. H. Self-reinforcement processes in children. *Advances in Child Development and Behavior*, 1974, 9, 151–188.

McArthur, M., & Hawkins, R. P. The modification of several behaviors of an emotionally disturbed child in a regular classroom. In R. Ulrich, T. Stachnik, & J. Mabry (Eds.), *Control of human behavior: Behavior modification in education*. Vol. III. Glenview, Ill.: Scott, Foresman, & Co., 1975. Pp. 342–352.

Meacham, M. L., & Wiesen, A. E. *Changing classroom behavior*. Scranton, Pa.: International Textbook Co., 1969.

Meddock, T. D., Parsons, J. A., & Hill, K. T. Effects of an adult's presence and praise on young children's performance. *Journal of Experimental Child Psychology*, 1971, 12, 197–211.

Meichenbaum, D. H. The effects of social reinforcement on the level of abstraction in schizophrenics. *Journal of Abnormal Psychology*, 1966, 71, 354–362.

Meichenbaum, D. H. The effects of instructions and reinforcement on thinking and language behavior of schizophrenics. *Behaviour Research and Therapy*, 1969, 7, 101–114.

Meichenbaum, D. H., Bowers, K., & Ross, R. R. Modification of classroom behavior of institutionalized female adolescent offenders. *Behaviour Research and Therapy*, 1968, 6, 343–353.

Meichenbaum, D., & Goodman, J. The development and control of operant motor responding by verbal operants. *Journal of Experimental Child Psychology*, 1969, 7, 553–565.

Meichenbaum, D., & Goodman, J. Training impulsive children to talk to themselves: A means of developing self-control. *Journal of Abnormal Psychology*, 1971, 77, 115–126.

Miller, N. E. Some animal experiments pertinent to the problem of combining psychotherapy with drug therapy. *Comprehensive Psychiatry*, 1966, 7, 1–12.

Montgomery, G. T., & Parton, D. A. Reinforcing effect of self-reward. *Journal of Experimental Psychology*, 1970, 84, 273–276.

Nay, W. R., & Legum, L. Increasing generalization in a token program for adolescent retardates. *Behavior Therapy*, 1976, 7, in press.

Nevin, J. A. Stimulus control. In J. A. Nevin & G. S. Reynolds (Eds.), *The study of behavior: Learning, motivation, emotion, and instinct*. Glenview, Ill.: Scott, Foresman, & Co., 1973. Pp. 115–154.

Nolan, J. D., Mattis, P. R., & Holliday, R. C. Long-term effects of behavior therapy: A 12-month follow-up. *Journal of Abnormal Psychology*, 1970, 76, 88–92.

O'Dell, S. Training parents in behavior modification: A review. *Psychological Bulletin*, 1974, 81, 418–433.

O'Leary, K. D. The effects of self-instructions on immoral behavior. *Journal of Experimental Child Psychology*, 1968, 6, 297–301.

O'Leary, K. D., & Becker, W. C. Behavior modification of an adjustment class: A token reinforcement program. *Exceptional Children*, 1967, 33, 637–642.

O'Leary, K. D., Becker, W. C., Evans, M. B., & Saudargas, S. A. A token reinforcement program in a public school: A replication and systematic replication (analysis). *Journal of Applied Behavior Analysis*, 1969, 2, 3–13.

O'Leary, K. D., & Drabman, R. Token reinforcement programs in the classroom: A review. *Psychological Bulletin*, 1971, 75, 379–398.

O'Leary, K. D., & Wilson, G. T. *Behavior therapy: Application and outcome.* Englewood Cliffs, N.J.: Prentice-Hall, 1975.

Orlando, R., & Bijou, S. W. Single and multiple schedules of reinforcement in developmentally retarded children. *Journal of the Experimental Analysis of Behavior*, 1960, 4, 339–348.

Orne, M. T. On the social psychology of the psychological experiment: With particular reference to demand characteristics and their implications. *American Psychologist*, 1962, 17, 776–783.

Orne, M. T. Demand characteristics and the concept of quasi-controls. In R. Rosenthal & R. L. Rosnow (Eds.), *Artifact in behavioral research.* New York: Academic Press, 1969. Pp. 147–179.

Osgood, C. E. The similarity paradox in human learning: A resolution. *Psychological Review*, 1949, 56, 132–143.

Osgood, C. E. *Method and theory in experimental psychology.* London & New York: Oxford University Press, 1953.

Packard, R. G. The control of 'classroom attention': A group contingency for complex behavior. *Journal of Applied Behavior Analysis*, 1970, 3, 13–28.

Palkes, H., Stewart, M., & Kahana, B. Porteus Maze performance of hyperactive boys after training in self-directed commands. *Child Development*, 1968, 39, 817–826.

Patterson, G. R. Behavioral intervention procedures in the classroom and in the home. In A. E. Bergin & S. L. Garfield (Eds.), *Handbook of psychotherapy and behavior change.* New York: Wiley, 1971. Pp. 751–765.

Patterson, G. R., & Brodsky, G. A. A behaviour modification programme for a child with multiple problem behaviours. *Journal of Child Psychology and Psychiatry*, 1966, 7, 277–295.

Patterson, G. R., Cobb, J. A., & Ray, R. S. Direct intervention in the classroom: A set of procedures for the aggressive child. In F. Clark, D. Evans, & L. Hamerlynck (Eds.), *Implementing behavioral programs for school and clinics.* Champaign, Ill.: Research Press, 1972. Pp. 151–201.

Patterson, G. R., McNeal, S., Hawkins, E., & Phelps, R. Reprogramming the social environment. *Journal of Child Psychology and Psychiatry*, 1967, 8, 181–195.

Peterson, R. F., Merwin, M. R., Moyer, T. S., & Whitehurst, G. J. Generalized imitation: The effect of experimenter absence, differential reinforcement, and stimulus complexity. *Journal of Experimental Child Psychology*, 1971, 12, 114–128.

Peterson, R. F., & Whitehurst, G. J. A variable influencing the performance of generalized imitation. *Journal of Applied Behavior Analysis*, 1971, 4, 1–9.

Phillips, D. Case history of a behavior-modification project in a public school. In F. S. Keller & E. Ribes-Inesta (Eds.), *Behavior modification: Applications to education.* New York: Academic Press, 1974. Pp. 63–106.

Phillips, E. L., Phillips, E. A., Fixsen, D. L., & Wolf, M. M. Achievement place: Modification of the behaviors of pre-delinquent boys within a token economy. *Journal of Applied Behavior Analysis*, 1971, 4, 45–59.

Quay, H. C., & Hunt, W. A. Psychopathy, neuroticism and verbal conditioning: A replication and extension. *Journal of Consulting Psychology*, 1965, 29, 283.

Redd, W. H. Effects of mixed reinforcement contingencies on adults' control of children's behavior. *Journal of Applied Behavior Analysis*, 1969, 2, 249–254.

Redd, W. H. Generalization of adult's stimulus control of children's behavior. *Journal of Experimental Child Psychology*, 1970, 9, 286–296.

Redd, W. H. The effects of adult presence and stated preferences on the reinforcement control of children's behavior. Symposium paper presented at the biennial meetings of the Society for Research in Child Development, Philadelphia, March, 1973.

Redd, W. H. Behavioral and cognitive-personality approaches to the transfer of skills following behavioral intervention programs with Head Start children. Unpublished manuscript, 1974. (a)

Redd, W. H. Social control by adult preference in operant conditioning with children. *Journal of Experimental Child Psychology*, 1974, 17, 61–78. (b)

Redd, W. H. The effect of adult presence and stated preference on the reinforcement control of children's behavior. *Merrill-Palmer Quarterly*, 1976, in press.

Redd, W. H., Amen, D. L., Meddock, T. D., & Winston, A. S. Children's compliance as a function of type of instructions and payoff for noncompliance. *Bulletin of the Psychonomic Society*, 1974, 4, 597–599.

Redd, W. H., & Birnbrauer, J. S. Adults as discriminative stimuli for differential reinforcement contingencies with retarded children. *Journal of Experimental Child Psychology*, 1969, 7, 440–447.

Redd, W. H., & Wheeler, A. J. The relative effectiveness of monetary reinforcers and adult instructions in the control of children's choice behavior. *Journal of Experimental Child Psychology*, 1973, 16, 63–75.

Redd, W. H., & Winston, A. S. The role of antecedent positive and negative comments in the control of children's behavior. *Child Development*, 1974, 45, 540–546.

Reisinger, J. J. The treatment of "anxiety-depression" via positive reinforcement and response cost. *Journal of Applied Behavior Analysis*, 1972, 5, 125–130.

Reiss, S. Transfer effects of success and failure training from one reinforcing agent to another. *Journal of Abnormal Psychology*, 1973, 82, 435–445.

Reiss, S., & Redd, W. H. Suppression of screaming behavior in an emotionally disturbed, retarded child. *Proceedings of the American Psychological Association*, 1970, 741–742.

Rincover, A., & Koegel, R. L. Setting generality and stimulus control in autistic children. *Journal of Applied Behavior Analysis*, 1975, 8, 235–246.

Rinn, R. C., Vernon, J. C., & Wise, M. J. Training parents of behaviorally-disturbed children in groups: A three years' program evaluation. *Behavior Therapy*, 1975, 6, 378–387.

Risley, T. R. The effects and side effects of punishing the autistic behaviors of a deviant child. *Journal of Applied Behavior Analysis*, 1968, 1, 21–34.

Rosenbaum, A., O'Leary, K. D., & Jacob, R. G. Behavioral intervention with hyperactive children: Group consequences as a supplement to individual contingencies. *Behavior Therapy*, 1975, 6, 315–323.

Ross, A. O. *Psychological disorders of children: A behavioral approach to theory, research, and therapy.* New York: McGraw-Hill, 1974.

Rotter, J. B. Generalized expectancies for internal versus external control of reinforcement. *Psychological Monographs*, 1966, 80 (Whole No. 609).

Rubin, B. K., & Stolz, S. B. Generalizations of self-referent speech established in a retarded adolescent by operant procedures. *Behavior Therapy*, 1974, 4, 93–106.

Schroeder, G. L., & Baer, D. M. Effects of concurrent and serial training on generalized vocal imitation in retarded children. *Developmental Psychology*, 1972, 6, 293–301.

Schumaker, J., & Sherman, J. Training generative verb usage by imitation and reinforcement procedures. *Journal of Applied Behavior Analysis*, 1970, 3, 273–287.

Schwartz, M. L., & Hawkins, R. P. Application of delayed reinforcement procedures to the behavior of an elementary school child. *Journal of Applied Behavior Analysis*, 1970, 3, 85–96.

Seligman, M. E. P., Maier, S. F., & Solomon, R. L. Unpredictable and uncontrollable aversive events. In F. R. Bush (Ed.), *Aversive conditioning and learning*. New York: Academic Press, 1971. Pp. 347–401.

Seymour, F. W., & Stokes, T. F. Self-recording in training girls to increase work and evoke staff praise in an institution for offenders. Paper presented at the annual meeting of the American Psychological Association, September 1975.

Shore, E., & Sechrest, L. Concept attainment as a function of number of positive instances presented. *Journal of Educational Psychology*, 1961, 52, 303–307.

Sidman, M. *Tactics of scientific research*. New York: Basic Books, 1960.

Siegel, L. J., & Steinman, W. M. The modification of a peer-observer's classroom behavior as a function of his serving as a reinforcing agent. In E. Ramp & G. Semb (Eds.), *Behavior analysis: Areas of research and application*. Englewood Cliffs, N.J.: Prentice-Hall, Inc., 1975. Pp. 321–340.

Simon, H. A., & Newell, A. A computer simulation of human thinking and problem solving. *Monographs of the Society for Research in Child Development*, 1962, 27, 137–150.

Skindrud, K. D. Generalization of treatment effects from home to school settings. Unpublished manuscript, Oregon Research Institute, 1972.

Skinner, B. F. *The behavior of organisms*. New York: Appleton, 1938.

Skinner, B. F. *Science and human behavior*. New York: Macmillan, 1953.

Skinner, B. F. Behaviorism at fifty. *Science*, 1963, 140, 951–958.

Skinner, B. F. Preface to paperback edition of *The behavior of organisms*. New York: Appleton, 1966.

Skinner, B. F. *The technology of teaching*. New York: Appleton, 1968.

Skinner, B. F. *Contingencies of reinforcement: A theoretical analysis*. New York: Appleton, 1969.

Snyder, L. K., Lovitt, T. C., & Smith, J. O. Language training for the severely retarded: Five years of behavior analysis research. *Exceptional Children*, 1975, 42, 7–15.

Solomon, R. W., & Wahler, R. G. Peer reinforcement control of classroom problem behavior. *Journal of Applied Behavior Analysis*, 1973, 6, 49–56.

Steinman, W. M. Generalized imitation and the discrimination hypothesis. *Journal of Experimental Child Psychology*, 1970, 10, 79–99. (a)

Steinman, W. M. The social control of generalized imitation. *Journal of Applied Behavior Analysis*, 1970, 3, 159–167. (b)

Steinman, W. M. The effect of instructions, discrimination difficulty, and methods of assessment on generalized imitation. Symposium paper presented at the biennial meetings of the Society for Research in Child Development, Minneapolis, March 1971.

Steinman, W. M. Implicit instructions and social influence in "generalized imitation" and other "go–no–go" situations. Symposium paper presented at the biennial meetings of the Society for. Research in Child Development, Philadelphia, March, 1973.

Steinman, W. M. Generalized imitation and the setting event concept. In B. C. Etzel, J. M. LeBlanc, & D. M. Baer (Eds.), *Contributions to behavioral research: Festschrift in honor of Sidney W. Bijou*. Hillsdale, N.J.: Lawrence Erlbaum Associates, 1976, in press. (a)

Steinman, W. M. Implicit instructions and social influence in "generalized imitation" and comparable nominative situations. *Merrill-Palmer Quarterly*, 1976, in press, (b)

Stokes, T. F., & Baer, D. M. Preschool peers as generalization facilitating agents, Paper presented at the annual meeting of the American Psychological Association, September 1975.

Tate, B. G., & Baroff, G. S. Aversive control of self-injurious behavior in a psychotic boy. *Behaviour Research and Therapy*, 1966, 4, 281–287.

Terrace, H. S. Discrimination learning with and without errors. *Journal of the Experimental Analysis of Behavior*, 1963, 6, 1–27. (a)

Terrace, H. S. Errorless transfer of a discrimination across two continua. *Journal of the Experimental Analysis of Behavior*, 1963, 6, 223–232. (b)

Terrace, H. S. Stimulus control. In W. K. Honig (Ed.), *Operant behavior: Areas of research and application*. New York: Appleton, 1966. Pp. 281–287.

Terrace, H. S. Extinction of a discriminative operant following discrimination learning with and without errors. *Journal of the Experimental Analysis of Behavior*, 1969, 12, 571–582.

Tharp, R. G., & Wetzel, R. J. *Behavior modification in the natural environment*. New York: Academic Press, 1969.

Thoresen, C. E., & Mahoney, M. J. *Behavioral self-control*. New York: Holt, 1974.

Turkewitz, M., O'Leary, K. D., & Ironsmith, M. Generalization and maintenance of appropriate behavior through self-control. *Journal of Consulting and Clinical Psychology*, 1975, 43, 577–583.

Ullmann, L. P., Forsman, R. G., Kenney, J. W., McInnis, T., Unikel, I. P., & Zeisset, R. M. Selective reinforcement of schizophrenics' interview responses. *Behaviour Research and Therapy*, 1965, 2, 205–212.

Underwood, B. J. Associative transfer in verbal learning as a function of response similarity and degree of first-list learning. *Journal of Experimental Psychology*, 1951, 42, 44–53.

Valins, S., & Nisbett, R. E. Attribution processes in the development and treatment of emotional disorders. In E. E. Jones, D. E. Kanouse, H. H. Kelley, R. E. Nisbett, S. Valins, & B. Weiner (Eds.), *Attribution: Perceiving the causes of behavior*. Morristown, N.J.: General Learning Press, 1972. Pp. 137–150.

Wahler, R. G. Oppositional children: A quest for parental reinforcement control. *Journal of Applied Behavior Analysis*, 1969, 2, 159–170. (a)

Wahler, R. G. Setting generality: Some specific and general effects of child behavior therapy. *Journal of Applied Behavior Analysis*, 1969, 2, 239–246. (b)

Wahler, R. G. Some ecological problems in child behavior modification. In S. W. Bijou & E. Ribes-Inesta (Eds.), *Behavior modification: Issues and extensions*. New York: Academic Press, 1972. Pp. 7–18.

Walker, H. M., & Buckley, N. K. Investigation of some classroom control parameters as a function of teacher dispensed social reinforcers. Unpublished paper, University of Oregon, 1971.

Walker, H. M., & Buckley, N. K. Programming generalization and maintenance of treatment effects across time and across settings. *Journal of Applied Behavior Analysis*, 1972, 5, 209–224.

Walker, H. M., Hops, H., & Johnson, S. M. Generalization and maintenance of classroom treatment effects. *Behavior Therapy*, 1975, 6, 188–200.

Walker, H. M., Mattson, R. H., & Buckley, N. K. Special class placement as a treatment alternative for deviant behavior in children. In F. A. M. Benson (Ed.), *Modifying deviant behaviors in various classroom settings*. No. 1. Eugene, Ore.: University of Oregon, 1969. Pp. 49–80.

Weber, S. J., & Cook, T. D. Subject effects in laboratory research: An examination of subject roles, demand characteristics, and valid inference. *Psychological Bulletin*, 1972, 77, 273–295.

Weiner, B. New conceptions in the study of achievement motivation. In B. A. Maher (Ed.), *Progress in experimental personality research.* Vol. 5. New York: Academic Press, 1970. Pp. 68–110.

Wheeler, A. J., & Sulzer, B. Operant training and generalization of a verbal response form in a speech-deficient child. *Journal of Applied Behavior Analysis,* 1970, 3, 139–147.

Whitman, T. L., Mercurio, J. R., & Caponigri, V. Development of social responses in two severely retarded children. *Journal of Applied Behavior Analysis,* 1970, 3, 133–138.

Wilcox, B., Meddock, T. D., & Steinman, W. M. "Generalized imitation" on a nonimitative task: Effects of modeling and task history. *Journal of Experimental Child Psychology,* 1973, 15, 381–393.

Williams, C. D. The elimination of tantrum behavior by extinction procedures. *Journal of Abnormal and Social Psychology,* 1959, 59, 269.

Winett, R. A., & Roach, E. M. The effects of reinforcing academic performance on social behavior. *Psychological Record,* 1973, 23, 391–396.

Winkler, R. C. Management of chronic psychiatric patients by a token reinforcement system. *Journal of Applied Behavior Analysis,* 1970, 3, 47–55.

Wolf, M. M., Phillips, E. L., & Fixsen, D. L. The teaching family: A new model for the treatment of deviant child behavior in the community. In S. W. Bijou & E. Ribes-Inesta (Eds.), *Behavior modification: Issues and extensions.* New York: Academic Press, 1972. Pp. 51–63.

Woodworth, R. S., & Schlosberg, H. *Experimental psychology.* New York: Holt, 1954.

Yates, A. J. *Behavior therapy.* New York: Wiley, 1970.

Young, J. A., & Wincze, J. P. The effects of the reinforcement of compatible and incompatible alternative behaviors on the self-injurious and related behaviors of a profoundly retarded female adult. *Behavior Therapy,* 1974, 5, 614–623.

Young, R. K., & Underwood, B. J. Transfer in verbal materials with dissimilar stimuli and response similarity varied. *Journal of Experimental Psychology,* 1954, 47, 153–59.

AUTHOR INDEX

Numbers in parentheses are reference numbers and indicate that an author's work is referred to although his name is not cited in the text. Numbers in italics show the page on which the complete reference is listed.

SUBJECT INDEX

A

Abstinence, self-report of, 86–87
Academic performance
  classroom behavior modification and,
    54–55
  modification in learning disabled children,
    189–193
  research in, 195–201
Analogue outcome research, 148–149,
    167–168
  desensitization with social anxiety,
    157–159
  relaxation
    in sleep-onset disturbance, 159–167
    in systematic desensitization, 149–156
Animal studies, 207–211
  of conditioned stimulus flooding
    with graded conditioned stimuli and
      competing responses, 228–229
    response prevention and, 220–223,
      224–228
  of contingent reinforcement, 230–231
  extinction
    with anxiety-competing responses,
      218–219
    with graded conditioned stimuli
      presentation, 217–218
  implications for behavioral treatment of
    humans, 231–235
  methodological issues in, 211–215
  of modeling, 229–230
  of response prevention
    conditioned stimulus flooding and,
      220–223, 224–228

extinction and, 223–224
  of systematic desensitization, 219–220
  versus response prevention, 220
Anxiety, social, desensitization with,
    157–159
Anxiety-competing responses
  conditioned stimulus flooding with graded
    conditioned stimuli and, 228–229
  extinction with, 218–219
  response prevention and, 226–228
Attitudes, comparison in hypnosis and
  behavior modification, 14–19
Aversion strategies, for smoking behavior,
    90–106

B

Bag of tricks model, for teacher training,
    57–58
Behavioral programming, for smoking
  control, 114–115
Behavior therapy, theoretical trends in,
    28–31
Brain dysfunction theories, of learning
  disabilities, 180–181
Bribery, modification techniques as, 66–67

C

Cigarette smoke, as aversive stimulus,
    94–104
Classroom behavior modification, 45–46,
    50–55
  future research directions for, 64–65
  with institutionalized populations, 46–47